BEYOND THE
WORLD'S END

DUKE UNIVERSITY PRESS
DURHAM AND LONDON 2020

T. J. DEMOS

BEYOND THE WORLD'S END

ARTS OF
LIVING

END

AT THE
CROSSING

Designed by Aimee C. Harrison
Typeset in Fengardo Neue and Quadraat Pro by
Westchester Publishing

Library of Congress Cataloging-in-Publication Data

Names: Demos, T. J., author.
Title: Beyond the world's end : arts of living at the crossing / T. J. Demos.
Description: Durham : Duke University Press, 2020. | Includes bibliographical
references and index.
Identifiers: LCCN 2019047895 (print) | LCCN 2019047896 (ebook)
ISBN 9781478008668 (hardcover)
ISBN 9781478009573 (paperback)
ISBN 9781478012252 (ebook)
Subjects: LCSH: Ecology in art. | Human ecology in art. | Social justice in art. |
Art and society. | Art—Political aspects.
Classification: LCC N8217.E28 D45 2020 (print) | LCC N8217.E28 (ebook) |
DDC 700.1/03—dc23
LC record available at https://lccn.loc.gov/2019047895
LC ebook record available at https://lccn.loc.gov/2019047896

Cover art: Arthur Jafa. Still from *Love Is the Message,
The Message Is Death*, 2016. Photographed at Store
Studios, 2017. Photo by Hugo Glendinning.
Courtesy of the photographer, the artist, and Gavin
Brown's enterprise, New York/Rome.

CONTENTS

ILLUSTRATIONS

INTRODUCTION

THE WORLD'S END,
AND BEYOND

We are entering the endgame—the terminal point of democracy, of liberalism, of capitalism, of a cool planet, of the Anthropocene, of the world as we know it. Catastrophic environmental breakdown, global pandemic, neocolonial extractivism, algorithmic governance, disaster and racial capitalism, antimigration populism, and endless war comprise some of the forces structuring this conjuncture. Given this socioecological crisis—informed by past colonial genocides, ongoing corporate ecocides, and transatlantic slavery—how do we conceptualize the aftermath? What of the many worlds that have already ended? Equally urgent, how do we represent the radical potentiality of the not-yet? How do we cultivate and bring into being emancipated futures? Addressing this urgent, multifarious, and world-historical subject, this book centers interlinked sociopolitical, economic, and environmental crises—a copious and rousing intersection capable of motivating and engaging interdisciplinary, comparative research and civic attention alike. Doing so, it focuses specifically on models of aesthetic practice where life is being reinvented in ways that not only critically identify the manifold problems that threaten existence as we know it; they also offer diverse approaches to a hopeful futurity, where hope joins speculative imagination to the material practice of living otherwise, capable of carrying us beyond the end of the world.

While the world of the world's end is multiply configured, just as its supposed end has been variously conceived and historically encountered in many ways, the aftermath has less frequently been addressed.[1] The task remains to investigate not simply the structural causes and violent effects of the end times, including what its symptomatic if superficial imaginary looks like, whether zombie apocalypse, alien invasion, planetary collision, or Hobbesian war of all against all—which Hollywood is so good at envisioning, even while it consistently fails to ponder any kind of emancipatory life beyond the current death spiral of advanced capital. But more, where are the forms of life, the creative visions and stories of substance, that will aid us in moving beyond the various terminal points, past, present, and future? Where are the rift zones between destructive and wholly unjust if not quite outmoded ways of organizing existence—within petrocapitalism, colonialism, anthropocentrism, sexism, and white supremacy—and alternative practices, narratives, and visions founded on social justice and radical multispecies flourishing, glimpsing decolonized futures of environmental sustainability?

Seeking answers to these questions, this book explores a range of artistic and cultural practices that, for me, provide compelling and radical propositions and actionable modelings worth considering at length, even while it acknowledges the provisional and necessarily incomplete purview of its investigation and the fact that there is always more to consider. Extending over seven interlinked chapters, my inquiry addresses the visionary video projects of John Akomfrah (in particular *Vertigo Sea*) and Arthur Jafa (*Love Is the Message, the Message Is Death*), each of which, but in different singular ways, expansively reconceives what climate means, drawing the term into inextricable relation with sociocultural ecologies of racial capitalism, slavery and its legacy, as well as current migration politics and mass species extinction narratives. Both experiment with the visuality of world-ending disasters in racial and more-than-human terms, conjoining biopolitics to geopower. In chapter 1, I consider Akomfrah's in relation to the sea's industrialization and militarization, threatening its sublime nonhuman alterity, as well as its Black liquidity, graveyard of slavery's wake, and present migration's mass grave. Jafa's comes up in chapter 6, discussed in terms of solar apocalypse, Afrofuturism 2.0, and the monstrosity of racialized violence, all posed against the dangerous white futurisms of geoengineering and the neoliberal Anthropocene. Jafa and Akomfrah each also glimpse emancipatory futures beyond the catastrophe of capitalism's ecology and its deathly in/human and racial objectifications, and proposing sites of necessary solidarity. My second chapter relatedly builds on that basis, addressing extraction as a fundamental logic of our ruling economic order—connecting resource mining to the governmentality of debt, unequal trade agreements to neocolonial financial domination—as diversely plotted in the video-based and sculptural projects of Angela Melitopoulos, Allora & Calzadilla, and Ursula Biemann. These variously investigate conflict geographies in such places as Greece, Puerto Rico, Canada's Tar Sands, and Bangladesh's Ganges-Brahmaputra Delta, revealing what Achille Mbembe terms the "becoming-black of the world," a complex proposition of precarious globalization, or the globalization of precarity, on which I elaborate as, alternately, a newly racializing logic of climate injustice, and a crepuscular aesthetics of postcolonial liberation.[2]

Over several chapters I consider the visual politics of climate refugees, a controversial and potentially objectionable term (especially for those who fall unwittingly into its embrace, as depoliticized objects of humanitarian rescue). As appearing in the anthropological work of the Collectif Argos (Argos Collective) and popular photojournalism, these migrant images often cloak the structural forces behind dislocating inequalities that would indict Western complicity, doing so by disguising them with media spectacle's familiar photography of faces and empathic personal-interest narratives. Against those tendencies, my third chapter highlights an experimental media visuality of causes and of creative beyonds, as materialized in the work of Audrey Quinn and Jackie Roche, Forensic Oceanography, and Teddy Cruz and Fonna Forman. While the technofixes of green capitalism, an increasingly dominant force and rising target of climate-justice activism, come under attack throughout the book, especially in the form of neoliberal climate engineering as considered in chapter 6, my analysis resists any flattening dissolve into a regressive antitechnological green, while it equally rejects any simplistic futurist accelerationism. It does so both by inquiring how justice itself defines a social technology of sorts and by opening my case studies in chapter 4 to the considerations of ecomedia and computer games as virtual sites of the progressive practice of political ecology, namely those of Public Studio (a Toronto-based collaboration of Elle Flanders and Tamira Sawatzky).

Midway through the book, in chapter 5, I address the animal cosmopolitics conceptualized in the experimental artwork of Laura Gustafsson and

Terike Haapoja, which integrates postanthropocentric politics and aesthetics in their proposed rebuilding of legal and cultural institutions, offering a radical sociopolitical composition for a world-to-come. This discussion extends the book's earlier material insofar as it builds upon its focus on racial exclusions and social violence by exploring ecologies of the more-than-human within an intersectionalist frame, which importantly links intrahuman exploitation and dehumanization with environmental destruction and nonhuman animal objectifications.

After considering Jafa's video ecologies of what he terms the "abject sublime"—an explosive mix of beauty and horror, justice and violence, as found in historical and ongoing state violence and resistant social movements—and placing these in relation to white environmentalism (what some might term ecologies of affluence that decline to address social injustice and inequality), in chapter 7, my last chapter, I attend to the sociocultural modes of nonextractive living, where organic agriculture merges with radical politics as an artistic form of life, as well as a life of creative forms, human and non. Here I also extend the discussion of cosmopolitics to creative areas of socioecological transition in actually existing artistic-activist mobilizations, including Standing Rock's #NoDAPL struggle, the international movement for institutional liberation (from petrocapitalism as much as more generally privatized toxic philanthropy), and Europe's largest autonomous zone and postcapitalist ecological experiment known as the Zad—emergent worlds all, each embedded in the depredations of the current dominant spread of global capital, every one growing out of traditions of the oppressed.

WORLDS AND ENDS

What is a world, given this preliminary overview of the book? While no simple (or even complex) answer suffices, my understanding begins by calling up an infinite assemblage of discursive representations and deep genealogies of meaning-making practices. Audiovisual narrations and literary constructions embedded in and shaping cultures supplement all manners of knowing and being, forming lifeways established over generations. These surely contribute to and emerge out of violent conflicts with other competitive worldings, some systematizing and domineering, each comprising geopolitical cosmologies, heterogeneous modes of habitation, collective forms of belonging, and structuring forces of temporalization. All imbue the world—however great or small, ultimately uncapturable in totality—with formative values and expansive significance. "Global capitalism," for instance, names one such modeling, according to Pheng Cheah's recent analysis, designating a politico-economic modality that "incorporates peoples and populations into the world-system by tethering them to Western modernity's unrelenting march of progress and capitalist time and violently destroying other worlds and their temporalities."[3] For Terry Smith, worlds mix intimate settings with distant powers, where existential meanings, embedded in everyday routines, resonate and conflict with supraspecific logics (neoliberalism, globalism, nationalism, Christianity, Judaism, Islam), while connectivity occurs, increasingly so within advanced technological modernity and contemporaneity, in multiple ways with varying intensities. In relation to all this, contemporary art becomes an intense site of assorted world-making activities, which implies the ambitious opening up of what art or—more broadly conceived and beyond the legitimating functions of dominant cultural institutions—aesthetic practice can be.[4] So too can it operate as a central site of world destruction and imperial violence, where domination is extended into and through visual practices operating at the convergence of knowledge and power, instituting and enforcing one group's rights over others, according to Ariella Azoulay. She proposes to move the date of the invention of photography back to 1492 for just this reason, to tie its development to the universalization of a new world order: "Among these rights are the right to destroy existing worlds, the right to manufacture a new world in their place, the rights over others whose worlds are destroyed together with the rights they enjoyed in their communities and the right to declare what is new and consequently what is obsolete."[5]

Still other theorizations emphasize worlds within worlds (to borrow the Zapatista demand for un mundo donde quepan muchos mundos, a world in which many worlds fit), including more-than-human ones, those forming across multinatural onto-epistemological divergences, liberating us all from the oppressions of one-world domination.[6] Postanthropocentric conceptions have even achieved geological nomenclature with, for instance, the Chthulucene, Donna Haraway's proposal for the tentacular down-to-earth world of interconnected multispecies being.[7] While its existence has always been there, if buried beneath the surface and generally disregarded by Western humanism and head-in-the-clouds idealism, that infinitely biodiverse, mutually constitutive, and increasingly threatened world, bearing its own life forms, cultures, and materializations, has increasingly been highlighted in the innovative social sciences of anthropology, ethnography, and animal studies. In doing so, it has been catching up with Indigenous traditional wisdom that has long emphasized humans' life-sustaining synergies with nature's web of life.[8] It is only tragic that this reworlding, this coming-into-prominence of the Chthulucene—itself a world of many worlds—is occurring at the very time of global crisis, given the ongoing current mass species extinction event, the biological annihilation driven by habitat destructions, petrocapitalist environmental destruction, and resulting climate breakdown, all of which contributes to the world-historical existential crisis we are now facing, putting life as we know it—including our own—at grave risk. "Climate change is now reaching the end-game," concludes Joachim Schellnhuber, head of the Potsdam Institute for Climate Impact Research. "The issue is the very survival of our civilization."[9]

Consequently, at the time of proliferating worlds, where the failure of global modernity's one-world domination—the world of "no alternative," of military neoliberalism, of posthistorical life beyond capital, and of Western science and technology—is everywhere apparent, we gaze upon an unstoppable cascade of unimaginable tipping points, leading to visions of an "uninhabitable Earth," the end of civilization as we know it, even a world without us, arriving as early as 2100, according to some researched views. That future is marked by heat death, with average temperatures raised five to ten degrees Celsius above present levels; the end of widely available food following massive agricultural failure; climate plagues emerging from melting ice, threatening biological collapse; unbreathable polluted air; endless war, with geopolitical conflicts exacerbated by these very environmental stresses and resulting resource scarcity; global economic collapse; and poisoned oceans.[10] The closest analogue for our forlorn situation—although the current circumstances are truly unprecedented—is the Permian-Triassic mass extinction event that occurred 252 million years ago, known as the Great Dying, a world-ending event that saw 97 percent of all life on Earth expire owing to a carbon-warmed environment. Compared to that, journalist David Wallace-Wells notes, "We are currently adding carbon to the atmosphere at a considerably faster rate; by most estimates, at least ten times faster. The rate is accelerating."[11] While Wallace-Wells' science reporting was accused of irresponsible alarmism—indeed one wonders, is such unblinking assessment politically helpful, or is it debilitating and counterproductive?—he has since doubled down, providing an annotated version with interviews with diverse climate scientists and links to further scholarly research in order to support his claims. For Christian Parenti, these observations contribute to what he terms a world-ending "catastrophic convergence" of climate transformation, expansive militarism, and growing impoverishment, making for a socioecological cataclysm.[12] Isabelle Stengers too reads a "coming barbarism" in our cards, where dominant capitalist political forces, at a time of threatening postdemocracy and fascist creep, instrumentalize the very threat of the end of the world to support their own financial interests, including technofixes that do nothing to address, and even worsen, socioeconomic inequalities, antimigrant xenophobia, and indeed demand further military interventions from the sector that is in fact the largest emitter of greenhouse gases.[13]

It is clear: we are in the midst of a world-historical, cosmological event, an event that is quickly making the world we once knew historical. I consider it as a great politico-ontological unraveling that challenges the limits of knowledge itself, my thinking aided by Déborah Danowski and Eduardo Viveiros de Castro's recent study, *The Ends of the World*. In it they observe how geology is converging with planetary mortality, such that "we are about to enter—or have already entered, the uncertainty itself being an evidence of runaway temporality—a regime of the Earth System that is quite unlike anything we have ever known. The near future becomes unpredictable, if not indeed unimaginable outside the framework of science-fiction or messianic eschatologies."[14] Time itself is endangered, as much as imagination. Their point recalls Amitav Ghosh's notion of *The Great Derangement*, his title referring not only to the current disruptions of Earth's natural systems and their temporalities regulated by seasons but also to the systemic inability of still-dominant Holocene modes of cultural production to represent those disruptions. These latter owe to now-outmoded stylistic conventions reliant on stable environments playing the role of secure backgrounds to human-focused storytelling. Modern fiction has thus failed to capture the extreme events and climate weirding of the Anthropocene emergence. Just why that is so, Ghosh suggests, "is perhaps the most important question ever to confront culture in the broadest sense—for let us make no mistake: the climate crisis is also a crisis of culture, and thus of the imagination."[15]

While I agree that this question is indeed urgent, this book takes a different tack. If we look more closely, and more specifically at experimental forms of contemporary art and visual culture—rather than limit our gaze to what Ghosh calls "serious fiction"—then we can see that cultural practices are indeed dealing with climate breakdown, including the endings of worlds and the inauguration of new ones, in all sorts of imaginative and inspiring ways.[16] Those practices are also undergoing radical transformation in doing so, which have possibly rendered them somewhat illegible, at least to conventional institutions of exhibition and art-historical analysis. But if we look closely, we can observe that in fact the most compelling examples of contemporary cultural production offer an acute lens on this expansive cosmopolitical event, as well as a creative laboratory of world-making, not the least of which involves reconfiguring the ultimate end—as both termination and emancipatory goal—of art at this critical stage of history.[17] At least that is what I will argue in the pages below.

APOCALYPSE NOW . . . AND THEN

Invoking the Anthropocene narrative—or rather particular understandings of that charismatic megaconcept—some have suggested that the source of the present climate event reaches deeply into geological time and *Homo sapiens'* evolutionary origins. As such, it both transcends modern economics and destabilizes anthropocentric juridico-political norms. These arguments recall, if at an oblique angle, Fredric Jameson's oft-quoted remark: "Someone once said that it is easier to imagine the end of the world than to imagine the end of capitalism."[18] That indeed seems true of much Anthropocene reasoning, in terms of not only the concept's increasingly dominant neoliberal framework, geologizing ethics, and naturalizing conceptions of humanity's "species being" but also its ideological mission where it works in tandem with green capitalism to support climate solutions based on technofixes—anything to avoid messing with our dominant economic system, even if it means placing the earth's life-support systems in jeopardy.[19] But given the globalization of disaster capitalism in recent years, Jameson's subsequent caveat seems all the more imperative to recognize as well: "We can now reverse that and witness the attempt to imagine capitalism by way of imagining the end of the world."[20] With the globalization of neoliberalism's shock doctrine taking form increasingly around sites of climate breakdown and its super hurricanes, massive flooding, wildfires, and rising seas, our policy makers, politicians, and corporations are indeed exploiting speculative economic opportunities in the ruins of catastrophe by forcing through further privatization mandates, "free"-trade deals, and the cancellation of social welfare systems.[21] If the end of the world proves profitable for some, then environmental humanities discourse invoking depoliticized geology only aids in further distraction.[22]

Against this trend, dating the Anthropocene's emergence otherwise—specifically *within* capitalist, colonial history—is politically enabling and provides an important perspective on end-of-world conceptions. Climate scientists Simon Lewis and Mark Maslin, for instance, propose 1610 as the epoch's boundary event initiating the Holocene's conclusion, when the geological implications of the European conquest of the Americas begun in 1492 culminated in a marked drop in atmospheric carbon.[23] In those hundred-plus years following first contact, some fifty million Indigenous peoples lost their lives owing to warfare, mass murder, communicable diseases, and forced labor, with colonization disrupting native agriculture and forest management to such a degree that there was a massive regrowth of vegetation, enough to impact the stratigraphic record and produce what geologists call the early seventeenth-century Orbis Spike. The new geological epoch, in other words, represents the genocidal ending of an earlier one, with the Anthropocene's origins being inextricable from early modern globalization, practiced through resource extraction, military conquest, and culture-erasing colonialism. One can rightly argue that the world's currently threatened end—that of catastrophic climate breakdown—has been rehearsed many times before, prepared through the long unfolding of capitalism's five-hundred-year-old history, that is, since the time of what Jason Moore calls the "long sixteenth century" and the formation of our current world economy. One might even propose it extends back further, into deeper premodern European traditions, and equally continual contestations—defined by all forms of sociopolitical oppression, far predating but equally preparing the ground for the last few centuries of economic globalization.[24] Nonetheless, countless worlds in the Americas were annihilated in the years after 1492, which defines the inauguration of the Anthropocene's political ecology, with which we must now contend.

Current fears of the world's end are thus importantly contextualized by Indigenous voices that view them as a mode of settler anxiety, haunted by those centuries-old histories of colonial violence, climate-changing brutality, and genocide-directed militarism—forces that have long disrupted fragile ecologies integral to native lifeworlds and continue to do so in the present. Indeed, Indigenous peoples have already lived through many such apocalypses, the term defining, for Lawrence Gross (Anishinaabe), what happens when "the lifeway of a culture has come to an end."[25] Surviving the genocide of conquest with tremendous cost, Native Americans have seen "the end of their respective worlds" and now suffer from "postapocalypse stress syndrome," entailing intergenerational shock waves on individual and socio-institutional levels requiring hundreds of years of recovery—that is, if recovery is even possible.[26] Kyle Whyte (Potawatomi) argues relatedly that the Anthropocene represents nothing less than the unfolding of his Indigenous ancestors' dystopian fears, the worst of past potential futures, in which their descendants are now living.[27] For multitudes, the world's end—measured in the radical rupture of transgenerational cultural traditions, the termination of secure relations to the land, the overturning of stable systems of sovereignty, and the cancellation of self-determination—has occurred repeatedly over the centuries.[28] Much the same could be said of the world-ending, and equally world-transforming, event of the centuries-long transatlantic slave trade for those of African descent.[29]

About these complex historical entwinements of worlds and ends, including the Anthropocene's, Zoe Todd (Métis) importantly asks: "What does it mean to have a reciprocal discourse on catastrophic end times and apocalyptic environmental change in a place where, over the last 500 years, Indigenous peoples faced (and face) the end of worlds with the violent incursion of colonial ideologies and actions? What does it mean to hold, in simultaneous tension, stories of the Anthropocene in the past, present, and future?"[30] Her answer—with which I agree—is to insist on seeing Anthropocene stories of multiple temporalities and geographies, of sequential world-ending events, as a progression of ruins that informs present anxieties and realities, a progression indissociable from current climate breakdown: "If Lewis and Maslin's Orbis Spike hypothesis is correct, then this compels humanity to tend to the interconnections between, first, Indigenous genocide and the violent enslavement of peoples from across Africa, the Pacific, Asia, and the Americas throughout the colonial period, and second, the contemporary economic, political, social, and cultural forces shaping current environmental and power relations."[31] In other words, it is imperative to reframe "climate change and environmental degradation through an anti-colonial lens," as Jaskiran Dhillon (Cree) adds.[32] We must think the multiple ends of multiple worlds somehow together in a comprehensive analysis that will best enable us to address current and future challenges.

With this view in mind, looking back on the fifteenth-century Anthropocene emergence not only is historically informative and offers a crucial explanatory diagnostics on our present circumstances but also helps predict likely near-future unfoldings of environmental transformation, which, in turn, must become sites of ongoing intervention and political mobilization.

Otherwise, our future stands colonized by the same forces that have exacted such a toll in eras past. The stakes, in their gravest sense, concern not only the character of analyses of the long unfolding of the world's end/s but present decisions about how we wish to confront and hopefully survive it/them. To geologize ethics otherwise—framing it within deep time and beyond the dominant economic regimes of the present—risks a false liberal universality, a speciesist neohumanism, which not only disregards the Anthropocene's historical coincidence with and integral relation to conquest, genocide, and slavery but also all too easily surrenders critical traction against current threats of authoritarian, and, at their most extreme, fascist modes of capitalist-corporate governance, ethnonationalism, and white environmentalism.[33] We can confront these interlinked crises, I am convinced, only from within the situated knowledge of our current political economy—as do the activist-artists whose work forms the case studies represented in this book—where it is not human nature that is the culprit but most immediately the greedy interests of racially defined, patriarchally encoded, and extraction-motivated petrocapitalism.[34]

MODELING METHOD

My approach rethinks political ecology as much as aesthetic practice in light of the great rift of climate breakdown and its world-ending event/s. The first step is to develop what I term ecology-as-intersectionality, necessary to overcome the various iterations of nature/culture binaries and oftentimes reductive framings of ecology as present in the diverse articulations of green capitalism, technoscientific rationality, and environmental art history.[35] I adopt it as well to challenge the anthropocentrism that often curtails social justice and antiracist politics and theory. Emerging out of Black feminism and African American jurisprudence, and their rejection of the artificial but institutionalized segregation of racism and sexism, intersectionality has brought focus to what Patricia Hill Collins terms a "matrix of oppressions," which equally demands interlinking comprehensive redress via entanglements of justice demands.[36] While theorized across a long history of writings by such authors as Sojourner Truth, Anna Julia Cooper, Alexandra Kolantai, bell hooks, Claudia Jones, the Combahee River Collective, and Angela Davis, Kimberlé Crenshaw's analysis formalized the term in pointing out the structural incompatibility of double discrimination claims for General Motors (GM) workers before the law, where Black women workers were unable to gain legal recourse in response to the simultaneity of gender and racial oppressions.[37] Yet whereas intersectional critique now extends to virtually all forms of oppression—including homophobia, transphobia, ablism, religious bigotry, and class exploitation—it seldom if ever incorporates discussion of environmental discrimination or climatological violence, that is, even while environmental racism has become a more or less common term within grassroots struggle and justice-oriented political ecology, where ecology's science of relations necessarily expands to include sociopolitical dimensions.[38]

Still, while Marxist critiques of capitalism have importantly integrated ecological considerations within their methodologies (for instance, in their dialectical materialist approaches to past and present understandings of the metabolic rift between Earth systems and social reproduction), there is little sustained discussion therein of the formations of racial and colonial oppressions, even while Black and Indigenous decolonial studies have pointed out substantial limitations in the former's class-centered priorities.[39] At the same time, while mainstream environmentalism—for example, that of 350 .org, MoveOn.org, Greenpeace, and Sierra Club—does important work addressing environmental justice concerns (related to climate breakdown's disproportionate impacts on, and exacerbating vulnerabilities particularly within, communities of color), there is often minimal intersectionalist thinking in their relentless focus on greenhouse gas emissions and atmospheric carbon. These tendencies operate to narrow the horizon of activism as well as the composition of stakeholder communities, create competitive factions, and weaken alliance-building efforts (partly by failing to overcome identitarian divisions). Against this tide, Kyle Whyte argues that decolonization and anticolonialism "cannot be disaggregated from climate justice for Indigenous peoples"—and, I would add, for all frontline stakeholders—who place "resistance to the nexus of colonialism, capitalism and industrialization at the vanguard of their work."[40] Delinking such concerns, in other words, is how "mainstream environmental justice politics are inherently preoccupied with the maintenance of settler state sovereignty and settler futurity," Jaskiran Dhillon concludes.[41] Lest we succumb to such risks—and at their worst, they include eco-fascism's blending of organic purity with ethnonationalism—we must take these concerns seriously and form solidarity across difference.

If, as the Combahee River Collective, based in Boston and working in the 1970s, once wrote, "we are not convinced . . . that a socialist revolution that is not also a feminist and anti-racist revolution will guarantee our liberation," then today, we could equally say, it is impossible to imagine any revolution that will not also be a socioecological one.[42] Not surprisingly, the Movement for Black Lives' 2016 "Vision for Black Lives: Policy Demands for Black Power, Freedom, and Justice" includes exactly this addition: "While this platform is focused on domestic policies, we know that patriarchy, exploitative capitalism, militarism, and white supremacy know no borders. We stand in solidarity with our international family against the ravages of global capitalism and anti-Black racism, human-made climate change, war, and exploitation."[43] If current emancipation politics do not center climate considerations, then structural discrimination will continue to determine how governments and policy makers respond to this existential crisis, circumscribing all possible worlds to come. With such a scenario, we face the continuation of international environmental racism in the developed world's refusal to share technologies and resources and assist poorer countries suffering years of neocolonial financial domination in protecting themselves from extreme weather, thereby worsening inequalities, and fortressing the wealthy against the pressures of climate migration, as life is made increasingly unlivable for (nearly) all.[44] For those of us, myself included, who are white, non-Indigenous citizens of the US, opposing white supremacy includes opposing eco-fascism and green capitalism, acting in solidarity with those who have experienced the oppressions and violence on which this country has been built, and working with all towards a just future.[45] In this regard, it is worth recalling the ethically unassailable words of Alicia Garza of #BlackLivesMatter, who argues that Black lives "are important to your liberation . . . [and] when Black people in this country get free, the benefits will be wide reaching and transformative for society as a whole."[46]

In regard to the above implied refusal to limit the significance of climate to the biogeophysical realm, my second methodological intervention is to expand the reach of "climate" and "environment" to sociopolitical and economic fields.[47] In this move I draw inspiration from such analyses as Christina Sharpe's, where, attentive to the wake of transatlantic slavery, she discusses "antiblackness as total climate," highlighting the "atmospheric density" of racism after the time when "slavery undeniably became the total environment."[48] Such a conceptualization resonates as well with Stefano Harney and Fred Moten's poignant response to the 2015 killing of Michael Brown in Ferguson, Missouri, shot twelve times by white police officer Darren Wilson, his dead body then simply left on the street for four hours:

"Michael Brown is the latest name of the ongoing event of resistance to, and resistance before, socioecological disaster," they write. "Modernity's constitution in the transatlantic slave trade, settler colonialism and capital's emergence in and with the state, is The Socioecological Disaster."[49]

To conceive of climate as antiblackness, or socioecology as antiracist resistance, is to make a major intervention within mainstream environmental discourses, refusing ecologies of affluence and its disciplinary specialization and rejecting the perpetuation of color-blind environmentalism, as when its definition is institutionally and conceptually restricted to nonhuman natures. I find these insights crucial on several counts, especially if we are to avoid perpetuating the false idealism of locating nature beyond, instead of firmly within, culture, politics, and technology (and certainly some Anthropocene conceptualizations do important work here in avoiding such binaries). It is not just that Black and Brown communities have been and still are disproportionately situated near toxic waste sites, landfills, and incinerators—as African American environmental justice advocates have pointed out since the 1960s.[50] It is not simply that US environmentalism has historically been a privileged affair of racial exclusion, dedicated to wilderness protection, with its conservationist modernity colluding with settler colonial policies of Indigenous displacement and occupation of Native lands, whether to secure them as national parks or to develop them for environmentally destructive extractive projects, as social justice critics have stressed.[51] And it is not only the associations of environmentalism with white leisure, ethical consumerism, and liberal elite morality that is the problem.[52] In addition to all these factors, I find that the theoretico-political insights of Sharpe, Harney, and Moten are essential in mobilizing an intersectionalist language in order to resist nature/culture divisions; to insist on structural critiques that link intrahuman racial/sexual/ethnic/discriminatory violence with wider environmental destruction; and to expand climatological conditions to such factors as psycho-affective weather, jurisgenerative atmospheres, and aesthetic-environmental materializations, some of which have been naturalized over time, and which all require sensitive analysis and critical scrutiny.

These speculative positions have only begun to be developed in relation to political ecology as a mode of entangled environmentalism and aesthetic practice. Forwarding such a project here, I am thinking alongside such like-minded cultural critics as Yates McKee, who, in "Climate Justice, Black Lives Matter, and the Arts of Decolonization," comes to a similar conclusion as my own: that such an intersectionalist grouping of practices "spell[s] the dissolution of 'environmentalism' as a specialized realm of activism into a broader horizon of antiracist collective liberation."[53] I also take my lead from artistic practitioners included in the following chapters, who have compellingly modeled diverse forms of aesthetic construction that underscore just these commitments of ecology-as-intersectionality, founded on convictions of both social justice and climate science. Though these connections might not always be explicitly theorized or intended by the artists under discussion, I take it as one task in this book to connect the dots, articulating and analyzing the expansive implications of their practice in regards to these very concerns.

My third methodological approach, related to the two above, is to artic-ulate and support the arts of political ecology and their justice-based frame-work, which, as we have seen, emerges from the history of environmental justice politics and more recent decolonial directions—challenging, in other words, the neohumanism and postpolitical Anthropocene positions arising out of select geology and environmental humanities research. Dipesh Chakrabarty, for instance, cites liberal humanist Yuval Noah Harari's *Sapiens: A Brief History of Humankind* (a favorite of the likes of tech giants Mark Zucker-berg and Bill Gates) in proposing a species-based etiology of climate change, originating in the evolutionary rift when *Homo sapiens* first adopted tools, jumping to the top of the food chain yet without the cultural preparedness, according to Harari, to assume the ecological responsibilities demanded of that role.[54] These speculations are predicated upon claims that the Anthropo-cene is somehow fundamental to humanity, which, if true, exceeds not only the bounds of current and historical economic systems but also "human-centered thinking about justice, and thus . . . our political thought as well."[55] The result, however, effectively naturalizes Anthropocene climate transfor-mation. As Andreas Malm and Alf Hornborg contend, "species-thinking on climate change is conducive to mystification and political paralysis," and, though Chakrabarty goes to length to defend against this criticism, I can only agree with the formers' charge.[56] Moreover, I find it untenable conceptually and politically to adopt any such perspective from outside our situated po-sition within advanced racial capitalist and colonial modernity that would allow speculative thought beyond our socioeconomic system—which is why I read this kind of science-based geological thinking ultimately as postpoliti-cal, carving out a privileged liberal preserve and dangerously encouraging the neoliberal Anthropocene's conceptualization of "human activities" as unavoidable, inevitably leading to profound climate injustices.[57]

Instead, a far better course is, in my view, to operate from within the framework of environmental and by extension climate justice, which stresses the differential impacts—racially and economically determined—of biogeophysical transformations. In addition, that framework locates causality in the long unfolding of capitalist reason, which turns everything into economic units, seeking to extract the last drop of value from the web of life, even to the point of placing short-term profits above life's very survival. In doing so, the conditions of the extractive present propel the transformation of biopolitics (which also flips into necropolitics) into what Elizabeth Povinelli has termed geontopower.

> As extractive, industrial, and informational capitalism continues to generate climate change and toxic hot spots, the governance of biopower is fraying and revealing a kind of governance that I call geontopower. Geontopower does not operate through the governance of life and the tactics of death but is rather a set of discourses, affects, and tactics used in late liberalism to maintain or shape the relationship between life and nonlife. I do not see geontopower as a power only now emerging to replace biopolitics. Instead, biopower (governance through life and death) has long depended on a subtending geontopower, a mode of power that polices and regulates the difference between the lively and the inert, and that has operated openly in settler colonialism and its related forms.[58]

I view Povinelli's geontopolitics as enabling important insights into the conflicts around Earth elements, such as water, soil and air, that increasingly inform struggles across the Americas—from those of the Tar Sands, Standing Rock, and the Bayou Bridge Pipeline to the contests over the Amazon's resources in Brazil, Ecuador, and Colombia—which pit the forces of petrocapitalism and its commodification of everything against those who defend the web of life and nonhuman elements on the basis of radically different values.[59] It remains crucial to strengthen these transnational alliances, to contribute further energies to this movement of movements, which begins not by limiting our understanding of climate to greenhouse gas emissions or by extending it to humanity as a whole, but by opening it to an intersectionalist politics of climate justice, one that also inevitably bridges, if never collapses, different conceptions of what the more-than-human world is (say, between Indigenous views of Earth's sacred being and environmentalists' secular notions of the ecological commons).[60]

The preceding examples beg the question: What is justice? It is a complex term for sure, far from coterminous with legality, as we learn from the discourses of Afro-pessimism, which variously observe how slavery was legal for hundreds of years in the West, its history dramatizing the structural disjunction between law and justice in the starkest of terms.[61] Indeed, justice proposes a triple bind, according to Jacques Derrida's analysis: once codified and instituted as law, it becomes inflexible, unfree, and a mere mechanistic calculation (its first aporia); if necessarily reinstituted, its singularity is haunted by the "ghost of the undecidable," by subjective and capricious reason detached from collective deliberation and democratic accountability (its second aporia); and if justice is nonetheless necessary, it always, to some degree, refers to a world to come, one never fully present and available in the now, its urgency never quite reaching finality (its ultimate aporia).[62] Against the risk of making emergency decisions in the "night of non-knowledge," it is all the more vital that choices be made not by individual morals or elite dictate but by wide consensus, which in the framework of climate justice necessarily includes the most vulnerable and disenfranchised frontline communities. Breaking through these poststructuralist aporias, Cornel West claims that "justice is what love looks like in public."[63] I find his poetic formulation moving, its atmosphere of collective affect precisely what is needed in expressing the intangible sense of justice's necessary embeddedness and ultimate defining role in collective struggles like the Black radical tradition, decolonial praxis, and climate justice activism. I am reliant on this formulation too in considering more expansive climates in relation to my own mapping of the ambitious claims of what the arts of political ecology mean in contemporary culture, what the arts of living beyond the end/s of the world might look like. "Transformative justice" offers another urgent category, distinct from the state's retributive forms, connecting to West's radical love: it acknowledges the realities of state and corporate violence; seeks alternative ways to address and interrupt cycles of harm without relying on privatized, individualized response; turns to organic and creative strategies that are community created and social-movement directed; and seeks to transform the root causes of violence and inequality rather than merely address their symptoms.[64] Contemporary aesthetic practices can aid in just these ambitions, as I will argue in this book.

These conceptual mutations of ecology, I argue, parallel contemporary transformations of art—as advanced by the practitioners considered here—into sites of expanded creativity, unbounded by commercial institutions that tend to discipline and manage its products as distinctive luxury commodities for wealthy clienteles (defining an increasingly outmoded form of cultural practice). Equally, my approach to aesthetic practice is distinct from models of ecocritical art history that inadvertently turn ecology into a thematic concern (often celebrating exclusively nonhuman realms), picturing and materializing ecology and thereby containing its radical relationality within the artistic frame. The result effectively discounts the transformative event of climate breakdown, contributing to institutional normalization, and disregards art's more ambitious interventions within socioecologies of racial capitalism and colonial extractivism. In my reading, art defines the experimental practice of world-making, generative of justice-based cultural values and creating thinking-feeling places of radical sensibility. Its practice includes speculative and critical knowledge creation, situated within or allied with communities of action and social movements, and always, most ambitiously, provoking and furthering an entanglement of insights, perceptions, affects.[65] In other words, these are what I have termed creative ecologies—practices that make new sensible materializations and connections (aesthetic, practical, jurisgenerative) between otherwise discrete realms of experience and knowledge, and that cultivate just worlds to come.[66]

In this regard, I am thinking alongside expansive theorizations of the intersection of aesthetics and politics, as with Jacques Rancière's conceptualizations where aesthetics proposes possible "framing[s] of the common world," "where the forms of collective life are produced and can be transformed."[67] These "forms of life," sensible ways of doing and making, intervene in and reconfigure worlds of shared experience, with commonality predicated upon political dissensus (really another kind of uncommons), materializing the terms of structural antagonisms that define the stakes of emergent collective composition and solidarity.[68] Building on this understanding, it is vital also to push beyond its anthropocentric limitations, drawing together its "forms of [human] life" with an expansive "life of forms," where semiosis and creativity are not enclosed within uniquely human cultures of commonality. How might the world-generating activity of aesthetics become multinatural, a multispecies affair, and not simply the reserve of human exceptionalism (as it remains in Rancière's philosophy, and by extension, in much conventional art discourse)? In addition, how might life itself be conceived as a mode of material meaning-making? There are growing conceptual resources in this domain, including the work of multispecies ethnography, posthumanist anthropology, and feminist speculative science studies, which also collectively produce new and exciting postanthropocentric intersections to forward multispecies justice claims.[69] These have been taken up in contemporary artistic experimentation with the invention of new forms of life, sensitive also to the life of forms, in innovative configurations of political aesthetics. If some of the artworks considered in chapters below propose justice-based ecologies, then these expressions often re-align (non)human and more-than-human worlds in ways that do not reach an easy resolution. The possibilities of coexistence must ultimately reckon with incommensurate ontologies and multispecies perspectives as much as the ongoing destruction of biodiverse existence by extractive industry and anthropogenic climate breakdown. In this regard, my understanding of commonality is premised on what Marisol de la Cadena and Mario Blaser call the "uncommons": "the heterogeneous grounds where negotiations take place toward a commons that would be a continuous achievement, an event whose vocation is not to be final because it remembers that the uncommons is its constant starting point."[70]

My present analysis traces, more precisely, three interlinked transformations occurring in artistic, or more broadly aesthetic, practice, as they diversely materialize ecologies of intersectionality. The first is the negation of conventional art's commodity function, targeting art's institutionalization and consequent depoliticization, its complicit participation in oppressive systems (even while acknowledging the impossibility of spaces of purity, contradiction being the overarching condition these days, even while some are more complicit than others). All the practices I write about in this book share in this project of institutional transgression on some level, challenging oppression in multiple ways. As the MTL Collective, whose work I discuss in chapter 7, asks:

> What if, as artists and cultural producers, when we speak of "art" and "activism," we put both under erasure? What if we strike art to liberate it from itself? Not to end art, but to free it from the circuits of capital, white supremacy, settler colonialism, and debt, and to unleash its powers to imagine that which is not immediately apparent. And, what if, as

we reject the specialization of activism we choose a never ending process of experimentation and questioning, or, we choose, as the Zapatis-
tas say, to "make the path by walking." Let art be training in the practice
of decolonial freedom.[71]

This endeavor does not entail the complete abandonment of past aesthetic
and critical approaches. Rather, it involves a strategic engagement with the
radical resources of avant-garde practice (from speculative documentary aesthetics to creative participatory practice and institutional critique), as much
as selectively drawing on the progressive politics of social movements and
theories of anticapitalism and decolonization. One exemplary expression is
the movement for institutional liberation, comprising those groups (including MTL) working internationally to strike against art's enclosure within petrocapitalism's political economy of operations, including its sponsorship,
patronage, governance, and financial systems, according to which, striking
against the Guggenheim, Whitney Museum, or Tate Modern, for instance,
constitutes a socioecological act of decolonial liberation.[72] The emphasis
here is not only placed on nonreformist reforms—immediately contesting
cultural institutions' sponsorship agreements with fossil fuel corporations
like BP (formerly British Petroleum) in order to revoke their "social licence
to pollute" whereby industry "artwashes" its activities—but also on the
practice of what MTL terms "collective liberation."[73] Additionally, for Not
an Alternative (the formerly New York–based collective whose work I also
discuss in my final chapter) "institutional liberation isn't about making institutions better, more inclusive, more participatory. It's about establishing
politicized base camps from which ever more coordinated, elaborate, and
effective campaigns against the capitalist state in all its racist, exploitative,
extractivist and colonizing dimensions can be carried out."[74] Within such
engagements I see a forceful expression of political ecology, which importantly strikes out as well against the institutional containment and insuf-
ficient political engagement of much conventional eco-art.

Second, I examine the transformations of aesthetic creativity in opening
up new worldings of justice-based ecologies. While there is a substantial
history of ecocritical art in the Euro-American context that has unfolded
over the last few decades, examples of justice-based environmental arts, or
aesthetic practices exploring entangled or intersectionalist socioecologies,
have been few and far between.[75] In this regard, I am building on framings of
artistic practice in my recent books, including *Decolonizing Nature* and *Against*

the Anthropocene, wherein I identified a range of experimental models that, in my view, have forcefully materialized formations of politico-ecological aesthetics and practice. The case studies given in the present volume build on those bases, including considering documentary's innovative complex forms in ways that are both representational (creatively portraying conflict geographies through innovative signifying systems) and affective (expressing emotional intensities and linking them to political ecologies through moving images), thereby working in tandem toward ambitious and collective interventions within forms of sensibility, critical thinking, and experimental modes of living otherwise. In this vein, I focus on complex aesthetic modalities that are relational, hinging cross-sectoral differences and multidisciplinary knowledge systems, in order to materialize connective intersections, with creative ecologies producing assemblages of new insights, embodied sensations, and transformative experience.[76] By foregrounding speculative imagination, these creative ecologies not only critically expose oppressive structures but also open up emancipatory futures, new worlds beyond catastrophic climate breakdown, colonial domination, and social injustice.

Lastly, I argue that the current and ongoing structural transformation of artistic practice—particularly in relation to climate justice politics—is happening most dramatically beyond art's conventional institutions, within social movements, where creativity is fueling the building of new worlds by using diverse and everyday materials and ideas couched in the struggles, images, and stories of collective liberation. This occurs, for example, when the Unist'ot'en camp in British Columbia constructs geontopolitical assemblages (including barricades) that reject Canadian sovereignty claims and assert political ecologies of decolonial land-based efforts committed to the protection of Earth elements; or when Standing Rock's #NoDAPL struggle forms collective choreographies of resistance to contest the expansion of petrocapitalist infrastructure on their sacred lands, placing bodies on the line against the settler atmospherics of state police gas attacks working for catastrophic oil extraction. With artists, media practitioners, musicians, and diverse accomplices contributing to these current world wars, we encounter some of the most meaningful rift zones in Anthropocene times. It is in these cosmopolitical rift zones that a future world of many worlds has already begun to emerge.

FEEDING
THE GHOST

JOHN AKOMFRAH'S
VERTIGO SEA

O*blique tales on the aquatic sublime.* The phrase, appearing as one of *Vertigo Sea*'s nine intertitles, is apt for this moving three-channel video installation, created by John Akomfrah in 2015.[1] Running at forty-eight minutes, the piece investigates the ocean as a multivalent site of geopolitical conflict, liquid nationality, and postnational uprooting, all set within still-unfolding histories of colonialism, migration, slavery, and environmental transformation. In terms of affect, the ocean appears as locus of terror and beauty, providing a vast expanse of resonant meanings and experiential sensations where incongruous narratives interact. Most notably these are of social injustice and environmental violence, a pairing not often joined in contemporary art but all the more important to do so to avoid the siloing of each, thereby minimizing significance and impact, and to mobilize the power of their intersection. In Akomfrah's rendition that opposes any such narrow approach, startling seascapes provide colorful imagery as well as haunting backdrops for the routes of colonial exploration and the transatlantic slave trade, the latter referenced by seconds-long clips of shackled Black figures lying on the dank bunks of a ship's hold. In other scenes,

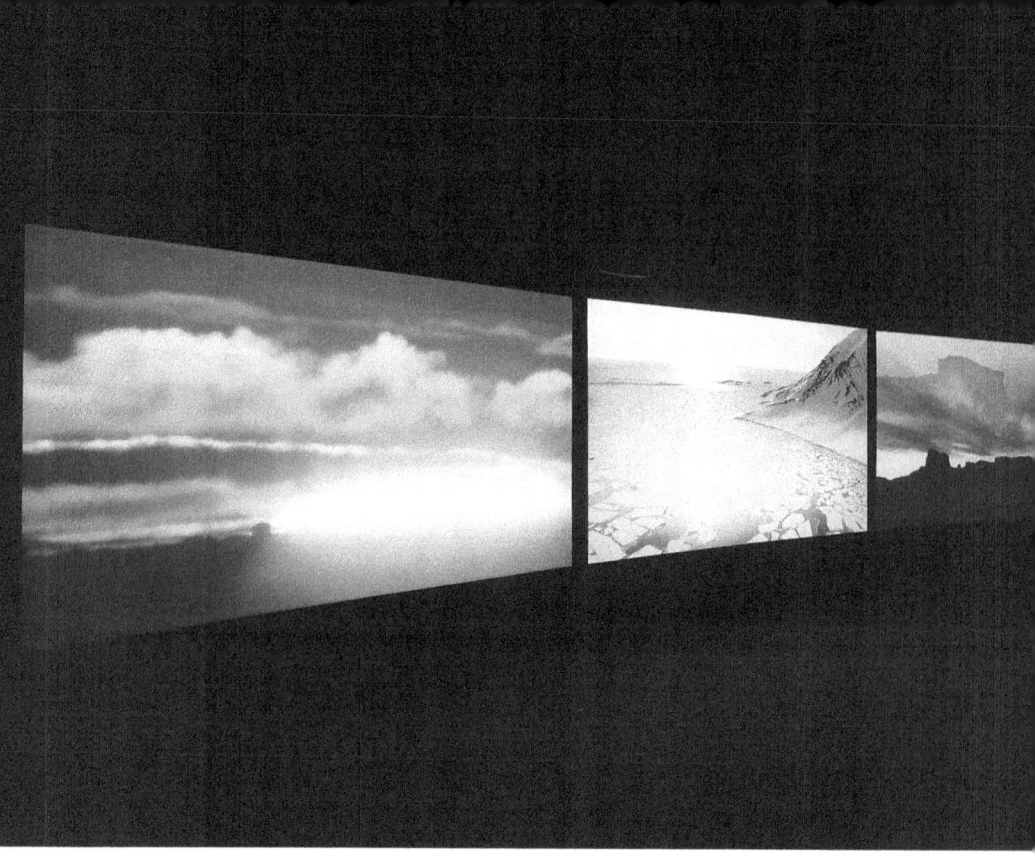

1.1 John Akomfrah, *Vertigo Sea*, 2015 (still). Three-channel HD color video installation, 7.1 sound, 48 minutes, 30 seconds. © Smoking Dogs Films. Source: Lisson Gallery.

stunning images of marine life, including dolphins and orcas, are interrupted by black-and-white passages of sailors killing whales and hunting polar bears. Gorgeous footage of mountainous Arctic icescapes competes with the brutal industrialization and militarization of nature, the sea serving as test site for nuclear bombs and extraction field for deepwater oil drilling, as well as sink for their leaks and backdrop for their fiery explosions. In this socioecological entanglement, oceanic signs of climate breakdown and global warming, appearing in footage of melting icebergs and calving glaciers, counterpoint shots of the sea as cemetery, where the bodies of countless Europe-bound migrants wash up on shore.

This panoply of images is partly drawn from the BBC's archive of nature films and television programs, including David Attenborough's sumptuous sea life documentary *The Blue Planet* from 2001 (updated in 2017 as *Blue Planet II*, notably including a final episode showcasing plastic pollution in

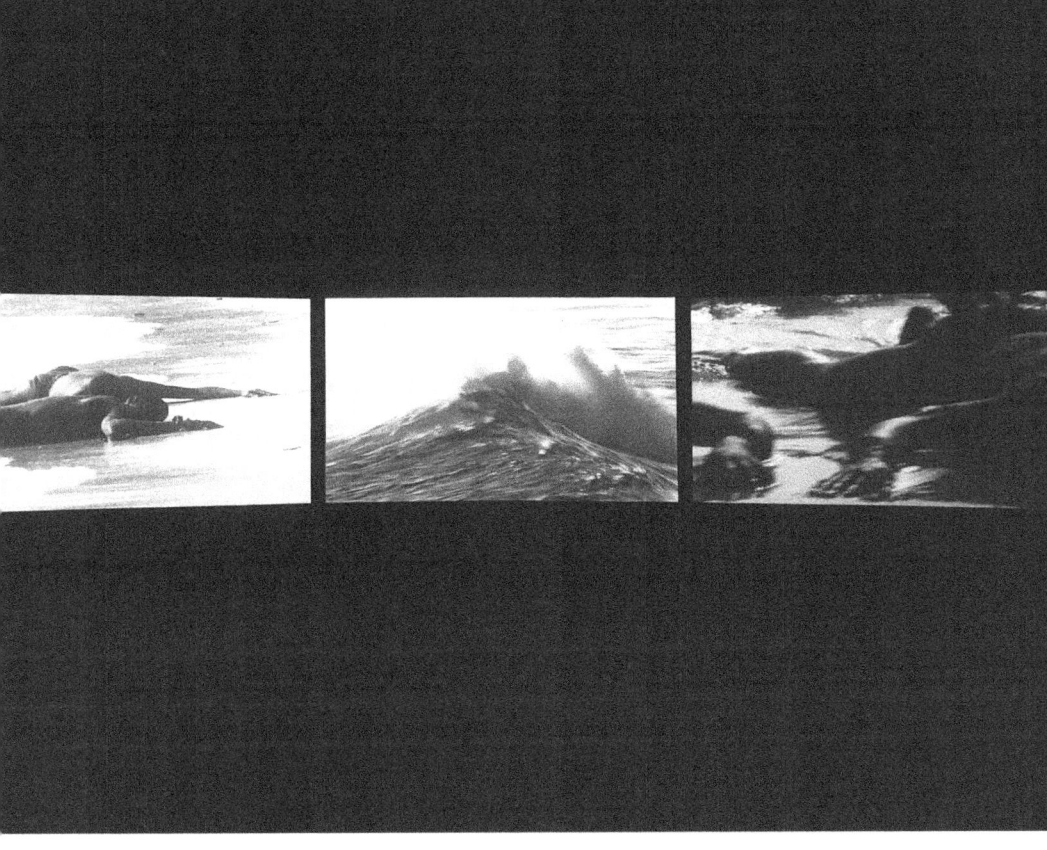

1.2 John Akomfrah, *Vertigo Sea*, 2015 (still). Three-channel HD color video installation, 7.1 sound, 48 minutes, 30 seconds. © Smoking Dogs Films. Source: Lisson Gallery.

the oceans). But in *Vertigo Sea*, these images appear delinked from their original narratives and explanatory voice-overs, where they functioned largely to dramatize the wonders of oceanography and marine biology as detached from all human life. In Akomfrah's treatment the footage becomes newly charged with intertwined social, political, and ecological impact and urgency.[2] Shifting the focus from nature documentary to socio-historical drama, the film adds footage shot by Akomfrah depicting Olaudah Equiano (1745–1797), the freed African slave and abolitionist who traveled the seas, explored the Arctic, and lived out his life in England. Equiano wrote an important autobiography detailing his opposition to slavery and in which the sea also figures as a place of multiple valences—of wondrous beauty, existential threat, and watery captivity alike—all of which serve as an important source of historical reference for the film.[3] Joined together in an immersive triple projection, Akomfrah's powerful montage is redoubled in the soundtrack (designed by longtime collaborator Trevor Mathison), where breathy strings of majestic and foreboding affect combine with whale song, interrupted at times with utter shock by the echoing shots of hunting rifles, the blasts of harpoon cannons, and whales' wailing. Indeed these images and sounds produce a powerful emotional score—what Akomfrah calls a transformative "affective economy" where "things and beings renew their relationship with each other"—although here the renewal produces a sense of devastating grief and sadness in view of the deathly outcome of biological annihilation and multispecies extinctions resulting from the insatiable modern industry and capitalist exploitation depicted in the video.[4] In *Vertigo Sea*, the intimation of renewal only comes after brutal destruction, giving rise to perhaps more of an emotional desire and yearning for reparation than showing any realization of post-apocalyptic flourishing.

Bringing these audiovisual elements together in conversation, including at times into painful conflict, Akomfrah offers a haunting meditation on fraught histories and visual cultures of Western modernity drawn from the perspective of the sea. At the same time, in defining a necessary historical ground for any future vision of emancipation and justice to be realized, any renewal to be initiated, it offers important lessons for how to live, perceive, and think sensitively and deeply in the present, steering clear of any emotionally manipulative forms of social documentary. Focusing attention on the intervals between projections as much as their interior images, the triptych, in Akomfrah's hands, proposes a cinema of spatialized relationality as well as an archival work of temporal correspondences that resists providing any simple message, moral, or partisan interpretation, even while it manifests an overdetermined space of what might be called the spectro-poetics of colonial violence, slavery, and multispecies death. While *Vertigo Sea* reveals unanticipated connections between narratives, none of them complete, and virtual openings that offer places where the unexpected appears and where discovery can occur, its drama is nonetheless devastating, implicating centuries of colonial conquest and slavery in the unfolding world-ending climate and environmental catastrophes of the present.[5] Indeed, Akomfrah pays homage to Equiano's own impassioned exposure of the horrors of bondage in his autobiography, if without dwelling on the abject re-presentation of its violences and daily abjection:

> Tortures, murder, and every other imaginable barbarity and iniquity, are practised upon the poor slaves with impunity. I hope the slave trade

will be abolished. I pray it may be an event at hand. The great body of manufacturers, uniting in the cause, will considerably facilitate and expedite it; and as I have already stated, it is most substantially their interest and advantage, and as such the nation's at large, (except those persons concerned in the manufacturing of neck-yokes, collars, chains, cuffs, leg-bolts, drags, thumb-screws, iron muzzles, and coffins; cats, scourges, and other instruments of torture used in the slave trade.) In a short time one sentiment alone will prevail, from motives of interest as well as justice and humanity.[6]

Part of Equiano's goal, in writing his Narrative, was to shed light on and thereby help put an end to the cruel and profitable practices of the slavery that had engulfed him (and the devastating effects of which he witnessed countless times in relation to others of African descent). Perhaps Akomfrah's aim is still greater: to strike out against contemporary forms of racial subjection and deathly exclusion that continue the legacy of the slavery Equiano fought so hard to overcome; and to show how that struggle has only expanded, inextricably connected now to challenging the world-destroying project of capitalist modernity that has brought about catastrophic climate breakdown, sweeping all manner of species into its destructive unfolding.

MIGRANT HISTORIES

In its audio track, Vertigo Sea cites several cultural and socioecological references. These include passages from famous literature that takes the sea as its subject, such as Herman Melville's Moby-Dick (1851) and Virginia Woolf's To the Lighthouse (1927); philosophical accounts of conceptual exploration, namely Friedrich Nietzsche's Thus Spoke Zarathustra (1883–91); and hymns dedicated to marine life, specifically Heathcote Williams's epic poem Whale Nation (1988). Although more often than not what results is a matter of visual and affective cinematic experience instead of informational communication typical of conventional documentaries. In addition, there are recent TV reports of unnamed refugee deaths at sea, which have become all too familiar in recent years, as multitudes from the Global South, particularly those from war-devastated areas where conflict has been exacerbated by climate breakdown and agricultural failure, risk their lives seeking European shores for economic opportunity or to escape desperate circumstances of military conflict and oppression. 2015 was a record year, with approximately one million migrants arriving in Europe, mostly from Syria, Afghanistan, and Iraq. Stand-alone audio elements, referencing the above, enter into the film intermittently, without proposing clear connections to the imagery or obeying a specific order or chronology, the piece being overall nonnarrative. As such, the film develops the aesthetic strategies found in Akomfrah's earliest productions with Black Audio Film Collective (BAFC), including *Signs of Empire* (1982–84), a sequential slide projection with a Wagnerian soundtrack that probes the visuality of Britain's colonial aftermath in cultural images, archival documents, and sculptural monuments, while mixing in prompting titles of critical speculation. They also build off his more recent post-BAFC productions, such as *The Nine Muses* (2010) and *Peripeteia* (2012), particularly in these latter attempts to foreground migrant experience by utilizing a mix of archival imagery and dramatized shots in meditative wintry landscapes that draw on an oblique and rare Western art history representing subjects of African descent often shown in the margins of paintings. In *Vertigo Sea*, audiovisual matter similarly unfolds to reveal a dizzying intersection of history, fiction, and philosophy, a vertigo of spaces and times, images and geographies, without clear boundaries between them, a fluidity of allusions that also works against the isolation of any given category or subject.[7]

As Akomfrah has explained in reference to the "unspeakable moments" sparked through similar juxtapositions in *The Unfinished Conversation* (2012), his film triptych installation addressing the life and work of late cultural theorist Stuart Hall, montage—manifested both *spatially* in relation to the multiplication of screens and projections and *temporally* in terms of the sequencing of footage over time—possesses the power to elicit "unconscious relations between the subject and historical forces" and "uncanny" affinities beyond the "literalism of historical causality."[8] Deploying montage's fundamentally migrant image, involving both images of the displaced and the displacement of images in ever new contextualizations and recontextualizations, *Vertigo Sea* builds on that precedent, defining an innovative cinematic methodology to endow the past, present, and future with new meanings.[9] On the one hand, the film's resulting chronopolitics constructs a fluid historical consciousness that bleeds into the present (and as we will see, impacts the future), by which it faces the difficulty of memorializing a past that is not yet past but which continues into the now, in the wake of what came before. That approach is particularly generative in relation to the history and present aftermath of transatlantic slavery; for if Akomfrah's *Vertigo Sea* is, in part, a meditation on its legacy, then it also enlivens a space "in

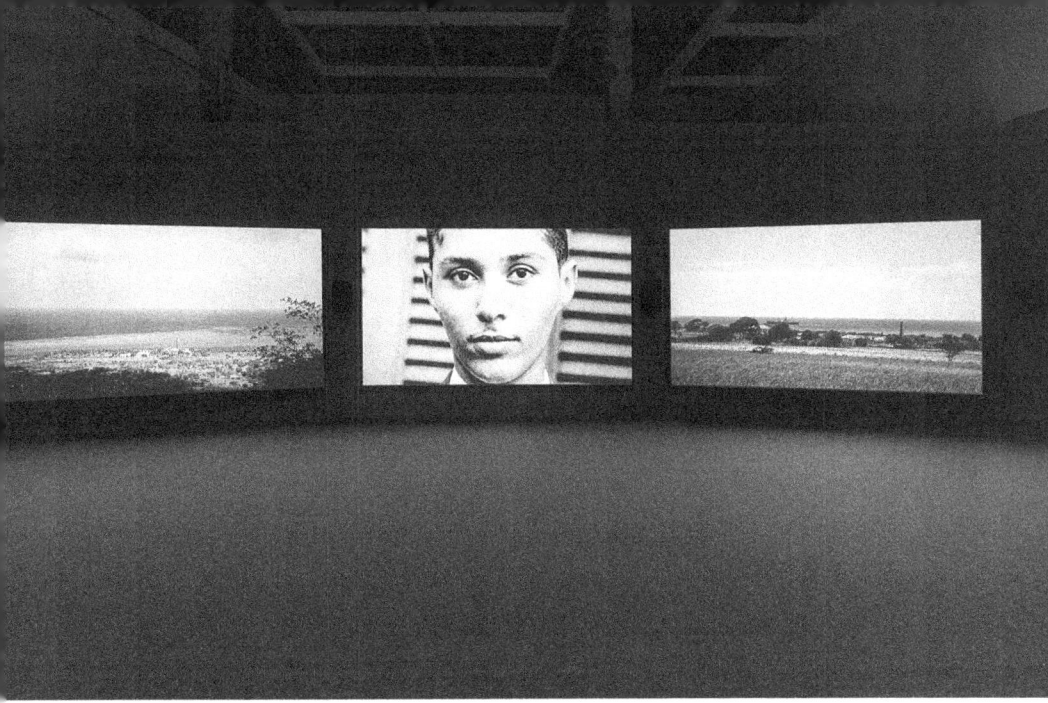

1.3 John Akomfrah, *The Unfinished Conversation*, 2012 (still). Three-channel video installation, 7.1 sound, 45 minutes, 48 seconds. © Smoking Dogs Films; Source Lisson Gallery.

the wake"—trailing the slave/migrant ship, mourning loss, keeping watch, coming into consciousness—that is a condition of contemporary Black existence, as discussed by Christina Sharpe. As Sharpe writes, "In the wake, the semiotics of the slave ship continue: from the forced movements of the enslaved to the forced movements of the migrant and the refugee, to the regulation of Black people in North American streets and neighborhoods, to those ongoing crossings of and drownings in the Mediterranean Sea, to the brutal colonial reimaginings of the slave ship and the ark; to the reappearances of the slave ship in everyday life in the form of the prison, the camp, and the school."[10] Akomfrah's work speaks to all these facets. Indeed these thematics continue in the poetics of Akomfrah's *Vertigo Sea*. At the same time, the film's vertiginous sea of references, times, and geographies includes novel approaches to the imaging and imagining of the Black Atlantic that also connects the history of slavery to the deadening Atlantic, a current threat resulting from the industrial destruction of marine life as well as the catastrophic transformation of environments and climate change into so many aquatic dead zones. It thus generates thematic flows not often conceptually joined together in contemporary art and discourse.

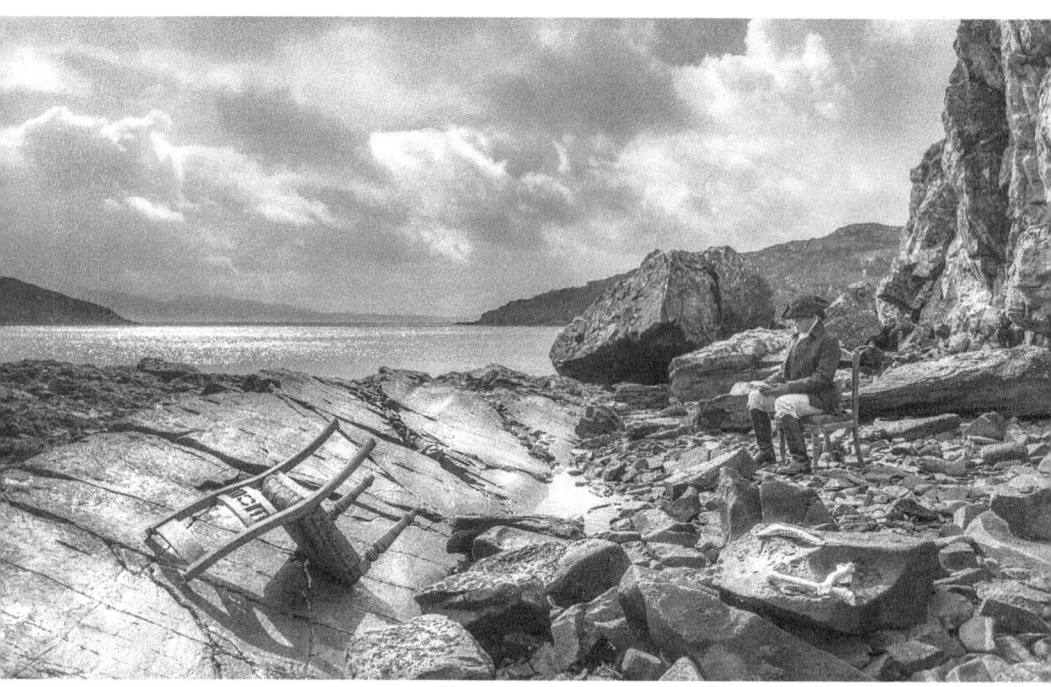

1.4 John Akomfrah, *Vertigo Sea*, 2015 (still). Three-channel HD color video installation, 7.1 sound, 48 minutes, 30 seconds. © Smoking Dogs Films. Source: Lisson Gallery.

The film's idea of vertigo—which characterizes the effects of Akomfrah's geo-historiographic methodology, including its aesthetic function that unleashes uncanny affinities and unconscious relations between Black death and ecocide—is further thematized by the footage of Equiano, who, as we know from his autobiography, was from the Igbo region of what is now southeastern Nigeria. In dramatic footage, *Vertigo Sea* pictures him statically in stylized tableaus, standing in eighteenth-century European attire on an unidentified northern coast gazing out at the sea. He appears in states of contemplation against ravishing backdrops of coastal mountains, bringing to mind the romantic paintings of Caspar David Friedrich, and also providing an analogue of the viewer's own position watching the film, initiating a slew of potential identifications, inviting a spectatorship associated with philosophic and historical inquiry mixed with natural science. There is equally a disidentificatory sense of standing apart from the wastelands of historical and ecological devastation, as if proposing an oneiric and distant being uncaptured by any single narrative, a figuring apart from the stream

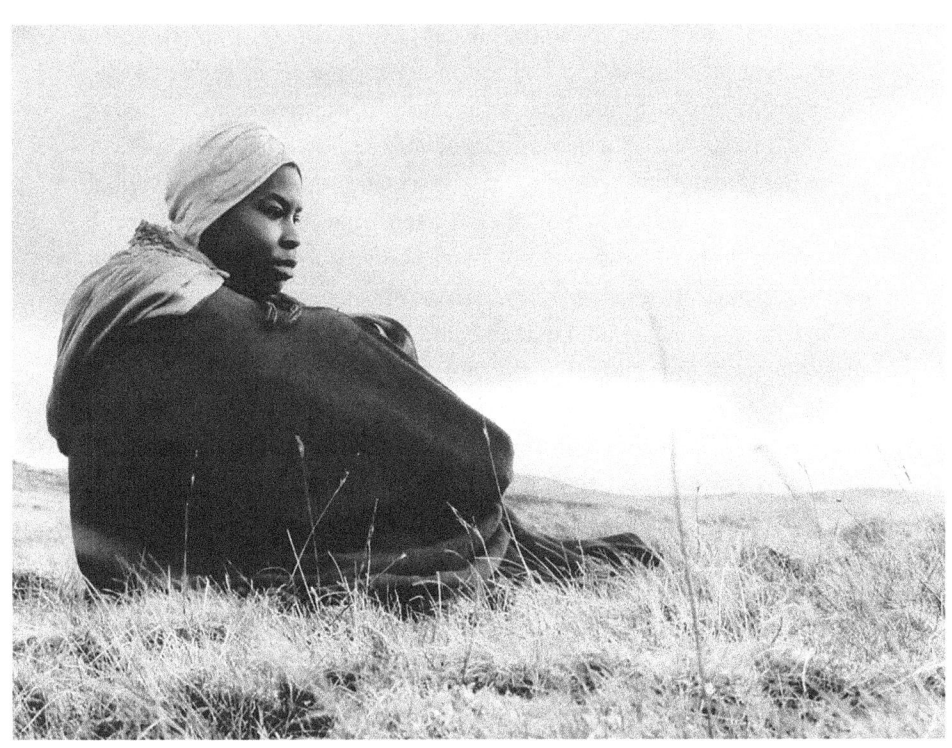

1.5 John Akomfrah, *Peripeteia*, 2012 (still). Single-channel HD color video installation, 5.1 sound, 17 minutes, 28 seconds. © Smoking Dogs Films. Source: Lisson Gallery.

of events, or even the brutal realities shown in the footage. In one scene, recalling Salvador Dalí's *The Persistence of Memory* (1931) but correlated with Akomfrah's modeling of his own version of Afro-surrealism, Equiano is shown amid a range of clocks, each set to a different time and strewn about on a beach; in another, evoking the ocean iconography of literary romanticism as found in Daniel Defoe's *Robinson Crusoe* (1719), he appears on the coast surrounded by assorted domestic items—an iron bed frame, a bicycle, a buggy—picturing the scene of a shipwreck, a migrant image (out of context, free-floating, unhinged) as much as an image of migration (of travel, displacement, dislocation). By referencing Equiano, *Vertigo Sea* continues the critically revisionary cultural history of Akomfrah's recent films, such as *Peripeteia*, which explores some of the earliest appearances of Black figures in Western painting, as found, for instance, in works by the sixteenth-century artist Albrecht Dürer. In Akomfrah's films, these figures become visible densities of imagination and mnemonic recovery, as well as dramatizations of knowing self-awareness and critical distance from context, contesting the consignment of Blackness to oblivion in the marginalia of such canvases and, equally, in the conventional art-historical narratives that continue to overlook them.[11] With these films, art history and literature—from Friedrich to Dalí, from Melville to Williams—are creatively reimagined and retold from an African diasporic point of view, one journeying through European cultural heritage and measuring it anew (including from the characters' own points of view) from that migratory, revisionist perspective.

In the case of *Vertigo Sea*, Equiano embodies a mobile site of deterritorialization, out of time and place, floating upon and confronting the vicissitudes of experiences and memories that the sea materially records and presents. The sea consequently becomes a vast field of dissolving bodies, and an abstract space of abstract liquidity, not easily connected or portrayed. That disjunctiveness has historical roots: while Equiano's *Narrative* describes its author's trials and trails in being violently ripped from his home by slavers, sold from one "owner" to another, and placed in abject servitude, it also describes his ability to purchase his freedom in his early twenties and relates how he subsequently lived an emancipated life of exploration (as much as was possible for someone like him then), seeing the world from the Arctic to Central America's Mosquito Coast.[12] At times this yielded thrilling experiences of far-flung places afforded by his travels, as recorded in his account. His description of Greenland's icescape is exemplary:

> On the 29th and 30th of July, we saw one continued plain of smooth, unbroken ice, bounded only by the horizon; and we fastened to a piece of ice that was eight yards eleven inches thick. We had generally sun shine, and constant daylight; which gave cheerfulness and novelty to the whole of this striking, grand, and uncommon scene; and, to heighten it still more, the reflection of the sun from the ice, gave the clouds a most beautiful appearance.[13]

In this regard, the radical ruptures and ambivalences in Equiano's life mirror the very incongruities he associated with the ocean, as a field of endless discovery but also a transit site of violence, even one of desired drowning to escape the perditions of the enslaved—of beauty but also terror, fear and attraction, absolute greatness and intense dread. If these associations evoke the eighteenth century's philosophical aesthetics of the sublime, the cultural framework of Equiano's Europe that *Vertigo Sea* takes up in turn, then they do so from a perspective sensitive to the experiences of one denied its privileged subjectivity.[14] Rather we see the sublime from below. Equiano's relation to the ocean was a matter of not only freedom and wonder but also existential threat, racial objectification, and social death. These shifting and flickering valences resonate with the more recent theorization of the "double consciousness" of migratory modernity, particularly that of the Black Atlantic according to Paul Gilroy's classic analysis. Viewing that complex experience through the writings of such figures as W. E. B. Du Bois and Richard Wright, Gilroy highlights in/voluntary transcultural identities resulting from trade routes and colonial invasion, discovery and expropriation, emerging through multiplying forms of perception, experience, and belonging—and indeed, Equiano is an exemplary case study for Gilroy.[15] Such a proliferating and disjunctive consciousness applied as well to Equiano's being and experience traveling between cultures, and the multiplying screens of Akomfrah's piece—a further perceptual zone of vertiginous audiovisuality—offer a cinematic approximation, a triple montage, of such complex aesthetic sensibility where migration, colonial conquest, and ecological transformation merge and divide, providing the structuring framework for that experience.[16] Equiano's *Narrative* was thus embedded in the historical dialectic between enlightenment reason and romantic expression, yielding what Fred Moten terms a literature engaging both thoughtful reflection and mediated feeling.[17] So too is Akomfrah's affective cinema symptomatic of his own, and our present, era's increasing confrontation with the impoverishment of information and data overload, necessitating new aesthetic approaches like *Vertigo Sea*: in poeticizing the image and removing talking-head commentary, it compellingly breaks through both media's boundaries of disciplinary silos and subjectivity's perceptual-conceptual divisions.

ECOLOGY AS INTERSECTIONALITY

In *Vertigo Sea* there is a further formation of double consciousness to which I have already alluded: namely, that which occurs in the entanglement of racialized social violence set within histories of rapacious slavery and deathly migration, and catastrophic climate disruption, invoking global tragedy unfolding in the human and more-than-human worlds, including the oceans. As such, with Akomfrah's work, ecology comes to define a mode of intersectionality, an approach insisting on thinking, being, and becoming at the cross section of multiple fields of sociocultural and techno-economic as much as politico-environmental determinations. Rather than repeating familiar constructions of the sublime, Akomfrah's film locates and thereby updates its perception within our own cultural-geological present, where modern society, no longer conceivable as separate from the natural world, has become a driver of disastrous environmental transformation over centuries of capitalist extraction and industry. The world that Equiano gazes upon—ultimately including our contemporary one—has colonized not only his own homeland (Portuguese explorers were among the first Europeans to conduct trade with the peoples of modern-day Nigeria, including trading bodies, at the port they called Lagos) but also, nature itself. This complex reality is what *Vertigo Sea* depicts and dramatizes. With natural and cultural zones now inextricable, and extractive industrialization increasingly determining the course of the Earth's biophysical cycles—what some call the Anthropocene; others, the Capitalocene—the incongruous categories of the sublime formerly located in the nonhuman realm now cross over into the cultural one too, each vertiginously corrupting the other.[18] Indeed, Akomfrah's film shows how the beauty of maritime nature becomes terrible under the sign of Western modernity and our capitalist present, even as the latter's horror—dramatized in scenes of the industrial destruction of whales and the collapse of the Arctic ecosystem—is grotesquely aestheticized, transfigured as a sort of cinematic geology but in no way acritically.

One effect of entering the geologic space-time of *Vertigo Sea* is that we lose our bearings—referentially, philosophically, perceptually—tipping into a nauseous loss of balance that is the very physiological enactment of vertigo. The disequilibrium occurs when we can no longer separate our own secure viewing space from that of the dizzying sight of the multitemporal real that surrounds us in Akomfrah's large-scale cinematic presentation (are we not a part of these geologies, are they not consuming us, reconfiguring our very environment and timescales, and are we not complicit, even if also victimized by these transformations?); nor do we have the distance to dissociate beauty from terror, as both combine and conspire grotesquely, horrifically, seductively. Of course Akomfrah's filmic image is not technically *the real* (as opposed to its symbolic representation, as in Lacanian psychoanalytic terms), but still, its mediation is powerfully immersive, as if it were. Taking as subject the expanded spatialization and extended temporality of the sea—a zone of unbounded scale and geological time that relativizes and displaces human epistemologies and representational capacities—Akomfrah attempts nonetheless to subject it to a frame, according to the monumentalizing terms of his triptych-based model of expanded cinema and his use of spectacular imagery, which propose a scenography of modern histories entangled with the natural, both beautiful and terrible in all of their historical resonances. The multiplying screens, the screens of multiplicity, of Vertigo Sea implies, for me, that its very filmic construction, its act of aesthetic presentation and capture, is also a visual component of Western modernity's violent project of seeing, owning, and dominating nature in the first place, as well as a resistance to that project.[19]

The film's recurring depictions of whale killing—a powerful and disturbing refrain, particularly at the present time of the sixth mass species extinction event, when we are losing some two hundred species a day at a rate one thousand times the historical average—figure as but one part of modernity's rampant colonization and destruction of the world.[20] "The way of killing men and beast is the same," reads another of Vertigo Sea's intertitles, as images mix scenes of majestic humpback and blue whales dying in watery clouds of their own blood, with those of drowned, shackled slaves washed up on beaches. Nature programs like Blue Planet, which can seemingly record every element of a whale's life and explore some of the most hidden spaces of the ocean, are here directly related to, and indicted in, the industrialization of the seas, by harpoon and camera alike: as such, the visualization of the aquatic sublime risks slipping into the socio-ecological grotesque, a case of human hubris asserting its dominance over human and nonhuman phenomena. Indeed, part of slavery's very horror resulted from the racial distinctions violently made between these two latter categories: between who is human and who animal. If aestheticization designates here a matter of the control and appropriation of nature for human pleasure (as with one common definition of aesthetics), then it parallels our horror when scenes of destruction (shipwrecks, slavery's Atlantic passage, whaling and polar bear hunting, migrants drowning) become spectacularized as filmic images, to be witnessed from a safe, mediated distance of privilege and security. Part of the horror is our powerlessness to intervene, not only in the social and ecocidal violence but also in the seemingly unstoppable imaging of its visual compulsions, the oceanic, in conventional versions and perhaps to some degree in Akomfrah's, proposing an overwhelming force of seductive obliteration and complicity with intolerable realities and images.

In this regard, beauty and horror converge. Recent marine biology and climatology research show how the seas have been transformed in modern

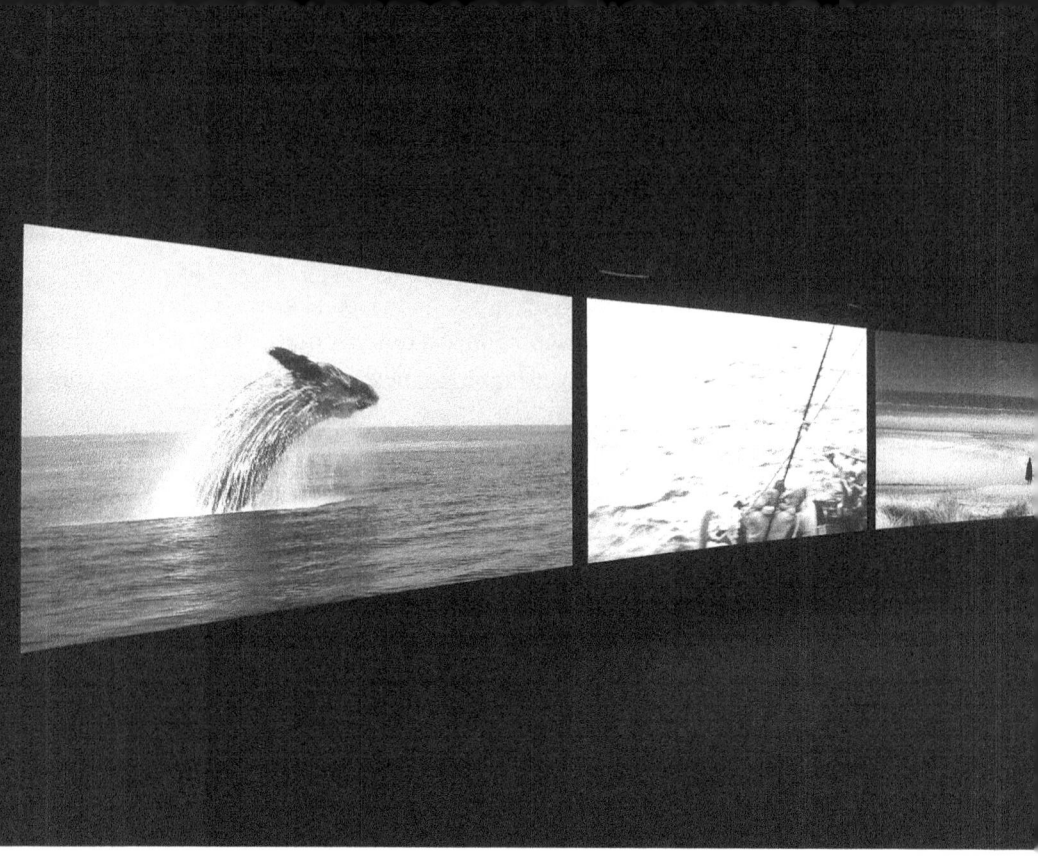

1.6 John Akomfrah, *Vertigo Sea*, 2015 (still). Three-channel HD color video installation, 7.1 sound, 48 minutes, 30 seconds. © Smoking Dogs Films. Source: Lisson Gallery.

times, especially since the Industrial Revolution. Half of all carbon emitted by modern society has ended up in the oceans, changing acidity levels to such a degree, perhaps more than in the past 300 million years, that it will take tens of thousands of years for ocean chemistry to return to pre-industrial levels. That makes shell formation and coral reef life increasingly stressed, even catastrophically impossible, leading to worldwide bleaching events, food chain collapse, fisheries loss, and the rise of jellyfish. With the biological annihilation that comes with bottom trawling, dynamite fishing, agricultural runoff, and oil spills like Exxon's and BP's, we face an unprecedented decline in marine life, glimpsed in spreading dead zones, initiating a global event of de-biodiversification—as if we are running evolution in reverse, according to reef scientists.[21] With massive driftnets and serial depletion of species one after the next, we are looking at the stark possibility of largely fishless oceans by 2048. In fact, when scientists search for historical analogies for our forlorn present mass extinction threat, they go back 55 million years to the Paleocene-Eocene Thermal Maximum, which saw an enormous release of atmospheric carbon, warming the Arctic by ten degrees Fahrenheit and corresponding to one of the worst of the planet's deep-sea extinctions. Or they reference the Crataceous-Tertiary Boundary Event occurring 65 million years ago when an asteroid six miles wide hit Earth, generating huge amounts of sulfuric acid, killing off more than three-quarters of species, with the effects lasting millennia.[22]

The darkening ocean, reflecting the winnowing of life, is upon us and offers a glimpse of our present global extinction event, despite the lushness of miraculous marine existence shown in Attenborough's *Blue Planet*, which in some ways figures as a compensatory reassurance that not all has (yet) been lost. The logic of such conventional documentary is familiar—if only we can appreciate the majestic beauty of nature, we will finally do something to prevent its collapse. Yet without massive social movements to challenge corporate-lobbied governance, the result may be more melancholy defeatism that only sharpens the pain of ultimate loss. In fact, the whales and orcas portrayed in Attenborough's series are now endangered, according to the World Wildlife Fund (WWF), owing to a multitude of causes, including industrial fishing and shipping, oil and gas development, sound pollution, like military sonar that can disrupt and damage whales' hearing and disturb critical feeding and breeding grounds, commercial fishing (more than one thousand whales a year are killed, still, for commercial purposes), and climate change's disruption of habitats and food chains.[23] Indeed, commercial fishing in the twentieth century—the industry's most effective era owing to diesel engine–powered factory ships and machine-launched exploding harpoons, as shown in Akomfrah's film—wiped out some three million whales, the largest culling of animal biomass in human history, depleting some populations, such as blue, fin, and sperm whales, by 90 percent (compared to sail-powered ships that dispatched around 300,000 sperm whales between 1700 and 1900).[24]

While showing elements of this ongoing maritime devastation, *Vertigo Sea* does not shirk from also portraying the unparalleled splendor of aquatic nature. This amounts to a courageous act of refusing the contemporary cynicism that has given up on beauty, even while that cynicism rightfully sees the latter as ever threatened, if not thoroughly colonized as some critics might claim, by consumerist spectacle, including where it operates as compensatory recourse against extinction dread.[25] As a result, the film courts the risk of providing sumptuous aestheticization of oceans that are also the scene of biological annihilation, as if proposing a hackneyed politico-ecological maneuver of critically juxtaposing nature's visual pleasure with terrible scenes of industrial exploitation. Yet ultimately, I would suggest, it evades that conclusion. If the film raises this possibility at all, it quickly moves on to further complexity by connecting to all of the historical relations discussed above, which resists any form of escapism. Plus, nature, one might rightfully respond, is intrinsically aesthetic—which is not necessarily a negative and more likely a positive thing, even a functional ecological matter—and beauty (defined in this case as sensory attraction between living forms, like a fish to a biodiverse reef) a part of life itself, which Akomfrah (and Attenborough) portrays in its fullest glory.[26] No doubt there is also a postcolonial, or rather anticolonial, reformulation of beauty as expressive of a form of life resistant to, struggling with, and existing beyond capture. This is directly relevant to Equiano's historical emancipation from bondage, as well as to *Vertigo Sea*'s aesthetic acknowledgment—through its various edits, cuts, and intervals within and between screens—of the ultimate limits of representation, and specifically of the limits of the human representation, capture, and comprehension of the infinity of the nonhuman worlds of the seas.[27] On the other hand, the film glimpses the annihilation of that beauty (its objectification and transformation into a commodity, a mere use to be exploited), especially where aesthetic delectation and the spectacular image mediate the destruction of a species, the violence of climate change, and the mass death of migrants.

Even if all of these currents are not fully resolved or brought to any final conclusion, the film reveals something key about our contemporary response to violence, whether environmental, human-nonhuman, or intrahuman, in this vertiginous sea of philosophical speculation. For when our image-saturated media invites us to enjoy scenes of violence through cinematic aestheticization, it is of course intolerable. This intolerability, as Jacques Rancière has noted in other contexts, identifies not only the unbearable reality that such images show (the destruction of whales, the murder of humans) but also the numbing, anaesthetizing capacity of such images, their ability to show but also to defuse, which can also be excoriating.[28] Whereas in past decades, political art and particularly documentary form directed intolerable reality against spectacularized appearance, in our current age of "disenchantment," we face "a single regime of universal exhibition" in our pervasive image economies and screen-based media, according to Rancière, and encounter the subsequent need to modulate earlier strategies that do not so much rupture that regime as participate in its endless shimmering flow.[29] *Vertigo Sea* interrogates both aspects—the intolerability of reality and the image of intolerability alike—showing their logic at work in scenes of slavery, ecocide, and migration. At the same time, it provokes a reconfiguration of the visible according to the imperative not to forget, not to rest complacent with the division of environmental violence from social violence, and, more, to put them in intolerable conversation.

HAUNTOLOGIES

Vertigo Sea intervenes, in other words, in cultural discourse at the time of the Anthropocene's geological turn. Doing so, it joins an expanding philosophy of the environmental humanities seeking to redefine the meaning of living when the interpenetration of human, cultural, and nonhuman milieus is stretching our "definition of 'self'-interest to include the flourishing of the complex system of bio-geologic processes," where that system also "encompasses the expanse of planetary time" beyond human history.[30] In this regard, *Vertigo Sea* not only mediates and meditates on the Black Atlantic and insists on connecting the deep history of the Middle Passage to current transmigration and its many deaths at sea within the wider border-zone contexts of institutionalized racism and militant xenophobia (during the year the film was made, more than 3,770 migrants died at sea trying to cross the Mediterranean, making 2015 among the deadliest on record to date); it also challenges the limitations of this largely anthropocentric framework, as tragic as it is. Indeed, if Gilroy mobilizes the ship as "novel chronotope" in order to "rethink modernity via the history of the Black Atlantic and the African diaspora into the western hemisphere," and references the story of Olaudah Equiano as a figure of "the rhizomorphic, fractal structure of the transcultural"—already a matrix of serious vertigo!—his important study simultaneously overlooks the violence occurring in the geological and nonhuman realms and the deeper links between them all in these contexts of death and destruction.[31]

While analyses focusing on race and diaspora tend to neglect considering the more expansive dimensions of social ecology (which sees structural parallels between intrahuman and human-nonhuman modes of domination, displacement, and violence), the geological turn and its new materialisms, at least in certain of their elaborations, limit their investigations to "the nature of reality independently of thought and of humanity more generally," as Levi Bryant, Graham Harman, and Nick Srnicek write in their introduction to speculative realism that serves as one such example.[32] In such cases, the insistently nonanthropocentric focus of object-oriented ontologies overlooks or simply disavows human-centered politics, including the histories of colonialism and racism, as beyond the scope of their analyses. That focus is, in turn, importantly contested in the work of writers like Fred Moten, whose argument provides crucial resistance to the potential depoliticization of these philosophical formations precisely by exploring the aesthetico-political conditions of subjectivity *within* objecthood, especially as revealed in slavery's objectification—and equally the objection—of the non/human within commodified and racialized bondage (even if he neglects ecological matters of concern in turn).[33] As one such dehumanized object/ion, Equiano, for instance, embodies something similar to what Moten characterizes as "the essential resistance of the object that manifests as lawlessness, as a kind of being against the law, as the lawless freedom and the struggle for freedom in unfreedom, in quite specific modes of discipline and regulation that we call slavery and colonialism."[34] That is a struggle, too, that manifests in the compelling inscription of Equiano's *Narrative*, materializing an aesthetic struggle, a self-authorization, and an insistent entrance into literature, against all conventions for the (formerly) enslaved, that becomes a powerful source, in turn, for *Vertigo Sea* and its own aesthetic materializations. Indeed, Moten's interest in "the universalization or socialization of the surplus, the generative force of a venerable phonic propulsion, the ontological and historical priority of resistance to power and objection to subjection, the old-new thing, the freedom drive that animates black performances," which he finds in works such as *The Narrative of Frederick Douglass, an American Slave*, is a force that can also be discerned, in its own singularity, in *Vertigo Sea*. But there it is not only sourced in the lawless articulations of the formerly enslaved and stolen life of Equiano but also located in the sonic expressions of the drama between harpoon shots, whales wailing, crashing glaciers, and the howling wind.[35] *Vertigo Sea* offers an ecology of entanglement *from below*, joining the socially excluded to the submarine.

With these in/human and geologic genealogies in mind, it is a mark of distinction that Akomfrah's *Vertigo Sea* invokes, interrelates, and complicates two central trajectories of what I am calling ecology-as-intersectionality. It incorporates more-than-human geologies of maritime life, geologies that have nonetheless been irrevocably impacted by human industry, technology, and militarism, and at the same time it refuses to relinquish the cultural memories, often unacknowledged hauntings, and ongoing significance of slavery, colonialism, and involuntary migration. The two trajectories have unfolded and continue to unfold in the same space-time as catastrophic climate breakdown, each, in complex ways, the cause and consequence of the other. *Vertigo Sea* thereby provides an astonishing, syncretic problem-space of cinema where these narratives and their manifold sensory elements movingly interact in ways that inspire new methodologies of political ecology and geocultural analysis.

Insofar as Vertigo *Sea* prompts a reshuffling and interlinking of times and places, it additionally disrupts the fixation on the presentness of the contemporary as the exceptional location of experience, according to which events (such as the death of lawless seafarers or the industrialization of marine life) may be partly shocking because they are misrecognized as new, even if they are always singular. Water is indeed an element that "remembers the dead," even though its abstract visibility suggests an empty screen, a blank continuous surface.[36] In this sense, the piece offers a continuation of Akomfrah's "hauntological" conjurings in his other recent films—such as *The Nine Muses, Transfigured Night* (2013), and *Tropikos* (2015)—which bring past horrors and injustices, sometimes from deep history, including scenes from the African diaspora and postcolonial transitions, into our own time, refusing to put them to rest. Their plays of in/visibility summon forth the non-negativity of absent presence (its refusal to vanish), even while its contradictory metaphysics of trace escapes easy or clear legibility. Connecting these "unspeakable moments" and "unconscious relations" to present developments, without simply collapsing them together, we experience the haunting of being as much as the being of haunting, a hauntology materialized in Akomfrah's eerie figurations, as much as an affect produced by the piece's audiovisual compositions of entangled geographies and histories.[37] These intertwined histories and persistent memories demand recognition and attention. Instead of allowing them to act out like unwieldy specters in our periphery, causing havoc where they may (or as incomprehensible hyperobjects), *Vertigo Sea* brings them into conscious regard, insisting on conversing with them—"feeding the ghost," as another of its intertitles reads. But Akomfrah's hauntologies are not simply about the past haunting the present—as if we, and some more than others, are haunted by nonbeing; rather, these specters refuse to rest because they are continually newly conjured and produced in the ongoing tragedies of the now, where the violence of slavery echoes in the brutality of and exacted upon involuntary migration and the persistence of racial capitalism.

Within this multiplicity and relationality of temporalities, *Vertigo Sea* also projects what Akomfrah calls an "afterlife of the image," according to which an image, any image, necessarily implies a future. This imaging and viewing-time-to-come define a utopian dimension intrinsic to image making, a virtual futurism embedded in cinema as a political ontology of endless materialization and anticipation. As such, cinema, in Akomfrah's hands, manifests a protest against finitude, as well as against the idea that representation can totalize experience and colonize significance, as if the image can ever be(come) complete or self-sufficient (which, as we have seen, informs his recent postanthropocentric filmmaking, as much as *Vertigo Sea's* triptych multiplicity). As Akomfrah contends, artists, as image makers who insist on emancipating the infinite, act as "custodians of a possible future," implying a future of viewership too, a future reality impacted by the artwork, as well as a future context unanticipated by the filmmaker, which also reveals the present as necessarily incomplete and non-totalizable.[38] Developing the same line of thinking, can we not also say that remembering past tragedies and imaging present wrongs—on the world-historical levels of slavery and colonialism, species extinction, nuclear war, and anthropogenic climate disruption—can also, in fact *must*, entail proposing, even cultivating, alternate futures? If so, perhaps what *Vertigo Sea* offers is, ultimately, optimism, if not without its cruelties: where past injustices have failed to utterly destroy their aftermath, we can maintain hope, despite all, of a different time to come. If that time will not necessarily redeem what has been, then at least, as dramatized by Akomfrah, it insists on holding historical failings within the realm of visibility—so that they will not ever be forgotten in the creation of future alternatives.

CHAPTER
TWO

BLACKOUT

THE NECROPOLITICS
OF EXTRACTION

In view of spreading sacrifice zones given over to resource mining, accompanied by exploitative international trade agreements and the finances of debt servitude, what newly mutated forms do the cultural politics of opposition take? And how are artist-activists materializing the images and sounds of decolonial emancipation against late-stage capitalism's rapacious commodification of anything and everything? With reference to the artworks of Angela Melitopoulos, Allora & Calzadilla, and Ursula Biemann, which variously consider geographies of conflict in such regions as Greece, Puerto Rico, Canada, and Bangladesh, this chapter considers a range of artistic approaches that adopt and extend further an aesthetics of entanglement, drawing together social justice politics and ecological matters of concern. Doing so, these practices reveal complex causalities and effects of global extractivism, offer new imaginaries of intersectionality, and propose forms of movement building and solidarity with those on the frontlines of opposition.

An epic four-channel video installation of 109 minutes, commissioned by and shown at documenta 14, Angela Melitopoulos's *Crossings* (2017) presents an interlinking of people and multispecies environments, matter and history, mutating finance and shifting agencies, defining a globalized political ecology of inequality and dispossession. Made with collaborators Angela Anderson, Maurizio Lazzarato, Pascale Criton, Oktay Ince, and Paula Cabo Guevara, the piece offers several complex intersections, which build complexity through images and sounds, one such intersection focusing on the financial interests arrayed around the planned industrial extraction of gold, copper, and rare earths from the Skouries mine in the Halkidiki Peninsula, near Thessaloniki in northern Greece. That extraction site has created a socioecological conflict with locals and environmentalists—as well as with forests, rivers, and their more-than-human inhabitants—that continues to this day. Those exploitative interests, seeking to dig out materials from the earth and transform them into economic value, are shown in Melitopoulos's work to connect directly to the EU-driven withdrawal of political agency from the Greek citizenry. As dramatized by the astonishing reversal of the 2015 bailout referendum by Alexis Tsipras of the formerly considered left-wing Syriza government—voted into office explicitly to challenge EU dominance of domestic policy—the popular rejection of austerity economics imposed by Brussels as the condition of continuing membership in the Eurozone was itself rejected by the government at the behest of European financial demands (what Syriza's former finance minister Yanis Varoufakis, a political casualty of that very reversal, likened to neocolonial "gunboat diplomacy"[1]). These two formations—the opening up of Greece to transnational mining interests and the betrayal of popular sovereignty by treacherous EU politics—speak to the global conditions of extraction today and enter into direct correlation, as well as conflict, in *Crossings*. In this regard, the video reveals a politico-ecological territory much like Akomfrah's *Vertigo Sea*, considered in chapter 1, but does so in ways much more analytical and discursive, particularly given its researched and theoretical voice-over commentary on the conditions it investigates.

In one of *Crossings'* passages, environmental activists are shown passionately protesting the wanton destruction of regional forests and rivers by mining companies, including Eldorado Gold of Canada and the Greek subsidiary Hellas Gold, and are seen to be brutally suppressed by

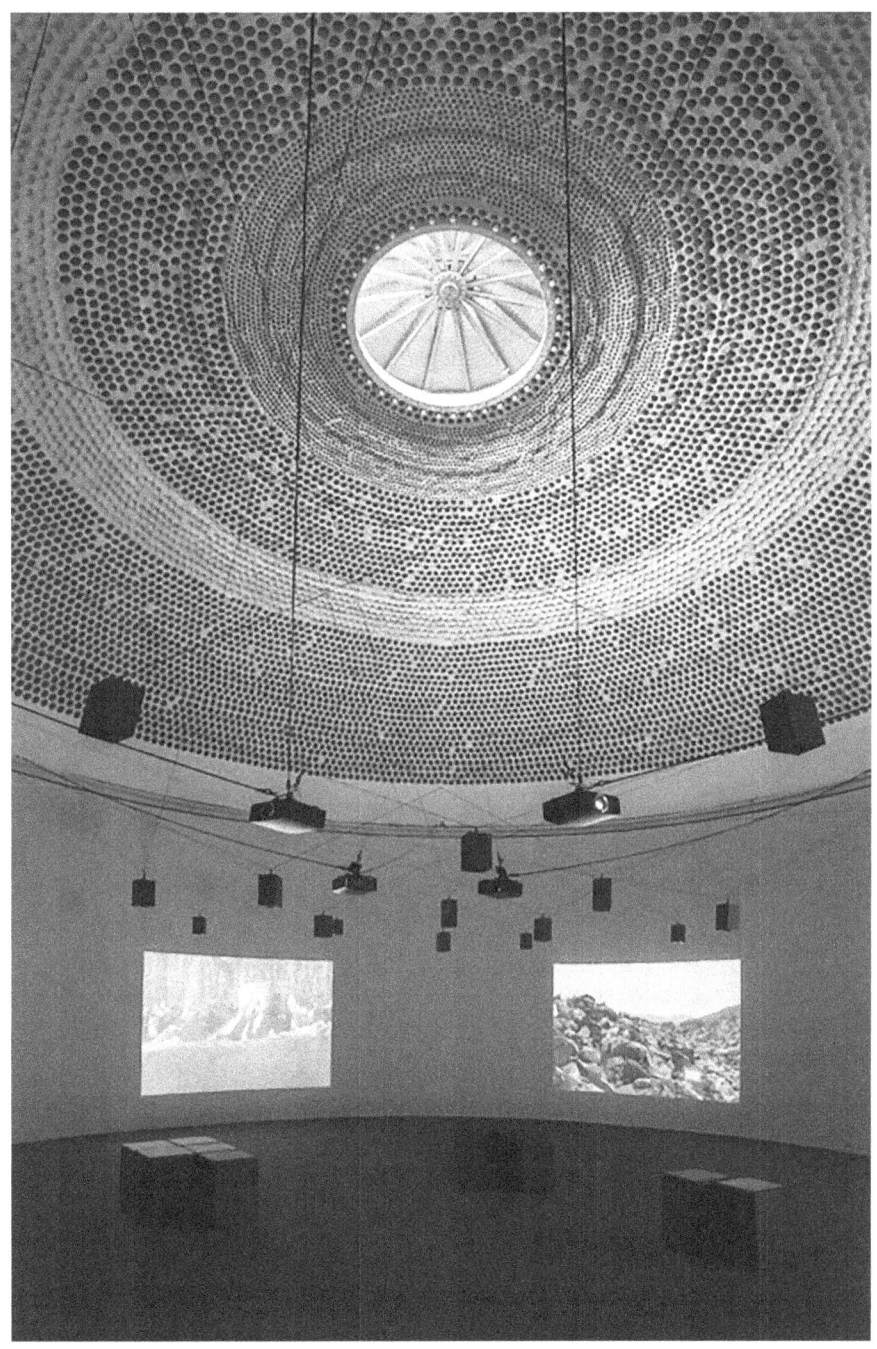

2.1 Angela Melitopoulos, *Crossings*, 2017 (installation, documenta 14). Courtesy of the artist.

militarized police. With these scenes, we confront the widespread fact that police charged with enforcing law tend to protect corporate power rather than defend democratic will, as state violence compounds the agonies of political disenfranchisement and material dispossession. As such, *Crossings* visualizes nothing less than the complex workings of extractivism, the dominant paradigm of advanced capitalism. According to theorists Sandro Mezzadra and Brett Neilson, extractivism identifies both historical and current modes of wealth accumulation based upon the withdrawal of raw materials and life forms from the planet's surface, depths, and biosphere in the production of financial value, which runs in coordination with expansive politico-economic and sociotechnological systems pledged to its operations.[2] Fundamentally, extractivism comprises a calculus of accumulation by dispossession, building on the terms of David Harvey, a withdrawal without corresponding deposit (except in the form of waste, disease, and death), which transforms whatever it touches—be that mines, forests, rivers, oceans, or human and nonhuman life—into economic value, employing whatever means at its disposal, including machinery, architecture, labor, finance, logistics, and media.[3] For Macarena Gómez-Barris, the global "extractive zone" identifies "the violence that capitalism does to reduce, constrain, and convert life into commodities."[4] While that extractive zone for her is largely located in the Global South, a more comprehensive analysis of its dispersed and interconnected processes would necessarily extend it to all reaches of the planet. Indeed, for Mezzadra and Neilson—whose take is useful particularly for their expansive definition not limited to resource mining—it includes virtual processes as well as dense materials, prison labor and debt servitude, bioprospecting, genetics, and informatics. It drives real estate speculation, tuition and rent increases, as much as structural neglect and privatization, and bends policy and trade agreements to its will. Extractivism consequently designates a common motivating logic of institutions, museums, universities, corporations, and states within late neoliberal capitalism, organizing their trade deals, social forms, labor policies, data mining, energy systems, and technologies. As a global formation, "the 'new urban frontier' is continually opening in diverse contexts, prompted by the appropriation and expropriation of spaces, values, infrastructures, and forms of life that are submitted to capitalist valorization."[5] It is this multivalent frontier that is the focus of *Crossings*.

While Melitopoulos's video may be focused on the case of Greece, the extractive logic it uncovers is pervasive worldwide in the global movement toward illiberal politics, authoritarian economics, and growing socioeconomic inequality. The current US administration is representative of this nexus, where disaster capitalism and expanding sacrifice zones converge under its reign, linking politico-financial and natural resource exploitation to the overwhelming benefit of corporate, elite wealth, facilitated by corrupt governance. Such an arrangement not only mobilizes disasters for further neoliberalization (particularly intensifying its investment logics of privatization, pro-corporate trade deals, and the elimination of welfare and social spending) but also produces countless disasters in its wake. For instance, the 2017 US tax plan, forced through Congress with little public support, lowers corporate rates from 35 to 21 percent, constituting a trillion-dollar transfer to the wealthiest, just as the same bill opens the Arctic National Wildlife Reserve to oil, gas, and coal drilling and exploration (with formerly protected US coasts to follow). The maneuver joins the pillaging of public finances to natural resource mining, moving the US toward historically unprecedented levels of environmental threat and economic disparity (a logic that was repeated in 2020 during the coronavirus pandemic).[6] According to this formation, again global in character, taxes are weaponized in asymmetrical class war, with the financial gains used to subsidize the fossil fuel industry. Politics become reduced to a massive police operation, as multitudes lose faith in representative systems, and not surprisingly, enviro-economic structural adjustments are accompanied by the gradual withdrawal of civil liberties and press freedoms.[7] At the same time, democracy, as a political project of popular sovereignty, regulatory authority, and accountability, becomes increasingly hollowed out by corporate power, economic inequality, and corruption, as civil activism becomes increasingly subject to control, repression, and illegality.[8] Indeed, environmentalists are exposed to growing state violence and extrajudicial killings, as dramatized by the case of Berta Cáceres in Honduras, who joined with the Indigenous Lenca people in waging a grassroots campaign that successfully pressured Chinese state-owned Sinohydro, the world's largest dam builder, to pull out of the Agua Zarca hydroelectric project in the Central American nation. She is one of thousands of activists murdered in recent years, and in a country operating under the US-supported 2009 deposal of democratically elected president Manuel Zelaya. Moreover, her case forms part of an international trend of increasing levels of state and corporate violence visited upon environmentalists, Indigenous activists, and independent journalists opposed to extractivism's current world order.[9]

In this antagonism that pits petrocapitalist states against land and water protectors and in many instances Indigenous peoples—from Greece to Brazil, Honduras to the Philippines, Indonesia to Russia—biopolitics (the governance of human lives) transforms into necropolitics (the administration of death) and scales up and down to geontopolitics (the governance of the relations between life and nonlife), constituting an ascendant politics of earth-being in our age of extraction.[10] Such is clear with the #NoDAPL struggle at Standing Rock, which figures as one recent hypervisible focal point of Blockadia, the expansive and transnational conflict zone meeting the extractive zone at every turn in which grassroots movements are set in opposition to petrocapitalist developments and the invasions of its infrastructure.[11] In 2016 members of the Standing Rock Sioux Tribe, part of the Oceti Sakowin, joined by numerous other Indigenous nations and countless allies, challenged the construction of the Dakota Access Pipe Line (DAPL), expressing popular resistance to both the exploitation of fossil fuels and their placing natural environments and water sources at risk, and the negation of Indigenous rights in the face of ongoing neocolonial land grabs and domineering corporate-state sovereignty. A central part of the struggle involved challenging the corporate-state complex's attempt to control and manage the difference between life and nonlife—specifically when it comes to oil and water. When water protectors insisted upon mni wiconi!, or water is life! / water is alive!, in the face of militarized police advances and private security assaults, shielded bulldozers, chemical weapons, and menacing police dogs, the event constituted both a biopolitical rift over human rights, with necropolitical implications, and a geontopolitical challenge to the neoliberal logic whereby elements, environments, and nonhuman life forms are violently reduced to commodities within the unfolding drama of an ecologically devastating and climate-changing economy of accumulation by dispossession.[12] In this case, the accumulation of financial wealth brought about the dispossession of ecosystem reproductive capacities and the dispossession of Indigenous self-determination.

At a time when contemporary politicians increasingly flirt with neofascist (alt-right) formations, events such as Standing Rock's #NoDAPL struggle speak to the delegitimizing of liberal electoral politics as it merges with antidemocratic corporate power. The situation continues to unfold

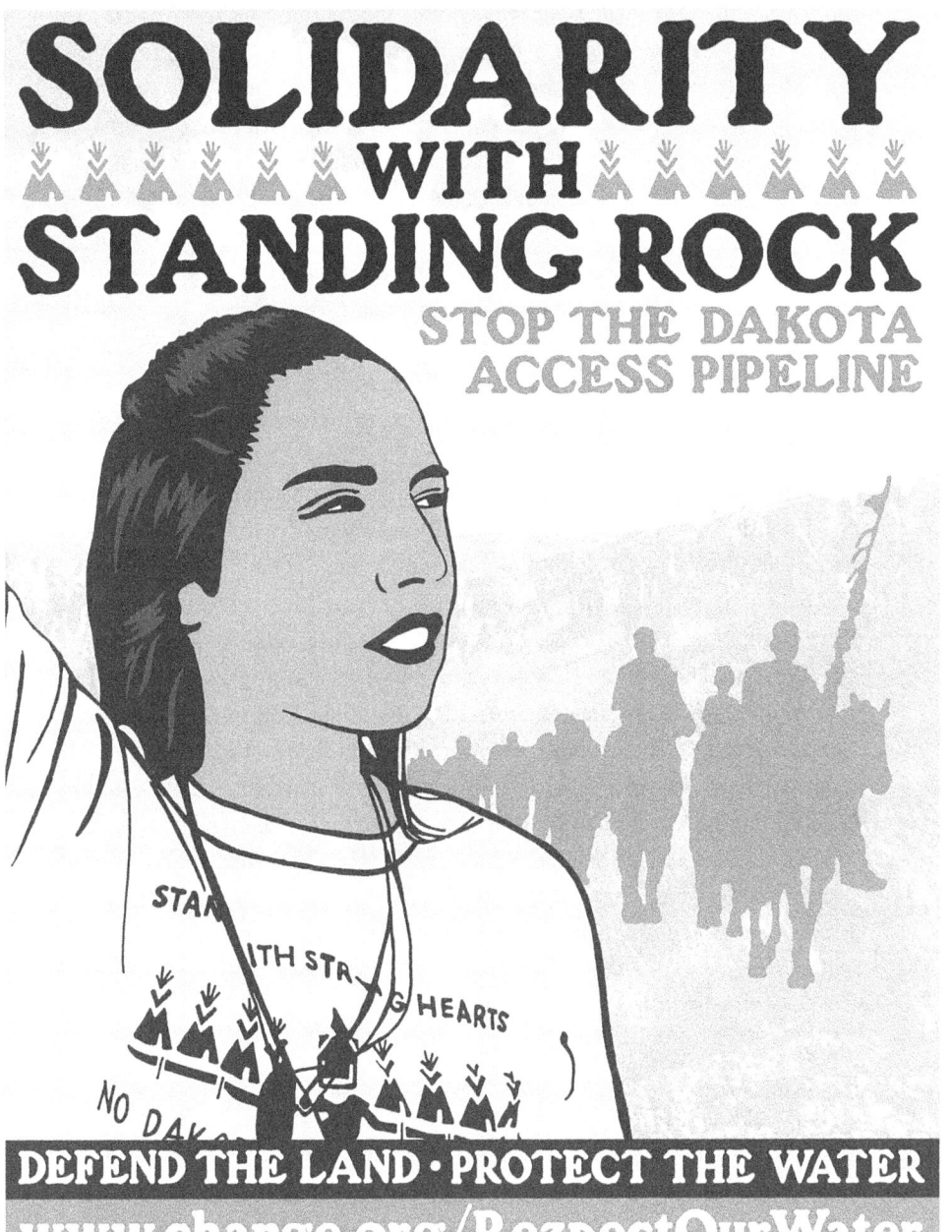

2.2 Jesus Barraza and Melanie Cervantes, *Solidarity with Standing Rock*, 2016. Courtesy of the Just Seeds Collective and the artists.

today with the spread of right-wing populism and authoritarian politics worldwide. Yet there has also been a growing intensity of thinking and living politically otherwise outside that domain—as at Standing Rock—which is to say in the civic realms of mutual aid societies, experimental cultures, and the community-based arts, where artists and activists are asserting a politico-aesthetic imagination that challenges petrocapitalist extractivism. In proliferating instances, aesthetic practices themselves shift character and modulate within this geopolitical framework; the artistic blurs with the aesthetics of social movements, producing an expanded field of artistic sensibility with cosmopolitical scope, focused on the formation of liberated desires and values, and joined in contexts where nothing less is at stake than a contemporary war of the worlds.[13] Against the extractivist logic of the Capitalocene—a world and future sacrificing the Earth itself to the interests of short-term profits—artists and activists, as well as communities set on doing politics differently, are restoring and inventing alternative forms of life and creative modes of ethical being-in-common. They are drawing on existing wisdoms and proposing new knowledges, remaking the world as we know it in imagination, representation, and practice. The artworks of Melitopoulos, Biemann, and Allora & Calzadilla do just that, covering a spectrum of cultural manifestations referencing and intervening in diverse sites in the Global North and Global South. Their practices include political documentary, speculative analysis linked to insurrectionary social movements, and gallery-bound sculptural and audiovisual experiments, which all give form to sociopolitical and environmental violence, as well as to inspiring sites of resistance.[14] Indeed, these are places of radical imagination where we can glimpse futures alternative to extractivism's wastelanding, debt prisons, and sacrifice zones.[15]

GOVERNING BY DEBT

Crossings places viewers uncomfortably in the crossfire of its four large screens, constructing an audiovisual confrontation approximating its warzone geography (even if this is ultimately unapproachable in the secure setting of a gallery environment). While the video provides interviews with Greek environmental activists who discuss the political and ecological stakes of their struggle, it also expands that rift zone to Greece's refugee crisis, including the views of migrants interned at the Idomeni camp, located north of Thessaloniki, and at the Moria Camp on the island of Lesbos, just off Turkey's coast. Migrants speak of life made impossible in the deteriorating conditions in their home countries of Turkey, Syria, and Iraq, each variously torn apart by US-supported political authoritarianism, endless war, ethno-religious conflict, and soul-killing impoverishment. It becomes clear that migration is itself symptomatic of the social breakdown that occurs in the face of political tyranny, economic inequality, and environmental-military violence—in other words, the very extractivist order that has had such devastating effects on homelands in the Middle East and Africa. Asylum seekers tell of desperate conditions in the infamous camps, the cruelty of police and guards, and the interminable waits that make their experience of dislocation (ultimately a dislocation from existential security) allegedly worse than life in places like war-torn Afghanistan. While these circumstances explain the many protests against camp conditions and migration policies—some of which are shown in *Crossings*—Melitopoulos's video also sees in these demonstrations contemporary echoes of ancient slave rebellions staged in the same region. The Laurion mines of southern Attica, like those in Halkidiki, were mined by forced labor more than two thousand years ago, as the video points out, and rebellions then, as now, materialize(d) demands for political transformation.[16]

The cries of resistance are thus the "signs and sounds of an epochal reconfiguration," as *Crossings* observes. "Where are we going? What has happened? Here we are in a land of passages where various wars are crossing: economic, strategic, racial, and sexual wars," runs Melitopoulos's voice-over near the beginning of the film. It continues its analytic progression, spoken over images of a Greek port and migrant transit point—one crossing portraying the microcosm of a world-transforming global event—before turning to the Skouries mine.

A territory that holds a double experimentation: the governance by the destructive force of debt, and the control of mobility of refugees and migrants. We are not witnessing a clash of civilizations but a war of subjectivities installed by capitalism. Those who struggle with the demons of national identity, racism, sexism, and xenophobia are facing the experience of departure, trials of poverty; they are the ones who have trust in the unknown. The "Wretched of the Earth" who trek towards the different Norths are halted by frozen and fearful European subjectivities. In the Chaosmosis of these times, they open possibilities that many others do not want to see. So they are surrounded by walls and shielded from vision. The imposed politics of debt is an economy that aims at the objects of war but with other means: Wars that are abandoning arms and military conflict. They become an affair of politicians, scientists, and even bankers. Wars that are not merely bloody, and the means of conducting them are not solely military. Economy, and notably financial economy, has replaced military means and given rise to "nonbloody" wars.

Adding to this incisive account of newly emerging economic warfare, Crossings includes interviews with refugee camp inhabitants who are members of the Partiya Karkerên Kurdistanê (PKK, Kurdistan Workers' Party), which continues to defend autonomous zones beyond state sovereignty and against extremist formations like the Islamic State in Iraq and Syria (ISIS) in northern Syria and Turkey. In these interviews, migrants discuss their revolutionary politics and affirmatively profeminist culture as well as their support for Kurdish leader and PKK founder Abdullah Öcalan, who, remarkably, was influenced by US social ecologist Murray Bookchin and his 1960s and 1970s anarchist theories of libertarian municipalism and environmental well-being.[17] Set in crisis conditions like these, the militant implications of current social movements become explicit. Just as one older Halkidiki-based antimining activist is shown admitting his hopelessness regarding the possibilities of conventional political transformation in the present antidemocratic EU system, speculating that violent resistance may be the only remaining response in Greece to current "nonbloody" wars, PKK refugee camp residents sing songs in praise of revolutionary guerrillas set to the Greek bouzouki. In the brutal conditions of war fought by economic means, wherein debt is a weapon of mass destruction and migration a descent into powerlessness, life must be defended by any means necessary. Such militant convictions lead Crossings to its unsettling concluding speculation: if democratic voting offers no effective means of politico-ecological phase shift—whether in ancient slave-holding states of patriarchal imperialism or in today's postneoliberal unfolding of authoritarian capitalism—then we must look beyond electoral politics, to a diversity of tactics, for ways of reclaiming justice, equality, and environmental livability, inventing new solidarities and collective efforts on those bases. In pointing this out, Crossings provides a crucial step in bringing these various intersections to the foreground, articulating both the stakes and the promise of emergent formations at the inextricable juncture of politics, economy, and ecology.

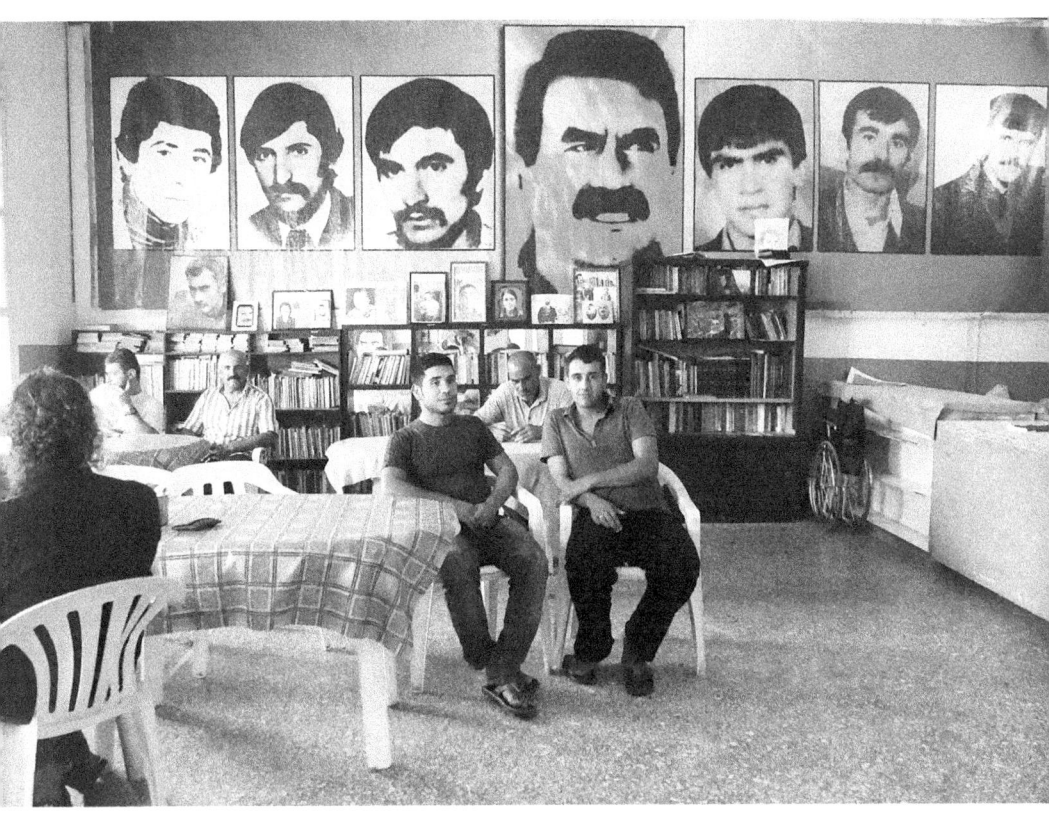

2.3 Angela Melitopoulos, *Crossings*, 2017 (still showing Lavrion migrant camp with PKK supporters and a poster image of Abdullah Öcalan). Courtesy of the artist.

CLIMATE CRIMES

Similarly advancing a relational geographies approach to global petrocapitalist extraction, and with an explicit focus on the politico-ecological entanglements between North and South, Ursula Biemann's short video *Deep Weather* (2013) begins by depicting the topography of Canada's Alberta Tar Sands, one of the greatest sources of climate disruption on the planet and another conflict zone. On the grounds of what was once a pristine boreal forest, corporations have industrialized an area roughly the size of England, mining dirty and hard-to-access hydrocarbons in the form of bitumen, a heavy, black oil mixed with clay, sand, and water, whose processing requires intense fossil fuel energy and leaves all sorts of toxic leftovers on the land. In the process of clearing the forest's biodiverse ecology—the critical zone

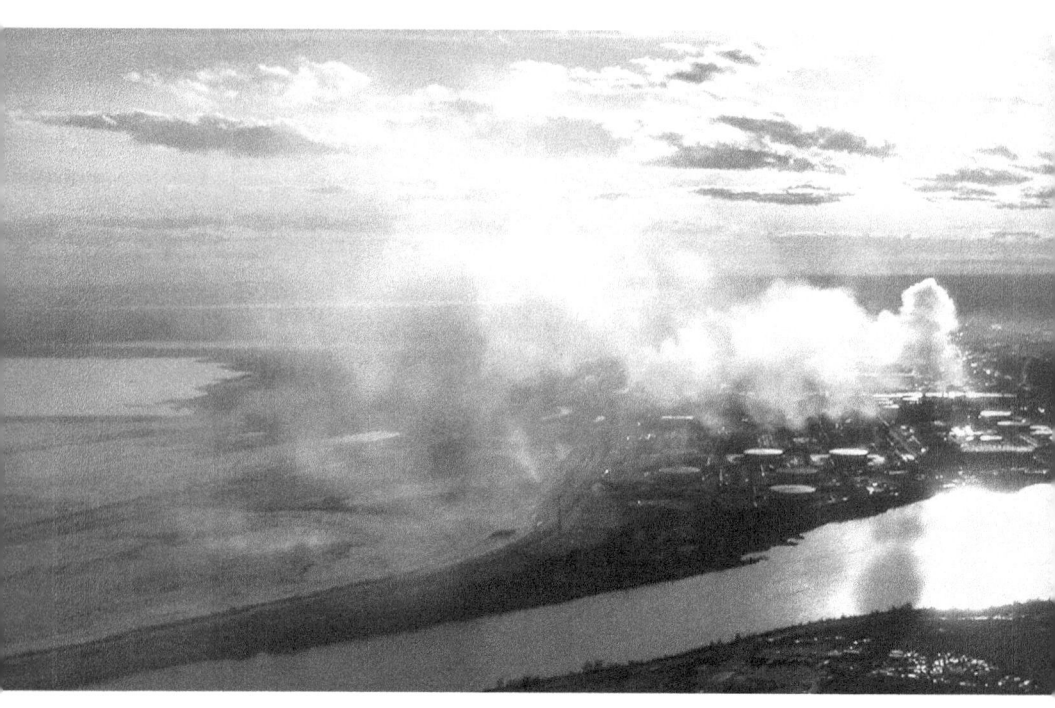

2.4 Ursula Biemann, *Deep Weather*, 2013 (still). Courtesy of the artist.

of life commonly denigrated as "overburden" by the mining industry—corporations have transformed the land into what Biemann's video terms so many "carbon geologies." Doing so, extraction firms such as Conoco-Phillips, Petro-Canada, and ExxonMobil have brought ruin to the natural environment and heavily impacted the lives of First Nations peoples who live nearby, among whom cases of cancer, asthma, diabetes, and mental illness caused by air and water pollution have risen dramatically over the last decade. This includes the Athabasca Chipewyan First Nation (ACFN), for whom "the land is the essence of the ACFN's culture, values, and spirituality," and who have filed grievances against Shell for practicing ecocide as well as against the Canadian government for reneging on historical treaties and failing to protect the health of Indigenous populations (though so far these lawsuits have been without success).[18]

Deep Weather forms part of Biemann's extensive research-based video practice that has investigated several other sites of extractivism—including *Forest Law* (2014), co-created with Paulo Tavares, which examines petrocapitalist drilling in the Ecuadorian Amazon along with Indigenous resistance

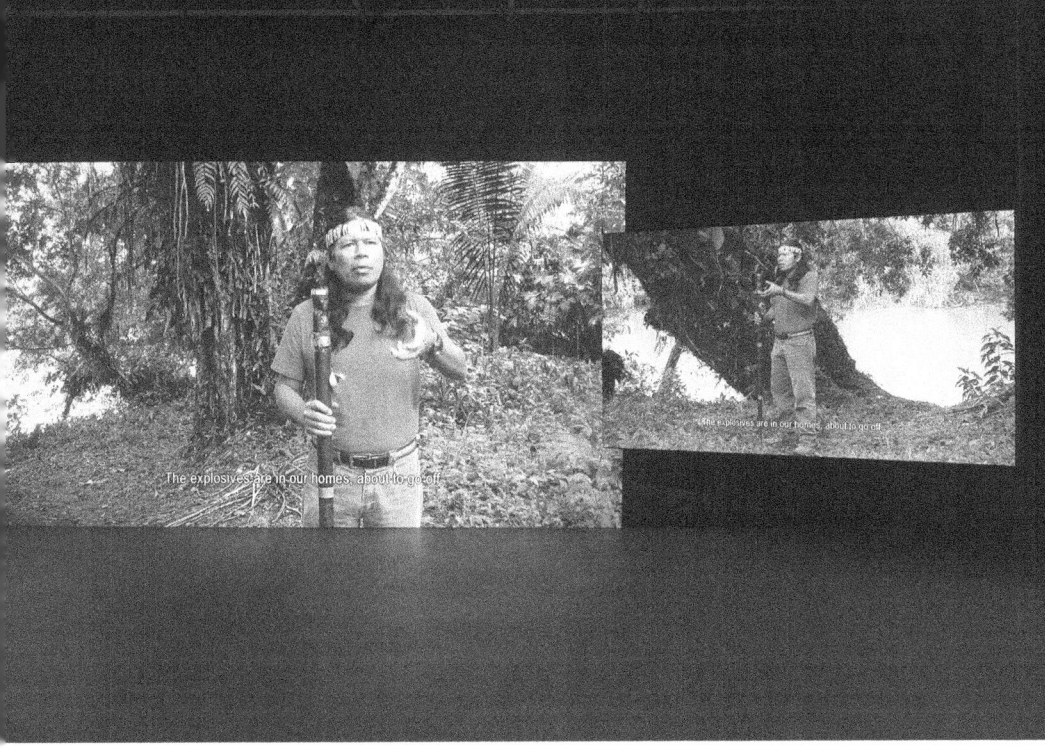

2.5 Ursula Biemann and Paulo Tavares, *Forest Law*, 2014 (installation shot).
Courtesy of the artists.

that adopts a rights-of-nature defense; and *Egyptian Chemistry* (2012), which considers water politics along the Nile and explores how water engineering relates to local agroecologies, the hydropower of farmer collectives, and revolutionary politics.[19] The video begins by providing aerial shots of the vast oil fields in the Athabasca River region. Narrated by the artist in a whispered voice-over (or rather, a hushed and humbled voice-under, as if personifying nonhuman being, or the Earth herself), the audio track speculates about the geological impacts of these corporate activities both locally and globally:

> Day and night they mine the black sediments and boil the Athabasca water to separate the tar from the clay. The toxic fluids collect in lakes where rhythmic explosions keep the birds from bathing in acid. The wildlife has retreated, the traplines are empty, the elders call the spirits, the young ones sing rap songs, and the acid wind's hissing, "Evolution isn't fast enough. Mutate!" For a hundred more years, there is enough stuff here for heavy fuel that will bring toxic clouds over the boreal woods and continue to warm and swell the seas, no longer to be witnessed but elsewhere, in equatorial zones.

Offering a meteorological visualization of similar environmental dynamics, research architect Adrian Lahoud has undertaken in a separate context a geospatial analysis-cum-artistic project linking aerosol emissions, including carbon and sulfates, in the Northern Hemisphere, with desertification and warming in Africa, Southeast Asia, and South America. His conclusions show how "climate change" is far from uniform in impact and results in unevenly distributed environmental consequences. Drawing on high-resolution NASA computer modelings of the atmospheric circulation of natural and industry-made particulates, as assembled by William Putman of NASA's Goddard Space Flight Center, this interconnected system constitutes, for Lahoud, "a new geopolitical cartography that ties together distant fates, linking industrialization in the North to deprivation [and climate disruption] in the South."[20] More, his modeling of forensic climatology provides a means for addressing what Lahoud calls "climate crime," where the perpetrators include not only the petrocapitalist industry but also UN climate negotiators who institute global warming targets based on uniform averaging, but which spell future disaster for underdeveloped regions in the South owing to higher predicted regional temperatures. Doing so, he, like Biemann, opens the term *climate* to juridico-political definition, one that in his case amounts to nothing less than a crime and transgression against African populations, against more-than-human life, and against the Earth. While 2 degrees Celsius warming may represent the internationally agreed limit for near-future global averages, different regions are predicted to be more or less affected. That abstract figure seems relatively innocuous. However, the difference between 1.5 and 2.0 degrees Celsius warming has been calculated to correspond to approximately 150 million human lives, designating people who would die from air pollution alone (disproportionately affecting the underresourced and impoverished), according to earth science professor Drew Shindell, which, as David Wallace-Wells points out, is the equivalent of twenty-five Holocausts.[21] Such daunting figures belie the celebratory tone of UN climate agreements, which generally exclude the voices of the powerless in underdeveloped nations. Yet the results will be profound. In the case of the common UN-agreed scenario of 2 degrees warming, "Africa will burn," according to Sudanese diplomat Lumumba Di-Aping and Nigerian environmentalist Nnimmo Bassey, whose activism has exposed a new order of politico-environmental violence practiced through "weapons of math destruction," indicting the abstract calculations of these selectively international deliberations (De-Aping's claim, made against negotiators

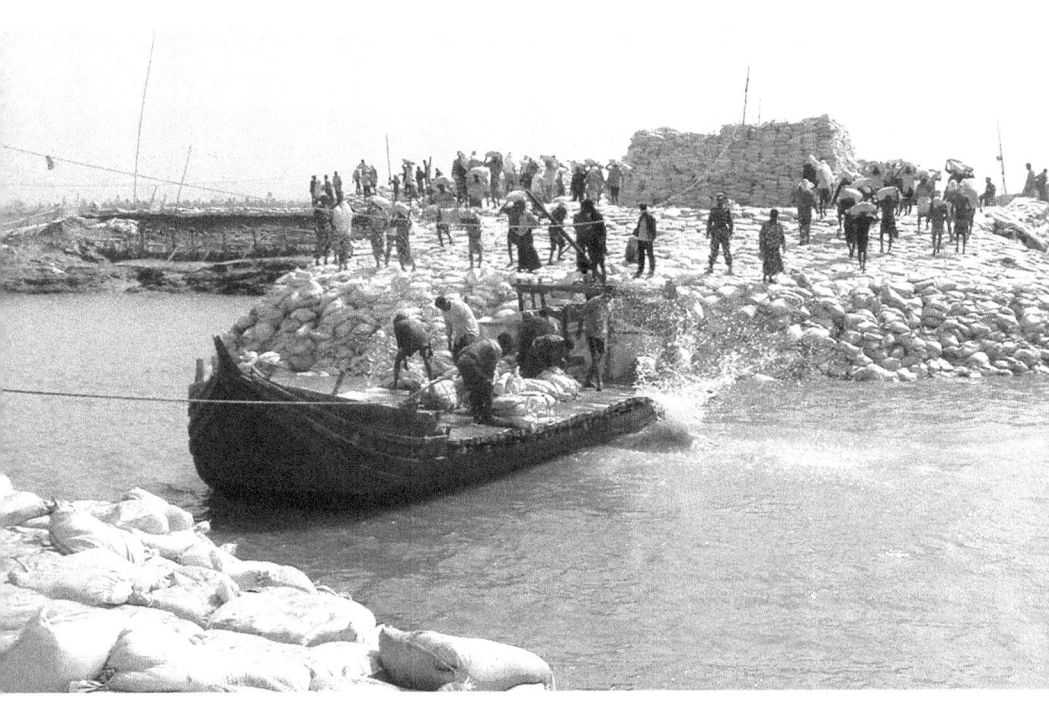

2.6 Ursula Biemann, *Deep Weather*, 2013 (still). Courtesy of the artist.

at COP 15, United Nations Climate Change Conference in Copenhagen in 2009, was part of the inspiration for Lahoud's project).[22] The problem is that, given their very obtuse character, the agreements and their implications seemingly surpass the ability of any court at present to prosecute the crimes—particularly at a time when agency and culpability are distributed across complex systems of information, regulation, and governance (which not only includes the antidemocratic power politics of transnational assemblies like the UN's but also increasingly cybernetic and algorithmic forms of artificial intelligence built into climate modeling systems).[23] Proposing cases for future justice, the visualizations of Lahoud are prefigurative, and Biemann's *Deep Weather* provides a case study of additional evidence.

One equatorial zone currently impacted by Tar Sands emissions is portrayed in the second half of Biemann's video, where the socio-environmental consequences of fossil fuel climate breakdown are witnessed in Bangladesh's Ganges-Brahmaputra delta. Bringing the camera down to a human-scaled ground level, *Deep Weather* shows the collective efforts of coastal communities to construct barriers against the rising seas. Some volunteers (generally women) are seen packing sandbags with mud by hand, while others (mostly men) deliver them to the growing seawall, slowly building up the buttresses to contain the water. Motivated to protect their homes and communities from submersion, their manual labor contrasts sharply with the high-tech extractive infrastructure in Canada, as the unequal access to technology and land-engineering resources is dramatically juxtaposed. Providing another version of forensic climatology, a climatology of techno-natural entanglement, Biemann's relational and speculative analysis demonstrates how disparate geographies are linked by industrialization and climate disruption. The monumental effort carried out by Bangladeshi collective labor represents nothing less, in Biemann's video, than a human externality of the oil industry, including the Tar Sands, a consequence generally disavowed by corporations and states alike (the distant climate change impacts of extraction, for instance, failed to mitigate the pro-drilling policies of both the conservative Stephen Harper and the liberal Justin Trudeau administrations in Canada[24]). Andrew Ross, in explaining the guiding principles of the climate justice movement, asks, "Is there a way to make rich nations pay climate debts to developing countries that have already felt the effects of climate change?".[25] Yet while this logic is solid, in envisioning a future of environmental justice, one wonders what form of debt could possibly repay such impacts as those shown in *Deep Weather*.

With a predicted sea-level rise of three feet—a low estimate for near-future impacts—20 percent of Bangladesh would be under water, displacing more than thirty million people, including Dhaka's coastal population of sixteen million.[26] Indeed, the Bay of Bengal is the largest delta region on Earth, and when its ocean surges fifty to sixty miles inland during storms, the ocean salinity already contaminates drinking water supplies and renders agricultural land less fertile. What is the cost of those lost homes and livelihoods? The result spells disaster for the region and will propel future waves of intensified climate migration. As Christian Parenti observes of this region, "perhaps the modern era's first climate refugees were the five hundred thousand Bangladeshis left homeless when half of Bhola Island flooded in 2005," not far from the delta where Biemann shot her footage.[27] By 2050, some twenty-two million people may be forced from their homes in Bangladesh owing to climate change. The response of neighboring India to this threatened social destabilization is to construct a militarized wall along its 2,500-mile border with Bangladesh, while the country's Hindu Right are mobilizing for the mass expulsion of Muslim immigrants in the present, initiating a massive project of ethnic cleansing. Although Biemann's video does not confront these precise developments, it does diagram migration's larger causes, placing them in visual relation to their effects. It thereby builds a framework for understanding displacement that implicates Western industry and petrocapitalism in relation to one flashpoint of militarized conflict and demographic upheaval in the Global South.

In recent years, the anthropogenic melting of Himalayan glaciers has at times swollen rivers that disastrously pour into Bangladesh from Tibet, Nepal, Bhutan, and India, even while the loss of ice threatens future water supplies. Swaths of the Sundarbans—the world's largest mangrove forest located in the Ganges River delta—have already begun to disappear in the rising seas. How can we visualize such scenes of territorial loss, as the Earth's topography transforms in ways that are incomprehensible in magnitude and infinite in complexity? Though Biemann's video helps in modeling artistic research methodologies, it is only a beginning. Climate breakdown defies the imagination and its representational powers, part of what the writer Amitav Ghosh calls our era of "the great derangement" of climates and culture alike, even while many artists are nonetheless making efforts at creative intervention, struggling against the tide.[28] Along with Brazil's Amazon, Montana's Glacier National Park, and the Congo Basin, the Sundarbans are considered vanishing geographies, which shockingly offer further sites of commodification via climate-change tourism, exemplifying extraction's general logic of destructive production and productive destruction—nothing less than a race to the bottom in a world of finite lands and resources. Faced with catastrophic territorial loss, our market system—"free" merely from regulation, in effect—can seemingly only see opportunities to intensify its economic logic of scarcity: the less land available, the more it will be worth. Indeed, the global travel industry is taking note, increasingly highlighting those areas as "destinations to see before they disappear," through its own aesthetics of destruction designed to attract disaster tourists.[29] Biemann's poignant analysis of the *causes* of climate disaster contests such fatalistic narratives: not only does *Deep Weather* depict the collective efforts to fortify geographical defenses, it also identifies the industrial sources of catastrophic environmental transformation, and, against them, portrays the building of the collaborative agencies of resistance.

An alternative to the documentary-essay approaches of Melitopoulos and Biemann—where video-footage making truth-claims unfolds within speculative-analytical frameworks of critical interpretation—Jennifer Allora and Guillermo Calzadilla's recent work assembles an audiovisual and sculptural poetics that draws together politics and ecology, particularly as they co-materialize in the scars of past and ongoing extractive violence in Puerto Rico. Theirs is also an intersectionalist aesthetic with materialist roots, formed of fragmented machinery and industrial architecture drawn from sites of international trade, transportation infrastructure, and energy generation. Their sculptural piece *Blackout* (2017) presents a large section of an electromagnetic power transformer that exploded in Puerto Rico in 2016. The explosion led to one of the many power failures that have plagued the island in recent years; scandalously, the one in summer of 2017, six months after the hurricane season hobbled the electricity system, left a majority of Puerto Ricans still without power. The fragments of ceramic insulators and transformer coils that appear in *Blackout* were sourced from the Aguirre Power Plant in Salinas, a station operated by the Puerto Rico Electric Power Authority (PREPA). Chronically (and possibly strategically) underfunded as a national utility set up in 1941, and nominated recently for privatization (where structural neglect primes the market for institutional investment), PREPA is also one of the largest bond issuers responsible for the island's current and growing $74 billion debt. *Blackout* draws these strands together, giving experimental form to the joining of debt servitude and energy production, as climate breakdown and petrocapitalism converge.

As the artists make clear in their research notes for the piece, creditors of the island's debt include US investment firms and vulture hedge funds that profit by recuperating dues, even if they come at the expense of brutal structural adjustments, not dissimilar to the debt subjection of Greece.[30] Consequently, Puerto Rico's economy, controlled currently by an unelected Financial Management and Oversight Board appointed by the US Congress in 2016, according to the stipulations of PROMESA (Puerto Rico Oversight, Management, and Economic Stability Act), siphons resources from the country's public university system, hospitals, pensions, infrastructure maintenance, and public schools (179 were closed in that year alone, and even more recently) and redirects the funds to creditors, effectively placing profits over people. The result is what some call the formation of a debt colony,

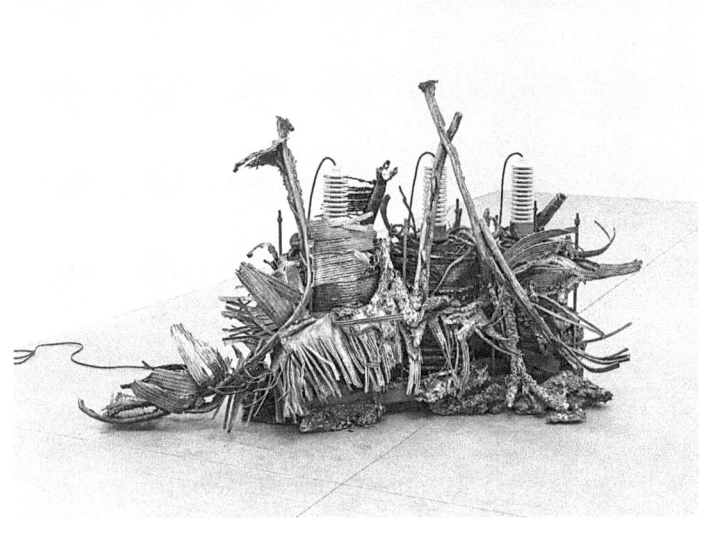

2.7 Allora & Calzadilla, *Blackout*, 2017. Courtesy of the artists.

which is only exacerbated by the island's environmental misfortunes.[31] Serving as a US colony from 1898 until 1952, Puerto Rico has existed as a commonwealth since then, one beholden to the mainland's interests according to the conditions of economic servitude. While the island's economic configuration, implemented over decades of US policy and constitutional law, has produced a situation of massive indebtedness, it simultaneously structurally excludes the option of declaring bankruptcy, which is commonly available to US cities and corporations in financial duress, and instead prioritizes loan repayments over social welfare expenditures.[32] The frayed, mangled, and corroded body of Allora & Calzadilla's resonant sculpture presents a state of material decomposition that sources and expresses this depraved politico-financial and socio-environmental situation, precisely embodying these unjust economic distortions, structural disfigurements, and legal maladjustments, revealing them for the massive failure they are.

Some activists believe that the overwhelming debt—approximately $123 billion, when factoring in the country's $49 billion pension burden—is simply unserviceable or even illegal. These opponents are demanding debt forgiveness or at least economic development first, though the Oversight Board, beholden to corporate stakeholders, will likely continue to do everything in its powers to guarantee immediate repayment before all else. Others contend that with ever more multitudes subjected to politico-economic disenfranchisement in a world of growing resource inequality—dramatized particularly in the postdisaster zones of Houston, Puerto Rico, Detroit, New Orleans, and Haiti, to mention only a few cities and countries in the Americas that form an interconnected web of structural and purposeful neglect—we are witnessing a spreading *blackout* that is socioeconomic and structurally racist in origin. Indeed, for Achille Mbembe, this system represents the geographical expansion to global proportions of the centuries-long economic violence of profound inequity that once characterized primarily the slavery of those of African origin. Now called "precarity" and released from strictly racial classification (though this is not to say that racial capitalism does not persist—it clearly does), blackout designates what Mbembe terms the "becoming black of the world": "Across early capitalism, the term 'Black' referred only to the condition imposed on peoples of African origin (different forms of depredation, dispossession of all power of self-determination, and, most of all, dispossession of the future and of time, the two matrices of the possible). Now, for the first time in human history, the term 'Black' has been generalized. This new fungibility, this solubility, institutionalized as a new norm of existence and expanded to the entire planet, is what I call the *Becoming Black of the world*."[33] The phrase designates the globalized blackout of impoverishment, necropolitics, and dispossession—the dispossession of the power of self-determination, of control over and belief in one's future, even the free access to time and the possible. To Mbembe's diagnosis of this new norm of precarious and defutured existence, I would add the material exposure to extraction's waste zones, befouled elements, colonized atmospheres, toxic externalities, and public health emergencies, where becoming black (in lowercase to connote its more-than-racial character) is evidenced in urban pollution, degraded water, mismanaged waste, and indebted and diseased bodies (even though this negativity does not totally define the category, as we will see). While its zones may be expanding globally, exposure is still based on differential vulnerabilities and unequal resources of protection, with the interconnected relations between the two inspiring further cycles of commodification (targeting health care, education, and housing as much as the primary elements of water, air, and soil, each encountering ongoing cycles of privatization and extraction).

In joining energy production with financial debt servitude, Allora & Calzadilla's *Blackout* identifies the key neocolonial logic of extraction, which is, as we have seen, operative in the environment of finance capital that has itself become globalized.[34] The two are indeed intimately connected, justifying their double metonymic referencing in the piece's literal inclusion

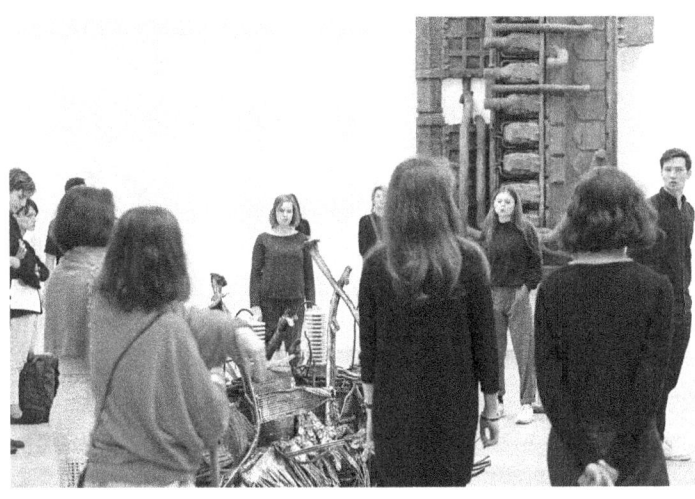

2.8 Allora & Calzadilla, *Blackout*, 2017 (installation with performers). Courtesy of the artists.

of the electromagnetic transformer from an indebted public utility—a transformer that can be understood here as being once a generator of both energy and financial flows, as well as of pollution, climate disruption, and debilitation. The fact that PREPA runs primarily on fossil fuels, despite being located on a Caribbean island rich in solar potential, and that its energy's high cost (three times what US mainlanders typically pay) is borne by Puerto Rico's captive consumers, only reinforces the significance of the connection of energy and debt production.[35] For Puerto Rico's debt is symptomatic of the global arrangement by which the world's eight richest people own as much wealth as the bottom half of the human population, some 3.6 billion, whereby enrichment is also cause and consequence of impoverishment.[36] We see this situation playing out further in Puerto Rico's dwindling population (some 135,000 left the island between 2013 and 2016 alone), as multitudes of these US citizens have moved to the US mainland for economic survival (creating yet another vanishing geography, a land with ever fewer people); meanwhile, a new class of upwardly mobile venture capitalists, crypto-currency speculators, and real estate developers are moving in to repossess the idyllic lands and benefit from tax advantages to do so.[37]

To these dynamics, Allora & Calzadilla add a sonic dimension, transforming *Blackout*'s transformer into an operative tuning device for a vocal-acoustic performance based on *mains hum* (2017), an original score by composer David Lang commissioned for the piece. It begins with a resonant quotation by US founding father Benjamin Franklin: "In going on with these

Experiments, how many pretty systems do we build, which we soon find ourselves oblig'd to destroy! If there is no other Use discover'd of Electricity, this, however, is something considerable, that it may help to make a vain Man humble." Franklin's words are ultimately rendered illegible in the music itself (as if nothing—neither history nor ethics—is freed from the transformer's distortions). But the irony, of course, is that this so-called humbling of man—referenced indirectly by the humming singers, who, in matching the humming pitch of the transformer, transform these words into a collective buzzing that builds off the sonic continuum of *Blackout*'s machine—has been far from the case. Even in the shadow of multiple power failures, including the recent period following 2017's summer of disaster, the burned-out mass of existing infrastructure on the island still inspires visions of yet more economic potential. Out of the ashes emerge ever-greater machinic monsters of wealth accumulation, and, as the paradigm of disaster capitalism expands, catastrophe affords further opportunities for advancing ever-more-intense neoliberal and extractive agendas, even as the social movements of opposition rise in turn.[38]

HOPE IN THE DARK

With these projects by Melitopoulos, Biemann, and Allora & Calzadilla, we encounter diverse approaches to extractive zones where exploitation simultaneously implicates natural resources and finances, where ecological and economic violence are inseparable. Abstract figures and calculations are simply idealist, serving to cloak all sorts of structural violence, inequalities, and uneven material consequences. The techniques of this exploitation include earthmoving machinery as well as operational logistics, trade agreements as much as legal arrangements, police brutality and coercive economics, tax evasion and offshore accounts, although the artistic projects discussed above tend to focus on community-scaled geographies of human and environmental costs. Nonetheless, these extraction and sacrifice zones formed at the intersection of extreme weather events, environmental de- or nonregulation, and creditor-debtor inequalities also offer scenes of what Rebecca Solnit has called "hope in the dark." For Solnit, the phrase describes acts of nonexploitative mutual aid, as when, in the absence of state or NGO assistance (or despite their often militarized formations), neighbors come to each other's support, form collective kitchens, deliver disaster relief, distribute essential services, rebuild homes, and save lives.[39] Perhaps most directly portrayed in *Deep Weather*'s account of Bangladeshi people

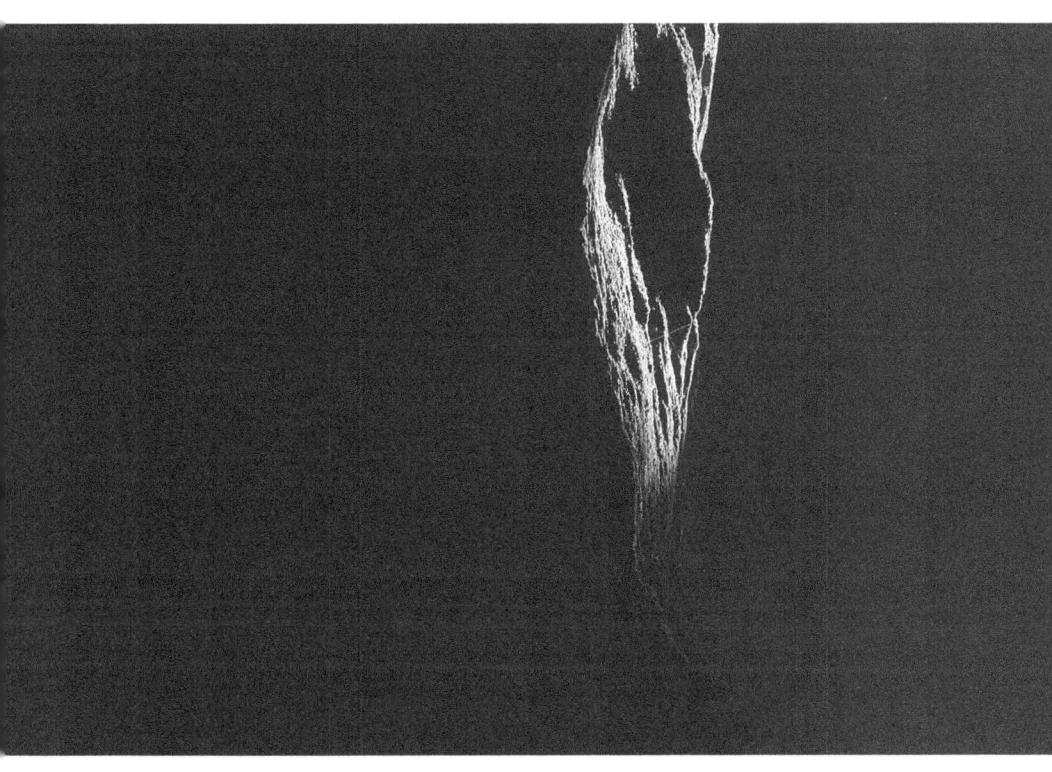

2.9 Allora & Calzadilla, *The Night We Became People Again*, 2017 (still). Digital HD video, color, sound. Courtesy of the artists.

fortifying their coastlines against storm surges, such practices also occur in the community-building and self-organized political education of Greece's refugee camps shown in *Crossings*, and in Puerto Rico's post-hurricane geographies of *autogestión*, meaning self-management, or more broadly, self-directed becoming, which is speculatively schematized in Allora & Calzadilla's cinematic visions of collective transformation.[40] In the latter's short film *The Night We Became People Again* (2017), the artists invoke precolonial Taíno cosmology as a resource for postcolonial survival. Its nocturnal scenery transitions between a cave of Indigenous mythological reference alluding to the beginning of time, and the dark interior of a decrepit Puerto Rican power plant, standing for world-destroying industrialization. The film's visuality features swirling bats and flickering stars, invoking the formation of new multispecies and astral worlds, which, in converging with a postapocalyptic imaginary of infrastructural breakdown and collective reinvention, charts out a new configuration of postanthropocentric, postextractive social being.[41] It cultivates, precisely, one sort of hope in the dark.

These practices reveal emergent spaces of potentiality, ones suggesting and building toward a politico-ecological paradigm shift, a self-governing leaderful movement overcoming the privations and manipulations of disaster capitalism, insisting on alternative futures where there were none at all. They even enliven modes of disaster communalism, or, as Ashley Dawson phrases it, disaster communism: "collaborative, altruistic, and often improvised forms of collective provision echoing Marx's dictum 'for each according to ability, to each according to need.'"[42] These forms glimpse new horizons of the possible and actively construct passage into the not-yet. By insisting on the ethical imperative of collective survival, they extend beyond loyalty to capitalism in expressing the dreams of decolonial transformation and emancipatory revolution.[43] If so, then in those areas of disaster communism emerging in the blackouts of the energy grid following extreme weather events, we also witness *Becoming Black* as a modality of decolonized subjectivation, a building of unrecognizable and ungovernable sovereignties, of prefigurative, postcapitalist mutual aid societies, inspiring a scaling up toward transnational solidarities and a coming movement of movements.[44] As with the recent socioenvironmental mobilizations at Standing Rock and Flint, Michigan, each threatened with the blacking out of their water sources, and extending to widespread and transnational activist networks such as Black Lives Matter and BlackOUT Collective, these are aesthetic, social, and political spaces where blackout is made to flip into positive expression, a productive discontent with pessimism where Blackness becomes "a symbol of beauty and pride," as Mbembe writes, "a sign of radical defiance, a call to revolt, desertion, [and] insurrection"; indeed, in such places, we can discern blackout as "an island of repose in the midst of racial oppression and objective dehumanization."[45]

That said, one would be right to question if these instances of volunteerist social mobilizations emerging in disaster zones—in colonized Greece, flood-risk Bangladesh, and posthurricane Puerto Rico—are not also symptomatic of neoliberal entrepreneurialism operating in the vacuum of governmental (un)accountability, where self-organization in defunded and indebted territories performs self-extracting unpaid labor, conveniently relieving the state of its responsibilities. Are these not instances where "recovery" ultimately means the return to capitalism's status quo and even more extreme versions of it, to its dependent sovereignties and unquestioned hegemony? If so, at what point do such collective efforts catalyze social emancipation beyond extractive capture, when blackout might designate radical degrowth economies, ecological downsizing, multispecies flourishing in postcarbon geographies—hope not only *in* the dark but also *of* the dark, a refuge of obscurity or strategic opacity resistant to surveillance, algorithmic capture, and media spectacle alike?

It is difficult to answer these questions, and to clearly separate hope from despair, especially when the topologies of revolt and normalization, desertion and capture, are so complexly intertwined, and where the effects and outcomes of these events are never simply punctual or secure. What remains clear is that we need more than ever a transnational movement answering and preempting the current distributive globalization of financial power, operating within and between nation-states that no longer function according to the logics of democratic representation and accountability, as is shown in Melitopoulos's *Crossings*. "Ultimately, the only way to begin dismantling imperialist relations of domination and truly liberate the new debt colonies from their economic subjugation is for the working classes and social movements of both the debtor and the creditor countries to become aware of their shared interest in building a unified front against the impositions of global finance," writes Jerome Roos.[46] What is required is greater sensitivity toward the entangled socioenvironmental conditions of contemporary extraction, as well as a renewed commitment to solidarity against and beyond inequality's multiple social fragmentations, including those isolating various identities.[47] As Rev. Dr. William Barber, co-chair of the Poor People's Campaign that has taken up Dr. Martin Luther King Jr.'s civil rights movement in the last few years, adds, "if you're poor, whether you're white, black or brown, and you can't pay your light bill, we're all black in the dark, so we need to stand together in the light."[48] It is exactly this need for solidarity within and through social difference that the work of the above artists show as pressing. In them—in their politics of aesthetics, in their critical pedagogies, in their amplified spaces of reception and engagement, in their liberated temporalities—we see some of the transnational social energies uniquely capable of challenging and transforming petrocapitalist systems of governance. In these blackouts of fossil and financial power, we witness the signs of radical defiance, a call to revolt, desertion, and insurrection.

THE VISUAL POLITICS OF
CLIMATE REFUGEES

Whether voluntary or coerced, or somewhere in between, migration responds to a network of forces that are rarely monocausal. Economic conditions connect with social factors, such as religious persecution or ethnic discrimination, and these join with biopolitical forces, including governmental legal frameworks and elaborate border control systems. In other words, migration too defines a site of intersectionality, which I am redeploying here as a politico-ecological analytic placed in relation to the discourse of climate refugees, wherein mobility expresses itself precisely through multiple and multiply entangled vectors of causality. This is especially the case when it comes to *images of migrants* that are also *migrating images*, endlessly recontextualized visual assemblages, as much at their origins as at their often transitory destinations, which may frustrate structural analysis of larger conditions. At a time when mainstream media defines the dominant conventions of migrant representation, it is urgent to overcome its tendency to focus on the faces and biographies of individuals and impacted communities—including children, adults, and families, at various points of passage—if we are to get at what lies behind migration in the first place.

When migration responds to environmental disturbances—including drought; sea-level rise; and extreme weather events, such as floods, fires, and cyclones—out of which emerges the recently proposed category of "climate refugees" (those forced to leave their traditional habitat, temporarily or permanently, owing to destructive climate transformation), we face a stubborn regime of visual representation that tends to occlude intersecting factors. This happens despite the fact that "there is no way to confront the climate crisis as a technocratic problem, in isolation. It must be seen in the context of austerity and privatisation, of colonialism and militarism, and of the various systems of othering needed to sustain them all," as Naomi Klein explains.[1] The problem is that many anti-austerity activists rarely discuss climate breakdown, and environmentalists seldom mention war, racism, or occupation, leading to compartmentalization on each side reinforced by the restrictive visuality of environmentally determined migration. That compartmentalization, also expressed visually, carries political implications in that migrants are typically viewed as disconnected from histories of socioecological entanglement that render many of our governments complicit in the very production and management of migration. And by ignoring those entanglements, it makes it easier for reactionary commentators, policy makers, and politicians, in acts of contemporary scapegoating, to situate the displaced as agents of injustice and themselves (somewhat perversely) as the victims.

In the near future, the stakes are set to grow more intense with what some are warning is a coming globalization of "climate apartheid," a system of institutionalized disparity regarding environmentally motivated displacement that will likely be exacerbated by racism and xenophobia.[2] Creating ever new possibilities for migrant labor exploitation founded on the material dispossession and political disenfranchisement of multitudes, "the insecurity of the migrant ensures the security of capital," argues Ashley Dawson, who observes how migration tends to drive down wages, produce a depoliticized mobile workforce, and spread precarity.[3] As such, the migrant represents the exemplary subject of corporate globalization. These circumstances will only worsen if we continue down the present path of growing neoliberal austerity, ethnonationalist populism, and unmitigated anthropogenic climate disruption. Against that eventuality, it becomes imperative to generate critical visual resources—central to the formation of a properly political analysis—in our activist and social movement responses, in order to aid in the collective transformation toward a just world.

Consider three examples of recent climate refugee photography that speak to the abovementioned concerns. First is that of the Collectif Argos (Argos Collective), a French group of photojournalists and humanitarians who presciently dedicated an image-text series from 2010 to climate refugees. In their portfolio depicting the low-lying Maldives—presented both on the collective's website and in their book *Climate Refugees*—the Indian Ocean lands appear threatened by rising seas, coasts subjected to erosion, and buildings collapsing on shrinking shores. The images portray inhabitants in scenes of flooding that are increasingly common these days, scenes where the Argos Collective plots the Maldives on the front lines of climate change migration. Moving beyond the science of climate change to its social implications, journalist and Argos member Guy-Pierre Chomette explains that "we wanted to emphasize the human dimension, especially for those most vulnerable."[4] Their images do just that, declining in the process, however, to represent the Maldivians' political agency in mobilizing support for critical climate response, including the responsive governmental policies of, and demands for justice-based decarbonization made by, President Mohamed Nasheed (in office at the time of their research). Their photos consequently tend to neglect the more complex *causes* of climate change located in the centuries-long fossil fuel development of industrialized countries, in favor of focusing solely on the world-ending *effects* in South Asia. In another series that operates according to a similar logic, the Argos Collective pictures the South Pacific island of Tuvalu, from a low perspective behind a wave, as if the land is already under water. Forming part of their series called "A Polynesian Requiem," images such as this transform future potential into alarming present reality, resonating with catastrophist narratives of humanitarian discourse. Not surprisingly, critics accuse its agents of construing victimizing identities for their subjects, abstracted from sociopolitical frameworks, in relation to which photographer-humanitarians model themselves as the heroic bearers of aid. Risking a self-serving mode of what Carol Farbotko calls "wishful sinking," these images correlate with a photography of fatalism based on climate determinism, where the future is already written and the past obliterated from the field of view.[5]

Second, take John Stanmeyer's *National Geographic* photography, specifically those that capture Syrian refugees in the midst of the notorious 2015 migration crisis. The images accompany "Fleeing Terror, Finding Refuge:

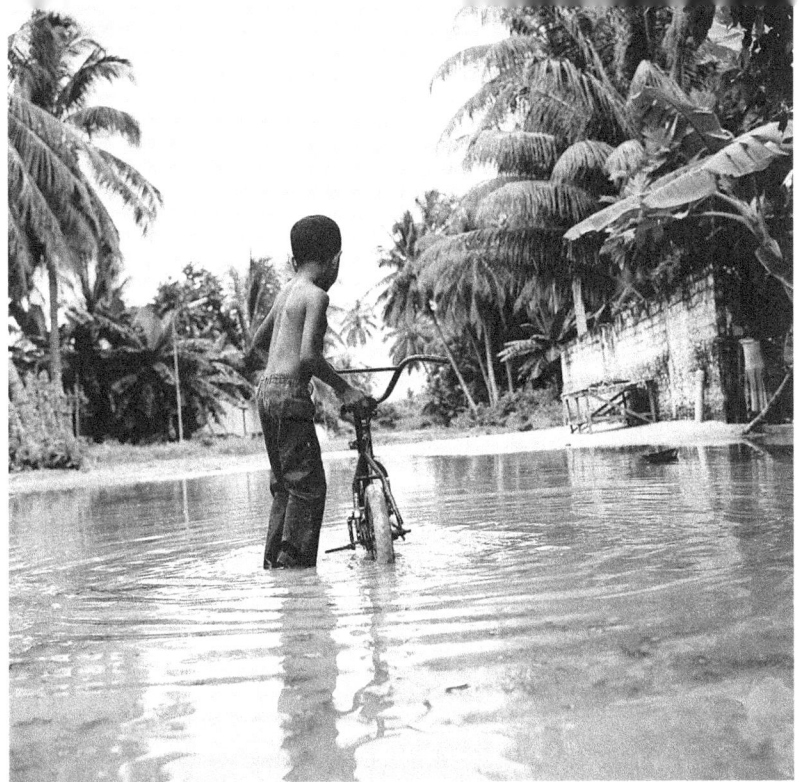

3.1 Guillaume Collanges / Collectif Argos, *Thudi (Laamu Atoll), Maldives*, January 2007. Courtesy of the artists.

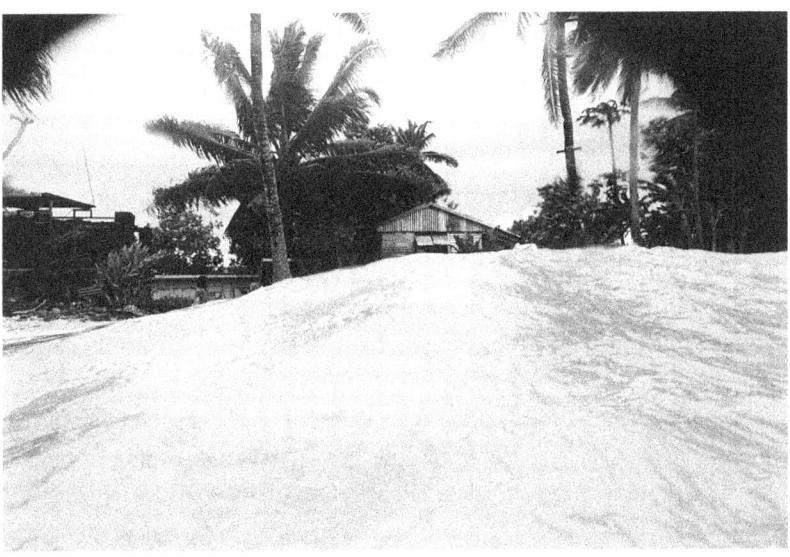

3.2 Laurent Weyl / Collectif Argos, *Funafuti atoll, Fongafale island*, February 2006. "The tsunami which struck Asia is on everybody's mind. Whatever their temperament, most Tuvaluans associate this catastrophe with what awaits them as sea levels keep rising. 01/02/2006." Courtesy of the artists.

Millions of Syrians Escape an Apocalyptic Civil War, Creating a Historic Crisis," an article by Paul Salopek that describes the conditions of some 100,000 displaced, including many ethnic Kurds, who crossed into Turkey near the Mürşitpınar border, many coming to occupy a refugee camp near Kilis.[6] The photographs, corresponding to what Salopek describes as "a vast panorama of mass homelessness," present what we can term a photography of faces—a system of representation that dramatizes the plight of the uprooted by focusing on their visual appearance with all possible pathos (what the Argos Collective calls the "human dimension"), but which is largely detached from the sociopolitical and geo-economic frameworks that complexly led to that homelessness.[7] The visualizations stress figurations of physiognomic and gestural affect, as well as their sympathetic environmental frames, including austere camp conditions, where resignation and dread are allegorized in the dark, cloudy atmospheres. The photography, in other words, transforms the dislocated into the readily consumable media category of refugees. It is true that the prevailing affect of melancholia is, in other images of Stanmeyer, mitigated by highlighting practices of creative survival in difficult circumstances, as when inhabitants are shown tending their small gardens, offering informal education for children, and providing everyday care for one another. However, the humanizing tendencies of these portrayals work to visually substantiate the article's abstract and abstracting statistics, as faces dissolve into numbers.

These photographs depict some of the approximately 1.6 million Syrian war refugees in Turkey, with another 8 million displaced internally within Syria (compared to a total 12 million dislocated in the Middle East overall as of 2015), according to Salopek's narrative. While the ravages of the Islamic State, the roles of Saddam Hussein and Bashar Assad, are briefly mentioned, Salopek foregrounds a quote by Jason Ur, a Harvard archaeologist who explains that "population displacements have a long and sad history in the region" and have occurred "repeatedly over the last 3,000 years at least," thereby further removing migrants from their historically specific circumstances.[8] The focus of the images too remains fixed on the refugees themselves, visually freezing the displaced into personal-interest stories. Contrary to Ur's *longue durée* perspective, it's as if we are looking through a telescope fitted with historical and political blinders—past Syrian geopolitics, decades of emergency rule, the transformative dynamics of globalization, uneven economic liberalization, petrocapitalist developments, uprisings of political Islam, chronic conflicts with Israel, contentious relations

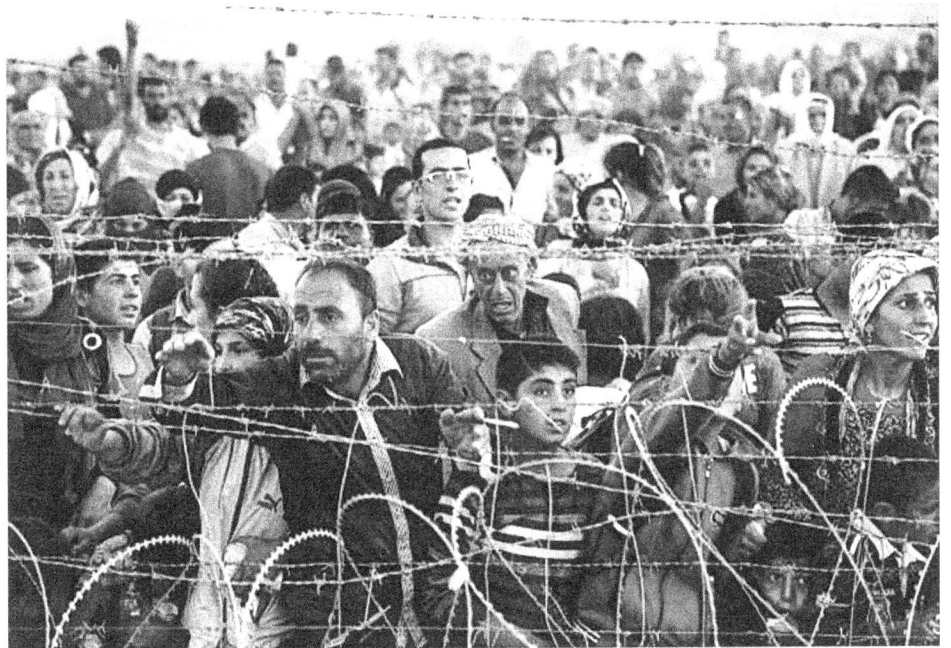

3.3 John Stanmeyer, photograph of Syrian refugees, September 2014. "Up to 5,000 Syrians from Kobani amass at the border with Turkey on Friday evening, next to the Turkish village of Dikmetas. On this day was the beginning of the exodus when 200,000 Syrians, mostly Kurds, crossed into Turkey in 72 hours." *National Geographic*, March 2015.

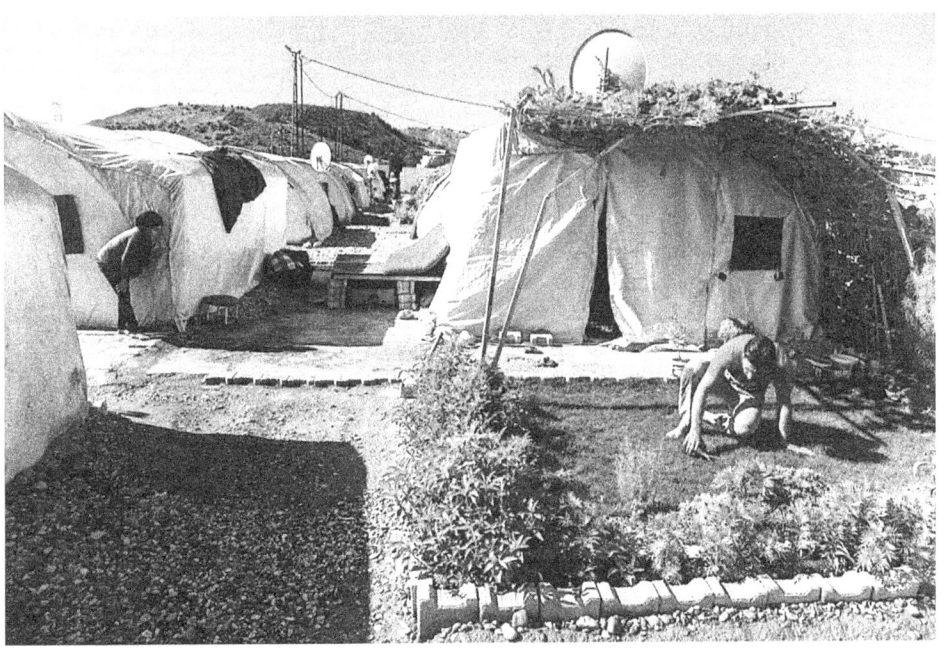

3.4 John Stanmeyer, photograph of the Nizip 1 camp, September 2014. "Mohammad Magelk grooms the oasis he has created in the dusty Nizip 1 camp, where more than 11,000 Syrians now live." *National Geographic*, March 2015.

with Iran, and interethnic and religious conflicts, all exacerbated by multiple years of environmental crisis, including a severe multiyear drought.[9] The ultimate point for Salopek is the visual construction of empathy, shaped by pronominal identification with the dislocated, which describes the intended photographic viewing process as well: "You take a step. You exit one life and enter another. You walk through a cut border fence into statelessness, vulnerability, dependency, and invisibility. You become a refugee." Like the Argos Collective's repertoire, Salopek's text and Stanmeyer's images invite Western audiences to identify with the subjects in mirror-image formation but one absent any visual infrastructure that would aid in revealing the inextricable complexities of the nonsubjective, geopolitical, and socioecological causes behind Syrian migration.

Third, consider images of the "first climate refugees" in the US, those located on the southern coast of Louisiana in Isle de Jean Charles, as captured in 2016 by photographer Josh Haner of the *New York Times*. The lavish color images show a landmass teetering at water's edge threatened with submersion, where more than 90 percent of the island has washed away since 1955. (The watery territory was appropriately the inspiration for "the Bathtub," the setting for Benh Zeitlin's Oscar-nominated 2012 film, *Beasts of the Southern Wild*, which tells a dystopian, enchanted tale of Delta survival in the midst of structural debilitation at the end of a climate-transformed world.) We learn in the accompanying text by Coral Davenport and Campbell Robertson that "human-caused climate change" has warmed the planet, bringing "rising sea levels, stronger storms, increased flooding, harsher droughts and dwindling freshwater supplies," in addition to more extreme and destructive hurricanes.[10] Isle de Jean Charles has been further harmed over the last few decades by water channels cut by loggers and carbon geographies terraformed (or better: petroformed) by oil companies, though none of these are identified in the text or shown in Haner's photographs, which instead focus on local residents, "among the nation's most vulnerable," including Native Americans of the Biloxi-Chitimacha-Choctaw tribe and the United Houma Nation. Violet Handon Parfait, her son, Reggie, and her mother, Theresa Handon, appear in one image standing on a raised wooden walkway just in front of the wreckage of Parfait's trailer house destroyed by Hurricane Gustav in 2008, a category 2 superstorm that wrought more than $8 billion in damage; and Marlene Autian, Laura Broussard, and Joann Bourg are pictured amidst a flowering field outside their home on Isle de Jean Charles, as if witnesses to their own undoing and facing an uncertain future. With

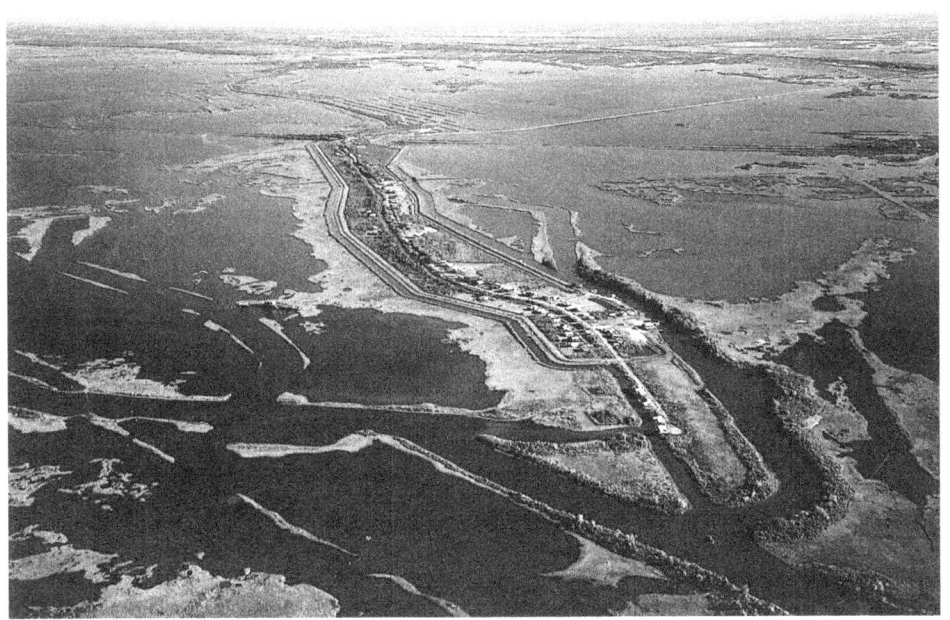

3.5 Josh Haner, aerial view of Isle de Jean Charles, 2016. *New York Times*, May 2, 2016.

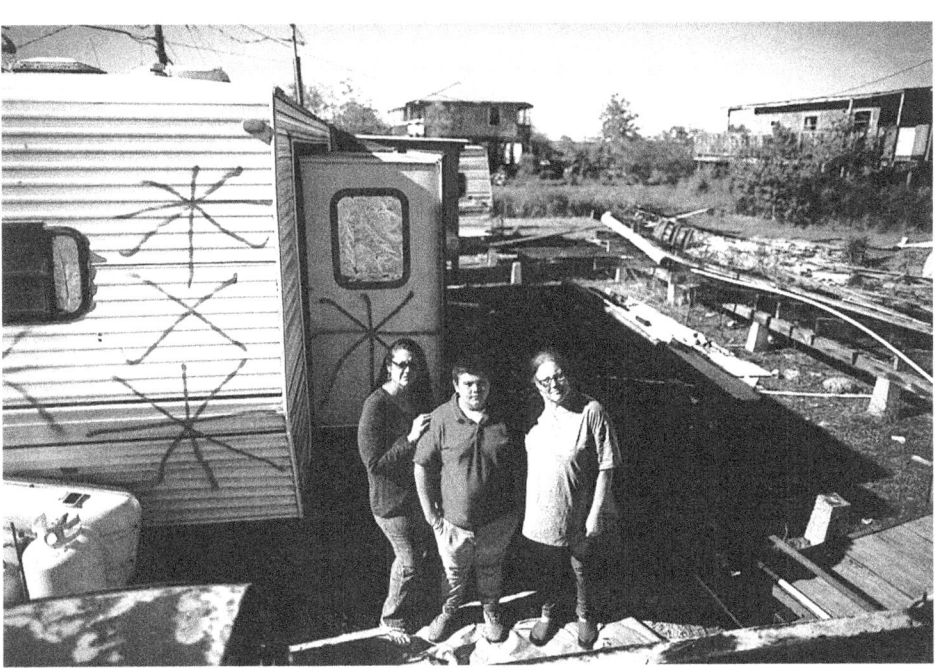

3.6 Josh Haner, Isle de Jean Charles, 2016. Biloxi-Chitimacha-Choctaw tribal members Marlene Autian, Laura Broussard, and Joann Bourg in front of their house. *New York Times*, May 2, 2016.

their figures typically facing the camera, appearing unsurrendered to their precarious situation, these images are on the whole less victimizing than the Argos Collective's Tuvaluans or Stanmeyer's Syrians, but they still focus in tunnel-like vision on the subjective effects of climate change. Neither the article nor the images mention or visualize the relation to earlier episodes of colonial displacement, going back centuries, or the impoverishment of local peoples within postindustrial neoliberalism. If they did, then climate would expand to sociopolitical dimensions, economic determinants, and military causalities. Nor do they comment on the fact that the very government that is funding the massive relocation effort of Isle de Jean Charles's population with $48 million in federal tax dollars is the same one that subsidized past fossil fuel development and land-engineering projects in the region that have rendered the coastline increasingly uninhabitable. The tremendous gulf between, on the one hand, US interior secretary Sally Jewell's fatalistic pronouncement ("We Will Have Climate Refugees") and, on the other, Chief Albert Naquin's dark premonitions of his people's defutured existence, one gradually blinded by dissolving transgenerational memory ("We're going to lose all our heritage, all our culture. . . . It's all going to be history") remains unaddressed.[11] That is the gulf of fatalism's violence.

THE SPECTACLE OF MISERY

A number of observations follow in relation to this admittedly brief but exemplary survey of the mainstream visual culture of climate refugees, where "mainstream" represents the doctrine of dominant institutions (corporate, governmental, educational, media), which tend to amplify and perpetuate narratives about "the way things should work" in the interests of the wealthy, privileged, and powerful.[12] Three general concerns rise to the surface. The first concerns the practice of figuration-over-contexualization in mainstream media representation, where images of climate refugees mirror the dominant media's visualization of refugees in general. We find therein a spectacle of victimhood seen through a voyeuristic lens that migrates figures from the ground of historical and structural causes, focusing instead on personal traumas, limited background contexts, and present physical circumstances. The situation parallels trends in international humanitarian law and human rights practice, which often produce figurations detached from complex structural determinations, as notes Eyal Weizman, director of the Forensic Architecture project: "They tend to extract an individual (victim or perpetrator, alive or dead) from the messy physical or political ground in which they were embedded." Conversely, "establishing field causalities requires the examination of force fields, causal ecologies, that are nonlinear, diffused, simultaneous, and involve multiple agencies and feedback loops."[13] By occluding "field causalities" and the complexity of their networked formation, mainstream media images of migrants—including those cited above—produce similarly incomprehensible abstractions, phantasms of social breakdown, and inexplicable forces of invasion, often narrated as threatening to European and North American reception. These fictions easily become weaponized, fueling and perpetuating extremist political rhetoric, further detaching migration from its compound determinants, which, were they taken into consideration to begin with, would introduce and require very different solutions and modes of address than the ones typically on offer.

My second observation is that the commercialized media of these conventional images tends to generate increasingly extreme narratives. During 2015, more than one million migrants reached Europe (mainly Greece and Italy) via the Mediterranean, as reports the United Nations High Commissioner for Refugees (UNHCR), charged with protecting the rights and well-being of displaced people worldwide. Of these migrants, 84 percent came from the world's recent top ten refugee-producing countries—including Syria, Afghanistan, and Iraq—informing UNHCR's research findings that most of those arriving in Europe were fleeing war and persecution.[14] The massive displacement was said to constitute "the greatest refugee crisis since the Second World War," the magnitude of which jeopardized the commitment of the European Union (EU) to open borders within its Schengen territory (the area comprising twenty-six European states that officially abolished internal passport controls in 1995 and which still, albeit increasingly precariously, remains in effect today).[15] Migration—or rather dominant perceptions of it—has also threatened the EU's welfare policies, its fundamental political cohesion, and its commitment to democratic principles. Meanwhile, the "crisis" has been manufactured and largely narrated by a corporate (anti)social media frenzy characterized by sensationalist reporting and imaging. These depend on algorithm-driven news feeds like Facebook that market and intensify affects of fear and outrage, often directed against migrants, designed to maximize online consumerist engagement without regulation or ethical compass.[16] Media ecologies of othering—constituting a mix of visual presentation and captioned extremism, progressively intensified by algorithms—lead in turn to right-wing hate speech making increasingly shocking and outlandish claims with ever greater visibility (including those of the UK's Nigel Farage and Boris Johnson, France's Marine Le Pen, the Netherland's Geert Wilders, and Hungary's Viktor Orbán).[17]

With this alarmist framing of migration, we face what some have called an "Islamic invasion"—a typical example of fear-mongering xenophobia once thought beyond the pale. But now, propelled by horrific terror attacks in Europe and the US—where in fact there has been greater right-wing neofascist violence, legitimated by the Trump administration, in recent years—and couched in a reactionary media environment, politicians feel increasingly licensed to draw generalizing and stereotyping conclusions about all migrants.[18] Their rhetoric is amplified particularly in the sensationalist press, alarming for its stoking the fires of apocalyptic populism, according to which adherents are willing to support drastic measures (such as bombing problems away) in anti-democratic expressions of world-destroying resentment.[19] Such extremist sentiment, needless to say, lends further support to building walls and militarizing border security—with full-spectrum dominance technology, including a near-future of automated weaponry with right-to-kill robotics and biotech applications that target genomic patterns keyed to ethnic traits—as the dominant framework with which to "address" migration.[20] Within this context, migration figures as a criminal menace attended to by a billion-dollar-a-year industry rather than as an in/voluntary mode of behavioral adaptation for human survival in complex and often insufferable emergency conditions predicated upon colonial injustice and structural racism, or as an opportunity for cosmopolitan hospitality and humanitarian empathy for those in desperate need.[21] Instead of locating the causes of migration in Western policies of austerity, unfair trade agreements, neoliberal structural adjustments, endless military interventions, and resource wars, migrants are alternately blamed for being responsible for their own displacement, or shown to be the victims of so-called natural disaster, in other words, crises devoid of context.[22] It is this process that is propelled by mainstream media's image regime.

The third point concerns the term *climate refugee*, which makes matters worse owing to its juridico-political nonrecognition, even while environmental dislocation stands to grow substantially in the near future. Measured in sheer numbers, recent demographic shifts may be relatively insignificant compared to what lies ahead. Already in 2019, there were approximately 17.2 million uprooted by weather-related events, compared to 10.8 million owing to conflict, according to the Internal Displacement Monitoring Centre.[23] With the looming global "climate departure"—the moment when we pass beyond the historical range of meteorological averages toward catastrophic environmental breakdown—set to occur in the mid-twenty-first century (should no mitigation of greenhouse emissions occur), we can expect between 250 million and 1 billion people to be on the move by 2050.[24] Owing to climate transformation, this event would produce 250 to 1,000 times the number of migrants who made it to Europe in 2015.[25] These future multitudes include subsistence farmers, fisherfolk, and coastal dwellers, most located in the Global South, who will move inland and northward in hopes of better lives, economic opportunity, existential security, and sheer survival. In addition, research now predicts that coming climate disruption will precipitate the largest transfer of wealth (northward and westward, exacerbating existing inequality) ever in the US and globally, should no mitigation take place and economic arrangements continue as they are today.[26] In this regard, environmental factors compound socioeconomic ones, leading to more violence and inequality and providing further motivating conditions for migration.[27]

If climate refugees are at the center of what Christian Parenti terms the "catastrophic convergence" of contemporary poverty, violence, and climate change, then it defines indeed "the most colossal set of events in human history."[28] That these elements are difficult to distinguish is highlighted by Rebecca Solnit, who argues that "climate change is violence," in the sense that environmental transformation results from criminally negligent behaviors in corporate and governmental practice, including the polluting and logging of tropical rain forests, failing to regulate healthy drinking water, and contributing to climate breakdown through fossil fuel extraction while funding climate denial (all continuous with long histories of colonial extraction).[29] Making matters worse is recent economic history. After decades of Western-led neoliberal structural adjustments, promoted by the International Monetary Fund, the World Bank, and the European Council, debtor states worldwide have been stripped of resources, their institutions of education, health care, housing, and infrastructure substantially defunded. They have been left with few provisions to help establish safe, secure, economically vibrant, and environmentally sustainable homelands, compromising as well their ability to adapt to environmental transformation. These factors then exacerbate poverty and violence, which leads to more migration in turn.[30]

There is, however, no easy solution for addressing climate migration in the framework of existing migration law, within which the climate refugee remains an invisible figure (the 1951 Geneva Convention, for instance, grants refugee status only to those fleeing persecution for reasons of race, religion, nationality, social association, or political opinion, representing the legal codification of separateness that an intersectional approach would challenge). Some legal theorists argue that recognizing environmental refugees under the Geneva Conventions would grant them international protections, independent of state law.[31] To that end, the term *environmental refugee* was proposed by Essam El-Hinnawi in a 1985 United Nations Environment Programme policy paper to identify "those people who have been forced to leave their traditional habitat, temporarily or permanently, because of a marked environmental disruption," which means "any physical, chemical, and/or biological changes in the ecosystem (or resource base) that render it temporarily or permanently unsuitable to support human life."[32] However, not only does this definition lack any traction in international law decades later, but there is still no operative climate refugee category. It also proves exceedingly difficult to formalize it, as well as distinguishing between intertwined causal elements in assigning climate refugee status. In addition, it is not currently legally possible to discriminate between environmental and climatological causalities, a situation exemplified and reinforced in dominant visual regimes of representation. Migrant images, as we have seen, tend to present spectacles of misery that overlook the complex determinants of socioenvironmental dislocation, which begs the questions to which I will return below: How might we conceive alternative representational systems that enable the juridico-political recognition of climate-based migration according to an expansive definition of what climate means?

THRESHOLDS OF INDISTINCTION

In addition to expanding the Geneva Conventions, recognition of climate refugees could also occur, analysts point out, by developing existing international law (the UN Framework Convention on Climate Change, for instance), or extending the mandate of the UNHCR.[33] There are nonetheless several reasons to question this route as an adequate response to climate-induced displacement, especially in a neoliberal era where political and legal formations manage the selective differentiation of migrants according to race, class, and religion. First, it is difficult, and even impossible, to define environmental causes and separate them from poverty, war, or any of the factors coextensive with the effects of climate change, as mentioned above. The climate refugee, by definition, represents an intangible figure, a relentlessly conceptually mobile one, owing to the impossibility of disaggregating its sources of displacement. Climate change exacerbates an already complex set of challenges for vulnerable populations, including uneven access to water, land, and infrastructure resources, as much as institutions, capital, and legal recourse.[34] Indeed, many political theorists remain skeptical of establishing further complex and likely confusing distinctions in classifying refugees, as "it will leave plenty of room for thresholds of indistinction that leave the final decision on the status of life up to sovereign power," which can then abuse ambiguity in oppressive ways.[35] Second, placing climate refugees under the UNHCR's jurisdiction will not simply grant rights to refugees; it also threatens to transform them into the victimized objects of humanitarianism, selectively recognized within liberal rights regimes, where aid can be withdrawn at any time, while larger structures of power and systems of inequality go unaddressed. Consider, for example, the displaced of Hurricane Katrina in 2005, some 400,000 people, including many African Americans with limited economic means who lived in New Orleans's Lower Ninth Ward, who encountered demeaning conditions in their Superdome-turned-camp environment in the days after the superstorm, with wholly inadequate federal assistance in subsequent years. That dystopian scenario—uniting institutional and environmental racism, economic precarity, climate change disaster, and militarized police response—foreshadows one potential future treatment of climate migrants worldwide.[36] Or take the migrants subjected to Trump's border regime, including the incarceration of children of divided families (there were approximately 70,000 migrant children held in federal custody during 2019). With that situation, we encounter the outright rejection of asylum claims amid the heightened militarized response to an overwhelming humanitarian disaster caused largely by decades of damaging US foreign policy (including environmental disaster) in Central America, constituting new extreme levels of postliberal, nationalist, and openly racist xenophobia.[37] Many migrants, commonly deemed "illegal," are in fact already subjected to a system of endless camps, bureaucratic hurdles, emergency temporality, and degrading circumstances. All of which feeds the telescopic presentism of disaster photography, which, in turn, exacerbates the defutured existence of the displaced.[38]

The third concern regarding the challenged climate refugee concept is that, as noted above, its legal nonrecognition follows the logic of much humanitarian visuality in addressing the effects of climate change rather than the causes. The problem is that, as discussed above, much visual culture—particularly the photography of mainstream media—tends to contribute to myopic portrayals of migrants, figures who appear abstracted from complex determinants, detached from the vector of intersectionality that is migration. In these portrayals, the human-interest story rules, the narrative that focuses on migrants themselves, with the media industry mining consumable biographies and their troves of moving affects for commercial ends. Many artists also participate in this iconographic machine, or go further, producing migrant images that offer well-intentioned empathic gestures but figure as guilt-relieving identifications, as when Chinese dissident artist Ai Weiwei had himself photographed posing as if dead on a Lesbos beach, representing Alan Kurdi, the three-year-old Syrian refugee who tragically drowned in 2016 while attempting to reach the EU. The image of Kurdi's body washed ashore near Bodrum, Turkey, was reproduced internationally. It is images like these that keep viewers entranced, with eyes fixed upon a photography of faces, while the structural causes remain invisible. Yet, as Slavoj Žižek observed in 2015,

> The first thing is to recall that most of refugees come from the "failed states"—where public authority is more or less inoperative, at least in large regions—Syria, Lebanon, Iraq, Libya, Somalia, Congo, etc. This disintegration of state power is not a local phenomenon but a result of international economy and politics—in some cases, like Libya and Iraq, a direct outcome of Western intervention. It is clear that the rise of these "failed states" is not just an unintended misfortune but also one of the ways the great powers exert their economic colonialism.[39]

One gets no sense of this complexity, however, from Ai's image, nor much more from the artist's film *Human Flow* (2017), which traces the migrations in recent years of vast numbers of people globally. To make the latter work, running at nearly two and a half hours, Ai visited more than twenty-three countries, including such war-torn hotspots as Iraq, Syria, and Afghanistan, as well as numerous refugee camps in Turkey, Greece, Lebanon, Kenya, Germany, and France. Using innovative approaches to filmmaking, including copious iPhone and aerial drone footage, the documentary highlights

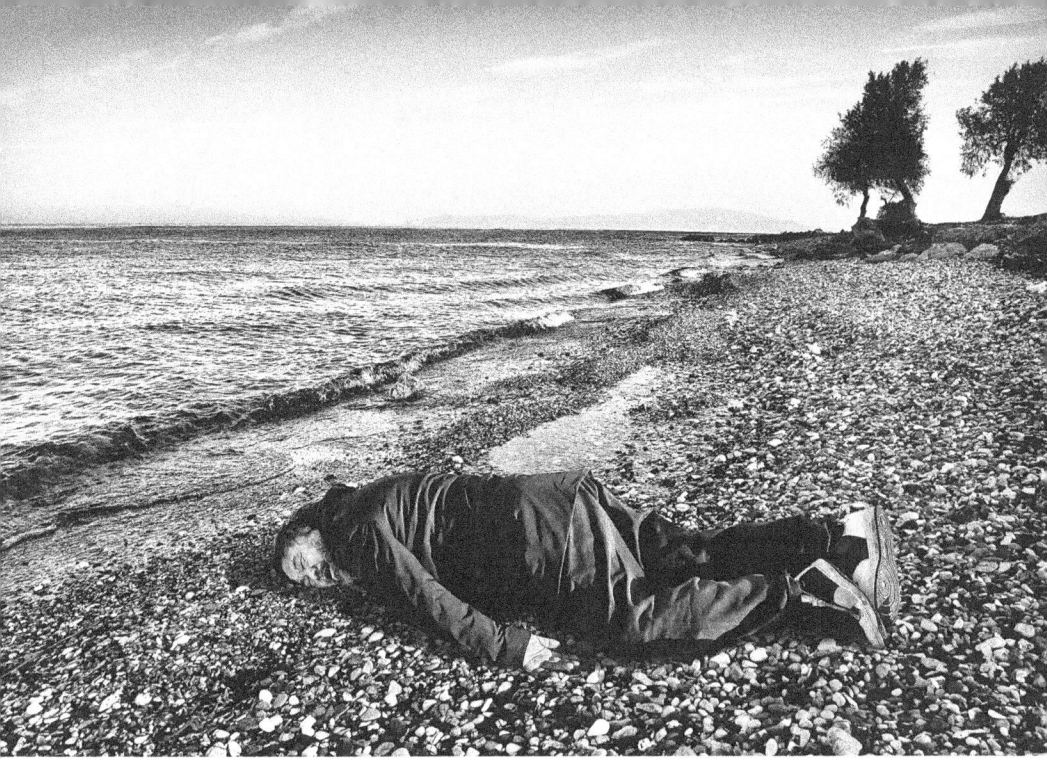

3.7 Ai Weiwei, posing as Syrian refugee toddler Alan Kurdi (whose body washed ashore in the Turkish town of Bodrum in September 2015), 2016.

scenes of wretched passage in miserable conditions, wherein migrants, living in makeshift tents and vulnerable to cruel border guards, appear hungry and unsheltered, beaten down and yet still determined. These images are set disjunctively within captivating cinematic displays of dramatic Mediterranean sunsets contrasting the Sahara's arid yellow-orange deserts with the deep-green tropics and the infinite blues of oceans. As such, the film marks a sea change in understandings of globalization. In contrast with 1989 and that subsequent era's erstwhile promise of a unified world of post–Cold War openness, when a mere eleven countries around the world possessed border fences and walls, thirty years later there are more than seventy, many protected with full-spectrum military surveillance systems and high-tech defenses, constituting a new epoch of nationalist xenophobia.[40] And matters seem to be getting only worse. While the ocean may appear to some as a navigable expanse of possibility, with new lands of opportunity on the horizon, it remains for the unfortunate an uncrossable barrier, and for all too many, a mass grave.

While its journalistic focus on the lives of migrants is a familiar human-interest trope in mainstream media, Ai's *Human Flow* nonetheless distinguishes itself as a cinematic feature. Yet its methodology is recognizable across the board: to portray the involuntarily dislocated as human beings who have stories to tell, feelings to share, grievances to be heard—in other words, the aim is to rescue these figures from the impersonal statistics and dehumanizing abstractions that invite invisibility and ignorance, and worse, xenophobia and racism, which in turn fuel the cruelties of securitization and militarization. Certainly a tragedy occurs when the most vulnerable become inescapably entangled in migration's carceral systems. Constituting human rights abuse, such brutal measures are unfortunately increasingly the rule, propelled by the collective intolerance on the rise in many parts of the world. *Human Flow*, in this regard, comes as an antidote. One of the film's areas of focus is the EU during 2015. As Boris Cheshirkov of the UNHCR explains in the film, we are living at a time of demographic shifts not seen since World War II, amounting to more than sixty-five million on the move, including refugees, asylum seekers, and internally displaced people. Yet rather than investigate the circumstances of this precarious situation, admittedly much less easily translated into cinematic form than subjective portrayals, the focus of *Human Flow*, as with the imagery of the Argos Collective, John Stanmeyer, and Josh Honer, remains largely on human effects.

As Dr. Hanan Ashrawi, head of the Palestine Liberation Organization (PLO) Department of Culture and Information—Palestinians being the world's largest group of refugees—poignantly observes in the film, "Being a refugee is much more than a political status; it is the most pervasive kind of cruelty that can be exercised against a human being by depriving a person of all forms of security, the most basic requirements of a normal life, by cruelly placing that person at the mercy of some inhospitable host countries that do not want to receive this refugee." Ashrawi's observation is affirmed by others in *Human Flow*: Ustaz Rafik, Rohingya community leader, speaks of campaigns of rape, pillage, and persecution against the more than 500,000 Rohingyas fleeing to Bangladesh, Thailand, and Malaysia; Peter Bouckaert, emergencies director of Human Rights Watch, discusses the internal chaos of Greece's Idomeni camp and the hardships of its diverse inhabitants; and Dr. Cem Terzi of the Association of Bridging Peoples, in Izmer, Turkey, where some three million Syrians have recently sought shelter (some pictured by Stanmeyer), explains how today's refugees are commonly deprived of international rights, offered no jobs, have little income, and are consequently vulnerable to authoritarian government policies and militarized controls. There is certainly an ongoing need to bring compassionate visibility to these figures—who on global average live for twenty-six years displaced from their homes—so that their representational erasure does not compound their geopolitical dislocation.

Yet *Human Flow* neglects the historical and present circumstances of migration; nor does it implicate its filmmaker or audience, other than in one singular scene in which Ai playfully exchanges his passport with a grateful Syrian migrant, telling him, "I respect you," speaking in a heartfelt manner. If only injustice could be repaired by individual ethical behavior alone.[41] While *Human Flow*'s exposure of migrant gloom is significant, offering an important wake-up call for those otherwise unaware, there is nonetheless all-too-little reflection on the structural forces driving migration beyond the familiar vague generalities of war and climate change. In this regard, *Human Flow* ultimately defines a cinema of liberalism: to manifest empathy for the wretched of the Earth in an effort to humanize the dispossessed and disenfranchised, but doing so in the absence of any proposals for structural transformation. While the formula offers reassuring visions of redemption, manifested in images of encompassing filmic splendor and Ai caring for the less fortunate, it leaves viewers with a nagging feeling of undefined guilt and no clear solutions. Empathy is a position few of us would oppose. But we also need to take matters deeper in terms of interrogating the causes of the oppressive conditions that make life miserable for multitudes and that propel displacement. Once those causes are understood, proposals can be more readily designed for structural changes to the systems that produce inequality in the first place. This is a basic recipe for a properly political film—political because it would challenge the systems of resource distribution, including the international trade agreements, inequitable access to technology, corporate monopolies, legacies and continuations of colonialism, and practices of institutional discrimination that maintain inequality. If climate change is, as Eyal Weizman argues, the telos of colonial modernity, rather than simply its accidental outcome, then what else would it mean to challenge its terms?[42] Such a film would have little to do with the vacant clichés of *Human Flow*, including its concluding proposal that "we must learn to live with each other," articulated by Dr. Kemal Kirişci, senior fellow of the liberal establishment Brookings Institution.

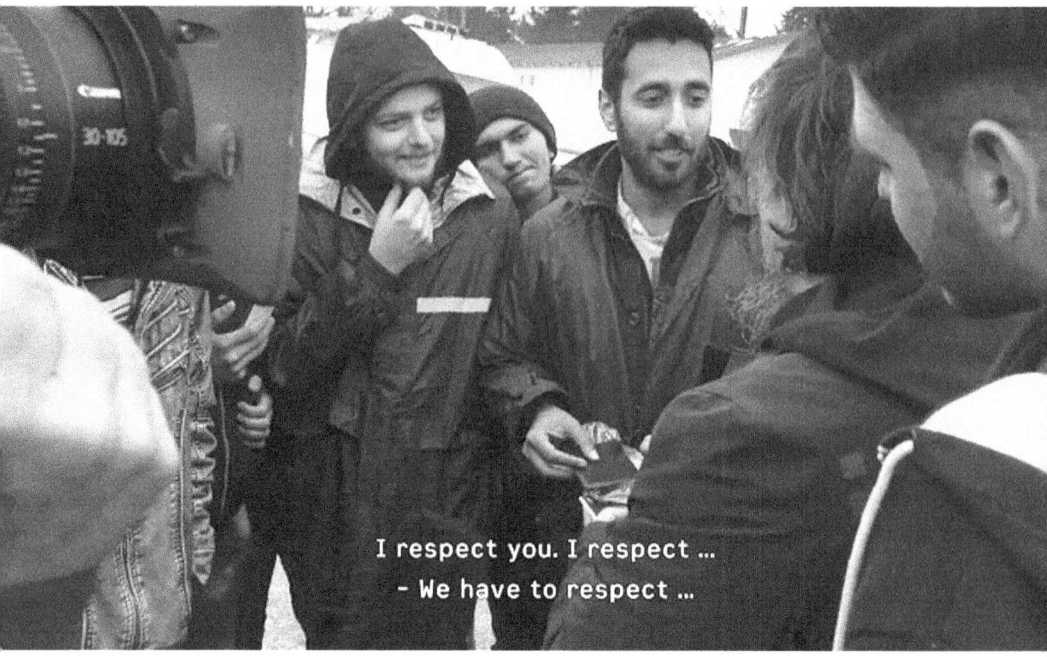

I respect you. I respect ...
- We have to respect ...

3.8 Ai Weiwei, *Human Flow*, 2017 (still).

In making such hollow suggestions, *Human Flow* in the end offers little to meaningfully challenge the material circumstances of inequality that are at migration's roots, circumstances that are only growing worse today. Indeed, climate breakdown, as *Human Flow* also points out, will only exacerbate drought, hunger, and ill health for millions in coming years. The next few decades of environmental transformation will likely provoke unprecedented migrations, pressuring all the world's borders, leading to even more extreme versions of insecurity, impoverishment, and suffering than those witnessed in 2015. For glimpses of that dystopian future, one need look no further than contemporary Mosul, Iraq's second largest city, as portrayed in *Human Flow*, where a half-million residents have recently fled ISIS's brutality, itself a complex manifestation of endemic poverty, authoritarian politics mixed with religious zeal, privatized militaries, and the West's disastrous Middle East policies. In one passage, Mosul's horizon appears as a conflagration of burning oil wells spewing purplish-black smoke into toxic skies. With this spectacle of disaster that holds life hostage to a living hell, one can begin to understand the warnings of Maha Yahya, director

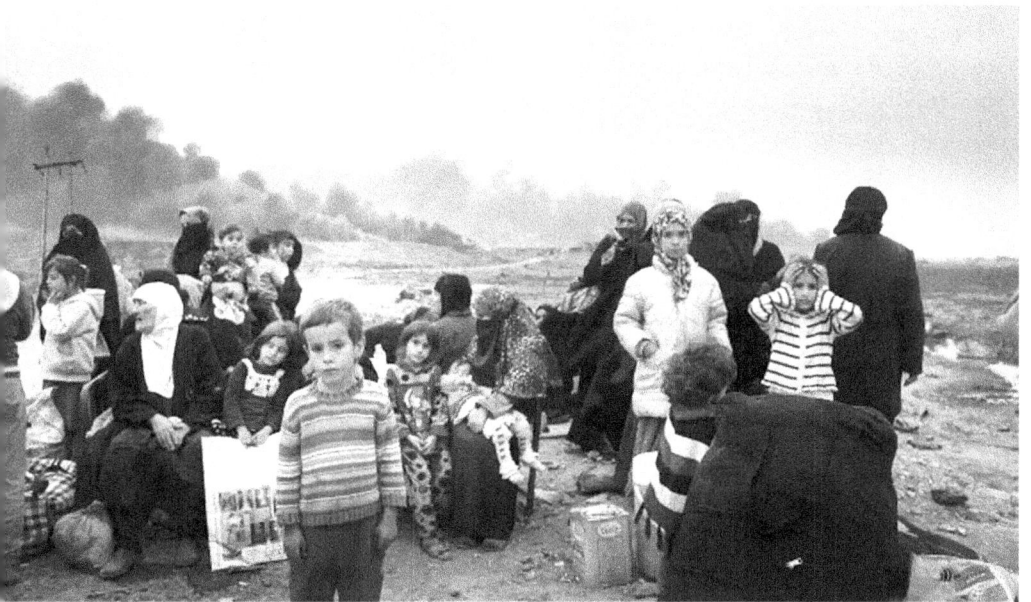

3.9 Ai Weiwei, *Human Flow*, 2017 (still showing Mosul, Iraq, October 2016, after Iraqi and Kurdish forces began a protracted battle to retake Mosul with American, British, and French support; ISIS fighters set fire to Mosul's oil fields as they retreated, with some 300,000 people displaced).

of the Carnegie Middle East Center, who observes how refugee children in Lebanon's expansive camps have no access to schools, grow up without optimism, and are thus vulnerable to exploitation and extremism. It is their future that is burning like the skies of Mosul, suggesting a living death beyond the end of the world. *Human Flow* appropriately quotes the late Palestinian poet Mahmoud Darwish in summing up the refugees' zombie-like outlook, with the poem's lines superimposed over a haunting full moon: "You killed me . . . and I forgot, like you, to die."

FROM EFFECTS TO CAUSES

In the preceding pages, we have encountered the Argos Collective's imagery of humanitarian fatalism, Stanmeyer's migrant photography, Haner's aesthetic of presentism, and Ai's cinema of liberal empathy—a veritable panoply of mainstream media and artistic visualizations of climate refugees. In the rest of this chapter, I consider three diverse approaches that challenge

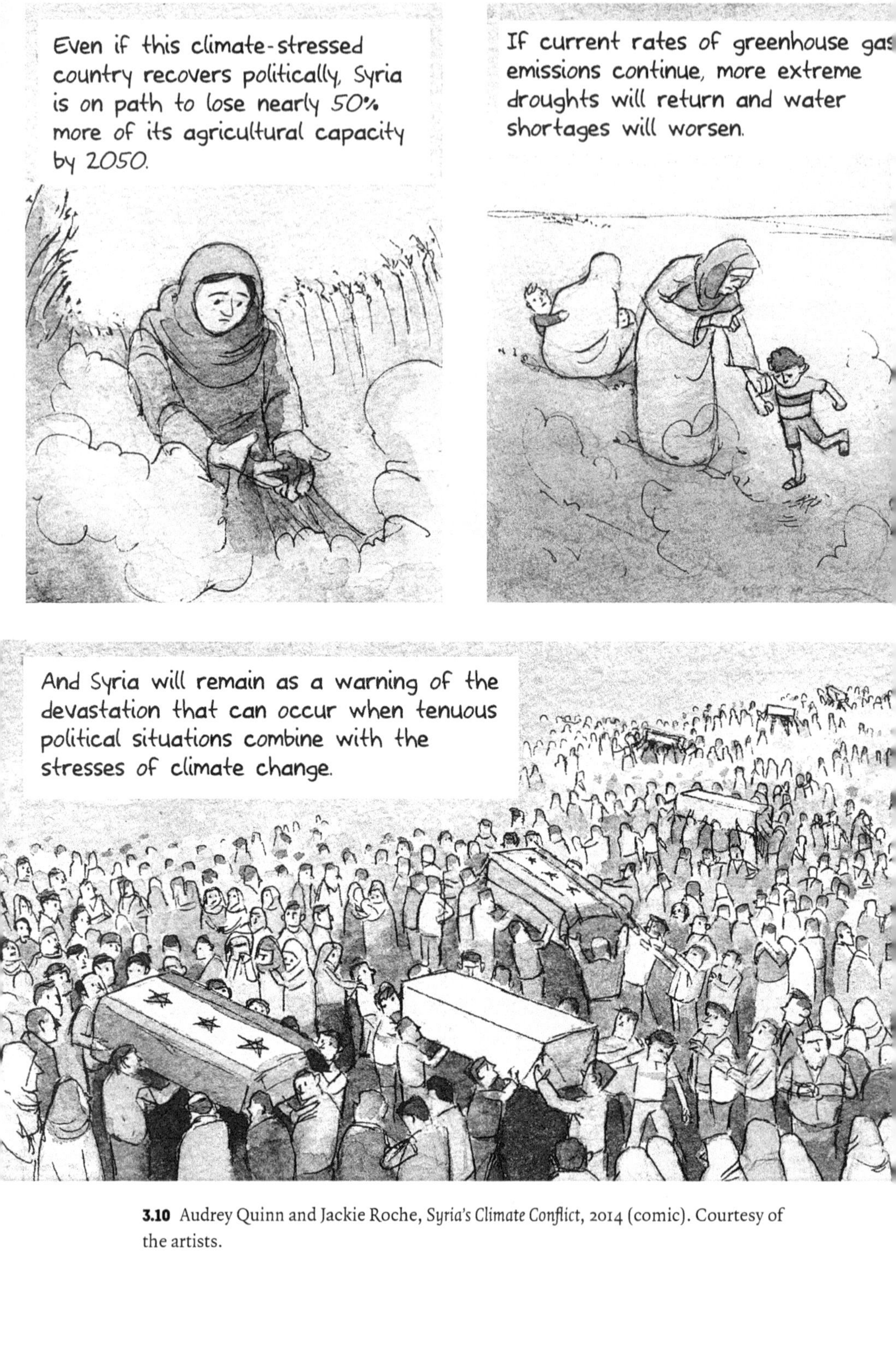

Even if this climate-stressed country recovers politically, Syria is on path to lose nearly 50% more of its agricultural capacity by 2050.

If current rates of greenhouse gas emissions continue, more extreme droughts will return and water shortages will worsen.

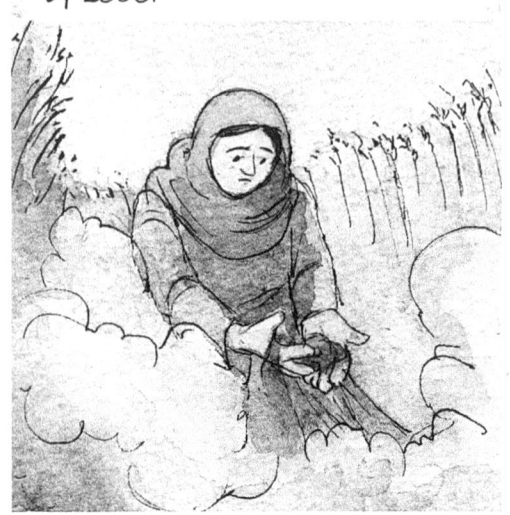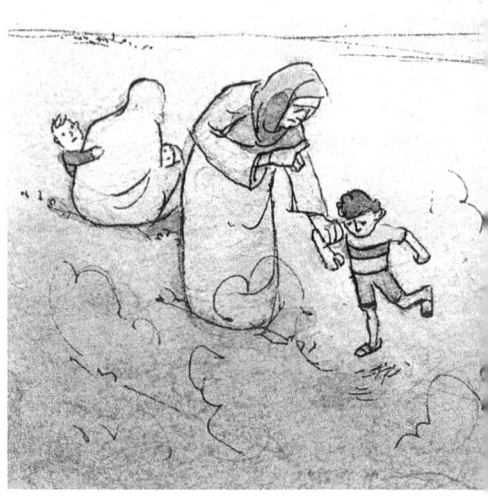

And Syria will remain as a warning of the devastation that can occur when tenuous political situations combine with the stresses of climate change.

3.10 Audrey Quinn and Jackie Roche, *Syria's Climate Conflict*, 2014 (comic). Courtesy of the artists.

the terms of photography's familiar spectacle of misery, voyeuristic imagery, and commercialized figures of decontextualization. By exploring the entanglements of socioecological genealogies of migration, these modelings also provide a compelling visual culture of causes. The first example is *Syria's Climate Conflict*, a nonfiction web-based comic from 2014 written by Audrey Quinn and illustrated by Jackie Roche. In this open-access work, the New York–based journalist and media artist narrate a story that tells how Syria was afflicted by a multiyear drought between 2006 and 2009, which wreaked agricultural disaster, driving urbanization and impoverishment. "Nearly a million rural villagers lost their farms to the drought. They crowded into overcrowded cities like Daraa. In the cities, the water problem became even more dire. There weren't enough jobs. Once prosperous farmers were lucky to find work as street sweepers," the text explains.[43] With their hand-made materiality still evident in the digital representation, the comic's constructed medium implicitly signals the absence or limited availability of critical visual analogues that are properly photographic and which might otherwise reveal the wider historical, geopolitical, and environmental intersections. As such, the piece speaks to the need to creatively develop and provide politico-ecological analysis of this and similar contexts in legible visual terms.

With Syrian cities deprived of their capacities for caring for the internally displaced, their inhabitants have been increasingly exposed to uncontrollable violence, eventually igniting civil war, despotic repression, international military intervention, and mass exodus—complex processes that are also depicted by Quinn and Roche in word and image. As recent research has shown, the intensity and duration of the recent Syrian drought have triggered enormous dislocation across the Mediterranean, forming a significant share of the origins of Syria's civil war.[44] While military rationality views climate change as a "threat multiplier," endangering present and future stability and reinforcing intensified security response, we have seen how images of climate refugees can easily aid and abet just this sort of reasoning. *Syria's Climate Conflict* offers the reverse, showing how the historical entanglement of "austerity and privatisation, of colonialism and militarism, and of the various systems of othering needed to sustain them all," in the words of Naomi Klein cited earlier, have produced migrant formations in the first place. Though seemingly simple visually, the comic's powerfully direct narrative offers surprisingly expansive historical depth, partly through the sequencing of images, a storyboard approach to organizing visual information that also offers affective and suspenseful narrative form. While a certain figuration organizes the storyline, the focus is rather on the historical and geopolitical framing of circumstances, moving from human flows to field causalities where anthropogenic weather too becomes an agent of the unfolding sociopolitical events. In this regard, the animated format of *Syria's Climate Conflict* proposes an experimental diagram for a relearning exercise in radicalizing historiography and visual approaches to the multiple intertwinements of socioecological displacement. Even if Quinn and Roche's project is short on some details, it nonetheless dramatizes a poignant intersectionalist account of climate migration in the choices for inclusion it does make.

My second example is Forensic Architecture's analysis of the Left-to-Die Boat, in which sixty-three migrants lost their lives on the Mediterranean in 2011 while trying to reach the Italian island of Lampedusa from Tripoli, Libya. The travelers, intent upon escaping the chaos of the civil-war-torn country, faced tragedy when the onboard motor broke down only a few hours into what should have been an eighteen-hour trip. They were consequently left adrift for fourteen days without receiving any assistance in one of the most intensely monitored seas on Earth, the NATO maritime surveillance area. Of the original seventy-two passengers, only nine survived, which became the focus of Forensic Oceanography, a component of the London-based research agency Forensic Architecture, which mobilizes interdisciplinary practice—spatial analysis, legal scholarship, art and filmmaking, software design, investigative journalism, and archaeology—in order to establish evidence that it presents in political and legal forums and human rights reports. This particular case focused on how the Mediterranean has lately been turned into a complex geopolitical zone of adjacent, overlapping fields of maritime ir/responsibility pertaining to NATO member states that are legally accountable to those in distress. However, that very geospatial complexity also enables criminally negligent state behavior—one type of field causality that leads to mass mortality. Producing a "selective militarized mobility regime," NATO members expose migrants to death at sea by nonassistance, even turning "the perpetual flow of currents into a deadly weapon" that allows boats to drift in and out of territorial zones, according to "Liquid Traces: The Left-to-Die Boat Case," a 2012 video of eighteen minutes put together by Charles Heller, Lorenzo Pezzani, and SITU Research.[45] This case still only taps the surface of catastrophe: indeed, since 2014, more than eighteen thousand migrants have died attempting to cross the Mediterranean, according to the Missing Migrants project (although the precise number of those who suffered nonassistance has not been established).[46]

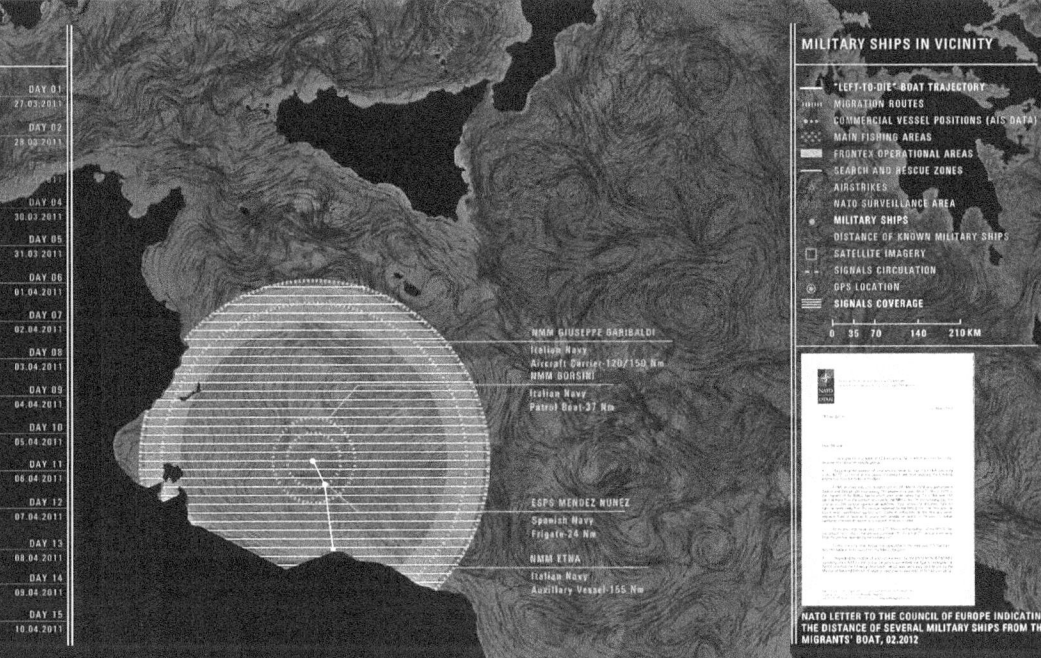

3.11 Forensic Oceanography (Charles Heller and Lorenzo Pezzani), "Liquid Traces: The Left-to-Die Boat Case," 2012 (still). Courtesy of the artist.

The video carefully reconstructs the route of the migrants in question and draws on available archival evidence (mainly videos and audio recordings) and satellite data to chart their vessel's progressive course, describe its circumstances, and investigate other ships they came across. While ultimately unable to determine responsibility for the disaster, but assembling a convincing accounting of systematic and widespread negligence, Forensic Oceanography's report has been used in a series of criminal legal cases filed in France, Italy, Belgium, and Spain, led by a coalition of NGOs attempting to hold NATO members accountable for the policies and practices that have contributed to thousands of deaths at sea. And while this specific case overlooks the root drivers of migration—the causes of displacement in the first place—the project does move beyond the human-interest stories and myopic focus on migrants' lives in much mainstream journalism, in favor of investigating the structural circumstances of the violence of dislocation.[47] In recent years, Forensic Oceanography has also explored subsequent developments around the intensification of Europe's—and specifically

Italy's—migration policies, as these latter have increasingly sought to delegitimize and criminalize NGO rescue operations and get North African countries to secure their own borders to prevent emigration.[48]

In addition to building intersectionalist diagrams, cartographic investigations, and field-causality analyses, artists and activists are also imagining futures absent of the criminalization of migration and that reinvent border zones as restored ecologies of open passage. Consider, in this vein, *Cross-Border Commons* (2018), a six-minute video and part of a larger urban research project of architect Teddy Cruz and political scientist Fonna Forman, who co-head the University of California, San Diego–based Cross-Border Initiative. The short video, largely schematic with mapping diagrams and pedagogical texts, shines light on the world's "political equator," more or less matching the Earth's geographical one, as a zone of conflict shaped by national borders, regions of economic inequality, and divided ecosystems— in other words, a diffractive spatialization of Parenti's "catastrophic convergence" of militarism, poverty, and climate change. Observing that the world's most contested borders—and showing those of US/Mexico, EU/Ceuta/Melilla, Israel/Palestine, Kashmir/India/Pakistan, and North Korea/South Korea—cluster along the same corridor of latitude, Cruz and Forman focus on the San Diego–Tijuana boundary in particular, which bisects a regional watershed and separates northern wealth, unsustainable sprawl, and a biodiverse estuary from southern wastelands, would-be-migrants, and dense informal settlements of impoverishment. As the largest binational metropolitan region in the world with more crossings than anywhere else, this border places nature and nation in direct conflict, one exacerbated by border regimes and military security, as diagrammed in the video by schematic aerial views of opposed sides of the wall. Remarkably, the two states share a watershed but have no collaborative ecological management, as we learn from Cruz and Forman's research. Instead, the area is ruled by unilateral and politicized spatial separation, intensified under Trump's harsh border policies, creating infrastructures of in/security between high-tech exclusion zones and recycled emergency shelters. The situation has also been increasingly worsened by the climate-transformed regions of Central America—running through Costa Rica, Nicaragua, El Salvador, Honduras, Guatemala, and Mexico—which have lost their agricultural capacities and sustainable economies owing to decades of US imperial policy. They are home to some ten million people, growing numbers of whom are joining the ranks of northward migrants.[49]

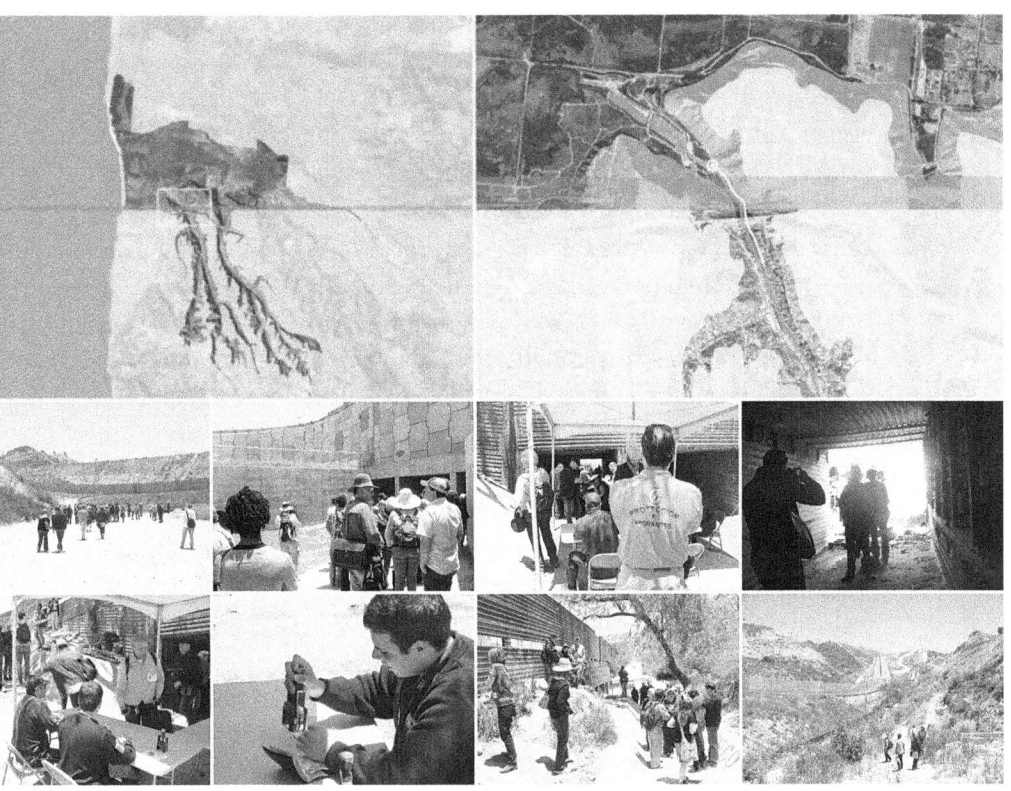

3.12 Teddy Cruz and Fonna Forman, "Cross-Border Commons," 2018 (still). Courtesy of the artists.

Instead of endorsing borders that produce migrants and proliferate artificial partitions in physical, psychosocial, and ecological ways, Cruz and Forman seek to "unwall" territories to germinate spaces of re-integrated, de-atomized forms of heterogeneous co-belonging.[50] With *Cross-Border Commons* they propose doing this in two ways. First, they experiment with rendering the border porous. With provisional permission from US Homeland Security (notably before Trump's election), Cruz and Forman worked in 2011 in collaboration with the NGO Alter Terra in transforming one of the normally secured border wall drains between San Diego and Tijuana into an official port of entry for twenty-four hours, with the video showing sped-up clips of people—prefigurative cross-border citizens—passing through the wall's aperture and getting their passports stamped, modeling a "social-ecological script for co-existence," according to the video's text.

As such, they suggest an alternate conception of human flow merged with temporary multispecies circulation, breaking down the wall instead of aestheticizing and dwelling on its devastating effects. At least temporarily, but also prefiguratively, the border became a "transnational commons," as the video explains: "a cross-border environmental 'conservancy' that connects the Mexican informal settlement with the American estuary, forming one continuous political, social, and ecological zone."

In their second act, Cruz and Forman created a "cross-border community station" on the Mexican side, one of several planned university-community knowledge- and resource-sharing bases providing infrastructure for youth empowerment and collaborative education across San Diego and Tijuana.[51] Showing images of happy kids gardening, the video explains that "children across the US-Mexico border are the cross-border citizens of the future." The aim is ultimately to cultivate new affordable housing within an innovative urbanism of support services and self-determinative collectivization, producing public space that integrates inclusive social, economic, and cultural practices for coming generations.[52] Moving away from a society that is antitax, anti-immigrant, prison obsessed, and ultimately antipublic, Cruz and Fonman's idea is to initiate "a bottom-up public" through architecture and design via everyday acts of resistance in marginalized communities everywhere.[53] In this regard, their modeling of architecture designates not so much the building of urban space but the designing of new socioecological political imaginaries supporting new modalities of transnational citizenship. Their aesthetic practice is crucial for its envisioning of commoning to initiate a debordered, denationalized world, one of transitional, translational multispecies ecologies (even while governments are generally moving in the opposite direction).[54] In other words, instead of getting states to recognize the legality of climate refugees, or representing empathy and respect, Cruz and Fonman conceptualize migrants as a force of postnationalization, inclusive equity, and ecocentric being. Generating a postanthropocentric sociopolitical composition, a community to come, their *Cross-Border Commons* supplants nationalist border zones that divide human and animal migrations alike, constituting new cross-border citizens—citizens not of states but of an increasingly urgent future of multispecies justice beyond the end/s of the current world.

Rather than endlessly fixating on the plight of the unfortunate through a photography of faces, those of us dedicated to structural transformation urgently need to redirect our energies toward critical investigation of the sources of climate migration. We also must imagine emancipated futures capable of inspiring communities of action in the present. The involuntarily displaced certainly deserve greater empathy and hospitality provided by institutions of transition and cosmopolitan hospitality, as well as legal protection and socioeconomic integration within a world of shifting climates and increased collective vulnerabilities. But the liberal reproduction of migrant categories, as we have seen, tends to isolate and fetishize subjective effects, conveniently releasing those who would choose not to care from both comprehending, and by extension implicating themselves within the deeper structures of political causality. Although progressive social movements offer an important way forward in demanding open borders, the global challenge of climate migration will remain unaddressed if countries in the Global North continue to help make lives elsewhere increasingly unlivable owing to environmental breakdown.[55] In the meantime, by transforming our approaches to migration from short-term crisis management to long-term and substantial system change—including not only decarbonization and habitat restoration but also greater equality and social justice for all—we can better advance the movement toward a world altogether different from the climate apartheid that awaits on the horizon of the present one.

GAMING THE
ENVIRONMENT

ON THE MEDIA ECOLOGY
OF PUBLIC STUDIO

One might think that media and ecology are diametrically opposed. It is true that traditional broadcast media such as radio and television, as well as new media—including algorithmic varieties, video games, the internet, and remote sensing and digital data—might seem distant from conventionally conceived environmental matters of concern, and of course all possess growing carbon footprints. Yet the exemplary media concepts of flow, convergence, and relationality spill over into both domains: environments are seen to materialize their own media of sorts, forming networks of biosemiotic meaning making that support multispecies life systems; and ecology increasingly represents a featured thematic engagement in technological approaches to the more-than-human world. Ecomedia is indeed a growing discourse, and understandings of the complex, if sometimes contradictory, correspondences between technology and environment, even in regard to video games, have reached advanced stages of theoretical depth and led to innovative practice.[1] One cannot generalize or make facile claims that, for instance, gamers are simply escapist and among the most prone to nature-deficit disorder, or that new media play—considering the sourcing of rare earths for computer technology, server farm reliance on fossil fuel energy, and the destructive disposal of e-waste—is exclusively environmentally damaging. For computer and console games may also advance, as some commentators argue, the positive values of botanical education, biocentric awareness, and perception-expanding creative learning, rendering gaming practice multifaceted at the very least.

Probing these complexities, the Toronto-based collective Public Studio, composed of filmmaker Elle Flanders and architect Tamira Sawatzky, have created a range of projects that investigate virtual, screen-based environments that build on this critical potential, and more, advance matters toward a politico-ecological basis of understanding. These include the exhibition *What We Lose in Metrics* (2016) and the video installation *Zero Hour* (2015), which I will focus on here. Both engage connections between media and ecology as a way to open a discussion on our precarious environmental situation, including drawing on and reconfiguring available technological resources that might aid in the construction of alternative futures beyond the dystopia of extractive capitalism. As gamers amount to nearly two billion of the world's population, the majority of whom live in urban areas— and those who interact daily with media environments doubtlessly number even more—such an intervention holds significant potential for making both environmentalism more accessible, socio-politically complex, and creatively engaging, and games an emerging site of climate activism.[2] Seizing that opportunity, Public Studio explores the hidden opportunities of gaming and screen-based ecologies to support a broad interlinking of environmental media and political aesthetics, imagining speculative futures of social and climate justice using technology often associated with fantasies of mindless killing and the visual spectacle of wars of all against all.

GEONTOPOLITICS OF GAMES

What We Lose in Metrics develops this investigation by collaborating with several players invited to explore a variety of recent commercial video games and consider their respective representations of forests. First shown in the Art Gallery of Toronto's York University, the carefully choreographed and architecturally designed exhibition comprises a multimedia and techno-organic environment, including videos and video projections, photography, and a collection of living tree saplings fed by a large text-flashing LED screen transformed into a giant grow lamp. Installed in a complex suite of

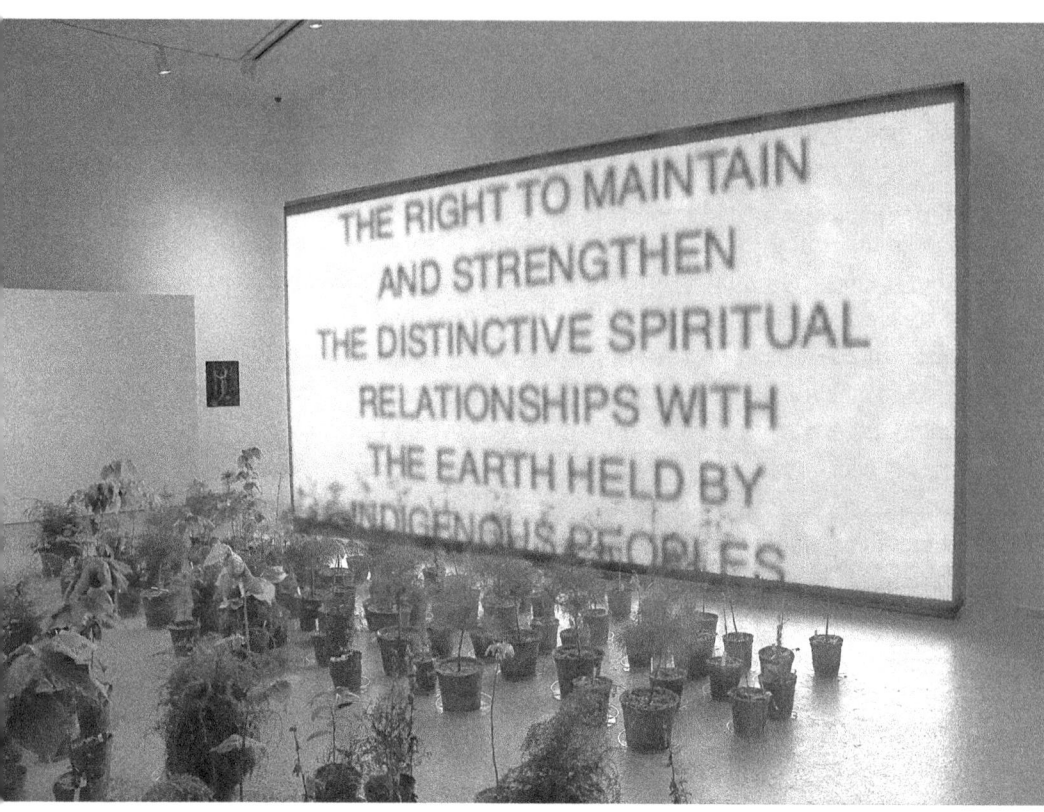

4.1 Public Studio, *What We Lose in Metrics*, 2016 (installation). Cheryl O'Brien. Courtesy of Art Gallery of York University (AGYU) and the artists.

rooms, it guides viewers in a predetermined direction through the layout, first passing through a long tunnel that spatializes the transition into the virtual realm. One then comes across a wood cabin interior that displays *The Darkness between Lives* (2016), a short video of appropriated clips from popular films, including *Bambi* (1942), *Apocalypse Now* (1979), *Rambo: First Blood* (1982), and *Avatar* (2009). The selected footage offers a representative pop-cultural panoply of cinematic dramas set in forest scenes, rendered by Public Studio in a silent and forensic black and white, supplemented by an electronic soundtrack designed by artist Anna Friz that provokes a sense of ambient disquiet and, at times, dread, lending aural affect appropriate to the diverse spectacles of ecocide and military violence shown in the films. Also included in the video is footage from Akira Kurosawa's 1950 classic *Rashomon*, which is key in its dramatizations of how truth depends on the teller, as four people recount differing versions of the story of a man's murder and the rape of his wife. By extension, considering this brief presentation of film history, the meaning of forest—whether enchanted place of magical discovery, threatening site of lurking evil, biodiverse lively ecosystem, set for social violence, or militarized source of industrial extraction—disconnects from any singular or definitive truth. While its etymology originates in the Latin word *foris*, meaning "outside," once implying the unknown realm of the fearful dark woods, especially within Euro-American mythology, here that zone of alterity seemingly opposite to human culture is discovered through the video screen.

In films like Francis Ford Coppola's *Apocalypse Now*, with its Vietnamese tropical jungles (actually shot in the Philippines), or Ted Kotcheff's *Rambo*, with its mixed conifer woodlands of the Pacific Northwest—both related to the US war in Vietnam and its traumatic aftermath—the forest generally figures as subordinated background to military activities, something to be fumigated and destroyed to clear the environment of guerillas and make way for troop advances, or alternately as weaponized against adversaries, with booby-trapped trees used as instruments against the enemy. But with more recent productions like James Cameron's *Avatar*, the assumed anthropocentrism of earlier films begins to be questioned: the forest glows in its biodiverse splendor, the spiritual locus of well-balanced multispecies living for the film's fictional Indigenous Na'vi, with whom viewers are invited to identify (particularly through the character of Jake Sully, a paraplegic former Marine who gradually switches sides via his avatar), taking up arms against the military assaults supporting the industrial extraction of valuable minerals by human colonists, which also includes the destruction of the natives' massive and ancient Hometree.[3] Aside from critiques of *Avatar*'s perpetuation of the white savior syndrome familiar in mainstream media's representations of colonial relations drawn with liberal Indigenous sympathies, the film gets at the defining opposition that Public Studio explores more deeply in *What We Lose in Metrics*: nature as a site of conflict between competing systems of value. Whether trees are reduced to natural resources, logged for timber, their worth calculated in currency according to financial metrics, on the one hand, or are appreciated intrinsically for their ecological, cultural, and spiritual values, on the other, is indeed a fundamental conflict of our time. It is more than biopolitical—the governance of life and lives, according to Foucauldian analyses, which tend to remain in the realm of the human—but rather concerns "geontological power," or "geontopower," which, according to Elizabeth Povinelli, corresponds to "a set of discourse, affects, and tactics used in late liberalism to maintain or shape the coming relationship of the distinction between Life and Nonlife."[4]

With the latter, the very nature of being, as well as the threshold between livingness and objecthood, or being (ontology) and nonlife (*geos*), is at stake, and specific understandings of which make a difference, determining potentially radically divergent forms of economic and political reason. In relation to one example, Povinelli draws focus to the far north of Australia, where a conflict has been brewing between the Aboriginal Areas Protection Authority and OM Manganese Ltd. over the deliberate damaging of an Indigenous sacred site known as Two Women Sitting Down located at Bootu Creek mine. At issue is how, and according to what criteria, the state would decide the fate of Earth elements such as rock and metal at the sacred/mine site—whether Two Women Sitting Down are two female dreamtime ancestors, as according to Aboriginal worldviews, or whether the Bootu Creek mine is composed of inanimate and therefore exploitable objects full of valuable manganese. The conflict is couched in the larger historical circumstances of settler colonialism and its long-standing unequal power relations, wherein the juridico-political system deciding the case is itself enmeshed within the very paradigm of oppressive geontopower that Aboriginal plaintiffs are attempting to contest.

Indeed, while "the new animism is extending Life into all entities and assemblages, Nonlife has remained fairly firmly sealed in its opposition to Life within extractive capital and its state allies," Povinelli observes, and thus the state-corporate complex had no problem consigning the Aboriginal worldview to a tolerated "cultural belief" that presented no reason to dig deeper into the sociopolitical and sacred ontology of matter.[5] Similarly, at the recent and ongoing Standing Rock oil pipeline conflict in North Dakota, as we have seen, nothing less remains at issue than whether the elements (water, trees, rivers) are fundamentally commodity objects, available for endless human exploitation supporting the capitalist economy, or rather represent life, are alive, and figure as part of an expanded community of beings that compose an interconnected world, make life possible, and demand reverence and care.[6] It is not that we live in multiple cultures sharing the same continuous nature, as a stable ground of homogeneous nonhuman reality; rather, cultures respond to completely different natures, and in fact to nature as a site of difference and differencing, populated by "perspectives" and activated points of view that extend well beyond the human, as Eduardo Viveiros de Castro describes Amerindian understandings in South America, which resonates with wider transnational Indigenous conceptions of the surrounding web of life.[7] In other words, multinaturalism's system of differences, its differing system, proposes so many antagonisms between governing onto-epistemological lifeworlds (as between colonial and Indigenous conceptions and situated forms of life), leading to properly geontological divisions—and worsening political conflicts. Indeed, Standing Rock, in addition to everything else it has represented (a struggle for native sovereignty, self-determination, and respect for historical treaties, and so on), was also an exercise in *"ontologies of decolonization,"* where land and water protectors asserted a view of water based on traditional Indigenous understandings of the elements. According to that perspective, water is not an object to be looked at or simply possessed and exploited as a commodity but a subject or being with an active gaze, constituting a "worldview" of its own, according to Melanie Yazzie and Cutcha Risling Baldy, whose characterization correlates somewhat with geontopolitics.[8] They specify further, stressing relationality, that somewhat "'worldview' is 'water view,' a view *from* the river not a view *of* the river," which defines "the condition of being-in-relation-to that water view instills in us."[9] In bringing up these geontopolitical rift zones, which have been spreading well beyond these two examples in Australia and the US, my point is to emphasize how nature has itself increasingly become an overdetermined and conflictual place of multinaturalism, that is at once anti/colonial, non/totalizing, and in/finite, which is not at all surprising in the extractive present. It is the goal of Public Studio to investigate these conflicts and expanding perspectives within the worldviews of mediated environments of popular computer games, seeking additional possibilities for cultivating critical awareness, transforming desire, and performing cultural intervention in ways that resonate with these ongoing anticolonial struggles and multinaturalist sensibilities.

What We Lose in Metrics probes these divisions and conflicts, initially by inviting experienced female players (a growing demographic of gamers) to interact with the five games presented in the exhibition—*Assassin's Creed III* (2012), *Dragon Age: Inquisition* (2014), *The Elder Scrolls V: Skyrim* (2011), *The Path* (2009), and *The Witcher 3: The Wild Hunt* (2015)—and in doing so, consider their virtual environments.[10] Performing "playthroughs" of popular releases (according to which players test a game's system and simultaneously record their experiences in videos with voice-over commentaries), the women transform the games into open systems of ecological exploration, the

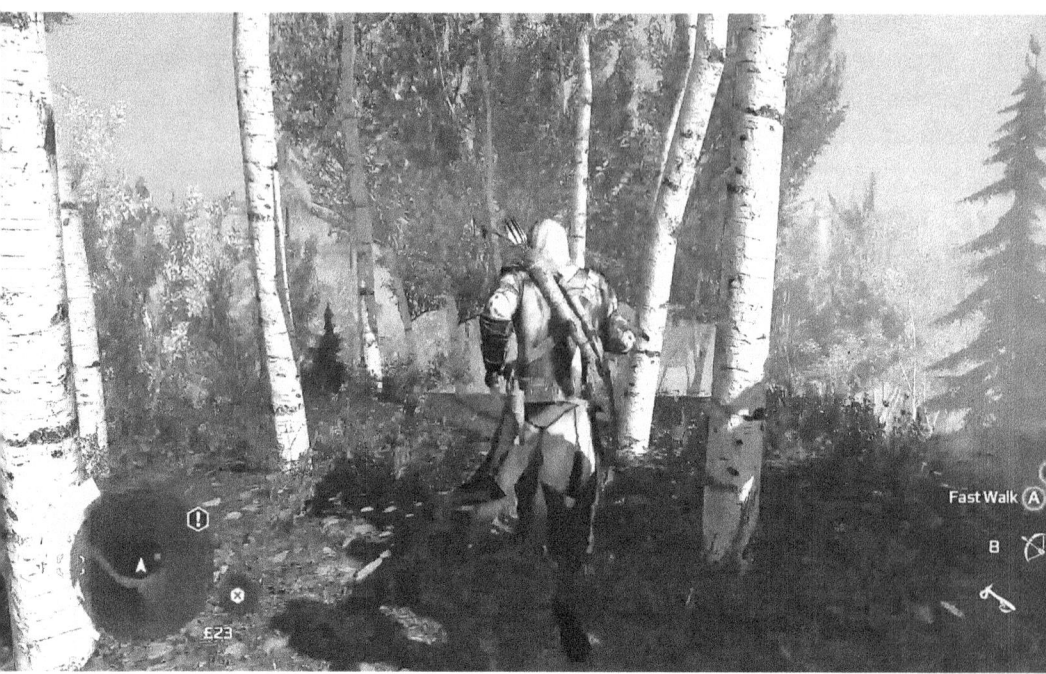

4.2 Public Studio, *What We Lose in Metrics*, 2016 (still from *Narrowing the Sky*). Courtesy of the artists.

practice of critical perception, and generating ecocentric ethics delinked from the game narrative's instrumentalized goals, including the frequent rampant sexism and violence of the entertainment's original design. Instead of considering games as the central portal for subjectivation within global capital's networked empire, according to which "virtual play trains flexible personalities for flexible jobs"—for instance, within the extractive economy or military sector, each founded on oftentimes competitive individualism and vicious domination—Public Studio intervenes to position play as an exercise in radical ecocentric sensibility, existential mutuality, and biodiverse perception.[11] During their sessions, they also recite verse by female poets, at Public Studio's invitation, linking the experimental poetics of environmental consciousness to the game's own specific aesthetic construction. For instance, in the video *Narrowing the Sky* (2016), Karolina Baran plays the action-adventure game *Assassin's Creed III*, set in the eighteenth century during the US Revolutionary War, and between her own observations of the platform's digital environmental representations, she reads occasionally from writer Louise Erdrich's "I Was Sleeping Where the Black Oaks Move" (2003).[12] The verse describes a destructive flood sweeping over a riverine landscape and its effects on local herons and the nearby forest habitat: "We watched from the house as the river grew, helpless and terrible in its unfamiliar body. Wrestling everything into it, the water wrapped around trees until their life-hold was broken. They went down, one by one, and the river dragged off their covering."

Meanwhile, Baran comments on the game's crisply rendered flora, comprising conifers and birch trees, grassy areas and wood pastures typical of New England. She critically observes how the game's design makes it difficult for players to run from predatory animals like bears or wolves, forcing them instead to engage and kill the beasts or die themselves (and begin the level anew). Still, and despite this goal-directed logic of destruction, Baran thoughtfully examines the game's presentation of an expansive audiovisual array that provides a virtual experience of sylvan nature—inviting players to listen to the wind and birdsong while exploring the landscape's wildflowers, trees, and waterways. In other words, she opens an audiovisual experience of the outdoors normally at the margins or background of the media platform, one otherwise likely overlooked by, for instance, the urban multitudes stuck in concrete environments playing the game more in keeping with its intended purpose.[13]

In *I Have Been Her Kind* (2016), another video component of *What We Lose in Metrics*, Nina Bakan plays *The Path* and reads "Her Kind" (1960) by poet Anne Sexton. While nongamers might assume that game platforms offer generic landscapes largely devoted to serving as backdrops for endless acts of virtual violence and endless conquest, recently designed systems are surprisingly attentive to realistic depiction, their portrayals even accurate in their regionally site-specific visualization of forests. *The Path* is one example. While noting its naturalistic details, Bakan nonetheless laments the unenlightened sexual politics of the game's scenario, which plays on stranger danger in order to allegorize the risks of the avatar's adventuresome adolescent femininity, even while her journey through the forest yields fascinating visual details about the sensuous flora. As in *Narrowing the Sky*, the playthrough produces a revealing appraisal of the game's gender politics, which figure as a destructive social ecology of sexism as much as ecocide. With quotes from Sexton's poem, the playthrough works to unlock female powers of the dispossessed and socially errant, proposing scenarios for peaceful survival with other species that counters the game's aggressivity.

> I have found the warm caves in the woods,
> filled them with skillets, carvings, shelves,
> closets, silks, innumerable goods;
> fixed the suppers for the worms and the elves:
> whining, rearranging the disaligned.
> A woman like that is misunderstood.
> I have been her kind.[14]

In the poem, kin(d)-based identification leads to solidarity in nonconformity, just as Public Studio takes video games that are commonly centered on navigating historical dramas of warfare and intrigue—generally perpetuating anti-environmental and socially violent tendencies—and redirects them toward enhancing critical and ecological sensitivities. In this regard, Public Studio is not alone. In fact, there are a growing number of progressive game designs being developed and released these days, ones that offer complex ecologies, affects, and decolonial experiences that promote non-anthropocentric values and creative life-enhancing interdependencies with more-than-human natures.[15] In this case, ecology is not simply a matter of the nonhuman outdoors but includes mediatic and sociocultural relationalities of immanence with that realm, overcoming binaries of nature-culture if in virtual terms, which is completely at odds with conventional game design. Most gaming environments, according to media theorist Alenda Chang, commonly divide into the two broad categories: "graphical spectacle" (providing sensuous landscapes as backgrounds to human conquest) and "terrains of resource extraction" (offering trees, mines, islands, and mountains as the object of competitive exploitation of natural resources).[16] By dehierarchizing figures and grounds, refusing the divisions between human/nature, Public Studio enacts an experiment in geontopolitical recalibration that is postanthropocentric and cultivates the sensibilities of more-than-human agencies and relational worldviews.

The mediated forest, in Public Studio's design, becomes a hybrid assemblage of human and humanlike characters (such as elves), and diverse flora and fauna—the forest as elemental media, an interconnected biophysical milieu, as well as a mediated environment of biosocial communication between assorted life forms, depending on the type of forest and in which game environment.[17] What these rejigged games of Public Studio aim at,

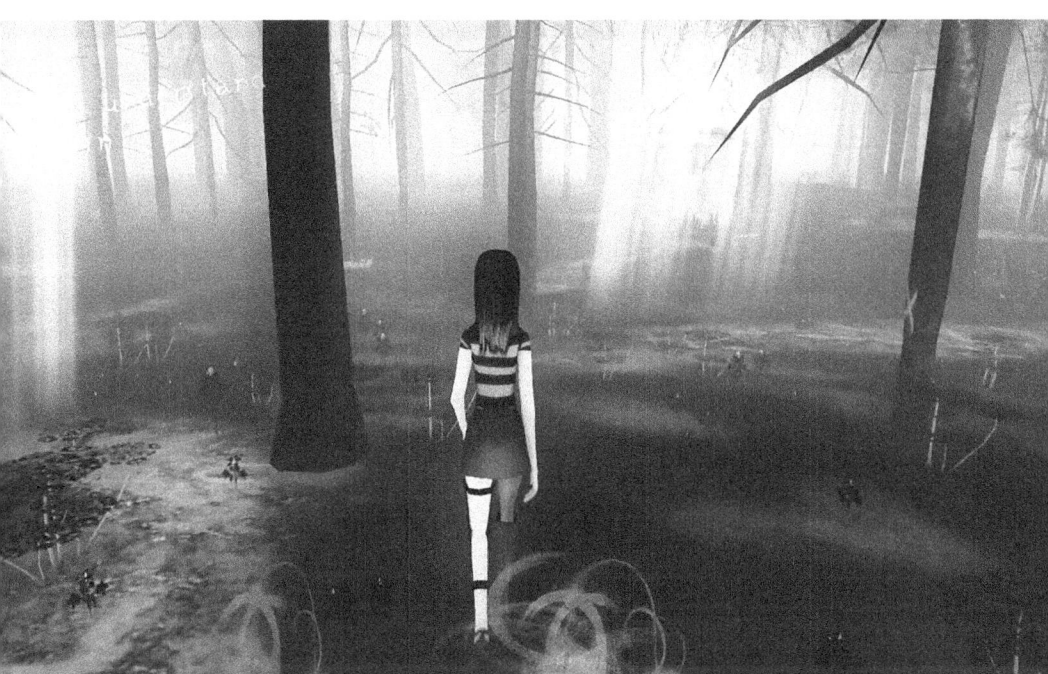

4.3 Public Studio, *What We Lose in Metrics*, 2016 (still from *I Have Been Her Kind*). Courtesy of the artists.

as we have seen, is the cultivation of heightened attentiveness to the environment's presence and complex media, including its relationality between diverse elements (biological, physical, semiological, ecological), in order to move away from a myopic human exceptionalism focused only on its own self, relegating all else to being either tools and objects of its own desire, or effectively nonexistent. This aim occurs in two ways. First, the playthroughs practice and perform sensitivity to the player's self (including its imagined and mediated avatar) and how it exists, changes, and transforms over time in ways that are context-dependent, synergistic with, and responsive to mediated natural surroundings. These experiments consequently open up conscious consideration of how the forest is not only a backdrop for, but also a determinative force of, subject formation. They provide containers for actions and transformations, revealing both pathways for exploration and an arena for self-conscious becoming in relation to the framing milieus of sensation and activity (this includes the recognition of limits too—for example, in *The Sea Is Another Story*, exploring the video game *Skyrim*, player

Kathryn Yani remarks on how her character cannot touch, feel, or smell the trees and flowers, and cannot move in spontaneous ways, noting the apparent sensory boundaries of the platform, even while she observes that animals are potentially rendered friendlier by the gamer's behavior). Second, the playthroughs produce an intensified awareness of the forest's existence, including its worldview and nonhuman agency through the artistic experiment's reduced focus on the character. This includes a fresh understanding about how the forest's elements might change as a result of the character's consequence-producing decisions and actions, as well as how the forest itself becomes a character of its own, or a multiplicity of characters. By suspending the player's concentration on the avatar and its instrumentalized behavior, the playthoughs generate newfound sensitivities to biodiverse subsistence and multispecies coexistence devoid of destruction and domination, where humans are no longer the sole possessors of agency and narrative drive.

Insofar as Public Studio effectively repopulates the game environment with complex beings and highlights nonteleological interrelations, the player comes to occupy shifting sites of ecological awareness, observation, and mindfulness, freed from the desire for total control and annihilating threats. With this newfound focus on nonantagonistic interactions with and between animals, plants, and images, by which player and platform coproduce multifaceted environmental assemblages and experimental narrative arcs, the game world transcends its otherwise limited role of exclusive playground and/or battlefield of and for humans. Rather, it becomes a virtual arena for the intricate intertwinement of diverse living and nonliving beings, approximating the biosemiotic environments and "thinking forests" shaped by more-than-human selves that Eduardo Kohn and Viveiros de Castro discuss in their respective postanthropocentric anthropologies.[18] Therein, the forest defines a theater of worldly interactions, perspectives, and lively representations. If, in Amerindian ontology, "the point of view creates the subject," as discussed above, and whatever is capable of having a point of view also possesses subjectivity, according to Viveiros de Castro's reading of Indigenous perspectivism, then digital media's techno-animism and its more-than-human avatars (animals, plants, mountains, even the planet itself) seem ideally positioned to creatively investigate the perceptual and experiential circumstances of multinaturalism, where nature defines a site of self-differing multiplicity and heterogeneity, irreducible to multicultural perceptual differences.[19] The acknowledgment of multiple ontologies means the world holds many worlds, the nature of trees being fundamentally different to that of humans, for instance (and of course different human communities can and do possess radically different natures as well, even where there may be continuities too). Closer to home, but not completely unrelated, the Public Studio project at times appears to take up the advice of Aldo Leopold, who, in *A Sand County Almanac*, famously encourages the reader to "think like a mountain"—that is, envision ecological processes as if one were a part of its interactions, sharing its point of view, its various becomings, and to consider the consequences of any interventions unfolding on its slopes.[20] These multinaturalist sensibilities, translating as well into a politico-ecological ethics, get at the very aim of Public Studio's elemental media: to endow the theater of worldly interactions with more intense vitality, agency, and complexity, ultimately so that life can be experienced and lived in ways that lead to greater awareness of the singularity, fragility, and interconnectivity of the human and more-than-human realm.

OPERATIVE IMAGES

In probing the landscapes of digitally animated games, Public Studio builds on the work of other critical media analysts, including the late Harun Farocki. In his four-part video installation *Parallel I–IV* (2012–14), Farocki shows how game animation has steadily evolved over the last few decades from two-dimensional schemas to photorealistic imagery, gradually taking over the veristic and objectivist ambitions once performed by photography and film. With reference to popular games such as *Grand Theft Auto* (1997), *Assassin's Creed* (2007), and *Minecraft* (2011), the *Parallel* series examines the shifting renderings of nature, the virtual infrastructure and border zones of game space, and the conventional range of avatar gestures. The work finds that increasingly complex and generative algorithms detach imagery from biomimetic appearance in forming a historically unprecedented idealist typology of naturalist visuality. With his earlier four-part video installation, *Serious Games I–V* (2009–10), Farocki additionally demonstrates how such gaming animation has entered US military applications, both training soldiers in virtual spaces of conflict in advance of real combat—wherein desert landscape designs mimic the environments of Iraq and Afghanistan—and treating them therapeutically in post-traumatic stress disorder simulations once they have returned from battle.[21] In this case, animation does not simply represent the termination of the image, as if merely referencing a preceding reality. It also founds a new visual regime inaugurated by

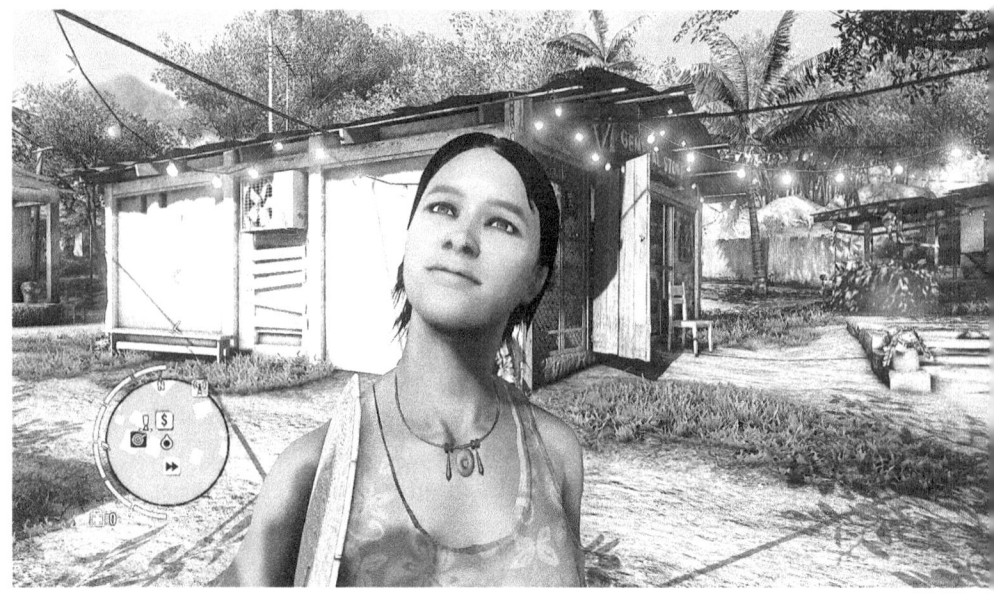

4.4 Harun Farocki, *Parallel I–IV*, 2012 (still). Source: Harun Farocki GbR.

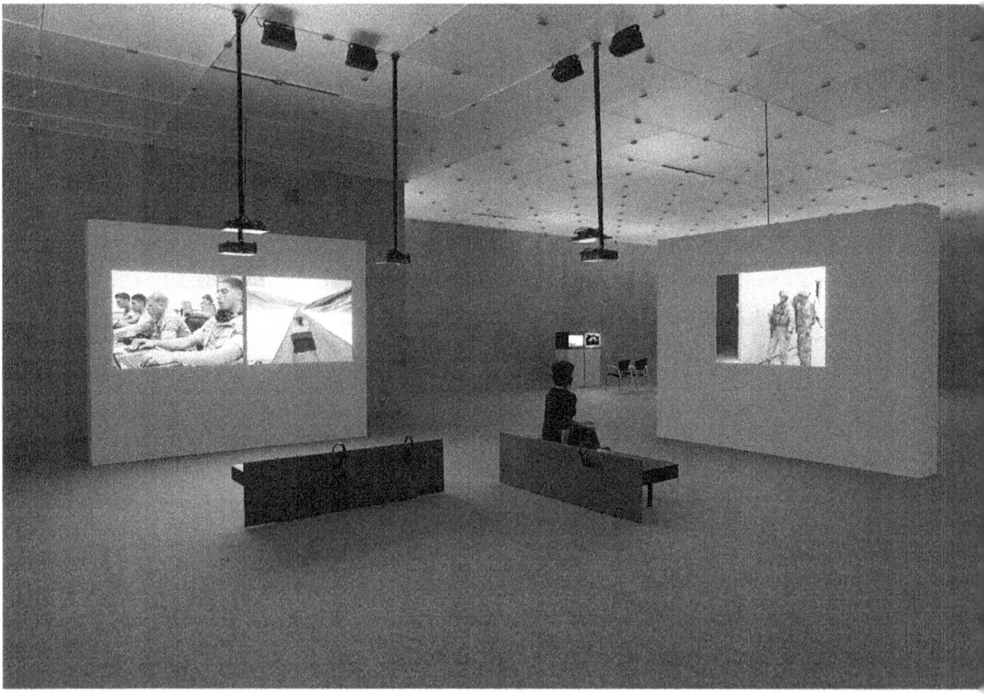

4.5 Harun Farocki, *Serious Games I–V*, 2009–2010. Installed at Kunsthaus Bregenz, Austria, "Weiche Montage / Soft Montage," October 23, 2010–January 9, 2011. Photograph by Harun Farocki. Source: Galerie Thaddaeus Ropac, London • Paris • Salzburg.

seeing-machines and smart bombs, introducing what Farocki termed an "operational image"—one that actively intervenes in the world after its production, becomes and creates (or destroys) new realities in its own right, even as it implies cybernetic processes increasingly invisible to the human eye (whether in military, consumer, political, or social media applications).[22]

Taking up related concerns as Farocki's, *What We Lose in Metrics* reveals how conventional video games produce operational images in two further ways, reinforcing extractivist reason as well as opening on to ecological consciousness in its expansive definition. First, they assist subjects in the naturalization and internalization of extractive relations to the natural world that, in destroying natural environments and deranging the climate, place life as we know it at risk; and second, they define a modeling of everyday life where militarized violence, existential threat, and power inequality according to sex and gender represent normative conditions, which might then, in turn, actually influence, reinforce, and transform behaviors in reality. Games provide ways to rehearse and practice reactions, feelings, and states that extend nuance, texture, and expectation into everyday life, as recent research is finding.[23] As such, they bear the potential to modulate present and future behaviors, even if not totally determining or rendering will automatic. At the same time, Public Studio intervenes in this logic by reprogramming operational images, transforming the supplemental aesthetic backdrops and instrumentalized sacrifice zones that appear in commercial video games into ecomimetic arenas of philosophical speculation, which, as discussed above, generate entirely different sensibilities. With the artists' work, viewers are offered socio-affective experiences promoting awareness of ecological functions, possibilities for exploring interrelations between humans and nonhumans, and opportunities for becoming self-aware of one's emotional connections to natural environments. According to their scenarios, virtual forests become, with the help of their players, more than generic frameworks or supplemental narrative architecture: they assume intrinsic value above and beyond the human dramas set within their midst that are otherwise focused on killing adversaries, racking up points, and advancing game levels, as well as reproducing heteronormative and petrocapitalist subjectivities based on those objectives.[24] Contributing to an ecofeminist critique of dominant games—and in this sense both extending Farocki's analyses and advancing the identity politics–centered game assessments of noted feminist media critics like Anita Sarkeesian who are shedding light on and working against misogyny in the media industry—*What We Lose in Metrics* stages a geontological state shift in an act of environmentalist transformation of popular media ecologies.[25]

A further gallery in Public Studio's exhibition offers the culmination of the installation's gradual movement from violent games that instrumentalize forests, including the selection of critical playthroughs discussed above, to a mixed-media presentation of biocentric transformation. *Everything Is One* (2016) comprises a range of potted tree saplings—including basswood, white pine, shag bark hickory, tamarack, burr oak, pawpaw, red pine, and honey locust—chosen in collaboration with the influential botanist Diana Beresford-Kroeger. Her writing in general explores the multivalent meanings of trees, pointing out the ecological, mythical, horticultural, spiritual, and medicinal value of forests.[26] In her book *The Global Forest: Forty Ways Trees Can Save Us*, Beresford-Kroeger addresses trees' significance as a global air-filtration system and explains how their decimation leads to the extinction of countless species, threatening by extension our own, as forests hold the potential to sequester carbon, mitigate global warming, and produce oxygen. Contesting outmoded oppositions between nature and culture, the installation dramatizes how trees and woodlands might be not simply threatened and destroyed by unsustainable media ecologies but also nurtured and protected by its gaming ethos wherein technology and ecology form relations of what Lynn Margulis and Donna Haraway call symbiogenesis.[27] This is literally the case in the installation, as the ten-by-twenty-inch LED screen turns into a massive grow lamp in the gallery for young trees that appear and evolve in the act, following their extensive video-based virtual introduction in the earlier part of the exhibition. Here media ecology modestly supports the massive reforestation project called for by Beresford-Kroeger as one way to mitigate the destructiveness of climate breakdown (its symbolic performance mitigating the fact that it draws on fossil fuel energy that contributes to destructive environmental transformation at the same time).

On the screen in front of the trees scrolls "The Earth's Covenant," a text proclaiming the rights of nature, presented in attention-grabbing all caps, written for the exhibition by Haida lawyer Terri-Lynn Williams-Davidson. Resonating with recent international calls for a legal paradigm shift toward a biocentric juridico-political system necessary to rescue ourselves and the Earth's other inhabitants from environmental catastrophe, and situated in the context of First Nations' decolonial claims for autonomy and Indigenous rights, the document evinces fundamental ecological principles: "that we [and nonhuman nature] are all one, that everything depends upon everything else, that we are all interconnected and interdependent and our fates are inextricably interlinked."[28] In positioning this declaration of unified rights and responsibilities before the assembly of trees, the piece stages the pronouncement of a new natural contract between human and nonhuman natures, outlining the necessary multispecies social composition and geontological legal arrangement to carry us beyond the anthropocen(tr)ic present. If this juridico-political revolution gains ground, formalizing in law the proposition that trees, rivers, and ecosystems have independent rights to exist and flourish—rather than being relegated to the category of human property and sources of wealth extraction—then coordinated mitigation efforts of carbon pollution could ensue within this new legal framework.[29] Industrial practices that contributed to ecocide could be legally regulated, with infractions prosecutable in courts of law, inaugurating a new age of Earth justice. According to Pablo Solón Romero, former ambassador to the United Nations of the Plurinational State of Bolivia, where the rights of Mother Earth were enshrined in the country's 2009 constitution: "If you want to have rights of nature, you have to fight against capitalism." He goes on to state: "To speak about Mother Earth's rights challenges the entire legal system on which this capitalist system is based. This is why we insist on talking about rights. Someone who kills someone else goes to jail, but if you pollute a river, nothing happens to you. We have to be accountable. The key issue is to make us accountable in relation to our Earth system."[30] While it may be true that (as David Harvey responded to Solón's provocation at a 2011 conference on the rights of nature at the City University of New York) it will take a mass social movement to ultimately bring about the necessary large-scale political transformation to achieve such ends—just as Indigenous activism drove Bolivia's own legal revolution—projects like Public Studio's contribute speculative insights to that movement, and their aesthetic platform provide spaces where the key elements of that ecocentric transition can be glimpsed, experienced, and sensed.

ZERO HOUR

Public Studio's *Zero Hour* gives further reasons why such rights are crucial at the present moment. Drawing together ecology and environmental poetics, the piece offers a digitally rendered video of destructive weather patterns projected onto a translucent dome ceiling. As a kind of collectively experienced alternative ecomedia presentation, it's as if the peripheral

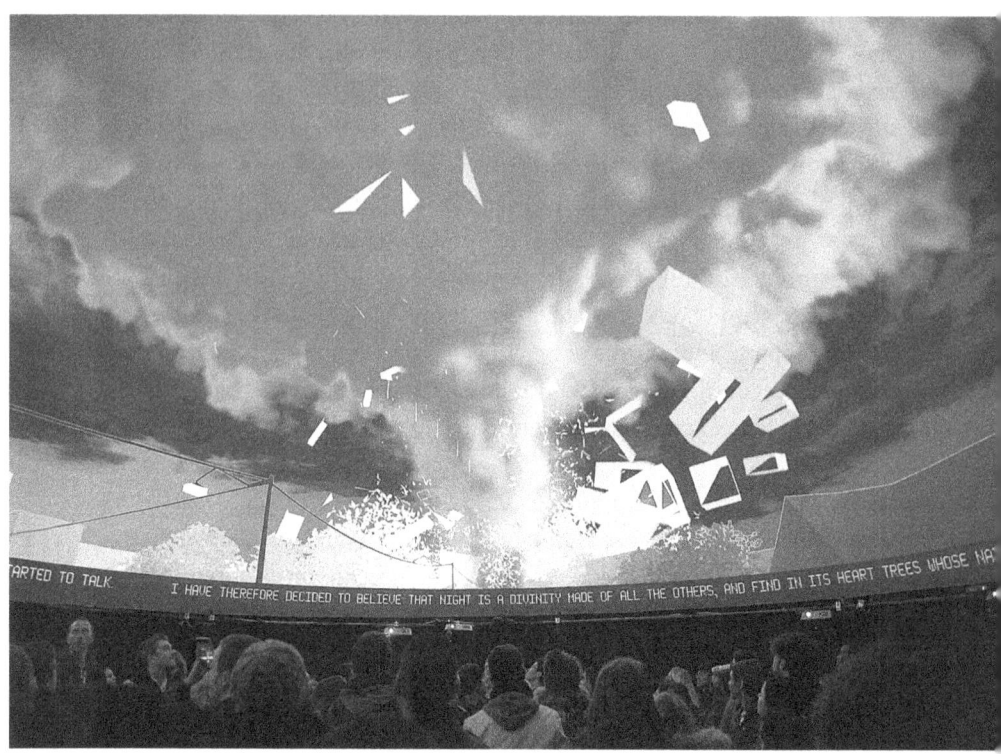

4.6 Public Studio, *Zero Hour*, 2015 (installation). Photograph by Dan Galbraith. Source: City of Toronto Nuit Blanche. Courtesy of the artists.

environment had been isolated from a game, here one of Public Studio's own, and projected into real space. Playing over twelve hours in looped succession, the ten-minute video commences with the depiction of a clear, star-filled night sky before transitioning to a gray cloudscape of atmospheric circulation, appearing later as if in a watery reflection, upon which rain-drops fall and dark debris floats. Soon, bordering buildings and trees frame a skyward view; the sun blackens as if in full eclipse, as flames erupt, birds fly overhead, and clouds agitate; until a tornado finally arrives and sweeps away the fragmenting, scattering infrastructure.[31] The scenario, created with game-design software, approximates the type of extreme weather event that is becoming disastrously common in the climate-changed Global South, suggesting what it might be like for such a calamity to befall Canada, a leader in fossil fuel extraction (the work was first shown in Toronto), even though recent real-life environmental catastrophes in the North tend to be warming and melting events, droughts, and terrible wildfires. Meanwhile, a text runs around the base of the visual projection like a ticker that announces natural-disaster statistics and relays, line by line, "Night," a poem by famed Lebanese artist and poet Etel Adnan commissioned specifically for this work.

The poem speaks of a nocturnal world centered upon trees existing beyond human exceptionalism, which provides a glimpse of one potential future beyond the end of the world, as depicted in the video. As Adnan's multinaturalist verse reads: "It's all because life, these days, has started to talk. I have therefore decided to believe that night is a divinity made of all the others, and find in its heart trees whose nature is a new reality." If "Night is the overflow of Being," as the poet intones at one point when her recorded recital of the poem fills the exhibition space, then it is because it exceeds us humans, has its own languages, defines new realities, and also represents a world without us. Adnan rejects any religious redemption or metaphysical human specialness that might save us from our displacement from centrality that multispecies social composition brings: "Rivers will run for as long as they have already done; it's wrong to think that we're loved." Considering the poem in relation to the apocalypse schematized in the video projection, the words imply associations with catastrophic climate breakdown that bodes gravely for human civilization, introducing the specter of what the late multispecies ethnographer Deborah Bird Rose calls "double death."[32] Double death defines a disastrous way of non/being—whether biological or governmental, agricultural or technological—that facilitates both mortality and the end of the possibilities of reproducibility. It is when a bird dies that is the last of its species, within an ecosystem that is itself no longer capable of supporting life; in other words, where death and extinction converge (as with the video of the male Kauai O'o, the last of its line, who sings to a mate who will never come, recorded by the Cornell Lab of Ornithology and presented in the 2015 film *Racing Extinction*). Adnan senses it as well, except in her verse the double death applies to humans, where *posthumanism* (forms of life beyond the human, including genetic and technological transformations of human life) may come too late to stop a *posthuman* era (one transcending human existence and its environmental possibilities altogether). At the same time, the poem's morbidity, and by extension that of Public Studio's *Zero Hour*, finds itself checked by the last line's affirmation of life beyond human existence: "There's a sweetness in the air that calls for death's coming. I try to deny the latter's presence because the birds, my brothers, have asked me to."

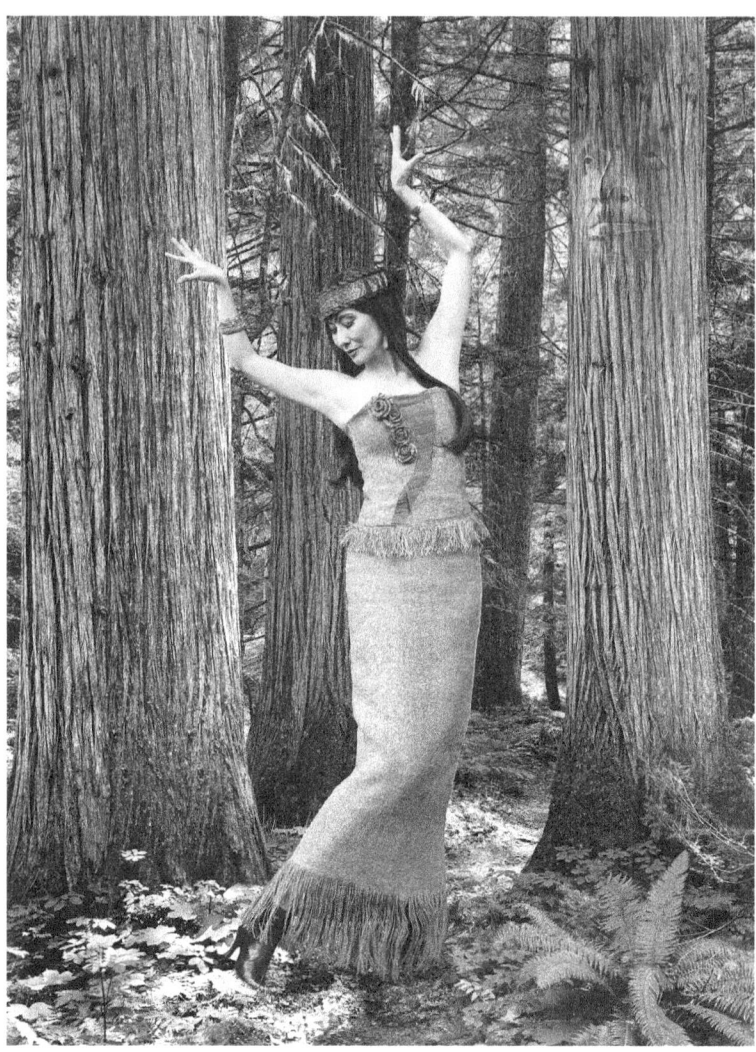

4.7 Terri-Lynn Williams-Davidson, *Cedar Sister, Ts'uu K'waayga*, 2016 (photograph).
Courtesy of the artist.

That more-than-human becoming is affirmed in the exhibition as a
whole, which includes in its final gallery *Cedar Sister*, a 2016 photograph
from the *Supernatural Beings* series by Terri-Lynn Williams-Davidson, the
First Nations lawyer and artist who wrote the rights of nature manifesto discussed earlier. According to Haida culture, the cedar tree is known as "every
woman's sister" and is understood as sustaining existence by supporting

biodiverse life, its roots extending into and nourishing salmon-filled streams, just as its bark and wood provide valuable medicines, housing material, and traditional tools that aid and protect human communities. Finding solidarity with trees is to "acknowledge the inter-relationship between the forests with the rest of the land and the surrounding marine environment," as Williams-Davidson observes in her explanation of the piece, drawing on ancient wisdom as a valuable inheritance for critical survival in a climate-stressed future.[33] It is an exemplary case of "making kin" across species lines "in order to cut the bonds of the Anthropocene and Capitalocene," as advocated by Donna Haraway and resonating with a belief long practiced within diverse Indigenous cultures who have been struggling for survival within the world-ending ecologies of colonialism long before those geological epoch names were proposed.[34] In the image of Williams-Davidson elegantly posed in modern-traditional hybrid dress, she stands amid a grove of cedar tree sisters with her arms raised and fingers outstretched, as if she herself is (becoming) a tree. With it, we glimpse one possible transition, although not at all guaranteed, toward multispecies flourishing in response to the ongoing contest—and ultimately more-than-a-game challenge—of world survival.

ANIMAL COSMOPOLITICS

THE ART OF GUSTAFSSON&HAAPOJA

In "State versus Perho Hunters," fifteen people from central-west Finland were recently put on trial for killing wolves. During the testimony and cross-examination of the defendants, the court heard extensive debate about whether the loss of life was justified, as the hunters claimed they were merely protecting the community's children and livestock from predators, maintaining public safety. Ultimately, however, the jury favored the prosecution's argument, taking into account the rights of the wolves to live out their natural lives and be spared unnecessary harm. The verdict found that the hunters violated those rights, leading to a choice between three possible sentences, depending on the perceived gravity of the crime: (1) life imprisonment for three "murders," if the destruction of life was deemed premeditated, cruel, or dangerous; (2) incarceration for at least eight years for the unnecessary "slaughter" of three wolves; or (3) imprisonment for four to ten years for the three "killings" committed under mitigating circumstances. Following deliberations, the jury chose the second option—a forgiving outcome, given the first alternative—one meant both to punish

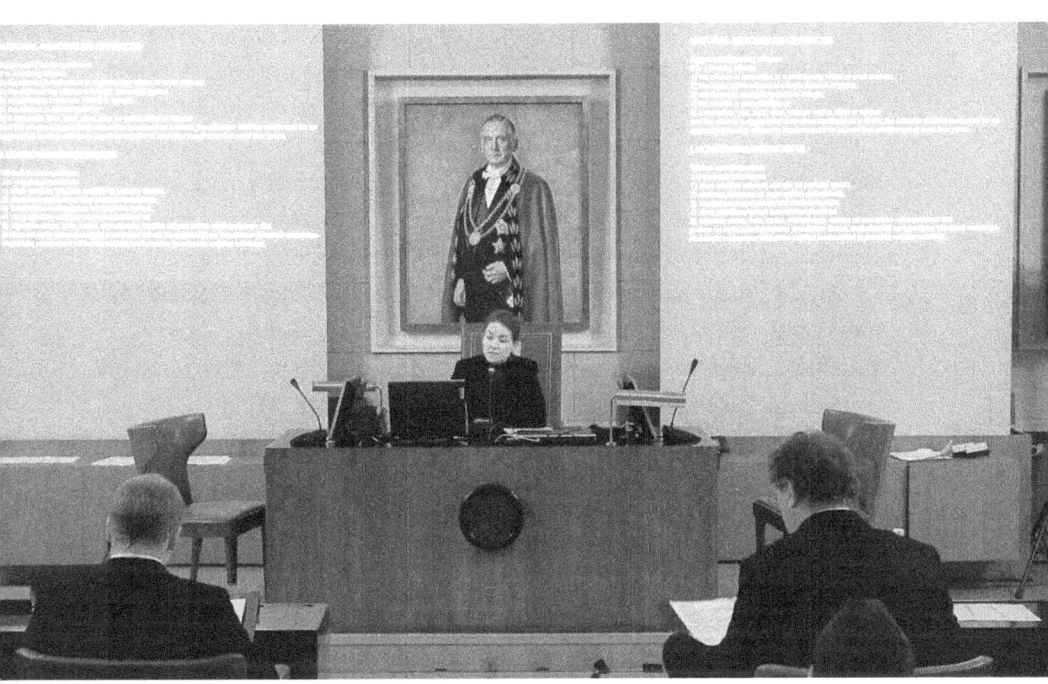

5.1 Gustafsson&Haapoja, *The Trial*, 2014 (performance). Courtesy of the artists.

the perpetrators for an irresponsible act and to deter future transgressions in a world ideally free of human exceptionalism.[1]

Of course this was not a real lawsuit but a theatrical enactment, as much as a speculative experiment, comprising a ninety-minute courtroom performance designed by writer Laura Gustafsson and artist Terike Haapoja in order to address the question of the legal rights of nonhumans, commissioned by the Baltic Circle Festival and first staged at Helsinki University in November 2014. Although fictional, *The Trial* was modeled upon an actual case that occurred a few years earlier in Kokkola in the Perho municipality, where thirty people took part in a wolf hunt that resulted in three kills, one of them a radio-collared alpha female. Haapoja reports that the poachers burned the carcasses to destroy the evidence, claiming the wolves were actually wolf-dog hybrids and thus unprotected by Finnish law.[2] Utilizing press material, legal documents, and research interviews, the artists' *Trial* began by acting out the case as it would have occurred under current law. But then they changed the rules midstream and introduced a new legislative framework based on recent scientific research and social justice principles that would protect the rights of nonhuman animals. As a result, the court reached a completely different verdict than the one initially expected (as it did each of the five times it was performed). As such, The Trial dramatized and demonstrated how law is ultimately mutable, with alternate versions creating very different conditions of life and what it means to live and die together, underlying and reaffirming in turn entire systems of values.

Legal transformation holds the potential to bring radically other worlds into being, which is ultimately the ambition of Gustafsson&Haapoja's collaboration, a research and artistic practice dedicated in part to conceiving and building experimental institutions devoted to those excluded from political visibility, including the more-than-human.[3] Providing a brief glimpse of future multispecies justice largely nonexistent in the present, their project offers a laboratory for thought experiments in imagining a biocentric future, thereby making it all the more possible to begin to bring it into realization in the present (and in this way it is complementary to the media ecologies of Public Studio considered in the previous chapter). In this regard, Gustafsson&Haapoja's project proposes something diametrically opposed to today's dominant forms of jurisprudence that privilege human economic interests and property claims, the legal infrastructure that supports corporate globalization, military neoliberalism, and the financialization of nature, including that of nonhuman animals. Their work reveals an entirely different world of justice and equality.

In granting animals legal standing, The Trial questions as well why nonhumans have no representation or intrinsic value in real courts. While the human consumption of meat and the industrialization of animal products remain contentious, creating divisions, for instance, between radical vegans and antiracists who might otherwise share opposition to the institutional and political operations of othering—what Haapoja defines as a historical and shifting divide between "legal subjects" with rights and "legal objects" without, or what Giorgio Agamben has identified as the construction of zones of inclusive exclusion that deny political being to some, making their lives killable—The Trial opens a creative space for the debate and critical consideration of the very logics and laws that would justify these circumstances.[4] Through its own juridico-political act of including the excluded within the category of rights-bearing subjects, The Trial's process and conceptualization also consider analogies within human history when oppression was practiced and abetted by representational erasure, which might very well be explicitly addressed in the piece's process of deliberation. When the state denies legal standing and a voice to certain groups of people—whether owing to gender, race, sexual preference, religion, or nationality—as well as to nonhuman animals, the implication is that those who fall into that category "can be legally owned, exchanged, and, if so desired, destroyed," justifying the cruelties of slavery, colonialism, and genocide.[5] By inviting the performance's audience to adopt the role of jury and to consider just these stakes, The Trial internalizes in its very participatory form open-ended debate of matters seldom addressed in, even structurally excluded from, conventional juridical contexts. According to the project's correlation of aesthetic form and political content, such discussion is enabled by the artists' reconstructed legal framework.

In The Trial's parallel universe, animals are not relegated to the status of natural resources available for limitless human exploitation, whether as food and materials for human consumption or as props in landscapes or zoos to be enjoyed aesthetically—all examples of anthropocentric practices common in our current world. That is, even if nonhuman animals are protected from unnecessary cruelty by liberal institutions in many regions, they are still generally available to industrial slaughter (save a number of protected species), a complex bind Gustafsson&Haapoja point out in their notes for The Trial.[6] By proposing to grant animals legal rights expressive of the intrinsic value of life in general, a principle opposed to current laws that subject nonhumans to human property claims, The Trial participates in the contemporary global movement working to establish the rights of nature, based within an innovative legal system expressive of Earth jurisprudence, or "wild law," as it is sometimes called, which is determinedly postanthropocentric. Indeed, in their notes the artists cite "Should Trees Have Standing? Toward Legal Rights for Natural Objects," the seminal essay written by Christopher D. Stone in 1972 about an actual court case laying out the groundwork for such a legal revolution, which has inspired much rights-of-nature legal activism ever since, including the work of NGOs and institutions like the Global Alliance for the Rights of Nature and the Nonhuman Rights Project.[7] The latter has fought to recognize the rights of their clients Tommy and Kiko, chimpanzees kept in squalid cages in New York by their human "owner" and "trainer," a case also cited as a precedent by Gustafsson&Haapoja for their own legal proceeding (although so far the attempt to persuade the court to bestow "legal personhood" on the chimps, a legal status entities such as corporations commonly enjoy, has been unsuccessful).[8] Such cases have also paralleled the Indigenous-led legal transformations in Ecuador and Bolivia where the rights of Mother Earth, or Pachamama, have been enshrined in their states' constitutions within the last ten years, initiating a movement that is now global in scope. Indeed, a number of recent international cases have successfully challenged existing law in asserting the rights of nature, including those of the Whanguanui River in New Zealand, recognized as a legal identity in 2012, and the Ganges and Yamuna rivers in India, both granted rights in 2017 by the High Court in Uttarakhand, although that decision was reversed by India's Supreme Court later that year.[9]

Offering a speculative artistic project that complements those international judicial shifts, *The Trial* also joins a host of recent artistic works that have experimented with legal institutions and practices, forwarding diverse ways of conceptualizing and realizing alternative juridical codes, forms of justice, and oppositional publics. These have also contributed to social movements organized around politico-ecological imperatives. Notable examples include *The Monsanto Hearings*, performed by Compass of the Midwest Radical Culture Corridor in Illinois and Iowa in 2012, which investigated the agribusiness giant and held it accountable for its environmentally damaging GMO, pesticide products and economic imperialism (featuring testimony from such nonhuman characters as corn and wolves, creatively performed by people). There is also Malian director Abderrahmane Sissako's 2006 feature film *Bamako*, whose production entailed a collaboration with community groups in placing the preeminent financial institutions of corporate globalization, the International Monetary Fund and the World Bank, on trial for the disastrous effects they have had on African economies and standards of living. Another example is the *Theatre of Negotiations*, organized by the art and politics lab of Sciences Po Paris and the Théâtre des Amandiers in Nanterre, under the co-leadership of Bruno Latour, Laurence Tubiana, and Frédérique Aït Touati, which, including some 200 students from 143 universities across the world, shadowed COP21, the UN climate conference in Paris in 2015, and creatively modeled ways to create a "parliament of things" in order to negotiate climate policy by giving legal voice to air, water, and the cryosphere along with other nonhuman elements. Lastly, there is the Inter-Pacific Ring Tribunal, a collaboration between research architect Nabil Ahmed and human rights organizations investigating ecocide in the Pacific, specifically in West Papua, seeking through its own prefigurative hearings to eventually prosecute that category of environmental destruction in the International Criminal Court.[10]

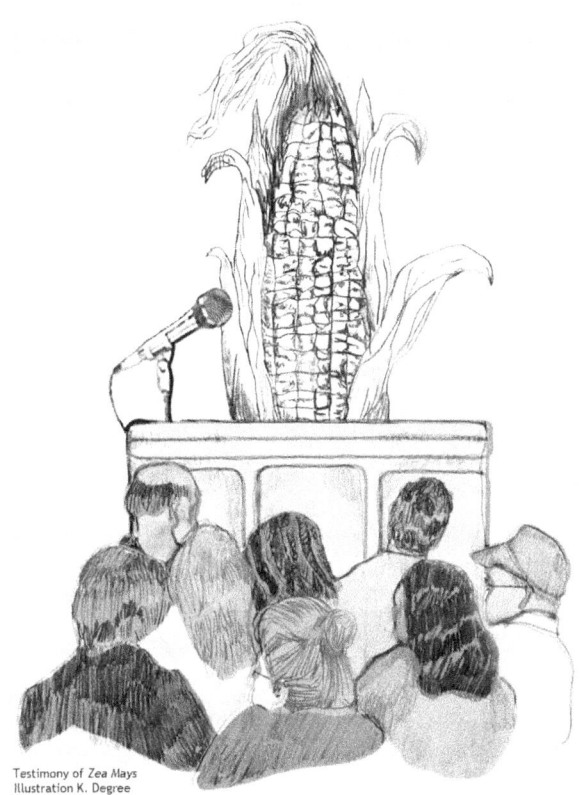

Testimony of *Zea Mays*
Illustration K. Degree

5.2 Compass, *The Monsanto Hearings— Testimony of Zea Mays*, 2012 (performance). Drawing by Kristen Degree. Courtesy of the artists.

Resonating with these aforementioned artistic, cinematic, and theatrical precedents in experimental legal institution building—each thoroughly interdisciplinary, activist oriented, and category defying—*The Trial* challenges the hidebound idea that we humans stand apart from the natural order. Animals' presumed basis in drive, instinct, and automatism, as distinguished from humans' possession of intelligence, language, self-consciousness, and free will, has granted us special status, an understanding that has been perpetuated over thousands of years of Western culture.[11] Seeking to overturn this regime, Haapoja&Gustafsson's project constructs what might be termed an innovative cosmopolitics via its experimental ways of instituting social relations, establishing a reconfigured commonality, and thereby reordering knowledge about the world.[12] As Haapoja puts it, "art and artists should have a far more central role in the society: not as engines of the creative economy but as creators of spaces where other worlds, other orders can become thinkable."[13] As we shall see, through their modeling of artistic play—in the shared senses of experimental theater, recreational pleasure, and the ludic activity that is sometimes conventionally understood as uniquely human, but which has recently been expanded to the more-than-human realm—they provide a remarkable reinvention of institutions, including legal forums, museums, and political parties, which are some of the central institutions where cultural values are shaped and maintained. Along the way, their work initiates a restructuring of fundamental and foundational social values, proposing paths forward for living in a world ultimately where "dehumanization is history."[14]

NATURES AT WAR

Gustafsson&Haapoja's collaboration to date includes a range of works dedicated to the nonrepresented. Including such projects as *The Party of Others* (2011), *The Museum of the History of Cattle* (2013), and *Museum of Nonhumanity* (2016–ongoing), these are intent on inventing new ways to counter political and representational exclusion. Broadly, each contributes to a rebellious conceptualization and materialization of an ethico-aesthetic paradigm, one that, through creative experiments with institutional constructions and juridico-political structures that interlink psychic, social, and institutional registers of experience, moves us beyond the grips of anthropocentrism. The terminology, which I find helpful in comprehending the stakes of their artwork, recalls that of Félix Guattari, circa 1989, as articulated in his texts *The Three Ecologies* and *Chaosmosis: An Ethical-Aesthetic Paradigm*.[15] These connect to powerful genealogies of thought that have continued to flourish in recent years, advanced alongside by such theorizations as Gilles Deleuze's rhizomes of immanence and Gregory Bateson's ecology of mind, and, subsequently, Rosi Braidotti's posthumanism, Donna Haraway's generative sympoeisis and multispecies justice, Eduardo Viveiros de Castro's multinatural anthropology, and Elizabeth Povinelli's geontologies. At the same time, Guattari's transversal methods—pioneering a cross-sectoral analytics operating across psychosocial and enviro-institutional spaces—provides a historical complement to recent discussions of intersectionality, as in decolonial thinking and African American commitments to antiracism and antisexism.[16] According to Braidotti, Guattari's writing remains at the center of this convergence between antihumanism and antianthropocentrism, where "living 'matter' is [considered to be] a process ontology that interacts in complex ways with social, psychic and natural environments, producing multiple ecologies of belonging."[17] For Kim TallBear and Zoe Todd, the philosophical and spiritual underpinnings of this "ontological turn" and its growing sensitivity to more-than-human animism are far from new, and in fact have long been an integral part of Indigenous cosmovision.[18] Mindful of these disparate trajectories, there is nonetheless much work that remains to be done in giving creative expression and formal articulation to this complex movement, a paradigm shift to which Gustafsson&Haapoja have contributed substantially.

Opposition to anthropocentrism is, as many know, increasingly ascendant in cultural discourse. Indeed, for Haraway, "human exceptionalism and bounded individualism, those old saws of Western philosophy and political economics," have "become unthinkable in the best sciences, whether natural or social," unthinkable owing to the growing recognition of the multispecies reciprocities at the basis of all life forms.[19] At the same time, it is increasingly clear that the systems of belief that place humans at the center of the world—with one such genealogy originating in the Judeo-Christian religious understanding of Earth as "man's" dominion—have sanctioned some of the worst forms of environmentally damaging practices, including current forms of extraction.[20] In the last few hundred years of modern capitalism, the political economy of endless growth (itself appearing like a modern religion) has taken the nonhuman environment as infinitely exploitable for human industry, causing untold havoc with the planet's biogeophysical systems.[21] As French philosopher Michel Serres contended around the same time as Guattari's call for an ethico-aesthetic paradigm shift, Western society has been "at war" with nature for centuries, with little to no consideration of how the various onslaughts of modernization—justified by scientific methods, religious beliefs, ethical assumptions, colonial missions, and corporate charters— have impacted the Earth's biosphere.[22] Today, as we have heard repeatedly, the situation is leading toward post-tipping-point climate catastrophe, which, considering recent super hurricanes and uncontrollable wildfires all over the planet, is in fact already upon us. It is this global system, led ultimately by capitalism's spiraling death machine, that Gustafsson&Haapoja's critique of anthropocentrism is ultimately up against.

Still, even though oil exploration in the Arctic, resource wars in the Middle East, fracking in the US and Europe, and mining and deforesting in equatorial regions all continue disastrously in the present, the underlying anthropocentric assumptions that help to rationalize such activity have increasingly been challenged over the last few years. In addition to the speculative models mentioned above, opposition has been mounting in the environmental arts and humanities, in such disciplines as science and animal studies, ecocriticism, cultural anthropology, posthumanist philosophy, cognitive ethology, and multispecies ethnography. In current research, *Homo sapiens* has definitively lost their evolutionary exceptionalism and biological integrity: "human nature is an interspecies relationship," contends Anna Tsing; "becoming-with, not becoming, is the name of the game," claims Donna Haraway.[23] At the same time, animal studies are gaining ground, viewing nonhumans increasingly as possessing their own distinct cultures, communication systems, and individual personalities—making the idea of granting wolves rights not seem so far-fetched after all. For instance, Hugh Raffles writes of insect "love" in *Insectopedia*; Thom van Dooren considers corvid ethics in *The Wake of Crows*; and Jennifer Ackerman discusses the technical wizardry, vocal virtuosity, and aesthetic aptitude of our avian kin in *The Genius of Birds*.[24] As well, diverse animals—birds, dolphins, wolves, apes—are increasingly understood as designers of complex ecosystems, while forests are seen to "think," realizing a transspecies and pluriversalist mode of world-building.[25] As more-than-human animals are increasingly situated, with or without consent, in intraspecies contact zones of naturalcultural intersection with humans—an emergent arena of "humanimalia"—it turns out that animal cultures have important things to teach us humans even about politics, according to Brian Massumi.[26]

In this regard, Gustafsson&Haapoja's work forms part of an expanding, interdisciplinary constellation of practice and thought, which is reconfiguring new ways of being in the world, where both "being" and "world" are at stake. The goal is nothing less than establishing the experimental terms of an emergent arts of living—as theorized initially by Guattari and modeled anew in the recent practices of multispecies ethnography—that goes well beyond the confines of anthropocentrism's conventional values. It is one based on a "curiosity [that] is an attunement to multispecies entanglement, complexity, and the shimmer all around us."[27] If so, then that reordering also means a certain abdication and negation of human centrality, mastery, and supremacy—the complexion of desires informing racism, sexism, and speciesism—a willing (of) renunciation, a mode of self-cancellation, along with a new accountability. These elements of postanthropocentric secession we find central in Gustafsson&Haapoja's pratice, an art of institution-building as much as one instituting new desires and subjectivities. As Haapoja writes, "What we [humans] know of the world, of its deep interconnectedness, of the intelligence and capacities of its inhabitants, of our mutual co-dependence of each other's wellbeing, should guide us directly toward one answer, one practical solution, that of withdrawal, respect and responsibility."[28]

THE PARTY OF OTHERS

Gustafsson&Haapoja's project comprises numerous elements, including exhibitions and publications, performances and experimental institutions. Bringing these together in gallery exhibitions, websites, and extensive catalogs, their multifaceted work investigates the lives and experiences of non/human animals and endeavors also to look at that history from perspectives beyond the human. By implying that others—such as cattle, the subject of some of their recent research—have existed in changing spatiotemporal conditions and possess a similarly transforming collective social life, their art adopts an innovative methodology that rejects the assumption that history and culture belong uniquely to humans, and by extension that nonhumans exist outside history. It also reinvents natural history institutions that have historically been responsible for maintaining the divisions between humans and nonhumans over hundreds, even thousands, of years. In a parallel analysis, Agamben calls such institutions part of an "anthropological machine," one responsible for determining the modern biopolitics that establish and regulate what is considered human and inhuman, dividing into *bios* and *zoe*, political life and animal life. It operates through various political assemblages and legal systems, modes of governance and popular mythologies, all interlinked ideologically and materially. It has also historically determined who is to be saved and who (may be) killed, forming a sociopolitical mechanism wielded at various historical moments to dehumanize certain groups of people (i.e., slaves, Jews, Indigenous people, women, persons of African descent, Muslims and so on) by their comparison to mere animals, rendering their destruction conceptually and legally enabled. As Agamben argues, "In our culture, the decisive political conflict, which governs every other conflict, is that between the animality and the humanity of man. That is to say, in its origin Western politics is also biopolitics."[29] Haapoja herself reiterates this point, explaining that the "foundation of violence" of modern society is constituted by that very "boundary": "this ungrounded division between us and them, which enables the use of two morals, one for the first, and another for the rest—a division that makes it possible to push anyone outside the boundary and 'treat them like animals.'"[30]

How we define ourselves, the world, and our place within it is continually valued, categorized, represented, and regimented through an assortment of institutions, such as governmental political bodies, legal forums, educational disciplines, prisons, and assorted museums—the very normative institutions (in a Foucauldian sense) that Gustafsson&Haapoja work across and intervene within. To counter the violent logic of such ontological divisions within conventional political composition (wherein the nature of the electorate is assembled and founded upon these divisions), in 2011 Haapoja created The Party of Others, an organization to assemble those who have no political representation in present systems of dominant governance, including animals, as well as such excluded humans as refugees, children, foreigners, convicts, the neuro-diverse, and the disabled.[31] As she wrote in her articulation of the party's platform, formed from a collective process of interviews with diverse stakeholders, "The Party of Others speaks for all those who don't have a voice in social decision-making but who are nevertheless affected by the decisions: production animals, pets, wild animals, natural diversity as well as ecosystems such as rivers, swamps, mountains or forests," which is itself a "logical extension" of granting rights to humans previously dispossessed of legal recognition in acts of xenophobic, religious, and racist othering.[32] As such, The Party, forming an ethico-aesthetic construction directed toward actual institutionalization (in ways that would radically question the fundamental assumptions and practice of human-centered governance), was unfurled in the course of Helsinki's 2011 parliamentary elections, working toward the recognition of and respect for the intrinsic value of animal life, natural systems, and diverse human inclusivity.[33] In the place of exploitation practiced through nonvisibility and dehumanization, and contesting the operations of the anthropological machine, The Party of Others created the conditions of expanded representation, of including the excluded. Doing so, it premised the joy and happiness of a radical sociability—as yet another connotation of party—upon the values of social equality, diverse inclusivity, and interspecies understanding based on political solidarity.

While the initiative raised much public interest and garnered appreciable media coverage, it did not ultimately receive enough support to register the party officially, which required five thousand signatures. However, it nonetheless contributed to an ongoing discussion about the marginalization of the voiceless, extending its reach further as an art exhibition presenting a

three-channel video with audio and text-based quotes drawn from interviews the artist conducted about the project and its aims with leading Finnish thinkers from the fields of animal rights, environmental politics, juridical theory, art, and politics. "What would a society that would not be based
on exclusion be like? What would the political structure of that society be
like?" she asked her respondents. For Birgitta Walhberg of Åbo Academi
University, who researches legislation and regulation regarding the welfare
of farm animals, "To acknowledge their legal rights would definitely require
a completely different set of concepts and a radical reorganization of legal
systems in order to be able to process them in courts and official proceedings"; for Leo Stranius, city council member and Green Party environmental activist, "It's not so much about giving up things than it is about receiving. How could a Party of Others bring this question up in the light that this
is not about giving up things or withdrawing, but that the more we give to
others and withdraw and divest from something we don't really even need,
we are getting something so much better in return?"[34] Leena Vilkka, philosopher and author of The Intrinsic Value of Nature, explains further:

> I think we need a new kind of ecological sensitivity in order to start
> listening to what the nonhuman world has to tell us. In fact they are
> speaking to us all the time, but their speech reaches us at these peaks
> of eco-catastrophies, in the form of storms and destruction and climate
> change, because we haven't heard their more subtle speech. We are get-
> ting feedback from the environment all the time. We get it as polluted
> food or toxic, unlivable land, and that speech we hear. But we haven't
> heard them telling us how we could live in this world in collaboration, in
> a community, before these crises that we've created come to us.[35]

In reaffirming these insights concerning radical legal reorganization, the
potential benefits of human withdrawal, and the need for greater ecological sensitivity and multispecies awareness, the project's video component
also plays with language, attempting to raise thoughtfulness about the ways
that pronouns ("us" and "them"; "he," "she," and "it") can divide, socially
and politically, in terms of gender and sexuality, but also fuel the anthropological machine.[36] In certain passages of the video, we see fields of dis-
articulated letters floating in space, both exerting the dispersive force of
the negative on conventional words and grammars (as well as indicating
how text might appear jumbled from a nonliterate perspective) and atom-
izing language, suggesting new possibilities of reassemblage. In this way,

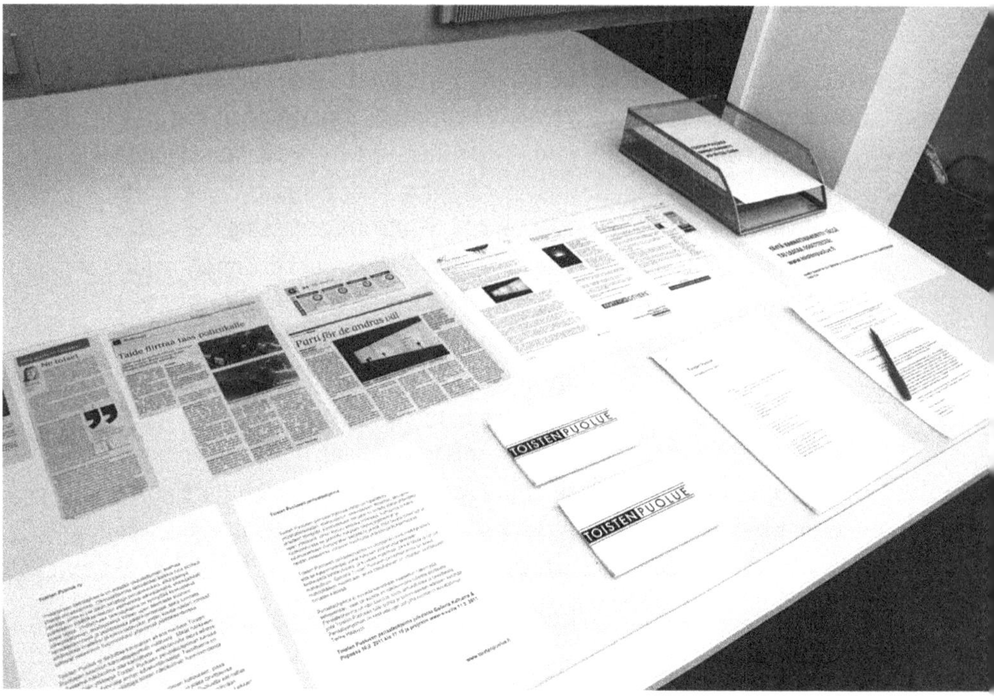

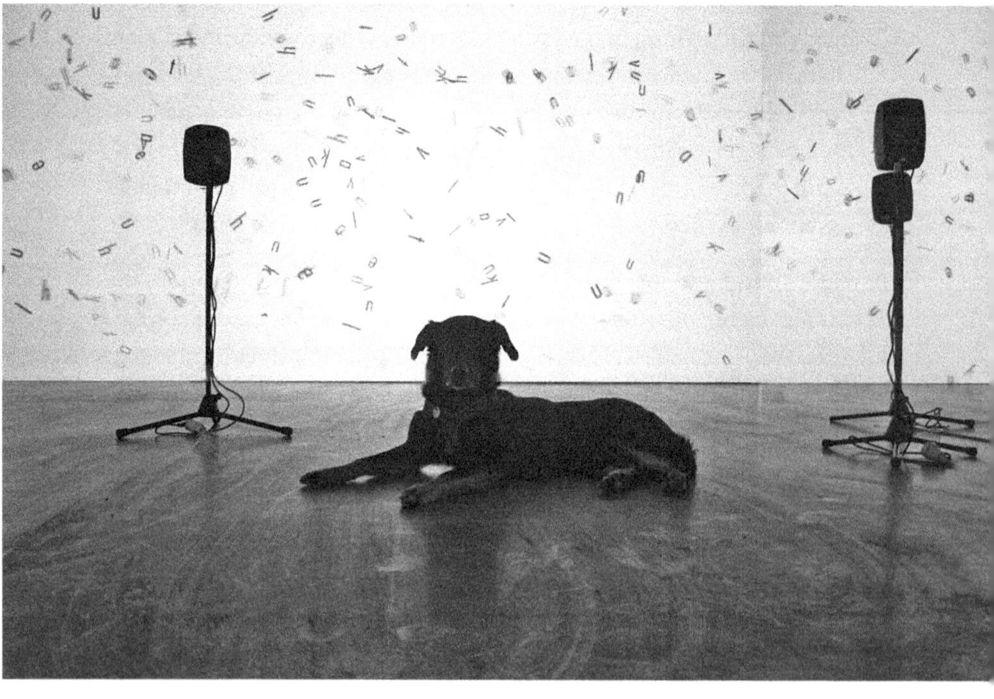

5.3a & 5.3b Terike Haapoja, *The Party of Others*, 2011 (installation). Courtesy of the artist.

the video experiments with a more inclusive pronominal politics, reaching out to those with limited or restricted voice—and indeed in one installation shot the piece appears being screened to Haapoja's own dog companion, as if inviting a small act of emancipation. As her "Platform" explains, "*The Party of Others* drives for structural changes to all stages of common decision-making so that the consideration of these silent parties would become a necessary phase in all social decision-making processes." This would extend to addressing such thorny questions as global population in a world of finite resources; possible economies beyond the growth paradigm; and new systems of rights, media, and education, where representation itself requires innovative forms of language and languaging—ultimately a new emancipatory poetics—"free of financial or other interests."[37]

To further theoretically position Haapoja's project, as well as her collaboration with Gustafsson, one might say that they answer contemporary calls for an innovative ecology of politics directed toward "the progressive composition of a common world," as Bruno Latour proposes, one we are desperately in need of in order to cultivate emancipated futures of multispecies flourishing.[38] *The Party of Others* does so via a newly inclusive legal system, reshaping commonality by extending representation and participation beyond the human. As such, it constitutes what Stefan Helmreich terms a "symbiopolitics" based on the "governance of entangled living things"—correlating with long-standing Indigenous views of relational ontologies and nonanthropocentric webs of being as the fundamental basis of life.[39] Whereas animals have been historically objectified and instrumentalized for human use and enjoyment, in Gustafsson&Haapoja's project, they are granted legal standing in courts of law and invited to join political parties, an approximation of the legal institutionalization of an entangled naturalcultural assemblage composed of distributed representation and expanded recognition of subjecthood.[40] In this regard, such an innovation challenges the destructive social, political, and ontological divisions that construct "Others," recognizing, as Haraway puts it, "the discursive tie between the colonized, the enslaved, the noncitizen and the animal—all reduced to type, all Others to rational man, and all essential to his bright constitution," which "is at the heart of racism and flourishes, lethally, in the entrails of humanism."[41] While intersectionality connects antiracism to antisexism and synergizes their struggles, the result, as I have argued in previous chapters, all too often resides in the zone critical of human biopolitics and racial capitalism yet without going beyond the human (or beyond the dehumanized, objectified human)—just as antispeciesism often remains blind to racial, sexual, and socioeconomic inequalities within the human.[42] Gustafsson&Haapoja's project importantly draws these threads together, finding structural traces of each in the other, and countering the anthropological machine that has engineered so many modern pogroms, genocides, and institutionalized modes of discrimination. By transporting "others" from the realm of "bare life" (stripped of political identity and killable on that basis) to a form of life where the biological is inseparable from the political, they oppose the anthropological machine's very structural function of division. As such, their work provides an artistic blueprint for an intertwined postanthropocentric and anti-discriminatory political legality, anthropology, and museology—an art of institution-building beyond the world of anthropocentrism.[43]

CATTLE-EYE PERSPECTIVE

Haapoja&Gustafsson's The Museum of the History of Cattle, initially shown in Helsinki in 2013, offers a further presentation of the ambitions described above, representing perhaps the world's first museum that addresses history from a nonhuman perspective. As Haapoja explains, "It does not claim to know what cattle think, or whether even their understanding of time is linear like ours. Instead, it points to a place from where the voice of cattle is missing, though the animal itself clearly is there: an absence, a hole in our narrative the shape of a cow."[44] The extensive display includes vitrines containing select objects relating to bovine culture, with text panels explaining the presentations, focusing on the naturalcultural assemblages that cattle, as much as humans, find themselves increasingly within. These include technological and scientific artifacts, such as milking instruments and insemination tools, through which species meet, catalyzing the development and transformation of each in turn. As Gustafsson and Haapoja explain, "The focus of our research . . . is to understand how the lifeworlds of [bovine] individuals have changed over time and how historical events may have been interpreted or perceived by non-human beings."[45] The museum's periodization, told from the collective first-person perspective of cattle, begins with the prehistorical time of the aurochs, ancestor of the modern bovine, who once lived on the grasslands of Eurasia and North Africa more than two million years ago (displays present samples of vegetation from grazing lands of the Indigenous Banteng populations, and Auroch footprints from nearly two million years ago). It continues with the historical

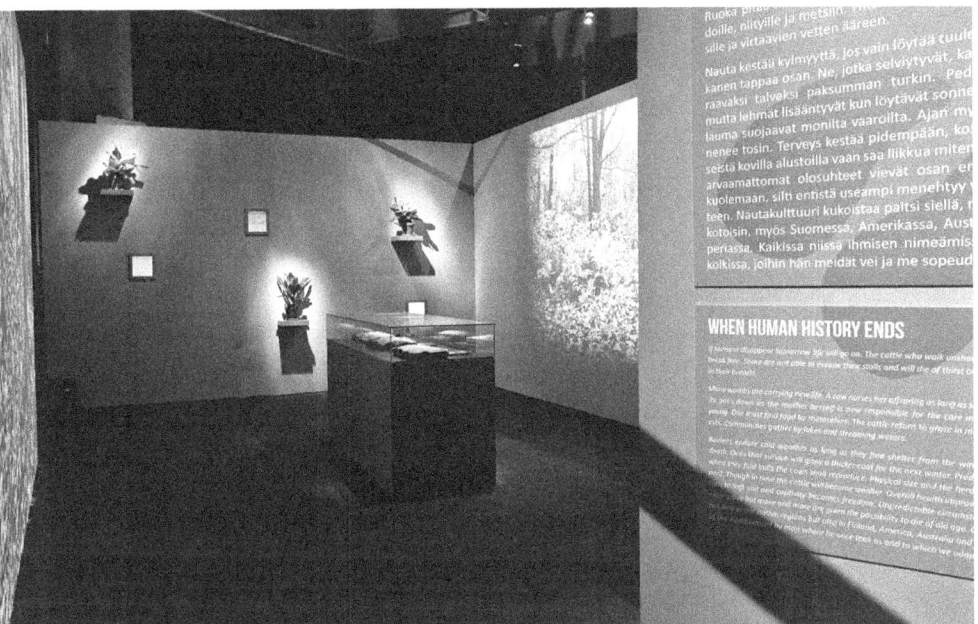

5.4 Gustafsson&Haapoja, *The Museum of the History of Cattle*, 2013 (installation). Courtesy of the artists.

epoch that commenced ten thousand years back with the first human civilizations, in regard to which the museum includes historical topologies of cattle development and narratives written from the viewpoint of individual cattle. Finally we come to the "ahistorical" era, when bovine time and space became deranged by the cyclical patters of industrialization, with cattle dissociated from family relations, collective social structures and shared memory, and natural seasons and environments, as they have been subjected to the enclosures of concentrated animal feeding operations (CAFOs), biotechnological applications, and mass-production-based slaughter. As one exemplary text panel reads from the perspective of cattle:

> Now we live inside the factory. It has become impossible to pass on any heritage. Calves are taken from us immediately after being born, and family lines are scattered out of our sight. We do so little that all our culture and habits have faded to nothing. We no longer learn from our mothers, but from the machine that tells our bodies how to stand and how to eat. Stuck in the industrial process, we live in collective isolation, cut off from all relations that could anchor us to time, history, or culture.[46]

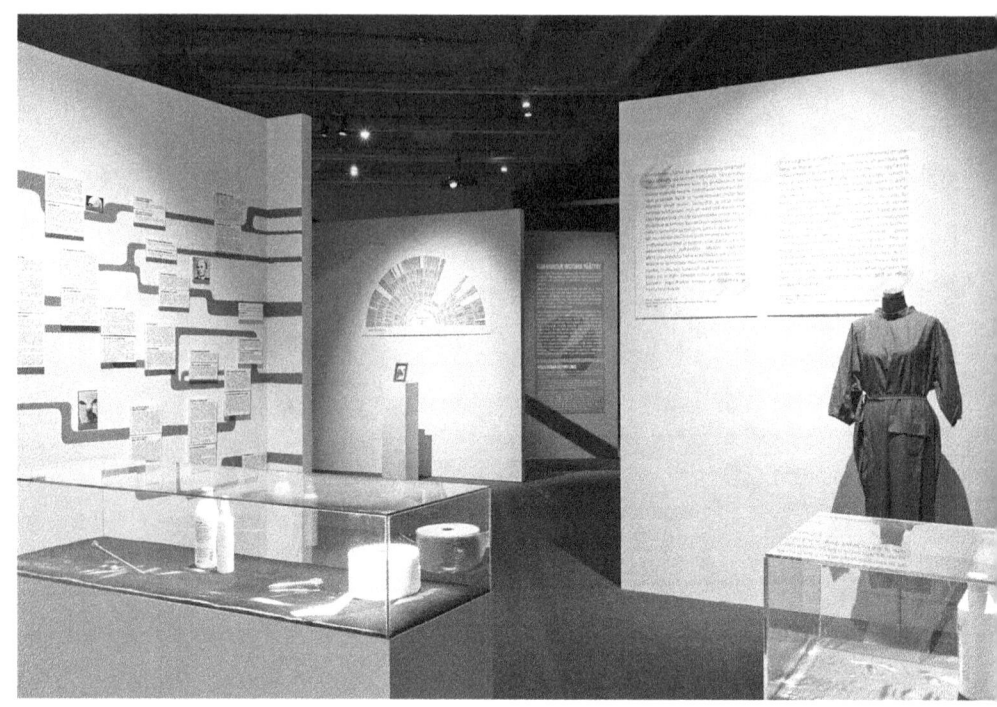

5.5 Gustafsson&Haapoja, *The Museum of the History of Cattle*, 2013 (installation). Courtesy of the artists.

Supplementing the documentation of this latter period are photographic portraits and family trees of individuals like "Haukilammen Joplin," bred as part of Finland's high-quality ASMO herd and producer of commercial embryos.[47] In addition, there are written accounts of cattle living on beef and dairy farms, and statistics on cattle demographics corresponding to different parts of the world that detail the growth of twenty-first-century populations in such places as India and corresponding declines in the US and Finland. This contemporary era further illuminates the recent history of multispecies entanglement and biopolitics in the commercialization of cattle—or better, a nonhuman animal necropolitics, designating the governance of life and death of cattle according to zoontological hierarchies of life. The wider context is the industrialization of livestock, where economics, technology, the architecture of feed lots, animal-based economies, and political organizations intersect, with major implications for the fate of cattle—or what Scout Calvert terms "cowborgs," adopted from Haraway's techno-organic hybrid, designating animal-machine assemblages increasingly designed genetically to enhance their productive capacities and performance in gender-divided sites of labor that deny their subjects any form of sovereignty, culture, or rights.[48] Given that background against the thousands of years of bovine formation, Gustafsson and Haapoja ask, "How might history look through the eyes of a nonhuman species—a species that has played its own contributory role alongside the human race in the unfolding plot that we call history?"[49] Addressing that question of nonhuman historiography, their project attempts to avoid falling into a naïve anthropomorphism (or perhaps it self-consciously adopts a strategic *anthropomormism* in order to challenge the larger reign of *anthropocentrism*). Equally it resists repeating the institutionalized disenfranchisement of animals, reduced to voiceless objects of human manipulation, abandoned to industrialized death worlds of cosmological autism—an existence restricted to an immediate experiential environment without communicative connection to other members of their own or other species.[50] How, in other words, can animals be viewed as more than mere machinic instruments denied subjective agency, culture, and history?

In providing a response to this question, *The Museum of the History of Cattle* considers history through the eyes and interests of animals in order to cultivate human sensitivity to what transcends human reference, even if it ultimately surpasses the possibility of complete human comprehension. While its presentations that document the history and experience of cattle are ultimately built for human visitors, they also remain attentive to the "gestures, experiences, feelings and subjectivities" of cattle, in opposition to the "objectified taxidermied animals that [are] displayed in museum cabinets," which reveal little about actual animal cultures, providing insights rather into human perspectives, values, and systems, as the artists point out.[51] At the same time, the museum accepts the limitations of its project. For instance, in employing human language and written texts in order to convey the experience and history of another species for human viewers, it also problematizes the ultimate inadequacy of that very gesture: "We may not be able to vicariously re-experience how cattle see the world, but we can at least distance ourselves from our normative perceptions of our fellow human beings and other animals," write Gustafsson and Haapoja in their introduction to the *Museum*'s catalog.[52] In fact, according to the artists, "It is the duty of art to expose our blind spots," including the profound difficulties of representing the voiceless and nonrepresented without falling into the traps of a colonizing anthropocentrism once again.[53]

At the same time, this, as well as the broader project of Gustafsson& Haapoja, inevitably raises the difficulty of "speaking for others"—a long-standing challenge regarding representation and unequal agency when it comes to the disparity between people who have the rights, social-class status, power, and education that afford access to speech and those who have no entrance to collective systems of communication, a disparity put in place by colonial relations and slavery and perpetuated through continued socio-economic inequalities.[54] But in the present case, it also concerns nonhuman speech. "Can the subaltern speak?" Gayatri Spivak famously asked in 1983, referring to those human populations that are socially, politically, and geographically located and kept outside hegemonic power structures. Attentive to interspecies relations of inequality and differential access to representation, Eben Kirksey and Stefan Helmreich have recently rephrased that question, asking, "Can the non-human speak?"[55] Avoiding the risk of becoming ventriloquists or defining nonhuman animals on the basis of lack, thereby reinforcing anthropocentric hierarchies, they ultimately avoid answering the question, suggesting a humble non-knowledge as postanthropocentric methodology (perhaps similar to the "withdrawal" Gustafsson&Haapoja advocate). In some ways this broader problem reiterates Jacques Derrida's query, posed in his late essay "And Say the Animal Responded?," questioning how we might reconsider the animal's lack of humanly configured communicative abilities as other than "privation."[56] Recent theorists have gone beyond that framework, investigating the communicative capacities of animals in innovative ways. For instance, Haraway discusses the question in relation to the research of bioanthropologist Barbara Smuts, whose essay "Embodied Communication in Nonhuman Animals" analyzes baboons' greeting rituals.[57] Or consider recent multispecies ethnographic work about "insect poetics," animal storytelling, and "narrating across species lines."[58] A common touchstone is Gregory Bateson's 1970s studies of animal play, which he saw less as categorically divisive than as definitional to multispecies being, subtending both human and nonhuman expression. Ludic form, in other words, is fundamental to both, a matter of gestural and audiovisual communication about relationships and the material-semiotic means of relating to others, all of which resonates with and informs Gustafsson&Haapoja's project's aims.[59]

Building on the above genealogies, theorist Brian Massumi has recently approached the question of whether the non-human can speak from another angle, arguing that human communication is itself grounded in animal play: "The prehuman, preverbal embodied logic of animal play," he contends, "is already essentially language-like."[60] If so, humans should be placed on the same continuum as animals rather than being set apart onto-logically, as the latter risks reifying divisions and hierarchies within institutional, legal, and discursive practices of discrimination within and beyond the category "human." Insofar as play differs from instrumental behavior (just as play-fighting is not actual fighting), ludic activity defines a communicative structure realized through aesthetics, materializing a metacommunication that supplements linguistic and written signs and exemplifies the expressive aspect of play. This capacity, for Massumi, is fundamental to animal creativity, sociability, and expressivity, whereby play does not so much fashion itself on real-life activities but defines an area of creative experimentation—composed of mimetic gestures, multisensory connections, patterns of movements—that constructs the very terms of those activities. Moreover, play opens a realm where reality and one's relation to it is in effect established, (re)constructed, and (re)defined.

It is on this basis that we can envision the realm of play as constituting "a different politics, one that is not a human politics of the animal, but an integrally animal politics" from which humans can learn.[61] Such a conceptualization differs from Latour's extension of human political representability to nonhumans, asking, for instance, what types of architectures, prostheses, and technologies of mediation can assist in composing a multispecies public. Conversely, Massumi proposes ways to resituate humans on an animal scale and constitute democracy on that basis. The conceptualization of animal play and animal politics is ultimately directed "to reassume and reintensify the nature-culture/human-animal continuum to invent unrepresentable movements of singularization constituting a revolutionary democracy in the act."[62] While this opens up a range of practical questions—for instance, how can we create a politics mediated by the singularities of human and nonhuman languages and play? And how would this recognition revise interspecies relations?—one lesson to be drawn from this discussion is that we humans should not so much strive to "speak for" our animal and more-than-human partners in the formation of a newly imagined and inclusive governmental politics, as learn to listen better to nonhuman languages in order to consider other forms of life and build a symbiopolitics on those grounds. Or as Haapoja writes, we should "work towards a time where we could hear the non-human world speak in its own tongues: towards an order we can now only imagine."[63] That process lends itself to constituting a milieu that is co-constitutive, opening new modes of becoming where we can no longer assume that our own form of communication is the only and best one. It is this experimentation that Gustafsson&Haapoja's projects initiate, acknowledging both its necessities, limits and its future challenges.

As such, Gustafsson&Haapoja's institutions, at their most experimental potential, propose a zone of indeterminacy between the human and the more-than-human, between institutions created by and for humans and those invented for and by new collectivities that surpass interspecies divisions. Such work does not simply expand human systems to the animal world. Rather, it queries and challenges the very borders between human and nonhuman, refuses to leave the conventional category human untouched, by enacting a form of aesthetic play—and indeed The Trial is ultimately a play of experimental theater—that is inherently animal. "Play is the arena of activity dedicated to the improvisation of gestural forms, a veritable laboratory of forms of life," writes Massumi.[64] In other words, play brings new worlds into being in the act, allowing us animals to test and innovate skills for understanding and operating within them and their provisional formations. Play functions as a creative engine that generates constructive real-life applications and operates at the basis of language itself. Play offers a generative zone, a place to create and test out new possibilities, free of real-life stakes and consequences, a training ground for emancipated futures. If so, then with this conceptualization of play, one expanded through diverse modes of institutionalization, we have an apt approximation of the broader creativity of multispecies aesthetics that Gustafsson&Haapoja advance—an experimental activity that is intrinsically animal. In opening up a series of questions about potential postanthropocentric worlds, it implicates us all in a series of creative multispecies becomings, reinventing play to remake the world.

TO SAVE A
WORLD

GEOENGINEERING,
CONFLICTUAL FUTURISMS,
AND THE UNTHINKABLE

The Anthropocene is proving to be an era of world war—or rather, worlds at war. Not that this is anything new. We are no doubt living in the continuation of long-standing onto-epistemological and politico-military conflicts set within (still unfolding) histories of colonial and global states of violence and dispossession. If catastrophe lies before us, then it flows from what has come before. Consider two ideological formations that speak to this current situation. First, the techno-utopianism of geoengineering, premised on climate-change fixes for the symptoms and increasingly alarming impacts of fossil capital's disastrous centuries-long transformation of the environment. Adherents suggest that solar radiation management and carbon capture—the two dominant forms of climate engineering, the first more extreme than the second—can stabilize temperatures so as to avert calamitous environmental breakdown, buying us time to come up with more long-term solutions (even though the technology is nowhere near implementation and at the necessary scales). With reference to this approach, the Breakthrough Institute, the California-based think tank advocating market-directed, pro-tech responses to environmental threat, offers a futurist vision of the "good

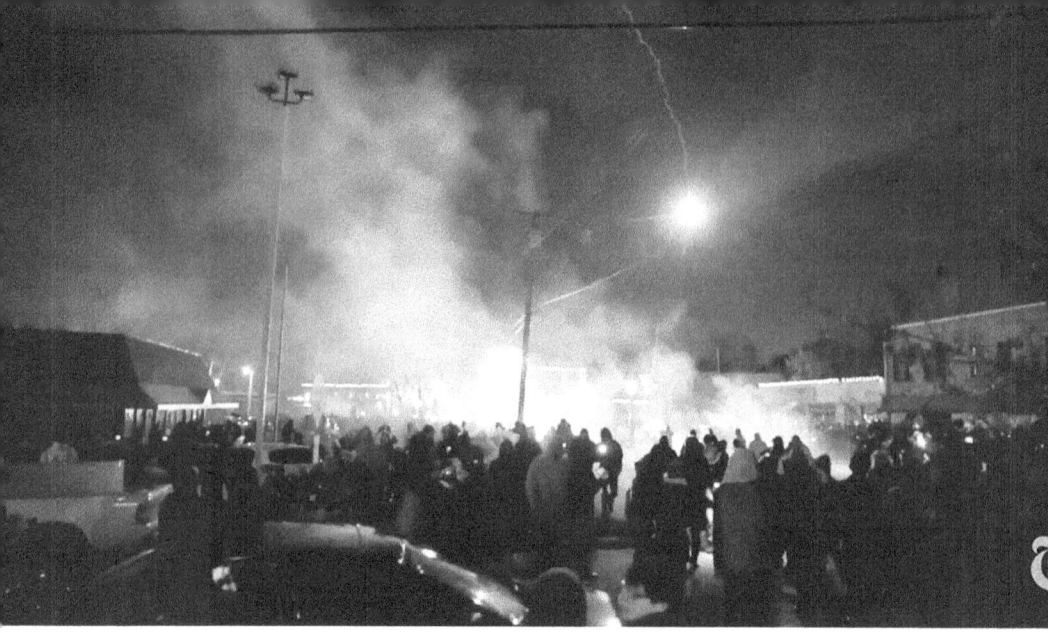

6.1 Arthur Jafa, *Love Is the Message, the Message Is Death* (video still), 2016. Digital color video, with sound, 7 min., 25 sec. Courtesy of the artist and Gavin Brown's Enterprise, New York / Rome.

Anthropocene," articulated as a potential near-future world where "humans use their growing social, economic, and technological powers to make life better for people, stabilize the climate, and protect the natural world."[1]

The second formation is the devastating racial violence appearing in Arthur Jafa's 2016 video *Love Is the Message, the Message Is Death*, which also answers that footage with a redemptive Afrofuturism. Proposing one model among Indigenous and anticolonial visions appealing to and embedded within social movements dedicated to justice-to-come, it foregrounds the heartrending violence against Black communities as the fundamental basis upon which any alternative—one of coexistence, equality, love, and peace— can be imagined. Resonating with the impulses behind the platform of the 2016 Movement for Black Lives, itself built on long-standing African-American approaches to socio-environmental justice that insist on correlating existential vulnerabilities with racial and economic inequalities, Jafa's video offers the occasion to bring far-reaching politico-ecological strands together in intersectional analysis.[2] It also offers the opportunity to counterpose that analysis against the technocratic framework and neoliberal values that guide climate engineering, which is increasingly becoming integral to dominant global climate policy within the framework of green capitalism.

The above two modelings of the future offer an expedient comparison—and more importantly a startling contrast—between the current technoscientific rationality of climate-change response and the socio-environmental justice concerns around racial capitalism. While the Breakthrough Institute's policies have very little to do with the matters addressed in Jafa's video, the latter does not explicitly or substantially reflect on climate breakdown, at least as conventionally conceived. This very segregation of concerns—between climate change and social justice—forms part of a problematic distribution of the sensible when it comes to the wider framework of environmental considerations, which I am intent on analyzing, challenging, and rearranging by drawing these distinct elements together into critical discussion. As such, the unlikely juxtaposition invites a much-needed discussion of competing approaches to what is to come, a future world that could potentially be locked in for hundreds, even hundreds of thousands, of years. That urgency is compounded by the fact that, while technocratic climate science tends to ignore or, at best, merely pays lip service to the differential impacts of environmental transformations on disenfranchised communities subject to ongoing racial and economic discrimination, social justice activism often shunts ecological matters to the side owing to an all-too-immediate and well-justified but ultimately limiting confrontation with police brutality, structural inequality, and political disenfranchisement. Perhaps part of the problem, which helps keep these multiple strands separate to begin with, is the very meaning of *environment*. Opening up that term, and resituating it through a recombinative politico-ecological analysis is urgent, and by doing so in the following pages, I hope to show that what is at stake in this improbable comparison is everything that matters.

OPTIMAL CLIMATES

In *Love Is the Message, the Message Is Death*, Arthur Jafa, a filmmaker by trade, unleashes a ferocious archive of citizen-journalist, dash cam, and social media video clips, wherein we see Black folks subjected to innumerable acts of state violence, but not just. Set to Kanye West's transcendent gospel-rap anthem "Ultralight Beam," the flurry of images quickly cycles through recent and historical footage of shootings, attacks, and beatings, also including intermixed shots of ghastly civilization-destroying aliens and monsters borrowed from Hollywood sci-fi and horror films. It would appear that through this eye-watering assemblage Jafa is proposing an allegory for the destruction of the world, where the systematic killings and unleashed brutality scales up to an apocalypse delivered by supernatural forces. More than that still, this world, shown as an agglomeration of social collapse and violent calamity, seems set on destroying itself, rising up in monstrous acts of suicidal catastrophe—one, in a parallel universe, where the catastrophe of racial violence is exchanged for climate breakdown, which geoengineering wishes to repair. Yet what we face with this comparison, between very different worlds and very different ends—which is so often not acknowledged as a comparison at all—is actually a missed encounter, which Jafa's intervention ultimately makes apparent: Technoscience's redemptive impulses appear wildly misdirected, just as horror movies picture far-flung catastrophes that often have little to do with our actual social reality. The challenge is to think these worlds together.

The Anthropocene thesis might be similarly criticized for its various problematic diversions.[3] These include its regressive and narcissistic neohumanism, its evasion of the differential causes and uneven effects of climate breakdown, its disavowal of petrocapitalist culpability, and its ecology of affluence, all of which are not unrelated to the present drama of self-destruction shown in Jafa's video. In past writings, my analysis has explored diverse visual-cultural expressions of photography and remote sensing data, the kind that offer "Whole Earth" utopian perspectives of the planet as if it were devoid of social conflict and safely in the hands of an emergent scientific mastery. These same tendencies continue to mark the mainstream theorization and unfolding reception of the Anthropocene today—despite parallel attempts to mobilize it critically, work progressively with its conceptualization, and also nominate additional terms to better comprehend current conditions, such as the Chthulucene and the Capitalocene.[4] If considered expansively, Jafa's video contributes to this discussion by powerfully elucidating the problems with environmental mastery from an unexpected point of view: by dramatizing the extreme costs of the social asymmetries that go unaddressed within much climate science and technological approaches to climate breakdown. If the neoliberalization of the Anthropocene is ascendant—which the last couple of decades of dominant market-based and high-tech approaches demonstrate with increasing clarity—then the growth of climate engineering theory and practice in fact threaten any future grounded in social justice, at least the kind that Jafa points us to. It behooves us to carefully consider the stakes of these competing visions for future worlds, particularly as their mutually exclusive realizations are already receiving substantial, if unequal, investments in the present. To that end, let me turn first to geoengineering.

Geoengineering in fact unfolds directly from the Anthropocene thesis, beginning with the latter's initial 2000 terminological proposal made by atmospheric chemist Paul Crutzen and biologist Eugene Stoermer to designate a new geological era where Earth's natural systems are increasingly determined by "human activities."[5] As Crutzen and Stoermer explain in that formative publication, "an exciting, but also difficult and daunting task lies ahead of the global research and engineering community to guide mankind towards global, sustainable, environmental management."[6] As Crutzen elaborates in his subsequent essay "Geology of Mankind": "Unless there is a global catastrophe—a meteorite impact, a world war or a pandemic—mankind will remain a major environmental force for many millennia. A daunting task lies ahead for scientists and engineers to guide society toward environmentally sustainable management during the era of the Anthropocene. This will require appropriate human behavior at all scales, and may well involve internationally accepted, large-scale geo-engineering projects, for instance to 'optimize' climate. At this stage, however, we are still largely treading on terra incognita."[7] Looking toward the future, Crutzen soon followed up with more explicit suggestions for large-scale engineering projects, including his own proposal for stratospheric sulfur injections.[8]

But in looking toward the past, we can draw important historical lessons that would lead us to question Crutzen's agenda. To begin with, much dispute remains over the dating of this post-Holocene epoch: whether it began with the nineteenth-century Industrial Revolution, or nuclear science in the 1940s, or again much earlier with the Orbis Spike of 1610, which remains the most compelling boundary event proposal within critical Anthropocene discourse. This last coincides, as we have seen, with the geological implications of colonization in the Americas, which unknowingly dropped atmospheric carbon levels, and with them global temperatures, owing to the large-scale afforestation of once-cultivated lands left depopulated following the genocide of Indigenous peoples (owing to epidemics, warfare, famine, and colonial atrocities). Indeed, colonization left upwards of 56 million dead by the beginning of the 1600s, or 90 percent of the pre-Columbian Indigenous population, around 10 percent of the Earth's population at the time.[9]

In other words, the selection of the era's boundary event determines what kind of discussion the Anthropocene thesis generates, whether one connected to the global formations of imperial violence and racial capitalism or one based in the technological developments of the Industrial Revolution or nuclear energy. In my view, most historically sensitive, politically enabling, and therefore compelling would be an expansive understanding that insists on seeing these formations within a mutually constructive entanglement unfolding within colonial, industrial, and capitalist modernity.[10] For now, it suffices to point out that the Anthropocene is not only far from innocent in historical diagnosis: it matters both geologically and politically when we date it. As well, the term's conceptualization, particularly given its apparently causal connection to geoengineering, may very well be preemptive in technoscientific prescription for future response.[11] Essentially, by interpreting the past, we determine the future—and vice versa.

For Crutzen, engineering may be a last resort to forestall the catastrophic breakdown of Earth's systems, where reducing emissions otherwise simply proves insurmountable politically and economically for global society; for others, however, it represents an attractive first option to advance "ecological modernization," merging climate solutions with tech-guided economic opportunity, creating the ideal climate for wealth accumulation. This returns us to the Breakthrough Institute's notorious proposal for a good Anthropocene, founded on the dubious "decoupling" of economic growth from environmental impacts, as if endless financial expansion, as long as it is decarbonized, can be considered independently of climate change effects.[12] Yet the ideological nature of this proposal should be clear. Indeed, this "leading big money, anti-green, pro-nuclear"—and pro-geoengineering—"think tank in the United States" was founded in 2003 by Michael Shellenberger and Ted Nordhaus, and they have long argued that economic growth in itself need not negatively impact Earth systems.[13] In their 2004 essay "The Death of Environmentalism: Global Warming Politics in a Post-Environmental World," Shellenberger and Nordhaus sought to dispatch what they term the "politics of limits"—the kind based in the regulatory environmentalism of the 1970s emphasizing Earth's finite carrying capacity—and replace it with a "politics of possibility" committed to technologically driven economic expansion put to task against climate breakdown.[14] The institute notably counts Carl Page, brother of Google founder Larry Page, among its funders, a detail symptomatic of the growing convergence of Big Tech with green economics, which has only expanded in significance in recent years, especially as climate modeling has become increasingly dependent on big data and computer processing

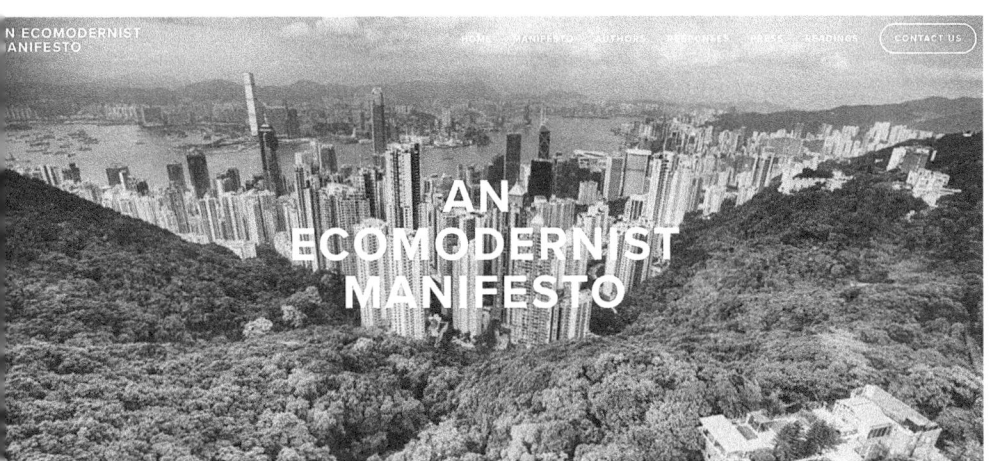

A MANIFESTO TO USE HUMANITY'S
EXTRAORDINARY POWERS IN SERVICE OF CREATING
A GOOD ANTHROPOCENE.

6.2 "An Ecomodernist Manifesto," 2015.

capabilities. This economic connection may also indicate the shared class-based interests of the well-resourced institute, which informs its climate policy. Indeed, according to critics, the institute remains singularly "dedicated to propagandizing capitalist technological-investment 'solutions' to climate change," but doing so in the absence of any evidence that ecological modernization is a credible thesis.[15] The clearest articulation of the Breakthrough Institute's recent position is "An Ecomodernist Manifesto," written by eighteen authors, including Shellenberger and Nordhaus, which attempts to justify their techno-solutions-based wealth-generating goal via eco-cultural claims: "More-productive economies are wealthier economies, capable of better meeting human needs while committing more of their economic surplus to non-economic amenities, including better human health, greater human freedom and opportunity, arts, culture, and the conservation of nature."[16]

Yet despite its familiar trickle-down economic theory and liberal-coated goodwill sentiment, which have been thoroughly debunked no less economically as ecologically, the manifesto's expansive spatiotemporal scales and abstract rhetoric—like much of the Anthropocene thesis's planetary imagery and deep-time framing—overshoot the figural, the local, and the experiential, where arts and culture actually reside.[17] It is not surprising, then, that the "politics of possibility" as articulated in the manifesto fails to mention the terms *race*, *equality*, or *justice*, which, if included, would at least help connect its future vision to the actual, even glaring, antagonisms, inequalities, and injustice of current social experience. In contrast, the lofty, liberal, and generalizing language of *human*, *technology*, and *growth* abound. By evading such key facets of justice-centered environmentalism—which they do their best to consign to the grave—ecomodernism's color-blind formulations reflect yet another version of what Van Jones has called "the unbearable whiteness of green," unbearable not only because the manifesto's enviro-economic utopianism utterly fails to consider the intolerable social conditions of current reality but also because it apparently seeks to extend those conditions infinitely into the future.[18] By disappearing the critical reflection on social inequalities in its performance of an ecology of affluence, ecomodernism implicitly commits justice and equity to the realm of the impossible or negligible. Meanwhile its priorities are confined to the biogeophysical and financial, conveniently not challenging its own socioeconomic privileges or those of its funders. Consequently, the manifesto's stated dedication to "stabilizing the climate" can only be read in this limited way—as a modality of "sustainable development," wherein "environment" is understood as an ideal, privileged bioeconomic realm.[19] Alternately, if we can describe Jafa's video as expressing an environmentalism of sorts—which I argue we can, although the video's reception to date has largely eluded such an analysis—then it is one attuned to what Christina Sharpe terms "antiblackness as total climate."[20] Indeed, Jafa's piece offers a compelling vision of how an environmentalism founded on that contention might enter into aesthetic form and poignantly contest the ecomodernist agenda and its underlying technoscientific reason.

GEOENGINEERING'S MONSTROSITY

In contrast to the many conceptual loopholes of "An Ecomodernist Manifesto," *Love Is the Message* is laser-focused on figurations distorted within and by the actual everyday environments of racial capitalism and its necropolitics, where climate policies impact real people in ways that are inextricable from sociopolitical differentials. Indeed, the dominant system's climate policies might be said even to produce and manage those differentials. Jafa's stream of rhythmic edits moves relentlessly through shots

6.3 Santiago Álvarez, *Now!* (publicity poster), 1965.

of police hitting, pummeling, punching, shooting, and brutalizing Black persons. In so doing, his video recalls and updates militant approaches of Third Cinema from decades past meant to operate as a cinematic weapon against imperialism, sometimes by re-presenting popular news media footage and showing its gruesome violence directly.[21] Specifically *Love Is the Message* evokes *Now!*, the 1965 short by Cuban revolutionary filmmaker Santiago Álvarez and its then-and-still-shocking portrayal of US racist policing set to Lena Horne's rousing civil rights musical number. Similarly visualizing the state's controlling of distinct climates of life and death premised on anti-Blackness but turning more toward our current era, Jafa includes scenes of the 2015 murder of Walter Scott in South Carolina, the abusive 2014 arrest of Kametra Barbour in her car with her four children in Dallas, and the cruel ground-tackling of fifteen-year-old, bikini-clad Dajerria Becton by a white police officer at a pool party in McKinney, Texas, in 2015. Going beyond this incisive acknowledgment of the continuation of civil rights–era racial violence, the sideways comparison with geoengineering allows further insights that invite an expanded reconceptualization of environment today.

Jafa's video clearly refuses clear distinctions between environmental management as a form of carbon capture and temperature modulation, on the one hand, and biopolitics as the governance of life and lives, on the other. These scenes of police violence, as contextualized in Jafa's piece, portray social engineering as a technique that joins the management of biophysical conditions (specifically through police batons, bullets, and fists) with the controlling of environments (state-produced milieus maintaining social order), which together organize and exacerbate race, gender, and class inequalities. These are, in other words, modalities of climate control, situating environmental conditions in longer-term patterns of historical duration and institutional management of biopolitics. If geoengineering seeks to regulate the state of regional environments, then the local determination of life-and-death conditions for individuals through remote precision drone attacks and aerial bombing, as shown in Jafa's *The White Album* (2018), his subsequent video of psychocultural environments of whiteness, represent further examples of militarized climate control. Elsewhere in *Love Is the Message*, Jafa contextualizes these climates of anti-Blackness with additional footage drawn from the historical archive (again resonating with *Now!*), depicting midcentury scenes of police fire-hosing Black protestors, striking civil rights activists with nightsticks, whites brutalizing lunch counter protestors in North Carolina, and imagery from D. W. Griffith's notorious 1915 film *The Birth of a Nation*, with its scandalous portrayals of Ku Klux Klan members and white actors in blackface. In other words, *Love Is the Message* offers a short lesson in US climate history, where environment has little to do with protected wilderness zones, global warming, or melting ice. Rather, it designates systematic patterns of institutional racism, unleashing the ambient violence of atmospheric anti-Blackness by referencing the affects, tonalities, rhythms, and spatial arrangements that generate discrimination and segregation in everyday life. Similarly drawing together ecology with racial politics, Alessandra Raengo asks, "What is the ontology of black lives, when they are so thoroughly wrapped in an atmospheric anti-blackness?"[22] *Love Is the Message* provides one answer.

Returning to ecomodernism, we can see that the Breakthrough Institute inadvertently contributes to the widespread invisibility and erasure of precisely those scenes Jafa highlights, disappearing from its imagined geo-engineered future what might be called the Black Anthropocene—wherein ecology is inseparable from the social terms of racial capitalism.[23] While engineering models aim for climate control at regional levels, as in its solar radiation management proposals, Jafa's video, which in fact exhibits tacit and sometimes explicit affinities with the fields of political ecology and climate justice, grounds environment as the realm of sociopolitical and techno-economic inequality, which also connects to the geophysical conditions of climate change.[24] This equation of ecology-as-intersectionality, which offers another way to comprehend this formulation, is most overt where his video includes passages of African Americans wading through the superstorm flood waters in the wake of Hurricane Katrina, a situation in which global warming's extreme weather became understood as inseparable in its effects from institutional racism and urban inequality.[25] For many New Orleanians, years of structural negligence, municipal and infrastructure defunding, systemic racial inequality, and impoverishment were compounded by that "unnatural" disaster, which cannot be extricated from its realization within the field of disproportionate impacts resulting from collective in/capacities and lack of access to resources. "In every phase and aspect of a disaster—causes, vulnerability, preparedness, results and response, and reconstruction—the contours of disaster and the difference between who lives and who dies is to a greater or lesser extent a social calculus," as Neil Smith wrote insightfully about Katrina.[26] In fact, taking that context writ large, geoengineering—as another form of disaster response—appears to be a technological construct mobilized in part precisely so as not to address social injustice, and more cynically, functions as a social calculus *of* social injustice, one wielded to restrict our understanding of environment to the biogeophysical realm. Showing how police brutality enacts the everyday and sometimes spectacular meanings of US environmental management, *Love Is the Message*, in contrast, brings climate control down to the racialized and classed figural scale, even as it opens onto historical formations dating back to conquest and slavery—in a way similar to how Stefano Harney and Fred Moten saw in the 2015 killing of Michael Brown in Ferguson, Missouri, the instantiation of "the ongoing event of resistance to, and resistance before, socioecological disaster," where "modernity's constitution in the transatlantic slave trade, settler colonialism and capital's emergence in and with the state, is The Socioecological Disaster."[27] With Jafa's video, too, we witness how white supremacy, disaster capitalism, and authoritarian neoliberalism, which operate climatologically at granular levels, were formed—even *geoengineered*, insofar as worlds were actively constructed, others destroyed—over centuries, since 1492. If these forces more recently have converged to represent the ruling order of Trumpist governmentality, then that is because the latter is itself a signature instance of the pathologies of late Anthropocene rationality.[28]

"Climate change is global-scale violence against places and species, as well as against human beings," Rebecca Solnit reminds us.[29] Naomi Klein extends that insight when she writes about how "the reality of an economic order built on white supremacy is the whispered subtext of our entire response to the climate crisis," a crisis that is far from accidental but rather "the result of a series of policy decisions the governments of wealthy countries have made—and continue to make—with full knowledge of the facts and in the face of strenuous objections."[30] It is within this broader matrix of mainstream climate policy that we can further situate the Breakthrough Institute and geoengineering's technofix proposals. Attacking the proclaimed goals and decision-making procedures at UN climate summits, the Sudanese diplomat and climate negotiator Lumumba di Aping, we recall, has predicted the results to be "climate genocide," where limiting warming to two degrees Celsius means accepting a global average that will translate into four to five degrees in some places, given differential impacts, meaning "Africa will burn."[31] Geoengineering, which (at least in its current guise) enables the fossil fuel economy to progress without major interruption, will likely make this eventuality ever more possible. Given the massive scales, delayed implications, and tremendous complexity of climate science, as well as its networked agencies built of depersonalized cybernetic systems, the challenge is urgent to render these critical insights into visual evidence capable of forming collective political subjects who act, so that we can shape the future we want to live in—at least while there is yet time left to do so.[32] Jafa's video aids in this critical project.

Even while *Love Is the Message* does not specifically reference geoengineering (at least in its conventional definition), it nonetheless offers a discernable cry of protest against the latter's ambition to sustain our present with no alteration to its governing sociopolitical and economic arrangements, with mitigation technology only intervening at the level of regional weather control, and atmospheric waste management as a matter of addressing carbon pollution. Yet it does propose connections between these diverse facets of reality. By virtue of its montage, Jafa's video joins passages of police violence to close-up shots of angry sun flares, as seen from NASA's International Space Station near-live feed, thereby establishing a link that resonates with environmental justice positions that view global warming as a threat multiplier, which, impossible to average and generalize, exacerbates social conflict and inequality. According to well-documented research extending out of environmental justice activism, disenfranchised and impoverished communities of color experience higher levels of exposure to toxicity, food and water shortages, major health risks, and other forms of environmental vulnerability and debility, all exacerbated by climate-related disasters and their aftermath.[33] Global warming aggravates the very social crises that, in the absence of social service provisions, invite security-based, and increasingly military-oriented, responses to the conflict. Indeed, according to Jasbir Puar, we are witnessing the globalization of debilitation as a spreading logic of inequality, where "debilitation is caused by global injustice and the war machines of colonialism, occupation, and U.S. imperialism."[34] Geoengineering, responding to a wider context of climate breakdown, stands to expand these modes of biopolitical control and neoliberal extraction, remaking the world according to those very forces.

In this vein, it is feasible to understand *Love Is the Message* as a powerful counternarrative and critical interruption to dominant climate policy. If the video unveils something like a world-destroying apocalypse, then it also performs the original meaning of that term as a modality of revelation. The video's appropriated footage of the creature's dripping secondary jaws from Ridley Scott's 1979 classic *Alien*, and those of the city-destroying monster from *Cloverfield*, Matt Reeve's 2008 faux-found-footage horror film, provide some of the elements of Jafa's hieroglyphic scaffolding of

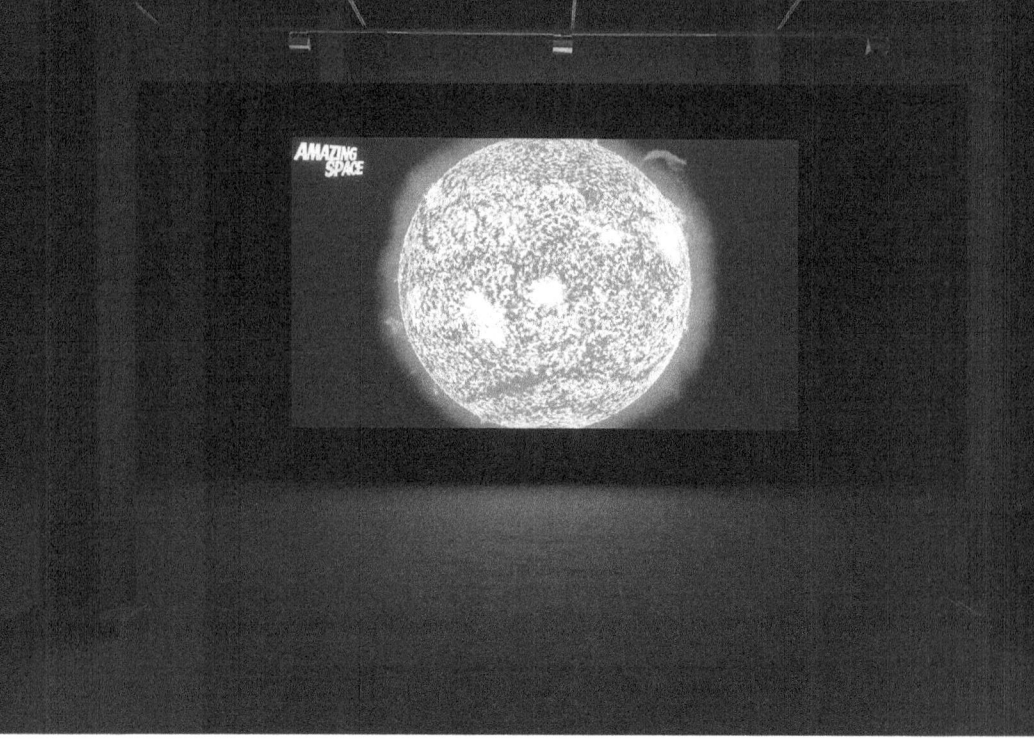

6.4 Arthur Jafa, *Love Is the Message, the Message Is Death* (video still), 2016. Digital color video, with sound, 7 min., 25 sec. Courtesy of the artist and Gavin Brown's Enterprise, New York / Rome.

meaning-construction around climate apocalypse, ultimately forming a rebus of excessive signification. It constructs an allegory serving to elevate the tragic-but-quotidian documents of police violence and racial oppression to the realm of cosmopolitical magnitude, the arena where worlds are annihilated and remade.[35] In other words, any given police attack cannot be seen merely as a stand-alone local event (a simple weather report); instead, by virtue of Jafa's stream of collected footage, each forms part of the systematic patterns of widespread violence, and further, that violence becomes a matter of civilizational threat akin to the horror of an alien assault on planet Earth. The monstrous tells a story of global warming driving racial injustice, a narrative of postnatural dystopia resulting from, or figuring as, runaway climate change. These scenes of invasion and annihilation propose so many film fables that might be read variously: whether as representing the greedy and senseless destruction of the world conducted by the rapacious power of carceral capital, bolstered by police climate control, the colonization of debt, and the chains of spectacle; or the radical and threatening otherness of racial difference, including whiteness, become a predatory behemoth; or alternately, a justice-seeking revenge fantasy upon white-supremacist culture (an overarching political, economic, and social system of domination) by what lies beyond recognition; or the materialization of contemporary fears of a genetically and geoengineered Frankensteinian science in creating postnatural dystopias and apocalyptic climate change. Or indeed it might suggest some element of each all mixed together without articulate or stable meaning: a figuration of intersectionalist ecology.

THE NEOLIBERAL ANTHROPOCENE

The Breakthrough Institute also references the monstrous, our "contemporary Frankenstein"—putting it to work and enlisting no less than Bruno Latour in its theoretical machinery. In his essay "Love Your Monsters," Latour argues that we must not disown the planetary monster we have created—the Earth of the Anthropocene—but learn to love and care for it through further technological acts of "modernizing modernization."[36] It is true that Latour subsequently came around to explicitly reject climate engineering—"as Gaia cannot be compared to a machine, it cannot be subjected to any sort of *re-engineering*. As the activists say: 'There is no Planet B.'"[37] However, his earlier position had already been put to task, and remains live on the institute's website (as of December 2019), continuing to support the latter's mission into the present. Responding to Latour's position, Naomi Klein overlooks his posthumanist call for an updated "compositionist" relearning as a necessary part of that modernizing modernization, entailing "a process of becoming ever-more attached to, and intimate with, a panoply of nonhuman natures," but she rightly criticizes the presumptuousness of his embrace of technology, especially where it aids in the institute's pro-engineering agenda: "The earth is not our prisoner, our patient, our machine, or, indeed, our monster. It is our entire world. And the solution to global warming is not to fix the world, it is to fix ourselves."[38] Adding to mounting opposition to geoengineering, she highlights the multiple problems of the practice, including its potential unintended side effects (e.g., interfering in monsoons in South Asia, exacerbating drought in North Africa, widening the ozone hole); the lack of any global regulatory protocol for climate interventions with transnational implications; the lock-in effect that makes it next to impossible to abandon the technology once it has been implemented, to the point where catastrophic temperature rise would occur as soon as its protective shielding came to an end; its antidemocratic basis in an era of unregulated globalism led by a handful of powerful developed nations; and, crucially, its directing of precious resources away from the causes of climate disruption, in favor of addressing its symptoms.[39]

Resonating with these critiques, in recent years popular resistance movements have formed around the theory and practice of climate justice, asserting the fundamental principle of "system change, not climate change," where justice means prioritizing equality, fairness, and the inclusion of the most vulnerable and frontline communities in the deliberation of climate solutions.[40] These areas of climate-justice activism are also invariably intersectional in their political ambitions: think of the ongoing battle in central France to stop the new airport and invent a noncapitalist commons at the territory known as the Zad; Standing Rock's ongoing opposition to the Dakota Access Pipeline and expression of Indigenous sovereignty and land-based environmental rights; the many examples of Blockadia pitted against fossil fuel infrastructure and extraction projects across the Americas, including mobilizations in Louisiana against the Bayou Bridge Pipeline, in British Columbia against the Trans Mountain Pipeline, and those in Ecuador against oil drilling in Yasuní National Park; and the proliferating European climate camps and the Ende Gelände (Here and No Further!) movement in Germany, where the state is currently threatening to tear down the ancient Hambach forest to dig for coal, evicting activists along the way.[41] More than mere anti–climate change protests, these are all pledged variously to the goal of reinventing forms of life dedicated to democracy, equality, and ecological flourishing, based on the refusal of the imperatives of capitalist growth and its market-based mechanisms for addressing climate breakdown. In other words, they seek to expand the social technologies of justice in the name of new climates of ecosocialism, cultivating environments of equality and self-determination as well as thriving multispecies life.[42] But despite growing momentum toward creative transitions, it is becoming clear with the ongoing development of geoengineering that massive resources and funding bodies are mobilizing that technology under the star of the neoliberal Anthropocene.[43]

Consider Breakthrough Initiatives—which has no relation to the institute other than sharing a trending term, one with alarming violent connotations, within the field of competitive tech development. It is one among many organizations trying to "save the planet," motivated in doing so by what some see as a $12 trillion opportunity.[44] Funded in part by Facebook's

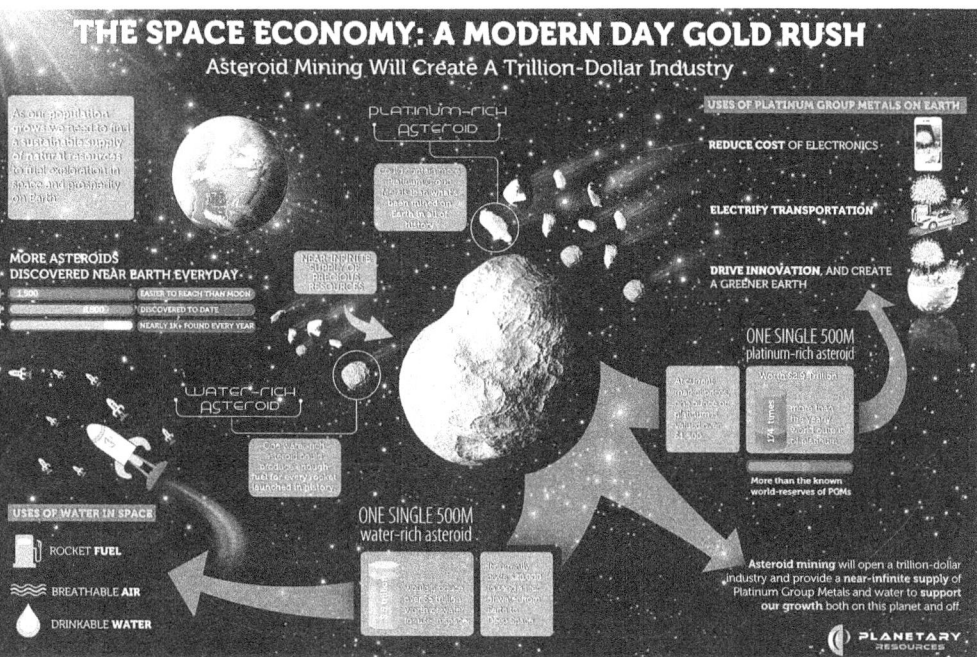

6.5 Planetary Resources, "The Space Economy," 2012.

Mark Zuckerberg and Israeli Russian venture capitalist Yuri Milner of Digital Sky Technologies, and counting the late Stephen Hawking among its collaborators, the project recently put $100 million into an interplanetary radio wave project to search for alien life.[45] Inspired by a techno-libertarian entrepreneurialism that derides the outmoded and bureaucratic state agencies of the Cold War including NASA, Breakthrough Initiatives is part of a growing "colonial futurism" premised upon the neoliberalization of outer space. It connects to the projects of Silicon Valley's modeling of "NewSpace," as in the rhetoric of Tesla entrepreneur Elon Musk, set on asteroid resource mining, terraforming other planets like Mars, and extending property claims far into the galaxy.[46] With the neoliberal corporate-military-state complex determined to occupy and settle the very space that many Afrofuturists have long sought in science and sonic fiction as an emancipated destination to escape colonized Earth, such starry-eyed fantasies stand to become grim off-planet industrial realities in years to come.[47] Yet if anything, this technoscience engineering formation parallels and joins the same forces that support the militarization and technologization of police functions, border security, and endless war. These forces also operate to expand economic inequality and generalized indebtedness, supporting the creation of for-profit prisons and security technologies, as well as the criminalization of protest, to the point where the state increasingly treats any opposition to this emerging global regime as terrorism.[48]

Other engineering initiatives focus their attention on Earth's climate, exemplifying how the same neocolonialist spirit haunts new-wave environmentalism. Consider SCoPEx, Harvard University's current $20 million "Stratospheric Controlled Perturbation Experiment," notable for its first-ever plans to test solar radiation management technologies outside the lab in the Earth's atmosphere, in this case above Arizona (representing a vertical politics of colonization above lands occupied by settlers long ago). Led by David Keith, Harvard professor of applied physics, founder and board member of the private corporation Carbon Engineering, and signatory of "An Ecomodernist Manifesto," the project is supported by Microsoft's Bill Gates and his Fund for Innovative Climate and Energy Research, as well as by the Hewlett Foundation and the Alfred P. Sloan Foundation (this last is a revealing beneficiary, considering that it is named for the longtime CEO of General Motors and indicating how fossil capital now fuels engineering as the favored response to climate threat and as a diversified strategy of wealth accumulation).[49] Notable as well for its funding model that joins university engineering and climate-science research to Big Tech capital, SCoPEx parallels a marine cloud-brightening field experiment in Moss Landing, California, led by the Joint Institute for the Study of the Atmosphere and Ocean (JISAO) at the University of Washington, directed by Thomas Peter Ackerman, professor of atmospheric sciences, with Paul Crutzen as a senior advisor. With $16 million in support from Gates and others, the project plans to shoot seawater droplets into the atmosphere from a ship with high-pressure nozzles, creating a solar shield to deflect sunlight, mitigating global warming.[50]

Recalling Achille Mbembe's diagnoses of creeping precaratization as "the becoming-Black of the world"—meaning the generalization of racialized dispossession, indebtedness, and loss of powers of self-determination under late capital—geoengineering's desire to save the world by *whitening the sky* dramatizes how completely detached color-blind technoscience is from the socioecological catastrophes currently occurring on the ground in the here and now.[51] While geoengineering may follow from love of Earth, its message is premised on the death of social justice, racial and economic equality, and democratic governance.

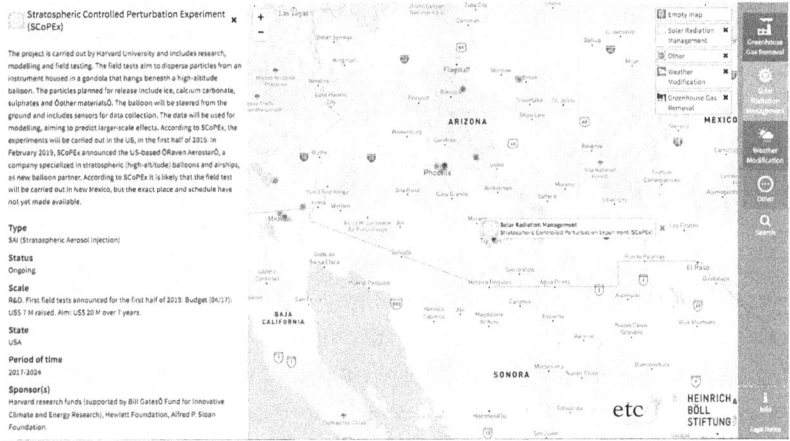

6.6 Geoengineering Monitor map showing Stratospheric Controlled Perturbation Experiment (SCoPEx), Arizona, 2019 (https://map.geoengineeringmonitor.org).

The go-to guide for Zuckerberg and Gates is Yuval Noah Harari's recent book *Homo Deus: A Brief History of Tomorrow*, which, tellingly, includes a chapter, titled "The Anthropocene," very much narrated from a pro-tech position (in fact Gates favorably reviewed the book for *The New York Times*).[52] Driven by an endless quest for "bliss, immortality, and divinity," *anthropos*, in this narrative, figures as ultimate and divine self-creator, for whom no challenge—climate change, agricultural failure, artificial intelligence, planetary hunger, even death and extinction—will be beyond technological overcoming, especially when matched to Silicon Valley capital. According to critic Joanna Zalinska, "There is a very clear sense in many of the science papers on the Anthropocene and their popularized media versions that the salvation from the Anthropocene's alleged finalism will come from a secularized yet godlike elsewhere: an escape to heavens (i.e., a planetary relocation), or an actual upgrade of humans to the status of *Homo Deus*. In both of these narratives Man arrives in the post-Anthropocene New Jerusalem fully redeemed—and redesigned."[53] In this regard, *Homo Deus* resonates with Breakthrough Institute affiliate and ecomodernist Mark Lynas's 2011 book, *The God Species: Saving the Planet in the Age of Humans*, itself an update of ecomodernist Stuart Brand's *Whole Earth Catalog* motto from the late 1960s: "We are as gods and have to get good at it."[54] It is easy to see how the likes of Zuckerberg, Gates, and Musk could be seduced by such delusions of grandeur. At the same time, the cost of this new world order, according to Harari's analysis, will be greater social inequality guided by technocracy, featuring an expanding useless class (formerly called the working class), a new religion of algorithmic "dataism," and the reduction of humanity to "biochemical subsystems" monitored by global AI networks.[55] More prosaically, the good—read: neoliberal—Anthropocene emerges in this and the Breakthrough Institute's narrations as the ideological mechanism of choice for accelerating geotechnology, specifically aiding in suspending contradictions between economic growth and climate solutions (another version of the "delinking" mentioned above). In fact, even climate change–denying Texas Republicans—part of "the most dangerous organization in human history, on the issue of climate change alone," according to Noam Chomsky—can get on board with geoengineering as a not-to-be-missed pro-tech economic opportunity, requiring no need to debate sources of environmental transformation or hold petrocapitalism responsible.[56] In the process, climate breakdown causality (and along with it, accountability and justice) is sacrificed on the altar of techno-solutionism.

The Trump administration has infamously defied the scientific consensus on climate breakdown, supporting fossil fuel deregulations at every turn (merging neoliberal extractivism with evangelical denialism, although those ties are beginning to fray). Its February 2018 budget, supported by many in the US Congress, included the first-ever tax breaks for new applications of atmospheric carbon capture, a key geoengineering technology (although this form may be one of the lesser evils, and even necessary for future drawdown, it still does redirect precious funding away from mitigating the causes of climate disruption). Meanwhile, the Hoover Institution, the Heartland Institute, and the American Enterprise Institute—all key conservative think-tanks—support this move, the latter hailing geoengineering as nothing less than "a revolutionary approach to climate change," where "climate change" seems synonymous with "regime change" in moving closer toward the new world order of *Homo Deus*.[57] Even more alarming is the current conceptualization by Keith and others of "counter-geoengineering," the tactical counteracting of the militarized weaponization of climate manipulation technologies as deployed by imagined rogue states or non-state actors.[58] This additional danger dramatizes engineering's ultimately ungovernable status and the potential for its destructive instrumentalization. Even more than biologically regressive, neohumanist and universalist, depoliticizing and neocolonialist, Anthropocene geoengineering may well prove most threatening where techno-utopianism merges with military unilateralism in proposing (and thereby helping realize) near-future global weather wars, going far beyond anything imagined during the Cold War.

THE ABJECT SUBLIME

The horror of those systems, expanding from depersonalized networks of political economy and technological assemblages to everyday acts of violence, are, as we have seen, devastatingly presented in *Love Is the Message*. Yet that's not all Jafa's video presents. It also powerfully intercuts those traumatic and traumatizing passages with scenes portraying the remarkable resilience, accomplishment, and beauty of African American culture—despite all—in activism, politics, speculative imagination, rhetoric, music, dance, literature, athletics, and, profoundly, quotidian forms of creativity. There is Martin Luther King Jr. riding in a car during a civil rights–era protest; Malcolm X speechifying; and Louis Farrakhan besting Mike Wallace on TV in 1996 during a *60 Minutes* interview. There are glimpses of Angela Davis from the 1970s, and of Black feminist scholar Hortense Spillers more recently. We see President Barack Obama singing "Amazing Graze" in Charleston after the racist shooting of Black churchgoers. Michael Jackson dances in the backseat of a car; gospel musician Mahalia Jackson sings and hugs Louis Armstrong. There are shots of Black Lives Matter protests. There are images of the Notorious B.I.G., Jimi Hendrix jamming, rapper Earl Sweatshirt performing. There is Serena Williams dancing after her 2012 Olympics tennis win, basketball wiz Stephen Curry in action, and legends Michael Jordan and Scotty Pippen celebrating on court. All of these, and more, intercut and interrupt the relentlessly unfolding images of anti-Black violence.

The positive and the negative, love and death, repeatedly and relentlessly oscillate and converge in explosive combination in this piece, proposing something like a singular Vine compilation of cutting philosophical import, or an Instagram feed of alternating soul-destroying and restorative affects. Jafa terms it "the abject sublime," an extraordinary rhythm of beauty and horror, issuing from a remixed archive of Black visual culture that seems infinite in its range of experiences.[59] For the filmmaker, this ultimately beyond-quantifiable record of being and becoming, of life and lives, a Black poetics in aesthetic form, stems from an ontological construction inseparable from the wake of transatlantic slavery, even while it unfolds in infinite acts of resistance and overcoming.[60] The video's description-defying vastness, its overwhelming multivalence, is signaled in Greg Tate's

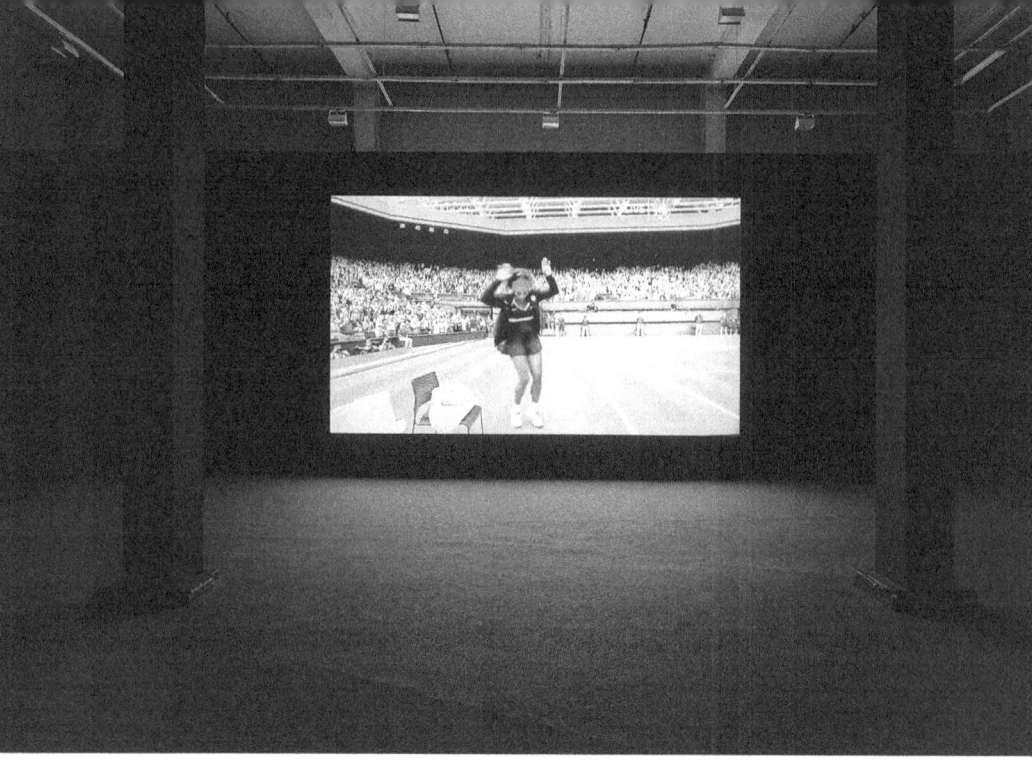

6.7 Arthur Jafa, *Love Is the Message, the Message Is Death* (video still), 2016. Digital color video, with sound, 7 min., 25 sec. Courtesy of the artist and Gavin Brown's Enterprise, New York / Rome.

appropriately transgressive grammar used in describing the piece: "The viral outgrowth of an aborted found-footage exercise, the 7-minute video is an alternately mirthful-cum-melancholic-cum-cardiac-arresting meditation on race-agency wrapped in a visually sermonic recitation of race tragedy wrapped in a nuanced and feverish exultation of diverse Black American lives at various states of collapse and regeneration."[61]

Yet even though the video offers an amazing and startling account of generative ambivalence and creative survival, and even while it also gives rise to encompassing hopefulness-in-action in collective moments of love, solidarity, ethical conviction, and collective justice-seeking, it simultaneously obliterates any consideration of extending or sustaining its world of horror—one of beyond-grotesque inequality, impoverishment, and violence that renders Black life and lives matterless by the state and its techno-human apparatuses. Unlike the Breakthrough Institute, which, as we have seen, proffers art and leisure as rewards for technofixed climate futures, Jafa's video grounds cosmopolitical magnitude within the vernacular instances of in/justice, of situated and embodied expressions that may be future-oriented but are intimately historically informed, which are dedicated to the reinvention of quotidian life, art, culture, politics, and mourning. It follows, then, that Jafa would extend solidarity to a younger generation of cultural practitioners and visionary thinkers by including reference to artist Martine Syms's 2015 "Mundane Afrofuturist Manifesto" in *Love Is the Message*. During her cameo appearance, she reads from her manifesto, which reprises the long-standing Black cultural aesthetic that draws on visions of a utopian time to come but in order to insist that it must be reached only by passing through the traumatic alienations, past and present, of racial capitalism. In other words, Syms's is a *mundane* futurism, founded in worldly experience where no simple time travel, off-planetary exodus, or easy shapeshifting is possible, especially if it means escaping from reality in an act of naïve utopianism. In this regard, "Mundane Afrofuturists recognize that we are not aliens," she explains while facing the camera seated behind a desk, responding to earlier generations of Afrofuturists, such as Sun Ra, who claimed to be from outer space and to understand it as an ultimate field of emancipation.

Jafa borrows that clip from Syms's manifesto that inspired the eponymous documentary shown online on KCET.[62] Over the course of its hour-long duration, Syms appears in various passages reiterating points made in her written account.[63] In it, she eschews the depoliticized fates of past Afrofuturisms, despite their important explorations of alien identifications within Black culture as allegorizing the historical experience of slavery's kidnappings and violent decontextualizations, even though these alien identifications have also come to symptomatize a problematic departure from current reality that may negatively reinforce racial difference.[64] According to Syms, classic versions of Afrofuturism have gradually sunk into hackneyed fashions, commodifiable styles, and stale pop-cultural spectacles severed from any radical imagination-inspiring collective liberation. Moreover, she warns against acritical escapism, as when "magic interstellar travel and/or the wondrous communication grid" lead to "an illusion of outer space and cyberspace as egalitarian," as if those places would not also extend earthly alienations and inequalities, as we have seen in the case of off-planet extractivism and neocolonial terraforming. For her, "jive-talking aliens," "reference to Sun Ra," and "Egyptian mythology and iconography" are all outmoded, and she calls instead for "a new focus on black humanity: our science, technology, culture, politics, religions, individuality, needs, dreams, hopes, and failings,"

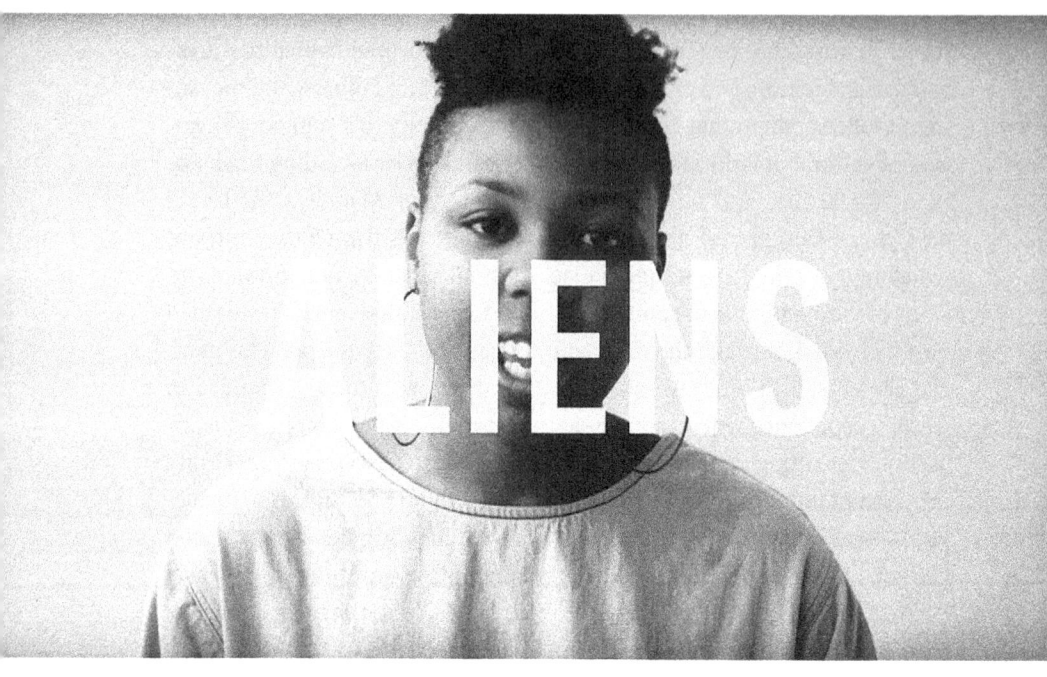

6.8 Ways and Means / KCET, *The Mundane Afrofuturist Manifesto* (still featuring artist Martine Syms), 2015.

explaining that "Mundane Afrofuturism is the ultimate laboratory for world-building outside of imperialist, capitalist, white patriarchy."[65]

While *Love Is the Message* conveys solidarity with the oppressed and excluded, both human and non, Syms's position rejects the simple equivalence between racial difference and the monstrous. In this vein, it resonates with what artist and writer Aria Dean diagnoses as the current conjunction of Afrofuturism with Black accelerationism, a superpositioning that entails both a catalytic movement toward "the end of the world" that is politically embraced (in order to stop injustice, to negate its abuses) and a revolution within and beyond the in/humanisms of racial capitalism (by inventing new forms of life, new futures, and new desires).[66] One can perceive precisely these in/humanisms—oscillating between abject dehumanizations and the sublime transcendence of those base circumstances in emergent forms of humanization as well as alien post-humanisms—as dramatized and materialized in the performative gestures, radical poetics, and scenes of revolutionary resistance re-presented and re-energized in Jafa's video. As such, a younger generation has elected to update Afrofuturism, or at least re-radicalize it, specifically via a double move that rhymes negative critique with positive transformation. Jafa in turn draws provocatively on these very dynamics, setting its complex energies to his own visual rhythms and "affective proximities" of audiovisual counterpoint.[67]

The goal here, for me, is bringing this vision, this aesthetic infrastructure of social critique and liberation, into explicit connection—and more importantly, direct conflict—with the neoliberal Anthropocene, and to mobilize the former to oppose the latter's threats of unjust climate control and extractive futurism. The ecomodernist agenda is, as we have seen, intent on shaping the world to come; and with deep resources and the political will to do so, it promises not only to set us on a track of unstoppable climate transformation for years to come but also to interminably extend forms of violent social inequality, including racial injustice and white supremacy.[68] If "capitalism seamlessly occupies the horizons of the thinkable," then we must move beyond those horizons.[69] Going beyond, we urgently need to invent and work toward cultivating futures beyond the world's end, an end that has occurred and will occur, and where that end is no longer unthinkable beyond the current dominance of sociopolitical and economic arrangements.[70] In other words, the challenge is to think, imagine, and create a world beyond imperialist, capitalist, white patriarchy and its technofixes of (false) socioeconomic sustainability.

Doing so, it is vital to ask, why should this challenge concern communities living beyond or outside the cultural traditions of Afrofuturism? While it may not motivate all who remain comfortably shielded by whiteness and benefit from the current narratives, practices, and economic arrangements that uphold its position and privileges, that challenge directly inspires solidarity among all those dedicated to tearing down the toxic machinery of racial capitalism and its climates of control. For only such a political composition of alliances that defines the construction of a diverse "we" is capable of transcending identitarian differences in the articulation of a common political horizon, one that struggles against the divide-and-conquer tactics of dominant corporate power and its oppression of all. In this sense, diverse communities—working class, white and of color, migrant, multiply gendered, socialist, LGBTQ, and Indigenous, and in all of their intersectionalist combinations—stand only to benefit from Black liberation. As Keeanga-Yamahtta Taylor writes, "While it is true that when Black people get free, everyone gets free, Black people in America cannot 'get free' alone. In that sense, Black liberation is bound up with the project of human liberation and social transformation."[71]

For those of us opposed to racial capitalism and its engineering technologies, we enter into solidarity because we remain committed to a shared world where "injustice anywhere is a threat to justice everywhere," as argued Dr. Martin Luther King Jr. That means bringing about an urgent disidentification from the white futurism, godly aspirations, and whitewashed Anthropocene entailed in the technosolutionist project of geoengineering. Expressing a radical justice-to-come with new politico-ecological purpose, Fred Moten, in a recent public conversation with Robin D. G. Kelley, has updated that famous ethico-political formulation of King (who, it should be remembered, makes an appearance in Jafa's video, and who consistently invoked the spirit of the indivisibility of justice). Moten posits the mission of contemporary Black studies as "on the most fundamental level to try to save the earth, and on a secondary level to save the possibility of human existence."[72] Kelley adds that this is a "project for liberation," a "transformative project," and, moreover, contends that if it does not mount a response to "the neoliberal, neo-fascist turn, then it's worthless." In equal measure, this project for liberation and transformation cannot but identify the overarching imperative of artistic practice today. If so—and I believe that it must—then art will name the practice of creative aesthetics that merges socioecological insight with political engagement in the hopes of not only saving what good we have left, but securing a flourishing and emancipated future for all.

THE GREAT
TRANSITION

THE ARTS AND RADICAL
SYSTEM CHANGE

With the rise of Trumpism, the US finds itself in nothing less than a state of emergency. We face a conflictual and volatile regime of postliberal plutocracy dedicated to corrupt wealth accumulation, fueled by patriarchal and white supremacist resentment. With repressive attacks on independent media and civil society, the empowered administration is mobilizing populist rhetoric to militarize borders, using lawfare to arm the courts with neoreaction and unleashing counterinsurgency forces to fortify its rule, dividing and conquering via a politics of racist, sexist, antimigrant, and religious extremism. Moreover, this political formation is joining and inspiring analogues in Europe, Asia, and Latin America in defining the current global ascendency of postdemocratic authoritarian capitalism (the Philippines, Brazil, Russia, China, Myanmar, and Israel come particularly to mind)—giving critics occasion to revive the term *fascism* in relation to our present.[1] Like those global examples, Trump's ethnonationalist fixation on domestic "greatness" is thoroughly extractivist—attempting to exploit all available natural and human resources in an effort to maximize elite profits at a time of grotesque economic inequality translated into racial insecurity and terror, even while he inspires (some) white working-class support with his "America First" rhetoric. Indeed, several unions have misguidedly backed his patriotic-cloaked rush to drill, mine, and build a wall, accepting his false claims that it will produce a new industrial age of fossil fuel–based prosperity. That agenda, tied to outmoded petrocapitalist industries, is global in scope and in some ways continuous with previous US administrations (with Trump being only the latest in a long line of "town destroyers," as Mohawk people refer to US presidents[2]). Constituting a contradictory politics symptomatic of today's dire situation of socioeconomic precarity, we are led to believe that there is no alternative to sacrificing the Earth if we are to have jobs, a proposal that is urgent to defeat if we are to transform conditions of life. Needless to say, this new wave of extractivism spells disaster for us all.

Adding fuel to the fire, current political shifts arrive at a time when we have entered an unprecedented geological interstice, when fossil-fueled climate breakdown has yet to deliver its full impacts owing to the temporal lag between anthropogenic cause and sociological effect. While to some degree already manifest, coming transformations—hotter temperatures, disastrous wildfires, spreading drought, rising seas, depleted resources, degraded lands and seas, species extinctions—will accompany and exacerbate social, agricultural, economic, political, and military crises, vulnerabilities, and inequalities. Not only will they worsen in the next few decades—the generally conservative Intergovernmental Panel on Climate Change (IPCC) has warned recently that we have approximately a decade before we enter a catastrophic cascade of world-destroying tipping points, complementing the World Wildlife Federation's report that the world's population of birds, fish, mammals, and amphibians has declined 60 percent already since 1970—but adding in the Trump factor, these negative predictions promise to strike with even more ferocity.[3] No doubt ours is the era of a great transformation—or what Amitav Ghosh has termed, provocatively, The Great Derangement—through which we (and future generations) will live, dream, and die with more or less inequality and violence, more or less suffering and injustice, depending on how aggressively we confront, or continue to ignore, the current crisis.[4]

We know that in any case climate breakdown will be distributed unevenly geographically, with regions in the Global South and impoverished areas in the North, including those with the least resources, hardest hit. As the worst wildfires in California's history burned through the land in 2018, rendering air quality dangerous, the critical difference was starkly dramatized between those who could afford the filters to breathe clean air and those without shelter who, unable to pay for housing, were abandoned to the toxic environment, even as their unhoused existence was in effect criminalized.[5] How will future analysts view this historically unprecedented situation, where our political systems are as out of whack as our ecologies are disturbed? When will our society recognize that our current growth-obsessed economic system—cloaked in the US myths of freedom and American exceptionalism—provides not the best hope for the continuation of life but instead the very cause of the politico-ecological catastrophe we now face? If culture designates the location where enduring social values are generated, where the narratives, images, and sounds through which we understand ourselves, our relations to each other and to the world we live in, are collectively created, then how can culture—or *cultures*, in their necessarily plural composition—contribute to sensing and comprehending the dangers to our present order? More importantly, how can we cultivate livable, desirable alternatives? How can the arts provide new perceptions and affects (for instance, those of justice, responsibility, and mutuality) through which life might be reinvented, avoiding game-over fatalism and commercial cynicism?

For some, these questions might smack of naïve utopianism, premised on a forward-oriented optimism that has itself been thoroughly corroded after decades of what Franco "Bifo" Berardi terms "the slow cancellation of the future."[6] In his book *After the Future*, Berardi explains that the psychological perception of and cultural expectations for a "progressive modernity" of gradual betterment of life conditions—shaped within genealogies of Hegelian-Marxist myths of Aufhebung and the teleology of Communism, as much as within bourgeois notions of techno-economic progress—have themselves fallen into disarray. Particularly in the face of the contradictory realities of endless war, growing inequalities, receding social provisions, state surveillance, and new media technologies of atomization and alienation, futurism appears today as an outdated luxury indeed. In his own subsequent writing, the late Mark Fisher connects Bifo's diagnosis to Jameson's earlier insights into postmodernism's "waning of historicity" according to the "cultural logic of late capitalism," whereby "neoliberal capitalism's destruction of solidarity and security brought about a compensatory hungering for the well-established and the familiar," which consumerism provides to the exhausted and overstimulated.[7]

Yet another reason Fisher highlights concerns production, where decades of structural austerity and the defunding of the arts and humanities have transformed cultural practice into the regime of making program-mable market outputs that mimic proven trends of success (witness Hollywood's endless stream of prequels and sequels, just as universities have increasingly embraced consumerist-oriented entrepreneurialism), with precarity threatening and punishing any alternative experimentation. Indeed, fetishized creativity tends to occur within increasingly privileged domains of elite arts education and commercial institutions, where specialist, individualist practice effectively privatizes art as a mode of luxury commodity production, justified as the seemingly only way to pay back mounting student debt (providing one response to the question asked by the collective BFAMFAPHD: "What is a work of art in the age of $120,000 art degrees?"[8]). In all these cases, the future—especially any vision alternative to the continuation of present economic arrangements—is effectively colonized by capital, which leads to the ultimate question: If we are concerned with life beyond the end of the world, then how do we decolonize what is to come?

BEAUTIFUL TROUBLE

Energizing some degree of optimism, if in a larger framework of legitimate pessimism given global events, we are also seeing the expansion of major social movement ruptures in the dominant regime in the current moment. These include the Movement for Black Lives, the massive Women's March on Washington and global #MeToo insurgency, the spreading sanctuary cities and No Borders resistance, Indigenous land-based struggles, environmentalist mobilizations (including recently Extinction Rebellion), and progressive artistic-activist formations of living otherwise—each of which is contributing to fundamentally challenging the extractive petrocapitalist order. And despite the 2016 US presidential election and global right-wing turn, we have also witnessed some undeniable gains, even if near-future pushbacks are already in motion: water protectors at Standing Rock temporarily stopped a nearly $4 billion oil pipeline from being constructed on their land and threatening their water sources in North Dakota, while rebel "kayaktavist" interventions associated with #sHellNo in Seattle's port contributed to the oil giant's abandoning of its plans to drill in the Arctic. Meanwhile, the London-based collective Liberate Tate, part of the international Art Not Oil Coalition, won a heroic six-year campaign to get the Tate Galleries to cut sponsorship ties with BP, and the allied group Not An Alternative organized a public petition signed by dozens of renowned scientists urging public museums in the US to sever links with fossil fuel corporate sponsorship, which led to the removal of billionaire oil-heir, right-wing philanthropist, and climate-change denialist David Koch from the board of New York's American Museum of Natural History. Additionally, radical farmers, climate activists, and diverse artists in western France—building on recent UK-based anti–fossil fuel Climate Camp occupations and inspired by the ongoing Zapatista revolution in Mexico—have been successfully defending their territory known as the Zad against the neoliberal state's plans, in cooperation with the French construction firm Vinci, to develop the area with a new airport, creating in its place a radical experiment in postcapitalist communing. The autonomous struggle complements international anti-state and municipalist formations in Rojava in Iraq, Baracha in Algeria, and Zumia in Southeast Asia. These various movements, situated variously between mutual-aid organizing, radical politics, and the arts of living, can be understood as diversely operating under the banner of decolonization, where "decolonization guides . . . efforts to become free through struggle—not as a ready-made program, but as a form of 'epistemic disobedience,' an immanent practice of testing, questioning, and learning, grounded in the work of movement building," in the words of the New York–based MTL Collective, itself involved recently in the successful grassroots campaign to remove Safariland CEO and teargas manufacturer Warren B. Kanders from the board of trustees of the Whitney Museum of American Art.[9]

These are certainly gains to be celebrated, even though they represent a small sampling of practices with greater or lesser stakes, assorted modes of engagement, and varying degrees of privilege and sacrifice. Yet all are exemplary of the spread of popular creative uprisings and joyful rebellions. Together they constitute growing massive resistance to the current political-economic impasse regarding global climate crisis as understood in its expansive socioecological dimensions. Still, even coupled with international movements for climate action, these formations are having admittedly all too little effect on the actual conditions of carbon-based environmental transformation under petrocapitalist governance, beholden as it is to the economic interest of the global fossil fuel industry. Measured over the last twenty years of UN climate conferences and associated social-movement activism, we have witnessed nothing less than the complete failure of climate governance to enact policies that would limit emissions to keep the Earth within one and a half to two degrees Celsius warming above preindustrial temperature levels. Indeed, CO_2 emissions are now more than

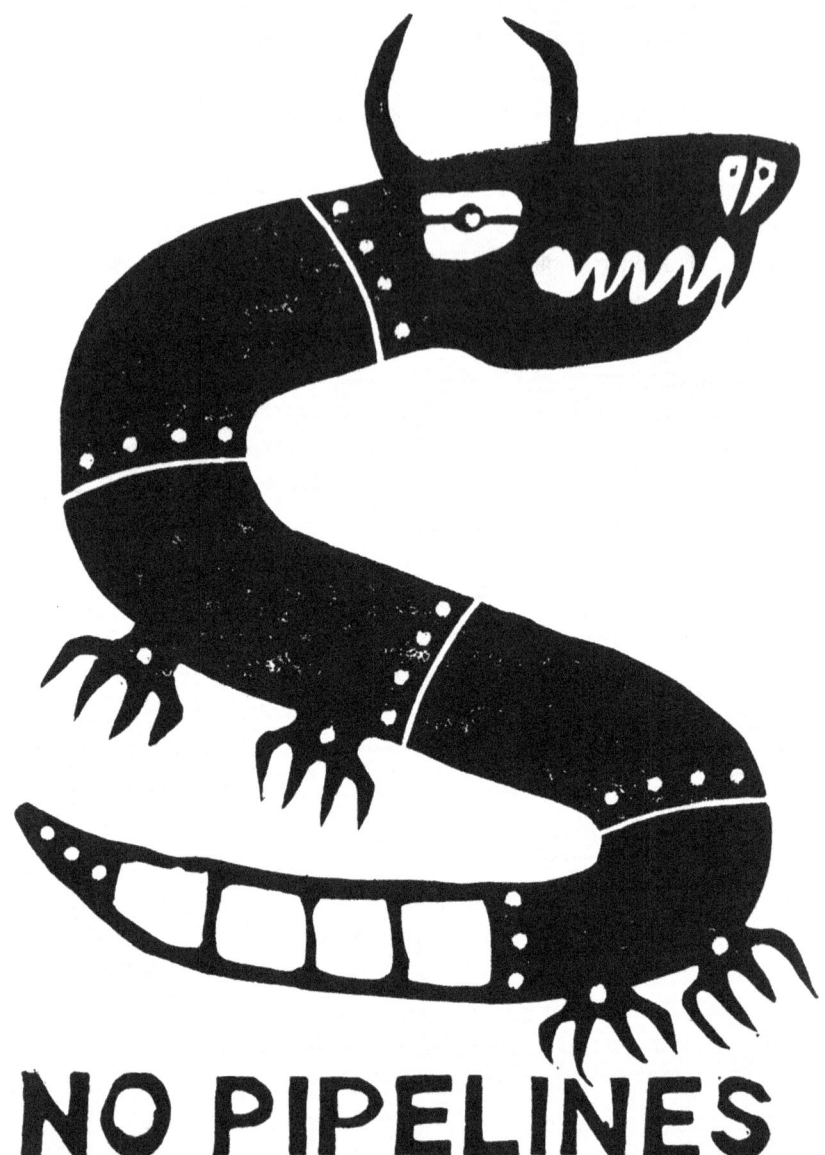

7.1 Dylan Miner, *No Pipelines on Indigenous Land*, 2016. Courtesy of the artist.

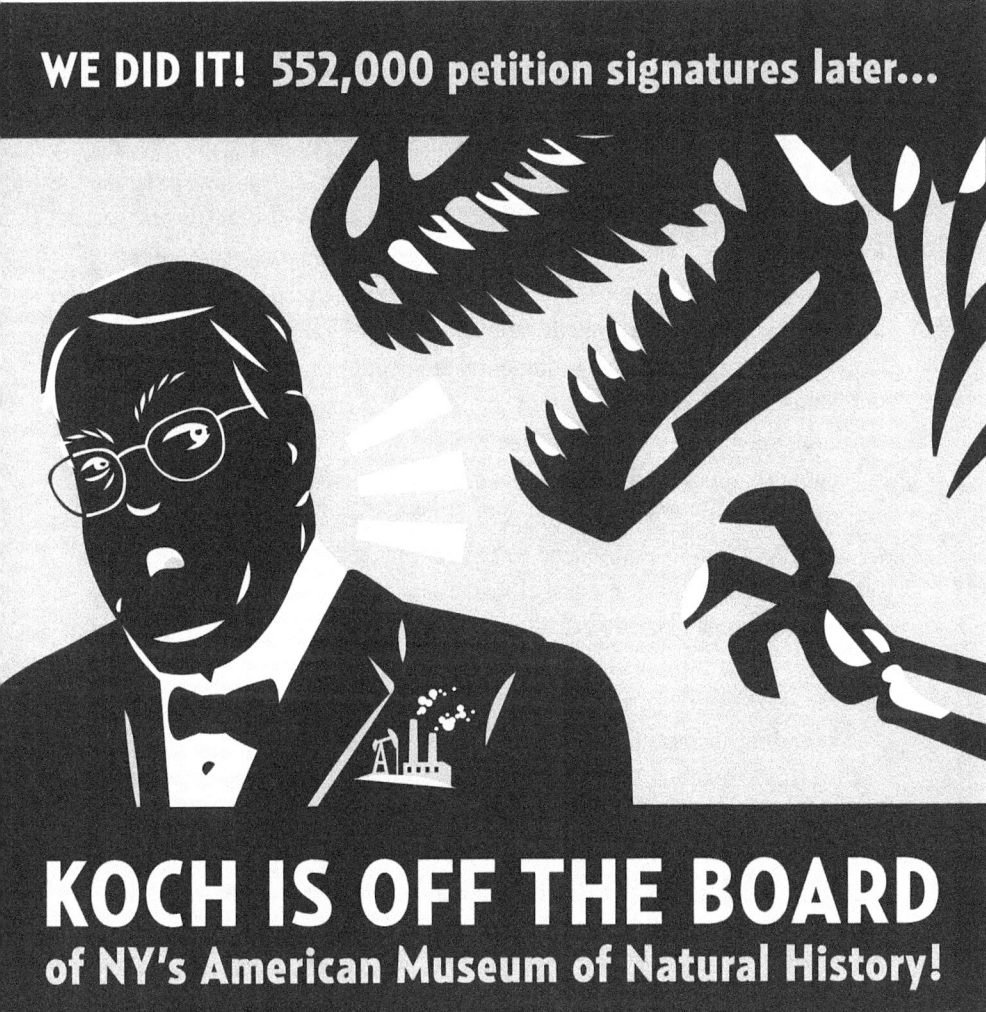

7.2 Not an Alternative, *Koch Is Off the Board*, 2016. Courtesy of the artists.

50 percent higher than in 1992 when the United Nations Framework Convention on Climate Change (UNFCCC) was signed at the Earth Summit in Rio by all UN members, who pledged to "prevent dangerous anthropogenic interference with the climate system."[10] Twenty-five years on, we face an insufferable contradiction between the yearly promises to limit global warming and the increasingly visible reality of our progression toward climate chaos, which, if anything, is contributing more energy to the slow cancellation of any livable future.

Unsurprisingly, the ultrawealthy are busy investing in million-dollar silos of escape in preparation for the coming apocalypse or in Mars terraforming projects, apparently not quite believing liberal policy makers who insist that climate solutions are compatible with continued economic growth. Meanwhile, organizations of scientists and physicians—not exactly known for their activism—have demanded radical system change, with more than 1,000 doctors, including 40 professors and several eminent public health figures, recently supporting widespread nonviolent civil disobedience in the face of the mounting environmental crisis.[11] Renowned climate scientist James Hansen disparaged the 2015 COP21 Paris agreement as a "fraud" for requiring merely voluntary contributions to emissions reductions, and subsequently appealed for nothing less than the construction of a new "revolutionary" political party.[12] Time will tell whether current proposals for a "Green New Deal"—supported by the actions of the ever-expanding Extinction Rebellion, Sunrise, and climate justice movements—will contain meaningful transformative effect or will instead succumb to the false solutions of green capitalism.[13] Nonetheless, the resistance is growing, with calls for insurrection sometimes coming from the unlikeliest of sources.

Defending an autonomous zone, blocking an oil pipeline, invading museums: this turn toward collective direct action and institutional liberation joins a long history of oppositional culture and anticolonial politics, creating what some have termed "beautiful trouble"—where aesthetic pleasure is wedded to politically directed disobedience guided by ethical conviction and radical demands.[14] The resurgence of joyful rebellion is not surprising today, given the circumstances cited above. When conventional governmental routes are shut down—corrupted by corporate, illegitimate, and antidemocratic influence—discontents are left to live according to a collectively determined ethico-political compass, which leads new questions to arise: How might current formations direct their energies in ways that are long-term, sustainable, and transformative, building on the gains of Occupy mobilizations, antipatriarchal and Black Lives Matter insurgencies, and Indigenous land and water struggles, even while they must operate at ever greater scales and in increasingly intolerant political environments? Given the limitations of representational politics, when many demonstrations seem to perform political emotion delinked from appreciable results within the corporate-beholden political process, how can activist cultures transcend what Elizabeth Povinelli notes as "the global expansion of explosive affect," which is only "intensified by the simultaneous expansion of the [expressive] individual via social media and the tight restriction of the same individual in terms of her imaginary socioeconomic future"?[15] Moving beyond what might be termed the current antipolitics of outrage, how can grassroots activist-led transformation lead to new forms of governance and ultimately to a transition beyond the current carbon regime? More specifically, how might cultural phase-shift infuse, energize, and direct new political organization, bringing militant and insurrectionary actions into relation with coalition-building and reclaiming an otherwise-corrupted electoral system?

Yet before we get ahead of ourselves, one important observation is that these resistant cultural formations are increasingly occurring outside the art-institutional system (even if sometimes directed at its makeover), which is not surprising given the increasing domination of the conventional arts by corporate wealth, what artist Andrea Fraser diagnoses as the art world's rule by "plutocracy."[16] At the same time, collective resistance is often derided or ignored as being merely activist, as if its explicit political engagement destroys any claims for its being dignified as anything else.[17] Activist art, or more broadly aesthetic practice with radical political horizons, thereby progresses deprived of the intellectual, educational, and institutional re-sources that would otherwise lend support to its engagements, covering over the ambitions of its creative world-building movements. But what if that is not our only option? What if these movement-culture practices— none of which are recognized or self-identified primarily or solely as art— were not simply slotted into the category of activism and dismissed as such by those in the privileged cultural sector but viewed, discussed, and taught as the most daring, bold, and courageous expressions of what art might be today? Certainly it would not be the kind of art that is commonly validated in well-resourced art institutions and supported by a generally elite and re-actionary patronage.[18] It would be something else entirely.

What if, moreover, those practices that do garner the greatest visibility in exhibitions and the media—typically (but not solely) dedicated as they are to individualist autonomy, self-expressive originality, duty-free creativ-ity, and visual spectacle—were to be seen as covering over a widespread cultural failure at addressing the most significant world-historical event facing contemporary civilization? What if, in the climate-changed future, those most visible art forms will be precisely the ones indicted for refusing or declining to engage with our contemporary state of emergency (itself an emergency of emergencies, where atmospheric carbon and colonization form two interconnected sides of the complexly entangled socioecological crisis)? I am reminded here of the argument Ghosh puts forward, where he reflects on the telling historical conjunction unfolding during the years of colonial and industrial modernity: the Anthropocene's emergence coincided with the establishment of modern fiction. Yet that conjunction was also a missed encounter. Ghosh notes how fiction, in failing to address climate change, has generally relegated the natural to oblivion. One can extend this insight to the larger coincidence of the Anthropocene with Western artistic modernism, premised on similar divisions and hierarchies that have broadly privileged culture over nature. Over the course of the nineteenth and twentieth centuries, as artistic avant-garde movements waged their campaigns toward advancing abstraction and medium specificity, they strove for aesthetic freedom premised on the complete overcoming of nature's contingency, determination, and finitude.[19] While that genealogy has changed course in recent decades—and certainly there are growing artistic exceptions to its narration—the engagement with ecology has been largely absent from advanced twentieth-century modernism and its histories. What if this nonaddress or missed encounter is part of the larger onto-epistemological problem of Western modernity from the point of view of climate breakdown, one dramatized further by the expanded perspective demanded by the Anthropocene? As Ghosh writes: "Indeed, this is perhaps the most important question ever to confront culture in the broadest sense—for let us make no mistake: the climate crisis is also a crisis of culture, and thus of the imagination."[20]

For just as the scientific basis and sheer complexity of climate change appears to wedge the latter's cultural address into the genres of nonfiction, as Ghosh observes, so too does it motivate an intensified relation to activism (often drawing on documentary and nonfictional representation) in the larger cultural sphere.[21] Yet both nonfiction and activism are equally liable to derision, both within the rarified literary institutions of what Ghosh calls "serious fiction" and by those who celebrate high-cultural forms of gallery- and museum-based art that is largely free of referential demands and political direction (though these latter are often wrapped up in irony, opacity, and contradiction). One limitation of Ghosh's book is that he does not seriously consider climate-conscious sci-fi—such as the writings of Margaret Atwood, Ursula LeGuin, Octavia Butler, Kim Stanley Robinson, N. K. Jemisin, and China Miéville—which might otherwise be considered as not only part but leading examples of "serious fiction." That said, he is clearly holding the gate-keeping literary institutions that maintain such genre divisions to account. But maybe it is the very conventional organization of culture—including the morbid continuation of these outmoded hierarchies that value autonomy and freedom above all else, in fiction and contemporary art alike—that has been thrown out of whack, and which represents further symptoms of the great derangement of which Ghosh speaks. If so, then with the previously mentioned examples of Blockadia, Indigenous resurgence, climate camps, and institutional liberation in mind, maybe we are witnessing not so much a failure of the imagination, but rather a structural transformation of the conditions of cultural practices—including a blurring of art, performance, media, theater, and architecture into world-building, social-movement formations—that are adapting to and critically negotiating the shifting challenges of life and living at the very moment when the violent reality of the Anthropocene and Capitalocene is sinking in.[22]

If so, we must then recalibrate our analytical methods and attune ourselves to these cultures of resistance, which are far from anti-aesthetic instrumentalized forms opposed to art's powers of creative invention. Rather, these are sites of aesthetic experimentation and engagement blended with emergent forms of life and infused with speculative energies, which are establishing new horizons of the possible in terms of what art can be. Indeed, I see the diverse examples cited above as wielding the "emergent strategy" of movement building by mobilizing "visionary fiction" for liberation, as adrienne mare brown argues in other contexts, and advancing "world-making through science fiction and activism," as Shelley Streeby contends elsewhere.[23] In doing so they are carving out pockets of justice-based futurity in the ruins of the capitalist present. At least that is what I am arguing here: that these formations are materializing and performing ongoing cultural mutations and disjunctions that, though easily misrecognized, rendered illegible or wrongly dismissed, are enacting the very ruptures most needed within our self-destructive petrocapitalist present.

WATER IS LIFE

The #NoDAPL protest unleashed at Standing Rock in 2016 represented not only a remarkable Indigenous convergence but also a structural transformation of the conditions of cultural practice. Most immediately, land and water defenders gathered to oppose the 1,172-mile-long Dakota Access Pipe

Line—commonly called the "black snake" by the Lakota people—designed to transport approximately 570,000 barrels of Bakken Shale crude daily from North Dakota to a terminal near Patoka, Illinois. The Sacred Stone and Oceti Sakowin camps were established in April 2016 by Standing Rock Sioux elders, including LaDonna Brave Bull Allard, responding to the proposed pipeline route that would disrupt sacred burial grounds (which were subsequently bulldozed despite opposition) and would cut under the Missouri River, threatening the water source for tribal members and for some eighteen million people downriver. The pipeline was eventually built in 2017. All would be impacted by the project of the Texas-based Energy Transfer Partners, representing only the most visible and recent large-scale investment in the ongoing expansion of fossil fuel infrastructure in the US since the battle over the Keystone XL pipeline, shut down by President Obama in 2015 and reopened by Trump two years later. Indeed, #NoDAPL connects with such struggles as #ProtectMaunaKea, #SaveOakFlat, the Navajo anti-extraction effort Nihigaal Bee Iiná, and the ongoing drive against the Bayou Bridge Pipeline with Louisiana's L'eau Est La Vie Camp in an area already impacted by the BP Gulf Spill in 2010. Like these other conflicts, Standing Rock is more than just a struggle over a pipeline. More expansively, #NoDAPL has figured as an expression of Indigenous sovereignty demands, continuing the battle against more than five hundred years of colonial incursion. As such, it also resonates with the broader aims of the Idle No More movement, founded in 2012 by Nina Wilson, Sheelah Mclean, Sylvia McAdam, and Jessica Gordon, that has energized and networked First Nations across Canada and the Americas in the collective struggle for First Nation rights, treaty enforcement, and self-determination. For Native American environmentalist and writer Winona LaDuke, #NoDAPL has represented as well a "battle for dignity and the future of a nation"—a claim that applies specifically to the Oceti Sakowin (often referred to by the settler-originated name "Great Sioux Nation") and Native Americans more widely, as well as more generally to us all, for a future of a nation (a nation of nations, a world of worlds, a future of futures) whose postcolonial character has yet to be realized.[24]

Over the course of the struggle, the #NoDAPL camps formed ground zero for direct actions and mobilizations around land and water protection, marked by prayerful nonviolent resistance to the brutal onslaughts of local and state police and private security acting in the service of the pipeline construction. These gatherings created remarkable and carefully improvised environments of collective solidarity and mutual aid, consisting of inclusive housing, shared food, free health-care clinics, and experiments in alternative education over the nearly year-long encampment.[25] Generating a multiplicity of representational, technological, and performative forms of decolonial opposition, the movement was also fortified by a wide array of militant protest graphics and print designs, mobilized in collective on-the-ground protests and spreading virally online, drawing on the creative resources of Indigenous artists and those acting in solidarity.[26] These insurgent aesthetic materializations were not simply reactive to repression but worked to define an alternative world of living together in support of physically defending the territory, the sociopolitical conditions of which were established on the basis of trust, cooperation, and solidarity, according to participants. Constituting as well subversive forms of defense linked to digital decoloniality that generated critical frames foregrounding the injustice of the pipeline and police oppression, Standing Rock's visual culture "mobilized individual acts of artistic expression, which politically align[ed] indigenous and non-indigenous protesters together in affective solidarity and artful resistance."[27] Yet the artistic component cannot be limited to these more or less conventional forms of protest.

Standing Rock also generated multiple modalities of unconventional creativity, including the collaborative processes of alliance-building, as when US Veterans for Peace, led by former army lieutenant Wesley Clark, son of former supreme commander of NATO general Wesley Clark, participated in a ceremony before a group of Sioux elders, including Chief Leonard Crow Dog, and movingly sought forgiveness for the US military's role in the centuries-long cultural destruction of Indigenous peoples.[28] Photographs and videos documenting that event circulated widely online. Meanwhile, dramatic footage of the encampments focused on their non-monetary economies of mutual care and support, in addition to documentation of the many courageous direct actions, including bodies locked on to construction equipment to halt their violent destruction, collective prayers resonating with drum rhythms, and frontline ceremonies that confronted militarized police armed with AR-15 assault rifles. Counterdrones, including the "Indigenizing technology" initiatives of Digital Smoke Signals and Her Eyes in the Skies, were launched to surveil police counterinsurgency and document instances of police brutality, subsequently used as evidence in cases of Indigenous legal defense.[29] To supplement mass gatherings, individual mirror-shields were developed by Cannupa Hanska Luger, artist and member of the Mandan, Hidatsa, and Arikara Nation, and were deployed as

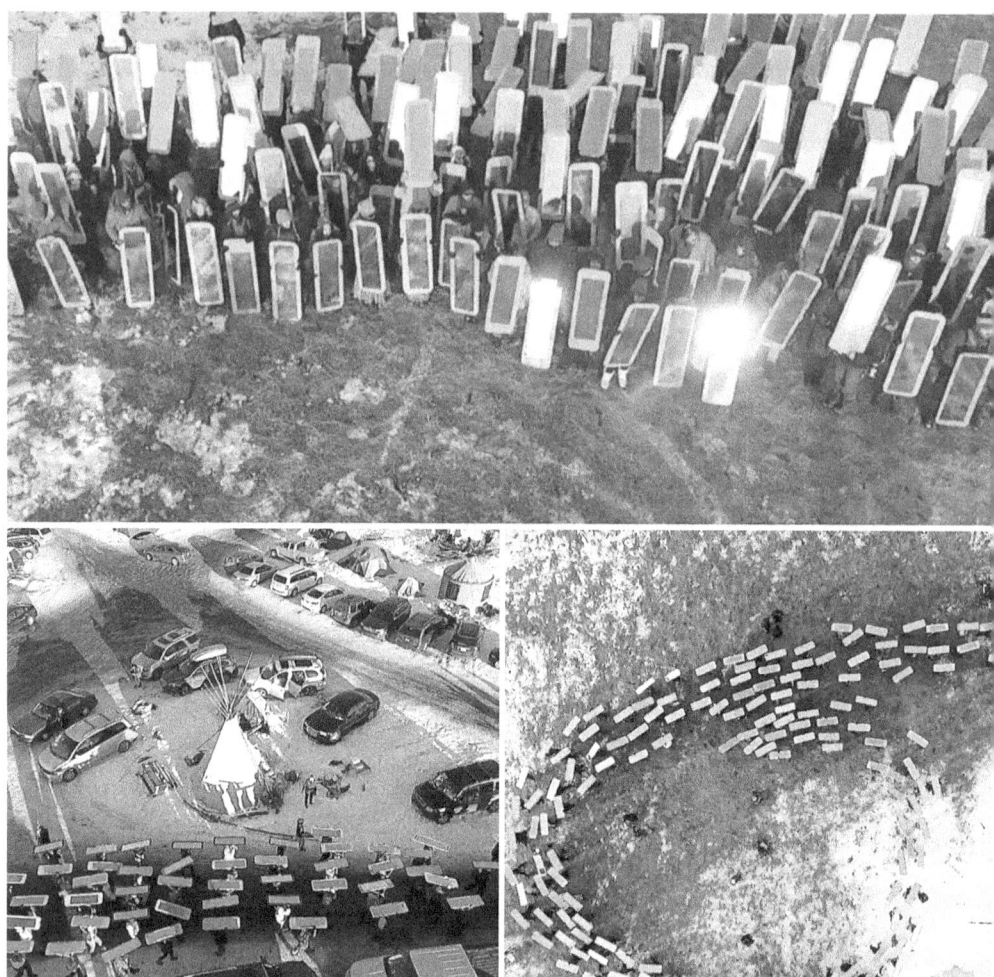

7.3 Cannupa Hanska Luger, *Mirror Shield Project*, Oceti Sakowin camp, Standing Rock, North Dakota, 2016 (drone operation/organization by Rory Wakemup). Courtesy of the artist.

tactical counterpower sculptures to defend water protectors from police batons and their weaponization of water and chemicals for crowd dispersal in extraordinary acts of settler atmospherics. Military actions drenched activists protesting nonviolently in freezing temperatures. The mirrors were also used to visually reflect the images of aggressive state violence back to the perpetrators in live-action image wars. These practices of Indigenous empowerment and anticolonial visuality produced critical shifts in perception and disidentification from state narratives of the conflict. They also promoted the insurrectionary knowledge—amplified in the widespread publicity of allied social movements such as 350.org, Greenpeace, Sierra Club, and the Movement for Black Lives—that this conflict, in which the bodies joined in defensive solidarity assembled against the forces of fossil corporate power, represented the continuation of the centuries-old Native American resistance to the practices of state-perpetrated genocide adapted now to the extractivist interests of the authoritarian capitalist present.

While each of these forms of collective mobilization and creative mediation are notable, even more so is the convergence of their visual, audible, and participatory forms, an aesthetico-political convergence that sought to rupture the symbolic order of contemporary state power. In this case, art, or more broadly aesthetic practice—designating here the images and sounds of collective resistance, decolonial justice, and self-determination—was integral to the process of cultural survivance and projective world making. At the same time, #NoDAPL was only the latest in a struggle unfolding over centuries of the colonization of the Oceti Sakowin, which, as Nick Estes (Lower Brule Sioux) has observed, has undergone "several apocalypses" over the years—including the settler fur trade's annihilation of native animals; the destruction of buffalo in order to starve Native Americans into surrender; serial violation of treaty agreements, including the 1868 Fort Laramie Treaty, resulting in land dispossessions and forced displacements; and the twentieth-century damming of the Missouri River, all of which has given rise to equally long traditions of Indigenous resistance to these and current US-abetted environmental catastrophes (where environment is sociopolitical as much biogeological).[30] The broad significance of #NoDAPL's diverse aesthetic practices has not been typically recognized, however, because, as Hanska Luger explained, "the media's general interest is in 'struggle porn,'" and "people have missed what is beautiful about [Standing Rock]."[31] What remains beautiful about Standing Rock refers not only to the forms of water protection the struggle unleashed but ultimately to the resurgence of people who have suffered a still-unfolding history of cultural destruction at the hands of settler colonialism, a conflict that is nothing less than cosmopolitical in its stakes. As such, Indigenous resistance over the last few centuries offers a road map for future collective liberation.

The central rallying cry of #NoDAPL was "Mni Wiconi," Lakota for "water is life," or "water is alive," which infused all the activity and death-risking conviction at Standing Rock, especially while the camps were active.[32] It also glimpses what botanist and Potawatomi Nation member

Robin Kimmerer and philosopher and environmental activist Kathleen Dean Moore claim to be "a story that is so ancient it seems revolutionary." They note that "the land is sacred, a living breathing entity, for whom we must care, as she cares for us. And so it is possible to love land and water so fiercely you will live in a tent in a North Dakota winter to protect them."[33] That love, that sacredness, that perspective, which views water as life, needless to say, is essentially different from the dominant capitalist valuation of oil, and indeed water, as a commodity to be possessed, hoarded, and profited from.[34] In fact, the beauty of this formulation of Mni Wiconi is, as Jaskiran Dhillon observes, "embedded within Indigenous epistemologies and ontologies that fundamentally challenge settler domination over nature and are inextricably linked to advancing decolonization."[35] Moreover, those beliefs are intrinsic to the ethos of "living well" within Indigenous practices of "radical relationality," which "bring together the multiple strands of materiality, kinship, corporeality, affect, land/body connection, and multidimensional connectivity coming primarily from Indigenous feminists" and are "deeply intersectional and premised on values of inderdependency, reciprocity, equality, and responsibility."[36] Indeed, as Kyle White notes, "the ceremonies at the #NoDAPL camps, expressions such as 'water is life,' the sacredness of the Black Hills, the leadership of women, and the many other moral claims about plants, animals, and ecosystems that protectors are making arise from the time-tested knowledges of Dakota and Lakota governance systems that preexist U.S. settlement."[37] If Standing Rock enacted the decolonization of water, then its ontology of being-in-relation both connects to long histories of Indigenous knowledge and reinvents emancipatory forms of being and ways of relating to one another and to the land, which offers a path forward to us all.

Toward the end of the feature-length documentary *Awake: A Dream from Standing Rock* (2017), directed by Myron Dewey, Josh Fox, and James Spione—its collaborative production exemplary of the intersectional alliances between environmentalists and Indigenous activists—the narrator sums up the lessons of the struggle and its future goals.

> What started in Standing Rock is now all over the world, and the battle wages on. Protest camps are being built to fight pipelines and fracking across the globe, to stop the Diamond Pipeline in Oklahoma, the Bayou Bridge Pipeline in Louisiana and in Florida. In Australia they are locking the gates to gas drilling. In the Amazon, Indigenous people fight

against the oil pipelines. In the UK, France, Spain, Poland, and Germany, in Africa and the South Pacific and in Asia, all over the world, water protectors and land defenders are rising up. We are planet protectors now. Global protectors. We have awoken. We will wake up millions more. Will you wake up? Will you join the millions of people that are taking their money out of banks that fund these pipelines in a massive divestment campaign? Will you join the water protectors rising up on the streets across the nation, in New York, San Francisco, Omaha, in every city in every corner of the nation, big and small?

#NoDAPL has opened an opportunity for the creation of transnational alliances across diverse conceptions of Earth elements, all critical of petro-capitalist extractivism and in support of Indigenous sovereignty and its modeling of land stewardship. Indeed, this may be the movement's most ambitious aesthetic act of reworlding: shifting perception and moving toward the revolution of forms of life, thereby making material and land-based transformations toward decolonial justice all the more possible.[38] Indigenous notions of water's sacred status, centering its living character and sensitive to its nonanthropocentric viewpoint, may ultimately differ from non-Indigenous environmentalist conceptions of the intrinsic value of elements as integral ecosystem components for biodiverse multispecies flourishing. Yet the two perspectives on divergent ontological natures nonetheless converge in the solidarity of opposition to fossil fuel infrastructure and its energy systems, petrocapitalist governmentality, and neocolonial domination, which threatens all. In other words, the convergence of planet protectors constitutes a site of the "uncommons" that Marisol de la Cadena foregrounds, which defines the challenge, and importantly represents the possibility of Indigenous and nonnative solidarity, that was realized (even if imperfectly) with Standing Rock.[39] This conceptualization helps avoid the problematic appropriation of Indigenous philosophies by non-Indigenous allies and accomplices in the shaping of an emergent world of many worlds, opposed to the hegemonic appropriations of capital. Indeed, according to Nick Estes, "for the earth to live, capitalism must die."[40] With his, and Red Nation's, proposed transformation of economic and ecological arrangements comes the necessary transformation of aesthetic modes of experience, and in that sense, #NoDAPL's accomplishment, even if yet to be fully realized, offers a glimpse of one possible emancipatory future and a vision beyond the end of one actually existing world.

The context and achievements of institutional liberation—perhaps most visible in Liberate Tate's successful six-year campaign, and recently in the work of Decolonize This Place—represent a struggle occurring within and around art institutions as well as public science and natural history museums in the case of Not an Alternative, all of which is distinct from the frontline Indigenous struggles for cultural survival in violent confrontation with the state-corporate complex. These groups nonetheless express solidarity with Standing Rock and likeminded Indigenous anticolonial insurgencies, and the movement for institutional liberation is similarly dedicated to a politico-ecological transition to a postcarbon future founded upon social justice and decolonial commitments. The difference is that they start with the emancipation of public cultural and educational institutions from petrocapitalist economics, sponsorship, and propaganda. More specifically, institutional liberation exposes and targets the cultural philanthropy—or "artwashing"—that grants corporations like BP, Shell, and Total a "social license to pollute," in the same way that others challenge the "greenwashing" by which industry manipulates the slippery rhetoric of sustainability to disguise their unsustainable practices.[41] The central question of institutional liberation is how to achieve transformative ends by mobilizing collective forms of creative direct action, defined by David Graeber as acting in an unjust society as if one were already free, according to one's ethico-political convictions, as if the desired future is now.[42] Operating within the cultural centers of Western state power and media publicity, these groups refuse the politics of representation alone by enacting unauthorized, or rather self-authorized, public performances of collective resistance to the fossil fuel cultural economy, where aesthetics as a politics of appearance is grounded in the insurgent bodies of social movements.

Key examples within their larger movements include: Liberate Tate's *Human Cost* (2011), the presentation of a human body soaked in an oil-like substance in a Tate Britain gallery so as to signify the biopolitical costs of petrocapitalism's uncontainable externalities; *The Gift* (2012), where the collective, in a surprise unofficial performance (and perhaps homage to Marcel Duchamp), delivered a 16.5 meter, 1.5 ton wind turbine blade to Tate Modern in an eco-interventionist offering, with the engineering part eventually being added to Tate's permanent collection; BP or Not BP's guerilla theater performances of counter-BP publicity enacted without permission before

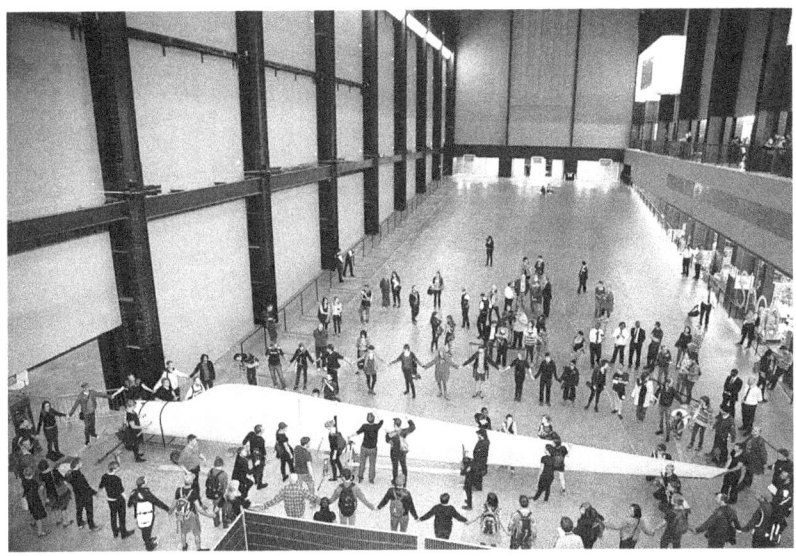

7.4 Liberate Tate, *The Gift*, 2012. Performance at Tate Modern. Courtesy of the artists. "On 7 July 2012 Liberate Tate installed a 16.5 metre, one and a half tonne wind turbine blade in Tate Modern's Turbine Hall in a guerrilla performance by over 100 members of the art collective. The artwork, called *The Gift*, was submitted to be part of Tate's permanent collection as a gift to the nation 'given for the benefit of the public' under the provisions of the Museums and Galleries Act 1992, the Act from which Tate's mission is drawn."

unsuspecting audiences at London's Royal Shakespeare Theater and the British Museum; and the coalition of groups, including Liberate Tate and Not an Alternative, arranging an oil spill intervention at the Louvre to challenge the flagship museum's sponsorship arrangements with oil multinationals Total and Eni at the time of the UN climate conference, COP21, in Paris in 2015. The alliance-building activities of these collectives effectively draw together scientists, environmentalists, artists, and diverse social movements, and point toward the formation of a "collective power" block that, according to Jodi Dean, member of Not an Alternative, "mobilize[s] in an emancipatory egalitarian direction, a direction incompatible with the continuation of capitalism and hence a direction necessarily partisan and divisive."[43]

With such divisive participation, *solidarity* becomes a key term, although an ever-endangered one, occurring in a socially impoverished context increasingly dominated by social media's info-bubble economy, precarity in the workforce, and ongoing attacks on organized labor. Ever more necessary to stem the tide of neoliberal social atomization and the mediascape of managed connectivity and enforced separation, solidarity, as at Standing Rock, proposes an embodied sociopolitical relationality of support and mutual care driven by shared political conviction across identities of difference, even if it is not wholly unified in every way.[44] Of course, theorists warn of the dangers of superficial alliances when decolonization becomes a mere metaphor, and, worse, it may symptomatize what Eve Tuck and K. Wayne Yang call the "white flight to innocence" when articulated by un-self-critical non-Indigenous activists without awareness of their own current and historical complicity in territorial displacements of Indigenous populations continuous with the long history of colonialism.[45] Similarly, Joe Curnow and Anjai Helferty have articulated the contradictions of solidarity, as when mainstream environmental movements participate inadvertently in forms of settler colonial behavior, even where climate justice activism displaces decolonial concerns and becomes a force of oppression.[46] But beyond these risks, solidarity remains an urgent instrument of collective empowerment, especially when "grounded in the practice of living," as the MTL Collective, the organizing body of Decolonize This Place, explains, "encompassing both daily acts of resistance, refusal, and sabotage, on the one hand, and economies of love, care, and mutual aid on the other," which extends beyond, even as it originates within, land-based struggles.[47] Solidarity also demands an intersectional approach that Angela Davis contends is crucial in the mutual support and transnational alliances of the scale and scope of movements necessary to enact meaningful global transformation, linking such groups as Black liberation struggles in the US, the Palestinian liberation movement, and Indigenous uprisings across the Americas.[48] As such, solidarity forms a fundamental element of the aesthetics of resistance.

While there is an important moment of negation in these activities of institutional liberation that assembles diverse participants, it complements the positive creation of an emergent shared culture of transformation. On the one hand, groups are resisting museum security and refusing to endorse its narrative, challenging the financial privacy claims of publicly funded institutions and opposing the extraction of cultural value to normalize destructive corporate operations. Artist-activists—forming an emergent hyphenated category of practitioner increasingly blurred and difficult, even impossible to pick apart—are intervening in the institutional context where the "exhibitionary complex" has been updated, moreover, in the era of the art system's plutocracy, commercial enclosure abetted by expansionist marketing and digital publicity, and strategic elite-networking philanthropy.[49] On the other hand, participants are also charging artistic interventions with the energies of social movements, reinfusing institutions with public interest and pushing museums into symbolic sites of what MTL calls places of "collective struggle" for "emancipation, equality, collectivity, and the commons," where the stakes of social well-being are waged against the narrow interests of financial elites.[50] Not only are cultural private-public sponsorship arrangements suddenly made strange and ethically questionable by these interventions; the everyday gestures and unexamined internalizations of such arrangements are consequently rendered intolerable— as has been the case with P.A.I.N. (Prescription Addiction Intervention Now), Nan Goldin's advocacy and activist-arts organization that has critically responded to the Sackler Family's philanthropic contributions to such institutions as the Guggenheim Museum, the Metropolitan Museum of Art, and the National Portrait Gallery, whereby they have artwashed their profits from their manufacturing and sales of the highly addictive and dangerous drug Oxycontin. Like Standing Rock, this movement preempts the ongoing reproduction of fossil capitalist culture, and more broadly the privatization of cultural institutions as machines of corporate publicity, decolonizing the future from its capture by short-term profit priorities, antidemocratic governance, and expanding zones of ecological sacrifice.

As Liberate Tate has explained, their practice builds on a long history of institutional critique in art—from Michael Asher's and Hans Haacke's interventions in the 1970s, developing minimalist and conceptualist approaches to broadly expose and challenge the art institution's often hidden economic functions; to Fred Wilson's and Andrea Fraser's subsequent installations, opposing the oppressive sociopolitics and white supremacist operations of cultural institutions more recently. Yet current practice after the Occupy movement signals a crucial difference from that genealogy, which generally privileges an exemplary individual artistic identity and tends to stay within the cultural economy. Instead it explicitly draws on the power of social movements in order to connect with their "instituent power": "activist-art's growing popularity marks an entry of social movement strategy into art's spaces" as well as infuses and draws upon the counterpublics and undercommons beyond and around them.[51] As such, institutional liberation goes beyond merely challenging fossil fuel sponsorship in this or that museum, even exceeding the liberation of art institutions in general as the ultimate goal (for instance, at recent events at the Whitney Museum, the immediate target of MTL's and Decolonize This Place's protest actions was the tear-gas manufacturer Safariland, whose CEO Warren Kanders sits on the museum's board; but ultimately it extended outward toward opposing the militarization of the US-Mexico border, US police departments and policing at Standing Rock, and the colonial violence of Israel's Defense Forces, which have all been supplied by that company's products[52]). At its most ambitious, institutional liberation joins formations like Standing Rock in defying petrocapitalism and creating "counterpower infrastructure," whose goals, expressed through a diversity of tactics and committed to international and global alliance building, are nothing less than the overturning of capitalism itself. In this framework, institutional liberation is linked in solidarity to movements like Black Lives Matter and Idle No More, and its mobilization acts in coordination with those struggles. As Not an Alternative explains, "institutional liberation isn't about making institutions better, more inclusive, more participatory. It's about establishing politicized base camps from which ever more coordinated, elaborate, and effective campaigns against the capitalist state in all its racist, exploitative, extractivist and colonizing dimensions can be carried out."[53]

AGAINST THE AIRPORT AND ITS WORLD

The Zad, while no art institution per se, is precisely such a politicized base camp, and it offers a more specific case of institutional liberation merged with land-based reclamation. At stake is a €580 million airport development slotted for the area near the rural village of Notre-Dame-des-Landes in central France. In deciding to realize its long-standing plans in 2008, the French state contracted the construction giant Vinci to begin creating a transatlantic "Great West" gateway to Europe, which would completely transform the low-impact farming region, threatening the area's biodiversity and the livelihoods of those who have lived there for generations.[54] Designated a "Zone d'aménagement différé" (zone for future development) by the state, the four-thousand-acre area was quickly renamed the "Zone à défendre" (zone to defend) by resident protesters, forming an increasingly politicized movement that has gained ground since a 2009 regional Climate Camp focused environmental concerns on the airport project. Now Zadists are intent on defending this region by political, juridical, media, and martial means if necessary.

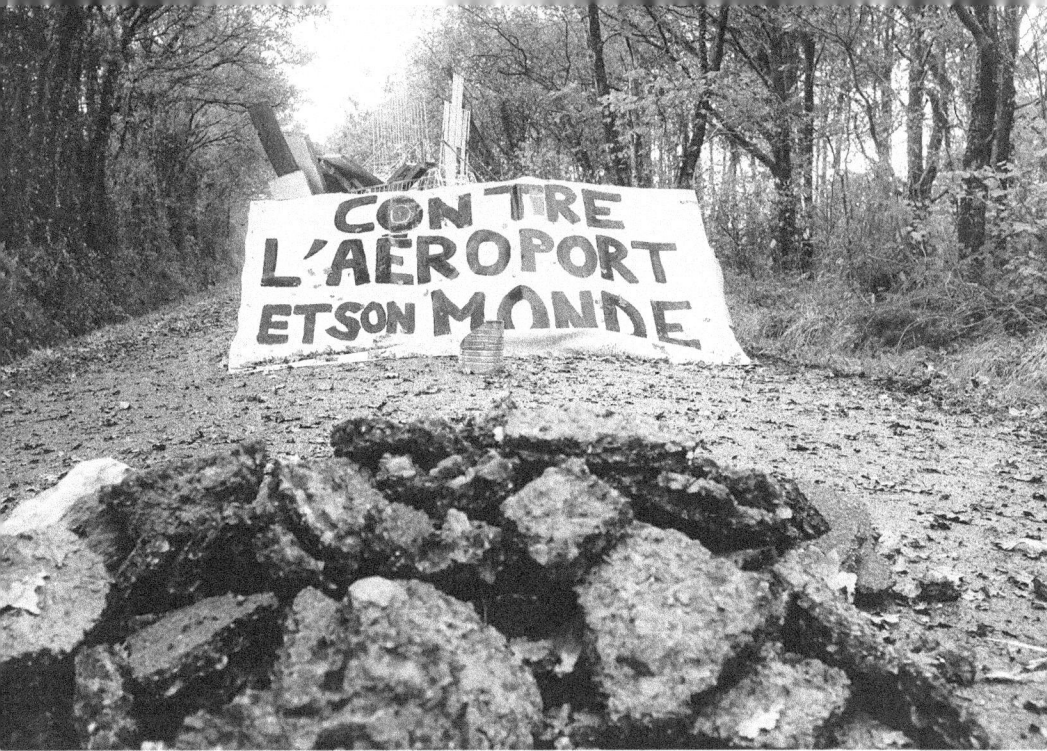

7.5 "Against the Airport and Its World," blockade on the Zad, 2016.

With the origins of the French airport development, and equally the political resistance, dating back to the 1960s, when the government first announced its plans, the conflict heated up once again in 2015 when those who live and farm in this biosensitive region of wetlands, fields, and forests were put on eviction notice. Since then they have repelled numerous attempts to clear the area by militarized police. Thousands of participants have joined the fluid, shifting, and growing movement, including trade unionists, pensioners, migrants, radical eco-activists, squatters, musicians, and engaged artists, all acting in defense of the territory and supporting its radical vision "against the airport and its world," as one road barricade, with dug-up asphalt, poignantly materialized the cosmopolitical scope of the struggle.[55] As the Mauvaise Troupe Collective, based on the Zad, explains, "The Zad is a space where different ways of inhabiting this world—fully and generously—are invented in the here and now. . . . It is a hope rooted in histories we hold in common, enriched by the momentum of tens of thousands of rebels and relationships woven thick by time . . . like blazing bearings for the future."[56]

Forming an experimental environment, the Zad includes much informal architecture—like huts, yurts, treehouses, and caravans, with recycled materials liberally shaped into a bricolage of spatial accumulations for inhabitation, gatherings, or blockades—that dots the landscape (although many of these were destroyed by the police during raids in April 2017).[57] Residents regularly hold "nonmoney markets" where fruit and vegetables, breads and flour are freely offered or exchanged in barter; organize collective meals prepared for celebrations; and guarantee that everyone has a place to sleep. With its bakeries, tractor repair workshop, brewery, banquet hall, medicinal herb gardens, weekly newspaper, flour mill, libraries, and lighthouse, the Zad operates as an ambitious social experiment in creative and noncapitalist collective living. Zadists publish their own books and texts, create images and videos, and maintain a website and a pirate radio station that offers programs in both French and English. Its collective decision making and communal practices contrast starkly with the authoritarian turn in French and European governmental politics, increasingly beholden to xenophobic fears and neoliberal austerity measures set within an unfolding crisis over migration and growing inequality in recent years. More globally, the Zad figures as a flashpoint in the network of Blockadia, glossed by Naomi Klein as "a roving transnational conflict zone that is cropping up with increasing frequency and intensity wherever extractive projects are attempting to dig and drill, whether for open-pit mines, or gas fracking, or tar sands oil pipelines," or indeed, to expand fossil fuel–intensive transport infrastructure.[58] Going beyond mere occupation with a short-term goal, Blockadia—which includes Standing Rock and connects to a broad network of international zones of anarchist organization—defines a revolutionary autonomous formation fighting for a society based on principles of direct democracy, gender equality, and environmental sustainability (much like Rojava, the Kurdish radical movement in northern Syria, with which the Zad expresses solidarity).[59] As an attempt to change everything, the Zad camp figures as a biopolitical assemblage, a convergence of bodies and signs, technology and media, spatial architectures and social networks dedicated to the reinvention of new forms of life.[60] Here aesthetics and politics converge in the construction of new worlds.

Counterposed against reified, commodified experience, the Zad's experiment in worlding dedicates itself to noncapitalist lifeways. These include shared collective living experiences, blurring the lines between political consciousness and the practice of everyday, intentional activities, and

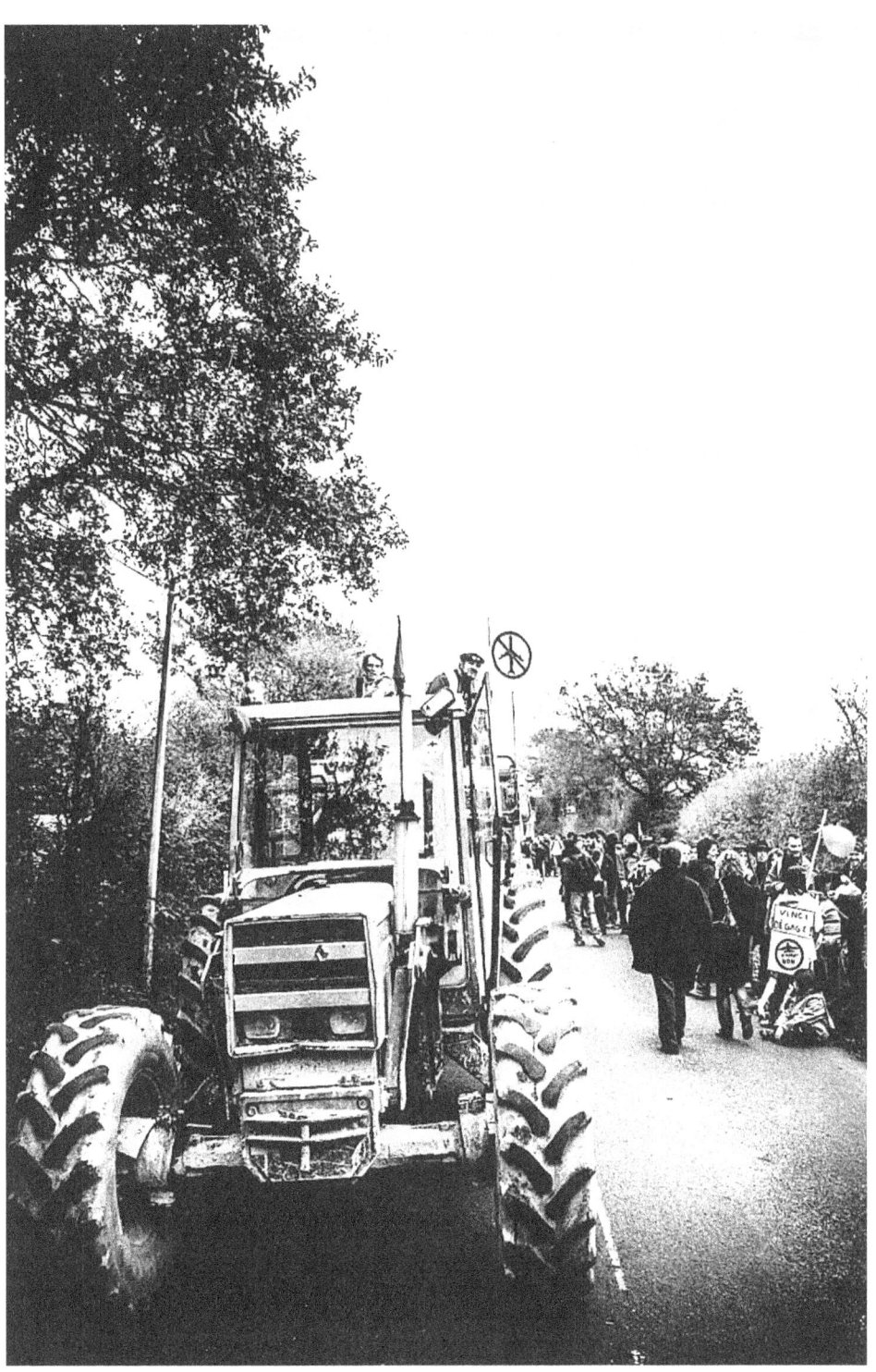

7.6 A tractor parked during a ZAD protest, fall 2012.

the blending of aesthetics with ethics, seeking to avoid contradictory relations between form and content, objects and process, representation and use values. The situated and endlessly negotiable beliefs in and practices of its socialist alternatives materialize a place of defense and self-invention, posed against the state's efforts at appropriation and extraction, defining an emergent site of sovereignty within the sovereignty of capital. The Zad's aesthetic practices unfold from symbolic forms of newspapers and subversive media imagery, graffiti and music, and assemblage and experimental DIY architecture, as well as include the creative invention of institutions of living, including the bakeries, gardens, libraries, community centers, and noncommercial markets mentioned earlier, all forms of autonomous self-governance reinvented with a difference from conventional examples. "Alternative ways of living with each other, fellow species and the world are experimented with 24/7," John Jordan explains. "From making our own bread to running a pirate radio station, planting herbal medicine gardens to making rebel camembert, a rap recording studio to a pasta production workshop, an artisanal brewery to two blacksmiths forges, a communal justice system to a library and even a full scale working lighthouse—the Zad has become a new commune for the 21st century."[61]

The Zad has paid dearly for proclaiming the end of petrocapitalism's world—an end not only to its spatial extension but also to its assumed infinitely unfolding futurity, an end to its ongoingness seemingly without end, and an end to a formation some have sought to naturalize as timeless. In doing so it has sustained cycles of state violence and police repression over the last decade. The most recent began in early 2018 when the centrist-right Macron government announced it was giving up on its airport plans (choosing to develop one in Nantes instead), which became a pretext to clear the Zad of activists who were thus deprived of their central grievance, seemingly leaving the zone's future in doubt.[62] While the airport development has been revealed to be politically and economically undesirable for the state, the self-declared autonomous zone proved intolerable, requiring normalization, most immediately by the return of the land to the individual-based regime of private property and profit-making enterprises. Police operations began in April, quickly demolishing a third of the zone's informal structures in three days with armored cars, helicopters, bulldozers, and thousands of riot cops, though leaving the rest otherwise intact, for now—an operation dubbed by Zadists as "revenge against the commons."[63] Meanwhile, one collection of groups authored a six-point plan for the zone's

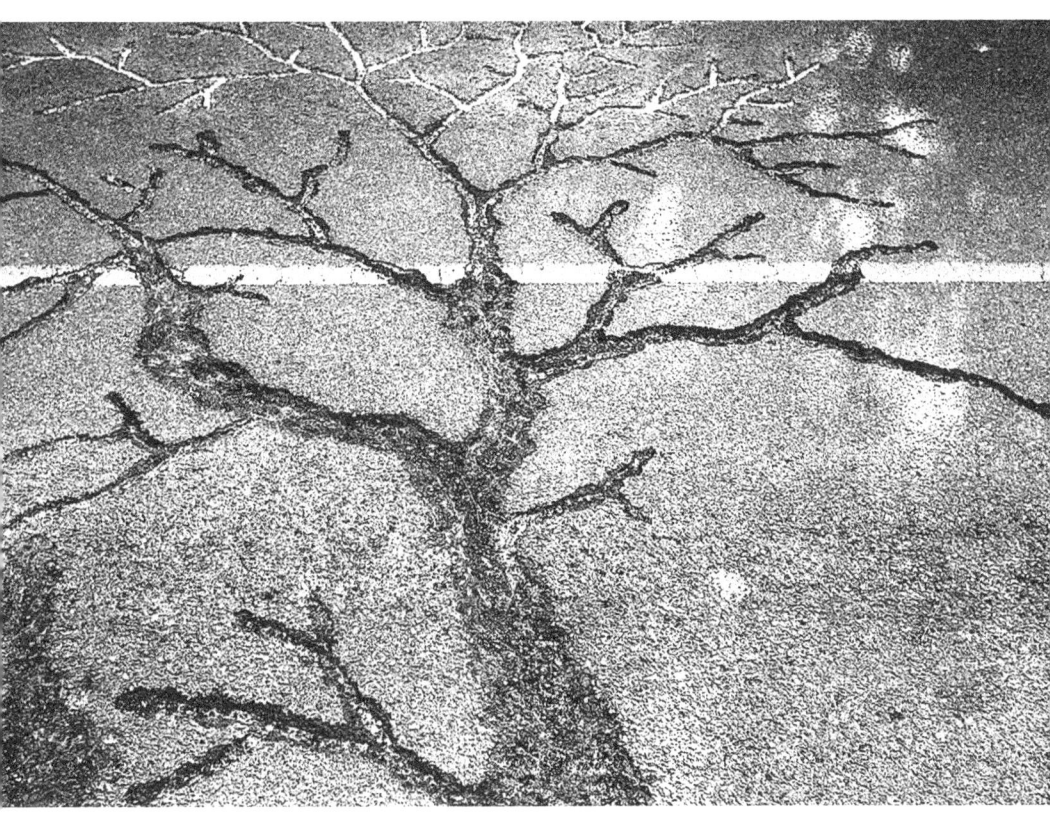

7.7 A tree relief is carved into the asphalt in the ZAD community, Notre-Dame-des-Landes, France, ca. 2015.

future, to be run as a commons together with rural farmers according to an "assembly of usages" (in distinction to commercial exchange value and its world of financialization), seeking to operate strategically within the state's framework but on a minimal basis in order for the Zad to survive.[64]

As such, the Zad undertakes the daily practice of creative disobedience—perhaps with elements of strategic uncivil obedience mixed in—which constitutes the zone's particular reinvention of the arts of living. As Martin Legall points out, the formation echoes the aims and strategy of the Invisible Committee (IC), the French anarchist collective (some of whom are based on the Zad) that advocates the arrest of capital at sites of opportunistic disruption rather than targeting national assemblies and political bodies directly.[65] Like the US group Deep Green Resistance, the IC calls for the formation of underground collectives such as communes, affinity groups, and strike forces to advance anticapitalist revolution in moments of political, social, and environmental crisis. Indeed, as the Zadists have it (echoing long-standing Zapatista strategy), "We call for the spirit of the Zad to continue to spread, taking a unique path every time, but with the desire to open cracks everywhere. Cracks in the frenzy of security measures, cracks in the ecological disaster, cracks in the tightening border regimes, cracks in the omnipotent surveillance, cracks in a world that puts everything up for sale."[66] Rather than advocating an exodus or disengagement with the world (as some communes of the past have done), the Zad actively connects directly with social movements beyond itself (including the still unfolding and politically indeterminate Gilets Jaunes, or "yellow vests" movement in France, rebelling against a newly proposed fuel tax, where the state's ostensible environmental policy not only fails to address growing economic inequality in the country but appears to be a way of extending and greenwashing disparities).[67] Intervening in capital's temporality of seeming infinite growth, the Zad mobilizes past potential futures—from the "communal luxury" claims of the nineteenth-century Paris Commune to anticolonial May '68 to the alter-globalization, anti-IMF Battle in Seattle—as a radical inheritance to inspire the creative and just reorganization of life now and in years to come.[68]

THE GREAT TRANSITION

With each new scientific report and critical analysis on the declining conditions of our intertwined political, economic, and natural systems, it is becoming clear that the leading challenge of our time is not only how to survive and make life livable in a world of capitalist ruins but how to stop the ongoing progression toward ever-greater forms of destruction while we still have the chance.[69] How do we advance the ethical principles of justice within the flourishing of life as much as on the way to extinction? These are the challenges that are driving the contemporary transformations of cultural engagements toward the practice of emancipation, toward the social-movement-based arts of living, and toward the merger of ethics and aesthetics, all premised on the delinking of the radical imagination from capitalism's stranglehold on futurity. Together, these transformations—which respond directly to anxious concerns about the supposed failure of culture to address climate breakdown—underline the imperative to enact a radical system change that will interrupt the seemingly inevitable movement toward an increasingly deranged world.

The engagements outlined in this chapter, in sum, are not simply oppositional to art, just as they are surely not collapsible into its conventional category. Instead, they draw on a diversity of aesthetic approaches in their ambitious redefinition of the possibilities and limits of what creative world making can mean today. In this context, radical aesthetic practices, emancipated from institutional enclosure and structures of commodification, form ways to reorganize the sensible realms of experience, rearranging in turn our perceptions and desires, which carry the capacity to reinvent the material, sociopolitical, and ecological conditions of life itself.[70] All are invested in generative alliance-building and tie art-making to collective solidarity and transformation; all are practicing a concerted unlearning of our relations to the elements as mere commodities, a rejection of public institutions as privatized spaces of corporate propaganda, and refusing community (dis)organization as ruled by the narratives of competitive individualism, market logic, and the militarization of everyday life. With Standing Rock, institutional liberation, and the Zad, we encounter the collective construction of the arts of living that cherish nature's intrinsic, relational values; that infuse a reimagined, postcolonial commons; that support self-determination and social justice; and that cultivate collective joy and love released from extractive instrumentality, initiating a creative break from the deathly economy of petrocapitalist maldevelopment.

Producing a rift zone between our current politico-economic disorder and available alternatives, these creative practices unleash "beautiful trouble," meaning, on the one hand, a radical reconfiguration of the otherwise conventional notion of beauty, revaluing it to name creative acts that contest capitalist realism, based on the idea that there is no alternative to the ruling economic arrangements.[71] On the other hand, beautiful trouble joins aesthetics to ethics, and social justice to climate solutions, in producing disobedient ruptures from the dominant regime. As such, its creativity is measured in temporal expansiveness, put to task against the slow cancellation of the future. Indeed, beautiful trouble generates "futurability," an ability to imagine futurity, to envision coming worlds worth living in, doing so from within the seemingly foreclosed current circumstances of agency, political composition, and imagination, which otherwise appear colonized by capital.[72] If utopian vision itself has been largely if not completely marked by instrumental, economic reason, then the present battle has shifted to reclaiming futurity itself. From the struggles of the oppressed, from the ashes of past destruction, a future of collective ongoingness and livability may be born. The above examples are, of course, only the most visible and mediagenic flashpoints of oppositional imagination, assembly, and (de)occupation practiced in recent years, but they form part of a rising tide of massive opposition wherein we witness the formation and growth of revolutionary energies.

Grounded in scientific consensus as much as political thought, recognizing the unfolding threat of disastrous socioecological breakdown—including and compounding all the other catastrophes and apocalypses experienced over the course of colonial and capitalist modernity—is undoubtedly the best motivation for a "Great Transition." Indeed, it is called for by leading voices within diverse and leading social movements to designate a systemic shift in social, political, and economic life toward a socially just, postcarbon, multispecies future.[73] According to ongoing formulations, correlating with visions for a radical Green New Deal joined to a decolonial Red Deal, the plan envisions a decarbonized nonextractive economy fueled by low-impact technologies and renewable energies, working in tandem with a global democratized politics that will eliminate poverty, ensuring a just transition for all workers, low-income communities, rural and urban, those of color, LGBTQ groups, and Indigenous peoples. For Kali Akuno, of the inspirational project Cooperation Jackson:

> This means highlighting grassroots, independent solutions in front-line communities: programs centering on reparations, decolonization and building a democratic economy through the advancement of the social and solidarity economy. For us at Cooperation Jackson, this is linked to a program of eco-socialist development. We are going to have to ultimately do a major overhaul in how things are produced, distributed, consumed and recycled back into the natural resource systems that we depend on. If we don't think about just transition in a long-term, holistic way, we are missing the point. To think we can make some tweaks to capitalism or expansive "carbon neutral" production—that is also missing the point. To address our deep problems, we have to shift wealth and power—it has to be moved from the United States and Europe to the rest of the world.[74]

To enact such a paradigm shift in fundamental desires and values may take generations to accomplish but will begin with the resources of past struggles as set within the emergency and deeply conflictual conditions of the present. With these creative ecologies of collective resistance fueled by radical imagination, we experience just that: new combinations of images and stories, music and participatory arts, solidarities and sacrifices, wherein this Great Transition has already been initiated. Now is the time to push this growing resistance further, advancing it into common sense in order for it to empower diverse allies, accomplices, and would-be participants to transform the world as we know it, so that an equally transformed "we" can survive beyond the world's end.

ACKNOWLEDGMENTS

A book is never written alone. In world-ending times of crisis, one's family, friends, and comrades are more valuable than ever, especially when one must become many. Thanks first and foremost to all the artists and practitioners whose compelling work and in some cases friendships and invaluable shared conversations have inspired my writing: John Akomfrah, Angela Melitopoulos, Angela Anderson, Jennifer Allora and Guillermo Calzadilla, Ursula Biemann, Adrian Lahoud, Collectif Argos, Eyal Weizman and Forensic Architecture, Ai Weiwei, Audrey Quinn and Jackie Roche, Charles Heller and Lorenzo Pezzani of Forensic Oceanography, Teddy Cruz and Fonna Forman, Elle Flanders and Tamira Sawatzky of Public Studio, Terri-Lynn Williams-Davidson, Laura Gustafsson and Terike Haapoja, Arthur Jafa, Martine Syms, Not an Alternative's Beka Economopoulos, Jason Jones, Steve Lyons, and Jodi Dean, Liberate Tate and Mel Evans, Dylan Miner, Cannupa Hanska Luger, Amin Husain and Nitasha Dhillon of MTL and Decolonize This Place, and John Jordan and Isabelle Frémeaux of the Laboratory of Insurrectionary Imagination and the Zad.

Infinite gratitude is owed to my many intellectual, scholarly, artistic, activist, and editorial interlocutors, too many really to name, who joined me in ongoing conversations about political ecology and aesthetic practice, including Emily Eliza Scott, Subhankar Banerjee, Ashley Dawson, Yates McKee, Ros Gray, Shela Sheikh, Fazal Sheikh, Susan Schuppli, Sarah James, Julia Bryan-Wilson, Alex Alberro, Emily Pethick, Nils Norman, Oreet Ashery, Iftikhar Dadi, Nabil Ahmed, Alessandro Zagato and Natalia Arcos of

GIAP (Grupo de Investigación en Arte y Política), Daniel Quiles, Béatrice Joyeux-Prunel, Eric de Bruyn, Sven Lütticken, Gopal Dayaneni of Movement Generation, Terry Smith, John Foran, Terri Weisman, Gene Moreno, Anton Vidokle, and Kaye Cain-Nielsen. I particularly appreciate their always and oftentimes tacitly reminding me that we are in this together. For their ongoing friendship, London-based hospitality, and discussions with endlessly expanding intellectual horizons, I thank Anjalika Sagar and Kodwo Eshun of The Otolith Group.

At UC Santa Cruz, I am fortunate to have many amazing and inspiring friends and colleagues, whose own work, writing, and shared discussions and the intersection of politics, theory, and cultural practice have been invaluable to me, including Donna Haraway, Karen Barad, Anna Tsing, Rachel Nelson and (formerly) John Weber of UCSC's Institute of the Arts and Sciences, Laurie Palmer, Jennifer González, Warren Sack, Beth Stephens, Annie Sprinkle, Derek Murray, Soraya Murray, Max Tomba, Banu Bargu, Anna Friz, and Miriam Greenberg. Many thanks equally to my UCSC colleagues Hunter Bivens, Mayanthi Fernando, Debbie Gould, and Matt O'Hara, who collaborated on and joined me for the Mellon Sawyer Seminar, *Beyond the End of the World*, which I directed at UC Santa Cruz, 2018–21, and which has also informed and benefitted this book. Much appreciation is due to Chessa Adsit-Morris, and the many participants in the Center for Creative Ecologies reading group, for the probing discussions and consideration of social-justice ecology and diverse aesthetic practices. Many thanks go as well to all the grad students, predocs, and postdocs whose work I have been involved with one way or another as supervisor, advisor, and/or examiner, and from whom I have learned much, including Amber Hickey, Sintia Issa, Zoe Weldon-Yockim, Matthew Harrison Tedford, Alex Moore, Elia Vargas, Gabriel Mindel, Martabel Wasserman, Siobhan Angus, Timothy Firstnau and Andrea Steves, Alison Dean, Ricardo Chaves, Chiara Sgaramella, Maija Lassila, Siobhan Angus, Isabelle Carbonell, and Hannah Martin.

A number of writers, thinkers, theorists, and activists have enabled this book's approach, political engagement, and conceptualization, including Naomi Klein, Beth Povinelli, Christina Sharpe, Fred Moten, Achille Mbembe, Eduardo Viveiros de Castro, Keeanga-Yamahtta Taylor, Isabelle Stengers, Kyle Powys Whyte, Zoe Todd, Kathryn Yusoff, Nick Estes, Melanie Yazzie, and Marisol de la Cadena. I deeply appreciate the various worlds they have opened up. I also thank my comrades in DSA (Democratic

Socialists of America) and particularly members of its Ecosocialist Working Group in Santa Cruz, who have helped me keep my theoretical discourse connected to on-the-ground struggles, sustained by solidarity and the collective practice of radical politics.

The book's chapters have been substantially revised from earlier publication, and much appreciation goes to all of the editors I have been fortunate to work with, and who contributed immeasurably to the improvement of my writing in all of its dimensions. Chapter 1, "Feeding the Ghost: John Akomfrah's *Vertigo Sea*," first appeared in *John Akomfrah: Signs of Empire*, ed. Thea Ballard with Dana Kopel (New Museum, 2018); chapter 2, "Blackout: The Necropolitics of Extraction," appeared in *Dispatches* 001 (October 1, 2018), edited by Gean Moreno; chapter 3, "The Visual Politics of Climate Refugees" was included in *Photography and Migration*, ed. Tanya Sheehan (New York: Routledge, 2018); chapter 4, "Gaming the Environment: On the Media Ecology of Public Studio" appeared in *Public Studio*, ed. Philip Monk (Toronto: Art Gallery of York University, 2019); chapter 5, "Animal Cosmopolitics: The Art of Gustafsson&Haapoja" was published in *Center for Creative Ecologies* journal, August 2016; chapter 6, "To Save a World: Geoengineering, Conflictual Futurisms, and the Unthinkable" was first written for in *eflux* Journal 94 (October 2018); and chapter 7, "The Great Transition: The Arts and Radical System Change" appeared in *e-flux* Journal (April 2017).

At Duke University Press, I am deeply indebted to Ken Wissoker for his ongoing support as a visionary commissioning editor dedicated to politically engaged and urgent scholarship, and for the many discussions we have had over the years. Appreciation goes to Nina Foster for her assistance, to Susan Albury for project managment, to Aimee Harrison for design, and to the anonymous readers for their incisive, ultimately helpful criticism. I thank UCSC's Arts Division for their support and the Center for Cultural Studies for its vibrant discussions. Finally, I express my heartfelt appreciation to family members—including Sandra Swanson, Kristin Demos, and Jim Demos—for their longstanding encouragement. My deepest gratitude—intellectually, politically, emotionally, and more—goes to my partner Joy Schendledecker, and to my daughters Zoë and Leila.

NOTES

INTRODUCTION

1. Déborah Danowski and Eduardo Viveiros de Castro, *The Ends of the World*, trans. Rodrigo Nunes (Cambridge: Polity, 2017). While this book was researched and written before the coronavirus, with its final editing completed during the shelter-in-place orders of April and May 2020, its argument, sensitive to world-collapsing events, in many ways anticipated the outbreak, including the cruel biopolitics of pandemic governance, especially in the US, where economic priorities and corporate profits have largely eclipsed concerns for public health and social welfare. While whatever comes next is unknown, we cannot return to the old normal, for that world was already broken.

2. Achille Mbembe, *Critique of Black Reason*, trans. Laurent Dubois (Durham, NC: Duke University Press, 2017).

3. See Pheng Cheah's useful overview in *What Is a World? On Postcolonial Literature as World Literature* (Durham, NC: Duke University Press, 2016), 19.

4. See Terry Smith, "Currents of World-Making in Contemporary Art," *World Art* 1, no. 2 (September 2011): 171–88; Terry Smith, *Contemporary Art: World Currents* (Upper Saddle River, NJ: Prentice Hall, 2011); and Sven Lütticken, *Cultural Revolution: Aesthetic Practice after Autonomy* (Berlin: Sternberg, 2017).

5. Ariella Azoulay, "Unlearning the Origins of Photography," in the series *Unlearning Decisive Moments of Photography*, Fotomuseum Winterthur blog, September 6, 2018, https://www.fotomuseum.ch/en/explore/still-searching /articles/155239_unlearning_the_origins_of_photography.

6. Mario Blaser and Marisol de la Cadena, "Introduction: Pluriverse; Proposals for a World of Many Worlds," in *A World of Many Worlds*, ed. Marisol de la Cadena and Mario Blaser (Durham, NC: Duke University Press, 2018), 1–22; John Law, "What's Wrong with a One-World World?," *Distinktion: Scandinavian Journal of Social Theory* 16, no. 1 (2015): 126–39.

7. Donna Haraway, "Tentacular Thinking: Anthropocene, Capitalocene, Chthulucene," in *Staying with the Trouble: Making Kin in the Chthulucene* (Durham, NC: Duke University Press, 2016). See also Bruno Latour, *Down to Earth: Politics in the New Climatic Regime* (Boston: Polity, 2018).

8. See, for instance, Anna Tsing, Heather Swanson, Elaine Gan, and Nils Bubandt, eds., *Arts of Living on a Damaged Planet* (Minneapolis: University of Minnesota Press, 2017); Eben Kirksey, Craig Schuetze, and Stefan Helmreich, eds., *The Multispecies Salon* (Durham, NC: Duke University Press, 2014); Robin Kimmerer, *Gathering Moss: A Natural and Cultural History of Mosses* (Portland: Oregon State University Press, 2003); and "Indigenous Peoples and the Politics of Water," ed. Melanie K. Yazzie and Cutcha Risling Baldy, special issue, *Decolonization: Indigeneity, Education and Society* 7, no. 1 (2018).

9. Quoted in Darh Jamail, "The Global Extinction Rebellion Begins," *Truthout*, November 15, 2018, https://truthout.org/articles/the-global -extinction-rebellion-begins/.

10. Recent literature and reporting includes David Wallace-Wells, "The Uninhabitable Earth," *New York* magazine, July 9, 2017, http://nymag.com/daily /intelligencer/2017/07/climate-change-earth-too-hot-for-humans.html; Darh Jamail, "Scientists Warn of 'Biological Annihilation' as Warming Reaches Levels Unseen for 115,000 Years," *Truthout*, July 31, 2017, http://www.truth-out.org /news/item/41425-biological-annihilation-trillion-ton-icebergs-warming-levels -unseen-for-115-000-years; and Will Steffen et al., "Trajectories of the Earth System in the Anthropocene," PNAS 115, no. 33 (2018): 8252–59, https://www .pnas.org/content/115/33/8252.

11. Wallace-Wells, "The Uninhabitable Earth."

12. Christian Parenti, *Tropic of Chaos: Climate Change and the New Geography of Violence* (New York: Nation Books, 2011), 7.

13. Isabelle Stengers, *In Catastrophic Times: Resisting the Coming Barbarism*, trans. Andrew Goffey (London: Open Humanities Press, 2015); Whitney Webb, "U.S. Military Is World's Biggest Polluter," *EcoWatch*, May 15, 2017, https://www .ecowatch.com/military-largest-polluter-2408760609.html.

14. Danowski and Viveiros de Castro, *The Ends of the World*, 12.

15. Amitav Ghosh, *The Great Derangement: Climate Change and the Unthinkable* (Chicago: University of Chicago Press, 2016), 9. For his own recent attempt to bring climate change into fiction, see Amitav Ghosh, *Gun Island* (New York: Farrar, Straus and Giroux, 2019).

16. Ghosh, *The Great Derangement*, 11.

17. On the philosophy of the event, see Alain Badiou, *Logic of Worlds: Being and Event II*, trans. Alberto Toscano (London: Continuum, 2009). On Badiou's views of nature and ecology, see Erik Swyngedouw, "Depoliticized Environments: The End of Nature, Climate Change and the Post-Political Condition," *Royal Institute of Philosophy Supplements* 69 (October 2011): 253–74. While Badiou

has evinced surprisingly little interest in mainstream environmentalism (even comparing it sneeringly to a postpolitical distraction as the contemporary "opium" of the people), his philosophy of the event nonetheless helps inform what I am implying here. The event—in its expanded theoretical sense—identifies the rupturing of the appearance of normality, opening a space of rethinking reality, producing new truths, subjects, and social systems, organized around a new naming regime in relation to what was once impossible, ultimately invoking, inaugurating, and describing the emergence of a new world. Beyond Badiou's own conceptions, we can call this event climate breakdown.

18. Fredric Jameson, "Future City," *New Left Review* 21 (May–June 2003): 76.

19. This is clear with the Breakthrough Institute, which I critically consider in chapter 6. For further consideration and examination of (anti-)Anthropocene discourse and visuality, see T. J. Demos, *Against the Anthropocene: Environment and Visual Culture Today* (Berlin: Sternberg, 2017).

20. Jameson, "Future City," 76.

21. See Naomi Klein's recent publications, including *The Shock Doctrine: The Rise of Disaster Capitalism* (London: Penguin, 2007); *This Changes Everything: Capitalism vs. the Climate* (New York: Allen Lane, 2014); and *The Battle for Paradise: Puerto Rico Takes on the Disaster Capitalists* (London: Haymarket, 2018).

22. For a repoliticization of Anthropocene discourse through a critique of "white geology," drawing on Black and Indigenous studies, see Kathryn Yusoff, *A Billion Black Anthropocenes or None* (Minneapolis: University of Minnesota Press, 2019).

23. Simon L. Lewis and Mark A. Maslin, "Defining the Anthropocene," *Nature* 519 (2015): 171–80.

24. See, for instance, Cedric Robinson, *Black Marxism: The Making of the Black Radical Tradition* (London: Zed, 1983).

25. Lawrence Gross, *Anishinaabe Ways of Knowing and Being* (New York: Routledge, 2016), 33.

26. Gross, *Anishinaabe Ways of Knowing and Being*, 33–34. Symptoms of postapocalypse stress syndrome, as detailed by Gross, include the following: abandonment of productive employment; increase in substance abuse; uptick in violence and domestic abuse; increase in mental illness and suicide rates; abandonment of religious practice; loss of hope and growing sense of despair; weakening or collapse of family structures, government and educational institutions, and health care delivery systems; loss of economic structures and forms of organization; and the weakening or loss of confidence in previous cultural worldviews.

27. Kyle Whyte, "Our Ancestors' Dystopia Now: Indigenous Conservation and the Anthropocene," in *Routledge Companion to the Environmental Humanities*, ed. Ursula K. Heise, Jon Christensen, and Michelle Niemann (New York: Routledge, 2017), 206–16.

28. For a history of these many endings, see, for instance, Roxanne Dunbar-Ortiz, *An Indigenous Peoples' History of the United States* (New York: Beacon, 2015).

29. Saidiya Hartman theorizes the "afterlife of slavery" as the enduring presence of bondage's racialized violence still present in contemporary society. See Saidiya Hartman, *Lose Your Mother: A Journey along the Atlantic Slave Route* (New York: Farrar, Straus and Giroux, 2007).

30. Zoe Todd, "Relationships," Theorizing the Contemporary, *Fieldsights*, January 21, 2016, https://culanth.org/fieldsights/relationships.

31. Todd, "Relationships."

32. Jaskiran Dhillon, "Introduction: Indigenous Resurgence, Decolonization, and Movements for Environmental Justice," *Environment and Society: Advances in Research* 9, no. 1 (September 2018): 3.

33. Jason Stanley, *How Fascism Works: The Politics of Us and Them* (New York: Random House, 2018). See also the special issue of *Third Text*, no. 158, dedicated to "Anti-Fascism/Art/Theory," ed. Angela Dimitrakaki and Harry Weeks, May 2019.

34. On related debates, see, for instance, Nathaniel Rich's much-discussed article and blaming of "human nature" for the failure of climate governance, "Losing Earth: The Decade We Almost Stopped Climate Change," *New York Times Magazine*, August 1, 2018; and the critical response of Naomi Klein, "Capitalism Killed Our Climate Momentum, Not 'Human Nature,'" *The Intercept*, August 3, 2018. On "situated knowledge," see Donna Haraway, "Situated Knowledges: The Science Question in Feminism and the Privilege of Partial Perspective," *Feminist Studies* 14, no. 3 (autumn 1988): 575–99.

35. See also T. J. Demos, "Ecology-as-Intrasectionality," *Bully Pulpit*, *Panorama: Journal of the Association of Historians of American Art* (spring 2019), https://doi.org/10.24926/24716839.1699.

36. Patricia Hill Collins, *Black Feminist Thought: Knowledge, Consciousness, and the Politics of Empowerment* (New York: Routledge, 1990).

37. Kimberlé Crenshaw, "Demarginalizing the Intersection of Race and Sex: A Black Feminist Critique of Antidiscrimination Doctrine, Feminist Theory and Antiracist Politics," *University of Chicago Legal Forum* 140 (January 1, 1989): 139–67.

38. Barbara Foley, "Intersectionality: A Marxist Critique," *Science and Society* 82, no. 2 (2018): 269–75; Sharon Smith, "A Marxist Case for Intersectionality," *Socialist Worker*, August 1, 2017; Mario Blaser and Arturo Escobar, "Political Ecology," in *Keywords for Environmental Studies*, ed. Joni Adamson, William A. Gleason, and David N. Pellow (New York: New York University Press, 2016), 164–67.

39. John Bellamy Foster, *Marx's Ecology: Materialism and Nature* (New York: Monthly Review, 2000); John Bellamy Foster and Paul Burkett, *Marx and the Earth: An Anti-Critique* (Chicago: Haymarket, 2017); Robinson, *Black Marxism*;

Glen Sean Coulthard, *Red Skin, White Masks: Rejecting the Colonial Politics of Recognition* (Minneapolis: University of Minnesota Press, 2014). Thanks to members of the Center for Creative Ecologies' reading group for critical discussions on this subject during the fall of 2018.

40. Kyle Powys Whyte, "Way beyond the Lifeboat: An Indigenous Allegory of Climate Justice," in *Climate Futures: Reimagining Global Climate Justice*, ed. Kum-Kum Bhavnani, John Foran, Priya A. Kurian, and Debashish Munshi (Los Angeles: University of California Press, 2019).

41. Dhillon, "Introduction," 3.

42. Combahee River Collective, "The Combahee River Collective Statement" (1977); quoted in *How We Get Free: Black Feminism and the Combahee River Collective*, ed. Keeanga-Yamahtta Taylor (Chicago: Haymarket Books, 2017), 20.

43. Movement for Black Lives, *A Vision for Black Lives: Policy Demands for Black Power, Freedom, and Justice*," 2016, https://policy.m4bl.org/.

44. Naomi Klein, "Why #BlackLivesMatter Should Transform the Climate Debate," *The Nation*, December 12, 2014, http://www.thenation.com/article/what-does-blacklivesmatter-have-do-climate-change/.

45. Sarah Manavis, "Eco-fascism: The Ideology Marrying Environmentalism and White Supremacy Thriving Online," *New Statesman*, September 21, 2018, https://www.newstatesman.com/science-tech/social-media/2018/09/eco-fascism-ideology-marrying-environmentalism-and-white-supremacy; Skyler Simmons, "Why Environmentalists Must Be Antifascists," *Earth First! Newswire*, April 21, 2017, https://earthfirstjournal.org/newswire/2017/04/21/why-environmentalists-must-be-antifascists/.

46. Alicia Garza, "A Herstory of the #BlackLivesMatter Movement," *Feminist Wire*, October 7, 2014, http://www.thefeministwire.com/2014/10/blacklivesmatter-2/; see also, relatedly, Nicholas Mirzoeff, "On Writing about Black Lives Matter while Not Being Black," in *The Appearance of Black Lives Matter* (Miami: NAME, 2017), 39–54.

47. This intervention resists, for instance, the natural-science-delimited definition of "ecology"—"the study of the functional interrelationships of living organisms, played out on the stage of their inanimate surroundings"—by environmental biologists Reinmar Seidler and Kamaljit S. Bawa, in "Ecology," in *Keywords for Environmental Studies*, ed. Joni Adamson, William A. Gleason, and David N. Pellow (New York: New York University Press, 2016), 71.

48. Christina Sharpe, *In the Wake: On Blackness and Being* (Durham, NC: Duke University Press, 2016), 21, 104. She explains: "I use the wake in all its meanings as a means of understanding how slavery's violences emerge within the contemporary conditions of spatial, legal, psychic, material, and other dimensions of Black non/being as well as in Black modes of resistance" (14).

49. Stefano Harney and Fred Moten, "Michael Brown," *boundary 2* 42, no. 2 (2015): 82 (emphasis mine).

50. See, for instance, the crucial work of Robert D. Bullard, including *Dumping in Dixie: Race, Class, and Environmental Quality* (Boulder. CO: Westview, 1990).

51. Traci Brynne Voyles, *Wastelanding: Legacies of Uranium Mining in Navajo Country* (Minneapolis: University of Minnesota Press, 2015).

52. See Ramachandra Guha, *Environmentalism: A Global History* (Oxford: Oxford University Press, 2000); Madhav Gadgil and Ramachandra Guha, "Ideologies of Environmentalism," in *Ecology and Equity: The Use and Abuse of Nature in Contemporary India* (London: Routledge, 1995); and Rob Nixon, *Slow Violence and the Environmentalism of the Poor* (Cambridge, MA: Harvard University Press, 2011).

53. Yates McKee, "On Flooded Streets and Breathing-in-Common: Climate Justice, Black Lives Matter, and the Arts of Decolonization," in *Strike Art: Contemporary Art and the Post-Occupy Condition* (London: Verso, 2016), 187. The following authors on political ecology have also been inspirational: Nick Mirzoeff, Subhankar Banerjee, Emily Eliza Scott, Heather Davis, Anne McClintock, Ashley Dawson, Not an Alternative, MTL Collective, Ros Gray, and Shela Sheikh (particularly Gray and Sheikh's *Third Text* special issue, "The Wretched Earth," 2018).

54. Dipesh Chakrabarty, "The Politics of Climate Change Is More than the Politics of Capitalism," *Theory, Culture and Society* 34, nos. 2–3 (2017): 27, 32, citing Yuval Noah Harari, *Sapiens: A Brief History of Humankind* (New York: Harper Perennial, 2018), 9.

55. Chakrabarty, "The Politics of Climate Change," 32.

56. Andreas Malm and Alf Hornborg, "The Geology of Mankind? A Critique of the Anthropocene Narrative," *Anthropocene Review* 1, no. 1 (2014): 67.

57. See Demos, *Against the Anthropocene*, for further related arguments.

58. Elizabeth Povinelli, "Acts of Life: Ecology and Power," *Artforum* 55, no. 10 (summer 2017): 131; see also Elizabeth Povinelli, *Geontologies: A Requiem to Late Liberalism* (Durham, NC: Duke University Press, 2016).

59. Particularly insightful here is Macarena Gómez-Barris, *The Extractive Zone: Social Ecologies and Decolonial Perspectives* (Durham, NC: Duke University Press, 2017); and recent special issues of *Decolonization: Indigeneity, Education and Society* on "Indigenous Peoples and the Politics of Water"; and *Environment and Society: Advances in Research* on "Indigenous Resurgence, Decolonization, and Movements for Environmental Justice."

60. On social movements of climate justice, see Bhavnani, Foran, Kurian, and Munshi, *Climate Futures*; and on nature as a site of onto-epistemological divergence and environmental alliance-building, see Marisol de la Cadena, "Uncommoning Nature," *e-flux*, 2015, http://supercommunity.e-flux.com /authors/marisol-de-la-cadena/.

61. See Frank B. Wilderson III, Saidya Hartman, Steve Martinot, Jared Sexton, and Hortenese J. Spillers, *Afro-Pessimism: An Introduction* (Minneapolis: Racked and Dispatched, 2017).

62. Jacques Derrida, "Force of Law," trans. Mary Quaintance, in *Deconstruction and the Possibility of Justice*, ed. Drucilla Cornell, Michael Rosenfeld, and David Gray Carlson (New York: Routledge, 1992), 3–67. See also the helpful gloss on Derrida in Leonard Lawlor, "Jacques Derrida," in *The Stanford Encyclopedia of Philosophy* (summer 2018 ed.), ed. Edward N. Zalta, https://plato.stanford.edu/archives/sum2018/entries/derrida/.

63. Cornel West, *Brother West: Living and Loving Out Loud; A Memoir*, with Davi Ritz (New York: SmileyBooks, 2009), 232.

64. Adrienne Mare Brown, *Emergent Strategy: Shaping Change, Changing Worlds* (Chico, CA: AK Press, 2017), 135.

65. My thoughts here are also indebted to Félix Guattari, *The Three Ecologies*, trans. Ian Pindar and Paul Sutton (London: Athlone Press, 2000), originally published as *Les trois écologies* (Paris: Éditions Galilée, 1989); and Haraway, *Staying with the Trouble*. For a useful genealogy of political ecology, see Blaser and Escobar, "Political Ecology," 164–66.

66. For more on "creative ecologies," see the Center for Creative Ecologies, accessed November 29, 2019, https://creativeecologies.ucsc.edu/.

67. Jacques Rancière, "From Politics to Aesthetics?," *Paragraph* 28, no. 1 (summer 2005): 18.

68. Jacques Rancière, *The Politics of Aesthetics*, trans. Gabriel Rockhill (London: Continuum, 2004), 26, 65.

69. See Eduardo Viveiros de Castro, *Cannibal Metaphysics*, ed. Peter Skafish (Minneapolis: Univocal, 2014); Eduardo Kohn, *How Forests Think: Toward an Anthropology beyond the Human* (Chicago: University of Chicago Press, 2013); Eben Kirksey, ed., *The Multispecies Salon* (Durham, NC: Duke University Press, 2014); Haraway, *Staying with the Trouble*; and Tsing et al., *Arts of Living on a Damaged Planet*.

70. Blaser and de la Cadena, "Introduction," 19. See also de la Cadena, "Uncommoning Nature."

71. MTL, "Questionnaire Response: Revolution at 100," *Center for Creative Ecologies Journal*, 2017, https://creativeecologies.ucsc.edu/mtl/.

72. See, for instance, the popular demand to remove Warren B. Kanders, owner and CEO of the tear gas and ballistic equipment manufacturer Safariland, from his position as vice chairman of the Whitney Museum's board of trustees, as reported in Hakim Bishara, "Over 120 Prominent Scholars and Critics Demand Removal of Whitney Museum Vice-Chair," *Hyperallergic*, April 4, 2019, https://hyperallergic.com/493611/over-120-prominent-scholars-and-critics-demand-removal-of-whitney-vice-chair/.

73. MTL Collective, "From Institutional Critique to Institutional Liberation? A Decolonial Perspective on the Crises of Contemporary Art," *October* 165 (summer 2018): 192–227.

74. Not an Alternative, "Institutional Liberation," *e-flux*, no. 77 (November 2016), http://www.e-flux.com/journal/77/76215/institutional-liberation/.

75. I consider additional examples in Demos, *Decolonizing Nature*.

76. Here the ambition of fictionalizing politics is crucial, as in the visionary writing of Octavia Butler, as well as the writers of subsequent generations associated with the collective Octavia's Brood. adrienne mare brown argues that such fiction is far from escapist imagination and instead germinates "strategies for organizers building movements for justice and liberation that leverage relatively simple interactions to create complex patterns, systems, and transformations—including adaptation, interdependence and decentralization, fractal awareness, resilience and transformative justice, nonlinear and iterative change, creating more possibilities." See Brown, *Emergent Strategy*, 24.

CHAPTER ONE: FEEDING THE GHOST

1. The piece was commissioned for the 2015 Venice Biennale, and also shown at the New Museum in New York, for which this chapter appeared in an earlier version as a catalog essay. See Thea Ballard and Dana Kopel, eds., *John Akomfrah: Signs of Empire* (New York: New Museum, 2018).

2. Akomfrah's implicit negation of Attenborough's voice, perhaps, by extension, also negates the latter's controversial neo-Malthusian environmentalist politics. A proponent of wilderness conservation, Attenborough, along with his colleagues at Population Matters, has been accused of running antimigration campaigns beyond his work on *Blue Planet*. For critical consideration of population in relation to climate justice, see Adele Clarke and Donna Haraway, eds., *Making Kin not Population: Reconceiving Generations* (Chicago: University of Chicago Press, 2018).

3. Olaudah Equiano, *The Interesting Narrative of the Life of Olaudah Equiano, or Gustavus Vassa, the African*, ed. Werner Sollors (1789; repr., New York: W. W. Norton, 2001).

4. See John Akomfrah in conversation with curator Rudolf Frieling at SF-MoMA, 2018, https://www.sfmoma.org/watch/artist-salon-john-akomfrah/.

5. Akomfrah discusses his aesthetic approach to history in an online interview accompanying a 2015 exhibition at the Bildmuseet, Umeå University, bildmuseet.umu.se/en/exhibition/john-akomfrah-vertigo-sea/20548.

6. Equiano, *The Interesting Narrative*, 292.

7. *Vertigo Sea* thus creatively inhabits the condition of what Jacques Rancière terms "documentary fiction," which "invents new intrigues with historical documents, and thus it touches hands with the film fable that joins and disjoins—in the relationship between story and character, shot and sequence—the powers of the visible, of speech, and of movement." That said, "intrigue" may be the wrong term when it comes to Akomfrah's important excavations, historical dramatizations, and creative representations of historical

and present in/justices. See Jacques Rancière, *Film Fables*, trans. Emiliano Battista (New York: Berg, 2006), 18.

8. Quoted in T. J. Demos, "Unspeakable Moments: An Interview with John Akomfrah," *Atlántica*, no. 54 (2014): 59.

9. For more on the aesthetics of migration, see T. J. Demos, *The Migrant Image: The Art and Politics of Documentary during Global Crisis* (Durham, NC: Duke University Press, 2013).

10. Christina Sharpe, *In the Wake: On Blackness and Being* (Durham, NC: Duke University Press, 2016), 21. If Sharpe also asks "how might we memorialize an event that is still ongoing?" (20), Akomfrah's work provides a compelling response.

11. Akomfrah's practice parallels the work of revisionist historians in recovering these figures from the art-historical archive, such as David Bindman and Henry Louis Gates Jr., eds., *The Image of the Black in Western Art* (Cambridge, MA: Harvard University Press, 2010). Of course, Akomfrah's collaboration with the Black Audio Film Collective was also invested in this critical historiographic project, reconstructing the history of Black subjects, from Martin Luther King Jr. to Malcolm X, focused largely on the twentieth century.

12. For further consideration of Equiano's *Narrative*, see Fred Moten, *Stolen Life* (Durham, NC: Duke University Press, 2018); and James Walvin, *An African's Life: The Life and Times of Olaudah Equiano, 1745–1797* (London: Continuum, 1998).

13. Equiano, *The Interesting Narrative*, 212.

14. The key references here are Edmund Burke's *A Philosophical Enquiry into the Origin of Our Ideas of the Sublime and Beautiful* of 1757 and Immanuel Kant's *Critique of Judgment* of 1790. For "Sublime Seas: John Akomfrah and J. M. W. Turner," the 2018 exhibition of *Vertigo Sea* at SFMoMA, Akomfrah selected J. M. W. Turner's romantic-sublime depiction of the biblical flood, *The Deluge* (1805), to be shown as reference and counterpoint.

15. Paul Gilroy, *The Black Atlantic: Modernity and Double-Consciousness* (Cambridge, MA: Harvard University Press, 1993). For developing discussion of the integral relations between capitalist speculation and racist objectification as figured in the slave trade, see Ian Baucom, *Specters of the Atlantic: Finance Capital, Slavery, and the Philosophy of History* (Durham, NC: Duke University Press, 2005).

16. Here I am in agreement with the late Okwui Enwezor, who laid out the filmic-to-postcinematic genealogy of Akomfrah's practice over nearly four decades as exploring the "emergence of the postcolonial subject in the single screen, to the diasporic ennui and Duboisian double-consciousness in the two-channel works, to the triangulation of slavery, migration, and ecological slaughter in the three-channel works"—that is, as long as that structuring formula does not become a too rigid interpretive rule. See Okwui Enwezor, "The Wreck of Utopia: Alienation and Disalienation in John Akomfrah's Postcolonial Cinema," in Ballard and Kopel, *John Akomfrah*, 86.

17. As per Moten: "Many of the early slave narratives [such as Equiano's] were also situated within this dialectic and, in this sense, they, too, were part of the transition from enlightenment to romanticism, prefiguring the reflection on feeling that is the hallmark, for instance, of William Wordsworth. The move, then, is toward a literature of reflection, a literature of mediated experience and emotion." Moten, *Stolen Life*, 277–78n97.

18. For my own critical analysis of Anthropocene discourse, see T. J. Demos, *Against the Anthropocene: Visual Culture and Environment Today* (Berlin: Sternberg, 2017).

19. One might compare *Vertigo Sea* to the construction of a "hyperobject," Timothy Morton's category of eco-philosophy, which describes "things that are massively distributed in time and space relative to humans," and about which "the more data we have . . . the less we know about them—the more we realize we can never truly know them," as found in *Hyperobjects: Philosophy and Ecology after the End of the World* (Minneapolis: University of Minnesota Press, 2013), 1, 180. However, Akomfrah's ethico-political approach to his material ultimately shows that powerful aesthetic experience is not only about overwhelming vertiginous wonder beyond grasp but also an urgent site of critically and carefully formed sensibility, expansive and generative relational thinking, and justice-based conviction responsive to historical and ongoing violence and inequality. Rather than reiterating the hyperobject's immobilization of thought and experience, it is about making a cut in the massively spatiotemporal distribution of things, with import, accountability, and conviction. Relatedly, consider the critique of Ursula Heise, who asks, when ultimately every object is a hyperobject, what useful work does the concept do? When accepting as final truth a world that is nebulous, mystifying, and filled with contradiction, as characterizes the world of hyperobjects—but not at all the films of Akomfrah—the abandonment of politics is not surprising. "Ursula K. Heise Reviews Timothy Morton's *Hyperobjects*," *Critical Inquiry*, 2019, https://criticalinquiry.uchicago.edu/ursula_k._heise_reviews_timothy_morton.

20. See Elizabeth Kolbert, *The Sixth Extinction: An Unnatural History* (New York: Henry Holt, 2014); and Elizabeth Kolbert, "The Darkening Sea," *New Yorker*, November 20, 2006.

21. Kolbert, "The Darkening Sea," 72; see also Terry P. Hughes et al., "Coral Reefs in the Anthropocene," *Nature* 546 (June 1, 2017): 82–90.

22. K. D. Burke, J. W. Williams, M. A. Chandler, A. M. Haywood, D. J. Lunt, and B. L. Otto-Bliesner, "Pliocene and Eocene Provide Best Analogs for Near-Future Climates," *Proceedings of the National Academy of Sciences of the United States of America* 115, no. 52 (December 26, 2018), 13288–93.

23. World Wildlife Fund, "Whale," accessed January 15, 2020, https://www.worldwildlife.org/species/whale#.

24. Robert C. Rocha, Phillip J. Clapham, and Yulia V. Ivashchenko, "Emptying the Oceans: A Summary of Industrial Whaling Catches in the

20th Century," *Marine Fisheries Review* 76, no. 4 (2014): 37–48. Dubbed the "most senseless environmental crime of the twentieth century," industrial whaling practiced by the Stalinist USSR in particular killed hundreds of thousands of whales, pushing Pacific sperm and North Pacific right whales toward extinction. Fictionalizing their reports so as to bypass the International Convention for the Regulation of Whaling, Soviet fleets included factory ships that could process an entire whale in thirty minutes (transforming the animal into materials for oil, canned meat and liver, and bone meal) and a number of smaller "catcher" vessels equipped with harpoon guns, all working tirelessly to meet the irrational demands of the Soviet economy. See Charles Homans, "The Most Senseless Environmental Crime of the 20th Century," *Pacific Standard*, June 14, 2017, https://psmag.com/social-justice/the-senseless-environment -crime-of-the-20th-century-russia-whaling-67774. For further consideration of experimental art and ecology under Soviet socialism, wherein unmastered nature figured as an "enemy of the people," see Maja Fowkes, *The Green Bloc: Neo-avant-garde Art and Ecology under Socialism* (Budapest: Central European University Press, 2015).

25. Contemplating the "'End of Art' or 'End of History'?," Fredric Jameson claimed more than twenty years ago that "the return of the Beautiful [in spectacle culture and art alike] must be seen as just such a systematic dominant: a colonization of reality generally by spatial and visual forms which is at one and the same time a commodification of that same intensively colonized reality on a world-wide scale." Fredric Jameson, *The Cultural Turn: Selected Writings on the Postmodern, 1993–1998* (New York: Verso, 2000), 87.

26. If "all life is semiotic and all semiosis is alive," as anthropologist Eduardo Kohn argues, then it also bears an intrinsic aesthetic element. See Eduardo Kohn, *How Forests Think: Toward an Anthropology beyond the Human* (Berkeley: University of California Press, 2013), 16.

27. This move has become somewhat of a refrain in my work over recent years, where I have argued on numerous occasions for a conceptualization of beauty as a sensory modality where formal materialization expresses and realizes liberation, drawing aesthetics and politics into creative alignment. See, for instance, T. J. Demos, "The Cruel Dialectic: On the Work of Nils Norman," *Grey Room*, no. 13 (fall 2003): 33–50; T. J. Demos, "Moving Images of Globalization," *Grey Room*, no. 37 (autumn 2009): 6–29; and T. J. Demos, "Ghostly Affect: Zarina Bhimji's *Yellow Patch*," in *Return to the Postcolony: Specters of Colonialism in Contemporary Art* (Berlin: Sternberg, 2013).

28. Jacques Rancière, "The Intolerable Image," in *The Emancipated Spectator*, trans. Gregory Elliot (London: Verso, 2009), esp. 84.

29. Rancière, "The Intolerable Image," 84.

30. Elizabeth Ellsworth and Jamie Kruse, "Making the Geologic Now: Intentions, Motivations, Provocations," in *Making the Geologic Now: Responses to*

Material Conditions of Contemporary Life, ed. Elizabeth Ellsworth and Jamie Kruse (Brooklyn, NY: Punctum, 2012), 245.

31. Gilroy, *The Black Atlantic*, 17, 4.

32. Levi Bryant, Graham Harman, and Nick Srnicek, "Towards a Speculative Philosophy," in *The Speculative Turn: Continental Materialism and Realism*, ed. Levi Bryant, Graham Harman, and Nick Srnicek (Melbourne: Re.press, 2011), esp. 3. The social ecology of Murray Bookchin (*The Philosophy of Social Ecology: Essays on Dialectical Naturalism* [Montreal: Black Rose Books, 1987]) compliments, for me, the intersectionality of bell hooks (*Feminist Theory: From Margin to Center* [Cambridge, MA: South End Press, 1984]) and Kimberleé Crenshaw ("Demarginalizing the Intersection of Race and Sex: A Black Feminist Critique of Antidiscrimination Doctrine, Feminist Theory and Antiracist Politics," *University of Chicago Legal Forum* 140 [January 1, 1989]: 139–67).

33. See Moten's moving reframing of Marx's speaking commodity in relation to *The Narrative of the Life of Frederick Douglass, an American Slave*: Fred Moten, "Resistance of the Object: Aunt Hester's Scream," in *In the Break: The Aesthetics of the Black Radical Tradition* (Minneapolis: University of Minnesota Press, 2003), esp. 1–24. As well, the projects of Donna Haraway, Karen Barad, and Elizabeth Povinelli insist on interlinking dramas of human politics and colonial injustices with those of the more-than-human and the geological, and, as such, are all indispensable guides and interlocutors for my analysis.

34. Fred Moten, "Knowledge of Freedom," in *Stolen Life*, 55–56.

35. Moten, "Resistance of the Object," 12.

36. See Elizabeth DeLoughrey, "Heavy Waters: Waste and Atlantic Modernity," PMLA 125, no. 3 (May 2010): 704; and Sharpe's discussion of the "residence time" for substances (including those of human bodies and specifically those of enslaved Africans) to enter and leave the ocean (measured in millions of years), in *In the Wake*.

37. "Hauntologies," referencing Derrida's coinage in his 1993 book *Specters of Marx*, was used as a title for Akomfrah's exhibition at Carroll/Fletcher in 2012. I have also investigated this haunting condition of cultural contemporaneity in Demos, *Return to the Postcolony*.

38. Akomfrah quoted in Bildmuseet interview, 2015.

CHAPTER TWO: BLACKOUT

1. See iLiana Fokianaki and Yanis Varoufakis, "'We Come Bearing Gifts'— iLiana Fokianaki and Yanis Varoufakis on Documenta 14 Athens," *Art Agenda*, June 7, 2017, http://www.art-agenda.com/reviews/d14/. For a critical analysis of Varoufakis's interpretation and more on the circumstances of debt in Greece and elsewhere, see Jerome Roos, "The New Debt Colonies," *Viewpoint Magazine*, February 1, 2018, https://www.viewpointmag.com/2018/02/01/new-debt-colonies/.

2. Sandro Mezzadra and Brett Neilson, "On the Multiple Frontiers of Extraction: Excavating Contemporary Capitalism," *Cultural Studies* 31, nos. 2–3 (2017): 185–204. See also Sandro Mezzadra and Brett Neilson, *The Politics of Operations: Excavating Contemporary Capitalism* (Durham, NC: Duke University Press, 2019).

3. David Harvey, *The New Imperialism* (Oxford: Oxford University Press, 2003). For an exposé of additional extractive processes of automation, Big Data, fee and fine farming, and services, all manifold ways to extract wealth from impoverished and indebted communities and comprising racialized forms of expropriation, see Jackie Wang, *Carceral Capitalism* (South Pasadena: Semiotext(e), 2018).

4. Macarena Gómez-Barris, *The Extractive Zone: Social Ecologies and Decolonial Perspectives* (Durham, NC: Duke University Press, 2017), xix. See also the 2018 special issue of *Social Text* dedicated to the topic: "Beyond the Extractive View," ed. Macarena Gómez-Barris, https://socialtextjournal.org/periscope_topic /beyond-the-extractive-view/.

5. Mezzadra and Neilson, "On the Multiple Frontiers of Extraction," 196. See also Jason W. Moore and Raj Patel, *A History of the World in Seven Cheap Things: A Guide to Capitalism, Nature, and the Future of the Planet* (Berkeley: University of California Press, 2017), which shows how the modern world has been made through seven cheap things: nature, money, work, care, food, energy, and lives, where "cheapening" has been, in part, a complex technology of capitalism involving debt, war, conquest, colonialism, and slave labor over five hundred years.

6. For an overview of President Donald Trump's deregulatory efforts to date, see Nadja Popovich, Livia Albeck-Ripka, and Kendra Pierre-Louis, "67 Environmental Rules on the Way Out under Trump," *New York Times*, January 31, 2018.

7. Maurizio Lazzarato, *Governing by Debt* (South Pasadena: Semiotext(e), 2015).

8. See Wendy Brown, *Undoing the Demos: Neoliberalism's Stealth Revolution* (Cambridge, MA: MIT Press, 2015); and Jackie Wang, "The Cybernetic Cop: RoboCop and the Future of Policing," in *Carceral Capitalism*, 253–59.

9. Global Witness "campaigns to end environmental and human rights abuses driven by the exploitation of natural resources and corruption in the global political and economic system." It also tracks the ongoing killing of land defenders. See the organization's website, https://www.globalwitness.org, for further statistics.

10. Achille Mbembe, "Necropolitics," *Public Culture* 15, no. 1 (winter 2003): 11–40; Elizabeth A. Povinelli, *Geontologies: A Requiem to Late Liberalism* (Durham, NC: Duke University Press, 2016).

11. See the Blockadia Map of the Environmental Justice Atlas project: "Originating from movements such as the Ogoni People against Shell in the Niger Delta since the 1990s and the Yasuni initiative in Ecuador to leave the oil in the soil, local people and activists are demanding we keep fossil fuels in the

ground. Today there are diverse and widespread resistances such as the Ende Gelände mass civil disobedience in Germany; the indigenous-led Standing Rock camp against the Dakota Access Pipeline; the movement in Kenya to 'deCOALanize'; and, amongst many others, the campaigns #BreakFree and #SaveTheArctic." "Blockadia: Keep Fossil Fuels in the Ground!," accessed December 17, 2019, https://ejatlas.org/featured/blockadia.

12. See Nick Estes, *Our History Is the Future: Standing Rock versus the Dakota Access Pipeline, and the Long Tradition of Indigenous Resistance* (London: Verso, 2019); and Nick Estes and Jaskiran Dhillon, ed., *Standing with Standing Rock: Voices from the #NoDAPL Movement* (Minneapolis: University of Minnesota Press, 2019).

13. For more on these stakes, see chapter 7; and Bruno Latour, *War of the Worlds: What about Peace?*, trans. Charlotte Bigg (Chicago: Prickly Paradigm Press, 2002).

14. While these case studies generally take conventional artistic forms and are exhibited most often in familiar art-world institutions like museums, galleries, and biennials, they operate in tension with the overriding commercial priorities of such contexts, mobilizing critical and emancipatory energies nonetheless within those systems. My analysis of the expanded field of aesthetic practices also extends beyond the conventional sites of contemporary art display—in documentary photography, activist social movements, and media and game contexts—in subsequent chapters. For a like-minded attempt to analyze this cultural transformation, see Sven Lütticken, *Cultural Revolution: Aesthetic Practice after Autonomy* (Berlin: Sternberg, 2017).

15. See Traci Brynne Voyles, *Wastelanding: Legacies of Uranium Mining in Navajo Country* (Minneapolis: University of Minnesota Press, 2015).

16. For an additional analysis of *Crossings* in its broader exhibition context, see T. J. Demos, "Learning from documenta 14: Athens, Post-Democracy, and Decolonisation," *Third Text*, August 23, 2017, http://thirdtext.org/demos -documenta.

17. See Alex de Jong's critical take on Öcalan's Bookchin-inspired libertarian municipalism, "The New-Old PKK," *Jacobin*, March 18, 2016, https://www .jacobinmag.com/2016/03/pkk-ocalan-kurdistan-isis-murray-bookchin/.

18. See Jenna Winton's report on one of the leading spokespersons of the ACFN, "Eriel Deranger: Fighting the World's Largest Industrial Project, the Alberta Tar Sands," *Cultural Survival*, February 4, 2014, http://www .culturalsurvival.org/news/eriel-deranger-fighting-worlds-largest-industrial -project-alberta-tar-sands (quoting Deranger from a 2014 presentation at Harvard); and Red Power Media, "Court Sides with Feds in Athabasca Chipewyan First Nation's Case," January 9, 2015, https://redpowermedia.wordpress.com /2015/01/09/court-sides-with-feds-in-athabasca-chipewyan-first-nations-case/.

19. For further discussion and context of Biemann's practice, see T. J. Demos, "Decolonizing Nature: Making the World Matter," in *Decolonizing Nature: Contemporary Art and the Politics of Ecology* (Berlin: Sternberg, 2016), 199–228.

20. See "Project focus: Adrian Lahoud: Climate Crimes," V&A, May 12, 2018, to November 4, 2018, https://www.vam.ac.uk/articles/project-focus -adrian-lahoud-climate-crimes.

21. See Drew Shindell, Greg Faluvegi, Karl Seltzer, and Cary Shindell, "Quantified, Localized Health Benefits of Accelerated Carbon Dioxide Emissions Reductions," *Nature Climate Change* 8 (2018): 291–95; and "Climate Denier to Head New Trump Panel Despite Once Comparing Climate Scientists to Nazis," *Democracy Now!*, February 21, 2019, https://www.democracynow.org /2019/2/21/climate_denier_to_head_new_trump.

22. "Project focus: Adrian Lahoud: Climate Crimes"; and Cathy O'Neil, *Weapons of Math Destruction: How Big Data Increases Inequality and Threatens Democracy* (New York: Crown, 2016).

23. Paul N. Edwards, *A Vast Machine: Computer Models, Climate Data, and the Politics of Global Warming* (Cambridge, MA: MIT Press, 2010).

24. Bill McKibben, "Stop Swooning over Justin Trudeau: The Man Is a Disaster for the Planet," *The Guardian*, April 17, 2017.

25. Andrew Ross, "Climate Debt Denial," *Dissent* (summer 2013), https:// www.dissentmagazine.org/article/climate-debt-denial.

26. See Robert Glennon, "The Unfolding Tragedy of Climate Change in Bangladesh," *Scientific American*, April 21, 2017, https://blogs.scientificamerican .com/guest-blog/the-unfolding-tragedy-of-climate-change-in-bangladesh/. For more on climate refugees, see chapter 3.

27. Christian Parenti, *Tropics of Chaos: Climate Change and the New Geography of Violence* (New York: Nation Books, 2011), 7.

28. Amitav Ghosh, *The Great Derangement: Climate Change and the Unthinkable* (Chicago: University of Chicago Press, 2016). I offer further critical consideration of Ghosh's text in chapter 7.

29. "20 Destinations to See before They Disappear," *Rough Guide*, November 29, 2016, https://www.roughguides.com/gallery/20-destinations-to-see -before-they-disappear/; Maxine Joselow, "'Last-Chance' Tourists Flock to Sites before They Vanish," E&E *News*, October 24, 2018, https://www.eenews .net/stories/1060104131.

30. The bondholders of Puerto Rican debt consist mainly of large-scale financial investment firms, including mutual funds (Oppenheimer Funds, Franklin Templeton) and hedge funds (Marathon Asset, Blue Mountain, Angelo Gordon, Knighthead, D. E. Shaw). In addition, Harvard University's endowment has substantial holdings in Puerto Rico's debt, according to David Dayen, "Harvard's Endowment Is Profiting from Puerto Rico's Debt as the Island's Schools Face Crippling Cuts," *The Intercept*, January 25, 2018.

31. For more on the current situation in Puerto Rico, see the work of Defend PR, a multimedia project designed to document and celebrate Puerto Rican creativity, resilience, and resistance (http://www.defendpr.com/);

Naomi Klein, *The Battle for Paradise: Puerto Rico Takes on the Disaster Capitalists* (London: Haymarket, 2018); and Roos, "The New Debt Colonies."

32. Juan González, "Puerto Rico's $123 Billion Bankruptcy Is the Cost of U.S. Colonialism," *The Intercept*, May 9, 2017.

33. Achille Mbembe, *Critique of Black Reason*, trans. Laurent Dubois (Durham, NC: Duke University Press, 2017), 6.

34. See Mezzadra and Neilson, "On the Multiple Frontiers of Extraction"; and "Extraction: Decolonial Visual Cultures in the Age of the Capitalocene," the conference organized by the Center for Creative Ecologies at UC Santa Cruz in 2017, https://extraction.sites.ucsc.edu/.

35. Ashley Dawson, "Let Sun and Wind Power Puerto Rico's Future," *New York Daily News*, October 11, 2017.

36. Gerry Mullany, "World's 8 Richest Have as Much Wealth as Bottom Half, Oxfam Says," *New York Times*, January 16, 2017.

37. See Klein, *The Battle for Paradise*.

38. Kate Aronoff, "Disaster Capitalists Take Big Step toward Privatizing Puerto Rico's Electric Grid," *The Intercept*, October 26, 2017; Naomi Klein, *The Shock Doctrine: The Rise of Disaster Capitalism* (London: Penguin Press, 2008). Hilda Lloréns asks when capitalism has not been a disaster. Indeed, "for Indigenous and Black communities in the Global South, the last 500 years have been a protracted disaster, one in which they have been at the mercy of cruel capitalism all along." Hilda Lloréns, "The Race of Disaster: Black Communities and the Crisis in Puerto Rico," *Black Perspectives* (blog), April 17, 2019, https://www.aaihs.org/the-race-of-disaster-black-communities-and-the-crisis-in-puerto-rico/.

39. Rebecca Solnit, *Hope in the Dark: Untold Histories, Wild Possibilities* (New York: Nation Books, 2004).

40. For more examples in Puerto Rico, see the websites of Mutual Aid Disaster Relief and Resilient Power Puerto Rico, bringing solar power to communities (https://mutualaiddisasterrelief.org/solar-power-to-the-people/ and http://resilientpowerpr.org/resilientpr/); JunteGente, which is resisting neoliberal capitalism and fighting for a just, solidary-based, and sustainable Puerto Rico (http://juntegente.org/); Boricuá Organization for Ecological Agriculture, which delivers seeds, soils, and permaculture skills to the island's farmers to support subsistence agriculture (https://www.facebook.com/organizacionboricua/); urban design nonprofit La Maraña, helping with postdisaster construction and repair (http://www.lamarana.org/); and the grassroots arts organization Beta-Local, supporting disaster relief (http://betalocal.org/).

41. For a more extensive analysis of this film, see T. J. Demos, "*The Night We Became People Again*: On Allora & Calzadilla's Art of Intersectionality," in *Blackout: Allora & Calzadilla*, ed. Hou Hanru and Anne Palopoli (Milan and Rome: Lazy Dog and MAXXI, 2018), 52–71.

42. On "disaster capitalism," see Klein, *The Shock Doctrine*; on "disaster communism," see Ashley Dawson, *Extreme Cities: The Peril and Promise of Urban Life in the Age of Climate Change* (London: Verso, 2017), 246. The key historical reference is Peter Kropotkin's "Mutual Aid: A Factor of Evolution" (1902), which, in arguing against social Darwinism and granting cooperation its own survivalist function, became a fundamental text in anarchist communism.

43. See the Center for Creative Ecologies' recent questionnaire on revolution, released on the centennial of the 1917 Russian Revolution: "Revolution at 100: A Questionnaire," October 2017, https://creativeecologies.ucsc.edu /revolution-at-100-questionnaire/.

44. See Naomi Klein, "The Battle for Paradise: Puerto Ricans and Ultra-rich 'Puertopians' Are Locked in a Pitched Struggle over How to Remake the Island," *The Intercept*, March 20, 2018. On the "life-affirming creativity" of "collective art-making" as a "connection-building process" in "laying the groundwork for a long-term infrastructure of movement culture," see Yates McKee, "On Flooded Streets and Breathing-in-Common," in *Strike Art: Contemporary Art and the Post-Occupy Condition* (London: Verso, 2016), esp. 209. For a comparative study of Caribbean islands where nonsovereign sites (such as Guadeloupe) might also be places where we can unsettle how we think of sovereignty itself, see Yarimar Bonilla, *Non-State Sovereign Futures: French Caribbean Politics in the Wake of Disenchantment* (Durham, NC: Duke University Press, 2015).

45. Mbembe, *Critique of Black Reason*, 47–48.

46. Roos, "The New Debt Colonies." Roos also states, "What is needed is a revamped popular internationalism that focuses all its energies on opposing the politics of dispossession and dismantling the rootstock of capitalist imperialisms both past and present: the structural power of finance."

47. For recent critiques of the fragmentations of identity politics, see Keeanga-Yamahtta Taylor, *From #BlackLivesMatter to Black Liberation* (Chicago: Haymarket Books, 2016); and Asad Haider, *Mistaken Identity: Race and Class in the Age of Trump* (London: Verso, 2018).

48. "Rev. Barber: MS Sen. Cindy Hyde-Smith Jokes about Hangings, but Her Policies Will Strangle the Poor," *Democracy Now!*, November 26, 2018, https://www.democracynow.org/2018/11/26/rev_barber_ms_sen_cindy_hyde.

CHAPTER THREE: THE VISUAL POLITICS OF CLIMATE REFUGEES

1. Naomi Klein, "On the Racism That Underlies Climate Change Inaction," *Saturday Paper*, June 25, 2016, https://www.thesaturdaypaper.com.au/opinion/topic /2016/06/25/naomi-klein-the-racism-that-underlies-climate-change-inaction.

2. Ashley Dawson, "Climate Apartheid," in *Extreme Cities: The Peril and Promise of Urban Life in the Age of Climate Change* (London: Verso, 2017), 230.

3. Dawson, "Climate Apartheid," 230.

4. Quoted in "Collectif Argos," MIT Press, accessed December 15, 2015, http://mitpress.mit.edu/contributors/collectif-argos; and Argos Collective, *Climate Refugees* (Cambridge, MA: MIT Press, 2010).

5. Carol Farbotko, "Wishful Sinking: Disappearing Islands, Climate Refugees and Cosmopolitan Experimentation," *Asia-Pacific Viewpoint* 51, no. 1 (2010): 47–60. For more on the Argos Collective, see Yates McKee, "On *Climate Refugees*: Biopolitics, Aesthetics, and Critical Climate Change," *Qui Parle* 19, no. 2 (spring/summer 2011): 309–25; and T. J. Demos, "Climates of Displacement from the Maldives to the Arctic," in *Decolonizing Nature: Contemporary Art and the Politics of Ecology* (Berlin: Sternberg, 2016), 63–100.

6. See Paul Salopek, "Fleeing Terror, Finding Refuge: Millions of Syrians Escape an Apocalyptic Civil War, Creating a Historic Crisis," *National Geographic*, March 2015.

7. In a discussion in 2002 prompted by the photography of Sebastião Salgado, art historian T. J. Clark proposed the need for a "photography of causes, not faces." Sebastião Salgado et al., *Migrations: The Work of Sebastião Salgado* (Berkeley: Doreen B. Townsend Center for the Humanities, 2002), 25.

8. Salopek, "Fleeing Terror, Finding Refuge."

9. On the socioecological determinations, see in particular: Francesco Femia and Caitlin Werrell, "Climate Change before and after the Arab Awakening: The Cases of Syria and Lebanon," in *The Arab Spring and Climate Change: A Climate and Security Correlations Series*, ed. Francesco Femia and Caitlin Werrell (Washington, DC: Center for American Progress, 2013), 23–32; Clemens Hoffman, "Environmental Determinism as Orientalism: The Geopolitical Ecology of Crisis in the Middle East," in "War, Revolt, and Rupture: The Historical Sociology of the Current Crisis in the Middle East," special issue, *Journal of Historical Sociology* (2018): 94–104; and Francesca de Châtel, "The Role of Drought and Climate Change in Syria in the Syrian Uprisings: Untangling the Triggers of the Revolution," *Middle Eastern Studies* 50, no. 4 (2014): 521–35.

10. Coral Davenport and Campbell Robertson, "Resettling the First American 'Climate Refugees,'" *New York Times*, May 2, 2016.

11. Davenport and Robertson, "Resettling the First American 'Climate Refugees.'"

12. See Noam Chomsky, "What Makes Mainstream Media Mainstream," *Z Magazine*, October 1997. The mainstreaming of much corporate media remains the case even though there has also been a proliferating networking of subcultural sites of mediation and news with the online formation of social media and independent outlets in recent years.

13. Eyal Weizman, "Introduction: Forensis," in *Forensis: The Architecture of Public Truth*, ed. Forensic Architecture (Berlin: Sternberg, 2014), 25, 27. Weizman adds: "Individual testimonies, recorded in voice or in bone, were indeed

useful in personifying histories of violence and making them affective. But by concentrating on the victim and by seeking to evoke identification and compassion, such accounts tended to mask the political context" (25).

14. Jonathan Clayton and Hereward Holland, "Over One Million Sea Arrivals Reach Europe in 2015," UNHCR, December 30, 2015, http://www.unhcr.org /5683d0b56.html. Of course, there are important terminological differences between migrants, refugees, exiles, and asylum seekers, each carrying varying degrees of agency, on which I elaborate in *The Migrant Image: The Art and Politics of Documentary during Global Crisis* (Durham, NC: Duke University Press, 2013).

15. Refugee Council Chief Executive Maurice Wren, quoted in World Maritime News Staff, "UK Halts Support to Mediterranean Migrant Rescues," *World Maritime News*, October 29, 2014, http://worldmaritimenews.com/archives /141298/uk-halts-support-to-mediterranean-migrant-rescue-operations. Wren's full statement reads: "The British Government seems oblivious to the fact that the world is in the grip of the greatest refugee crisis since the Second World War. People fleeing atrocities will not stop coming if we stop throwing them life rings; boarding a rickety boat in Libya will remain a seemingly rational decision if you're running for your life and your country is in flames. The only outcome of withdrawing help will be to witness more people needlessly and shamefully dying on Europe's doorstep. The answer isn't to build the walls of fortress Europe higher, it's to provide more safe and legal channels for people to access protection." I consider this proposal further in the following pages. The Schengen territory has also represented a "recolonization" of Europe through its regime of citizenship that has helped produce the new category of illegal alien, as Étienne Balibar has observed, in *We, the People of Europe? Reflections on Transnational Citizenship* (Princeton, NJ: Princeton University Press, 2004), 43.

16. See Amanda Taub and Max Fisher, "Facebook Fueled Anti-Refugee Attacks in Germany, New Research Suggests," *New York Times*, August 21, 2018; Zeynep Tufekci, "We're Building a Dystopia Just to Make People Click on Ads" (TED talk, September 2017), https://www.ted.com/talks/zeynep_tufekci_we_re _building_a_dystopia_just_to_make_people_click_on_ads#t-1363376; Karsten Müller and Carlo Schwarz, "Fanning the Flames of Hate: Social Media and Hate Crime" (University of Warwick Working Paper, May 2018), https://warwick.ac .uk/fac/soc/economics/research/centres/cage/manage/publications/373-2018 _schwarz.pdf; and Siva Vaidhyanathan, *Antisocial Media: How Facebook Disconnects Us and Undermines Democracy* (New York: Oxford University Press, 2018).

17. Gholam Khiabany, "Refugee Crisis, Imperialism and Pitiless Wars on the Poor," *Media Culture Society* 38, no. 5 (June 2016): 759. See also Jakob-Moritz Eberl, Christine E. Meltzer, Tobias Heidenreich, Beatrice Herrero, Nora Theorin, and Fabienne Lind, "The European Media Discourse on Immigration and Its Effects: A Literature Review," *Annals of the International Communication Association* 42, no. 3 (2018): 207–23.

18. See "The Perfect Storm," ed. Sven Lütticken, Julieta Aranda, Brian Kuan Wood, Stephen Squibb, and Anton Vidokle, special issue, e-flux, no. 76 (October 2016), http://www.e-flux.com/journal/76/; "Cornel West on Donald Trump: This Is What Neo-Fascism Looks Like," Democracy Now!, December 1, 2016, https://democracynow.org/2016/12/1/cornel_west_on_donald_trump _this; Halim Rane, Jacqui Ewart, and John Martinkus, Media Framing of the Muslim World: Conflicts, Crises and Contexts (New York: Palgrave Macmillan, 2014); and Zeynep Tufekci, Twitter and Tear Gas: The Power and Fragility of Networked Protest (New Haven, CT: Yale University Press, 2018).

19. Wendy Brown, "Apocalyptic Populism," Eurozine, August 30, 2017, https://www.eurozine.com/apocalyptic-populism.

20. See Todd Miller, "The 21st-Century Border," in Storming the Wall: Climate Change, Migration, and Homeland Security (San Francisco: City Lights Books, 2017); Steve Wright, "Preparing for Mass Refugee Flows: The Corporate Military Sector," in Surviving Climate Change: The Struggle to Avert Global Catastrophe, ed. David Cromwell and Mark Levene (London: Pluto, 2007), 82–101; and Ben Hayes, "The Surveillance-Industrial Complex," in Routledge Handbook of Surveillance Studies, ed. Kirstie Ball, Kevin Haggerty, and David Lyon (Abingdon, UK: Routledge, 2012).

21. That said, humanitarianism certainly has its dark sides in justifying war and the state, and increasingly "humanitarian aid and humanitarian warfare operate in tandem in an uneasy, but necessary, alliance between saving lives and killing—or letting die." Kelly Oliver, Carceral Humanitarianism: Logics of Refugee Detention (Minneapolis: University of Minnesota Press, 2017), 5.

22. Ryan Harvey, "Will the US Own Up to Its Role in Europe's Refugee Crisis?," Truthout 27 (March 2016), http://www.truth-out.org/news/item/35383 -will-the-us-own-up-to-its-role-in-europe-s-refugee-crisis.

23. Internal Displacement Monitoring Centre, "Global Internal Displacement Database," accessed December 16, 2019, http://www.internal -displacement.org/global-report/grid2019/.

24. Camilo Mora et al., "The Projected Timing of Climate Departure from Recent Variability," Nature 502 (October 10, 2013): 183–87.

25. Julia Conley, "Lancet Study Warns of Global Health Crisis and 1 Billion Climate Refugees by 2050," Common Dreams, October 31, 2017, https://www .commondreams.org/news/2017/10/31/lancet-study-warns-global-health-crisis -and-1-billion-climate-refugees-2050; Solomon M. Hsiang and Adam H. Sobel, "Potentially Extreme Population Displacement and Concentration in the Tropics under Non-Extreme Warming," Scientific Reports 6 (2016), http://www.nature .com/articles/srep25697.

26. See Solomon Hsiang et al., "Estimating Economic Damage from Climate Change in the United States," Science 356, no. 6345 (June 30, 2017): 1362–69.

27. See Saskia Sassen, "A Massive Loss of Habitat: New Drivers for Migration," Sociology of Development 2, no. 2 (2016): 204–33; and Richard D. Wolff,

"How Capitalism Perpetuates Immigration," *Truthout*, October 2, 2016, http://www.truth-out.org/opinion/item/37831-how-capitalism-perpetuates -immigration. As Wolff writes: "The uneven development of capitalism, coupled with its drive toward colonialism, has consistently produced the extreme conditions and extreme inequalities that sustain successive waves of migration. A real 'cure' for the horrific processes of migration lies in a real confrontation of capitalism's uneven development."

28. See Christian Parenti, *Tropics of Chaos: Climate Change and the New Geography of Violence* (New York: Nation Books, 2011), 5; Vincent Emanuele, interview with Christian Parenti, "Climate Change, Militarism, Neoliberalism and the State," *Truthout*, May 12, 2015, http://www.truth-out.org/news/item/30666 -christian-parenti-on-climate-change-militarism-neoliberalism-and-the-state; and Christian Parenti, "Make Corporations Pay for the Green New Deal," *Jacobin*, March 13, 2019, https://www.jacobinmag.com/2019/03/green-new-deal -private-investment-energy.

29. Rebecca Solnit, "Call Climate Change What It Is: Violence," *The Guardian*, April 7, 2014.

30. Daniel Robicheau, "The 'MENA' Region and the International Monetary Fund," *London Progressive Journal*, April 23, 2013, http://londonprogressivejournal .com/article/view/1474/the-mena-region-and-the-international-monetary -fund; Naomi Klein, *This Changes Everything: Capitalism vs. the Climate* (New York: Allen Lane, 2014).

31. See Simon Behrman and Avidan Kent, eds., *Climate Refugees: Beyond the Legal Impasse?* (New York: Routledge, 2018).

32. Essam El-Hinnawi, *Environmental Refugees* (Nairobi: United Nations Environment Programme, 1985), 4. Notice how El-Hinnawi's definition of ecology restrains it to the biogeophysical.

33. See Behrman and Kent, *Climate Refugees*; and John R. Wennersten and Denise Robbins, *Rising Tides: Climate Refugees in the Twenty-First Century* (Bloomington: Indiana University Press, 2017).

34. See Carol Farbotko and Heather Lazrus, "The First Climate Refugees? Contesting Global Narratives of Climate Change in Tuvalu," *Global Environmental Change* 22, no. 2 (2012): 382–90.

35. Angela Oels, "Asylum Rights for Climate Refugees? From Agamben's Bare Life to the Autonomy of Migration" (lecture delivered at the 49th Annual Convention of the International Studies Association, San Francisco, March 26, 2008). Also see Oliver, *Carceral Humanitarianism: Logics of Refugee Detention*.

36. Oels, "Asylum Rights for Climate Refugees?": "The social practice of the politics of migration in Europe shows that such 'exceptions' are becoming more and more the rule."

37. Christopher Sherman, Martha Mendoza, and Garance Burke, "US held record number of migrant children in custody in 2019," *AP News*, November 12,

2019, https://apnews.com; Jonathan Blitzer, "How Climate Change Is Fuelling the U.S. Border Crisis," *The New Yorker*, April 3, 2019, https://www.newyorker.com.

38. As explains Laura Paul, founder of Lowernine.org, a nonprofit dedicated to rebuilding neighborhoods affected by Katrina to the benefit of original inhabitants, "Worrying about the future is a luxury for privileged people. My friends here are worried about putting dinner on the table tonight, not what is going to happen in the city 20 or 30 years from now." Quoted in Jeff Goodell, "Welcome to the Age of Climate Migration," *Rolling Stone*, February 25, 2018.

39. Slavoj Žižek, "We Can't Address the EU Refugee Crisis without Confronting Global Capitalism," *In These Times*, September 9, 2015, http://inthesetimes.com/article/18385/slavoj-zizek-european-refugee-crisis-and-global-capitalism. Of course the "great powers" of the West might equally be considered failed states—verging increasingly on antidemocratic authoritarianism—if of a different sort than those that Žižek considers.

40. See Sandro Mezzadra and Brett Neilson, *Border as Method, or, the Multiplication of Labor* (Durham, NC: Duke University Press, 2013); and Wendy Brown, *Walled States, Waning Sovereignty* (Cambridge: Zone, 2010).

41. For a cutting artistic investigation of just this sort of uneven relationality, see Renzo Martens's documentary *Episode III: Enjoy Poverty* (2008), which self-critically uncovers misery's exploitation by humanitarians, photojournalists, and artists alike, himself included, in the Democratic Republic of the Congo; and T. J. Demos, "The Haunting: Renzo Martens's *Enjoy Poverty*," in *Return to the Postcolony: Specters of Colonialism in Contemporary Art* (Berlin: Sternberg, 2013), 97–124.

42. Fazal Sheikh and Eyal Weizman, *The Conflict Shoreline: Colonialism as Climate Change in the Negev Desert* (Göttingen: Steidl, 2015).

43. Audrey Quinn, *Syria's Climate Conflict*, Years of Living Dangerously, February 2011, accessed December 15, 2016, http://yearsoflivingdangerously.tumblr.com/post/86898140738/this-comic-was-produced-in-partnership-by-years-of.

44. Colin P. Kelleya, Shahrzad Mohtadib, Mark A. Canec, Richard Seagerc, and Yochanan Kushnirc, "Climate Change in the Fertile Crescent and Implications of the Recent Syrian Drought," *Proceedings of the National Academy of Sciences*, January 30, 2015, http://www.pnas.org/content/112/11/3241.full; Femia and Werrell, "Climate Change before and after the Arab Awakening"; Hoffman, "Environmental Determinism as Orientalism"; and de Châtel, "The Role of Drought and Climate Change."

45. Forensic Oceanography, "Liquid Traces: The Left-to-Die Boat Case," April 11, 2012, http://www.forensic-architecture.org/case/left-die-boat/.

46. Missing Migrants, "Total of Deaths Recorded in Mediterranean," accessed January 2, 2020, http://missingmigrants.iom.int/region/Mediterranean.

47. However, in other cases, Forensic Architecture does investigate the causes of environmental- and climate-based displacement—owing to military

violence ("Genocide in the Ixil Triangle," Guatemala, 2013; "The Drone Strikes Platform," Afghanistan, 2012; and "Torture and Detention in Burundi," 2018); colonial policies of ethnic cleansing ("Killing in Umm Al-Hiran," Israel, 2017), extraction and land grabs ("Ecocide in Indonesia," 2015), and more. See Forensic Architecture, https://forensic-architecture.org/, accessed January 2, 2020; and Forensic Architecture, *Forensis*.

48. See Forensic Oceanography, "Sea Watch vs the Libyan Coast Guard," May 5, 2018, https://forensic-architecture.org/investigation/seawatch-vs-the -libyan-coastguard.

49. See Jonathan Blitzer, "How Climate Change Is Fuelling the U.S. Border Crisis," *New Yorker*, April 3, 2019.

50. Tanvi Misra, "The Border Is a Way of Reinforcing Antagonism That Doesn't Exist," *Citylab*, January 11, 2017, https://www.citylab.com/equity/2017 /01/the-urban-laboratory-on-the-san-diego-tijuana-border-teddy-cruz-fonna -forman/512222/.

51. Misra, "The Border."

52. See Teddy Cruz and Fonna Forman, "The Cross-Border Public," in *Public Space? Lost and Found*, ed. Gediminas Urbonas, Ann Lui, and Lucas Freeman (Cambridge, MA: SA+P Press and MIT School of Architecture and Planning, 2017), 169–85.

53. Teddy Cruz and Fonna Forman, "A New Public Imagination!," *Metropolis*, September 27, 2017, https://www.metropolismag.com/cities/teddy-cruz -fonna-forman-manifesto/.

54. Of course, borders are devastating to migrating multispecies ecologies, with 134 mammalian, 178 reptilian, and 57 amphibian species living within approximately thirty miles of the US-Mexico border, of which some 50 species are globally or federally threatened. See Cally Carswell, "Trump's Wall May Threaten Thousands of Plant and Animal Species on the U.S.–Mexico Border," *Scientific American*, May 10, 2017; and Eliza Barclay and Sarah Frostenson, "The Ecological Disaster That Is Trump's Border Wall: A Visual Guide," *Vox*, October 29, 2017.

55. On open borders, see Natasha King, *No Borders: The Politics of Immigration Control and Resistance* (London: Zed Books, 2016); April Humble, "Open the Borders! Welcoming Climate Refugees," in "System Change," special issue, *Roar*, no. 7 (autumn 2017); and Suzy Lee, "The Case for Open Borders," *Catalyst* 2, no. 4 (winter 2019), https://catalyst-journal.com/vol2/no4/the-case-for-open-borders.

CHAPTER FOUR: GAMING THE ENVIRONMENT

1. Among the growing literature, see "Green Computer and Video Games," ed. Alenda Chang and John Parham, special issue, *Ecozon@: European Journal of Literature, Culture and Environment* 8, no. 2 (2017); Stephen Rust, Salma Monani, and Sean Cubitt, eds., *Ecomedia: Key Issues* (New York: Routledge, 2016); Nicole

Starosielski and Janet Walker, eds., *Sustainable Media: Critical Approaches to Media and Environment* (New York: Routledge, 2016); and Sean Cubitt, *Finite Media: Environmental Implications of Digital Technologies* (Durham, NC: Duke University Press, 2017).

2. See Luca Morgantia et al., "Gaming for Earth: Serious Games and Gamification to Engage Consumers in Pro-environmental Behaviours for Energy Efficiency," *Energy Research and Social Science* 29 (July 2017): 95–102; Lauren Woolbright, "Game Design as Climate Change Activism," *Ecozon@: European Journal of Literature, Culture and Environment* 8, no. 2 (2017): 88–102; and Bradon Tam Lynn Smith, "Resources, Scenarios, Agency: Environmental Computer Games," *Ecozon@: European Journal of Literature, Culture and Environment* 8, no. 2 (2017): 103–20.

3. For an ecocritical reading of *Avatar*, see Joni Adamson, "Indigenous Literatures, Multinaturalism, and *Avatar*: The Emergence of Indigenous Cosmopolitics," *American Literary History* 24, no. 1 (spring 2012): 143–62.

4. See Elizabeth Povinelli, *Geontologies: A Requiem to Late Liberalism* (Durham, NC: Duke University Press, 2016), 4.

5. Elizabeth Povinelli, "Can Rocks Die? Life and Death inside the Carbon Imaginary," in *Geontologies*, 34, 46.

6. For an overview of the literature on the #NoDAPL struggle, see NYC Stands with Standing Rock Collective, "#StandingRockSyllabus," 2016, https://nycstandswithstandingrock.wordpress.com/standingrocksyllabus/.

7. See Eduardo Viveiros de Castro, "Multinaturalism," in *Cannibal Metaphysics*, Univocal 20, by Eduardo Viveiros de Castro, ed. and trans. Peter Skafish (Minneapolis: University of Minnesota Press, 2014), 65–76. As he explains further: "Cultural relativism, which is a multiculturalism, presumes a diversity of partial, subjective representations bearing on an external nature, unitary and whole, that itself is indifferent to representation. Amerindians propose the inverse: on the one hand, a purely pronominal representative unit—the human is what and whomever occupies the position of the cosmological subject; every existent can be thought of as thinking (it exists, therefore it thinks), as 'activated' or 'agencied' by a point of view—and, on the other, a real or objective radical diversity. Perspectivism is a multinaturalism, since a perspective is not a representation." (72).

8. Melanie K. Yazzie and Cutcha Risling Baldy, "Introduction," in "Indigenous Peoples and the Politics of Water," ed. Melanie K. Yazzie and Cutcha Risling Baldy, special issue, *Decolonization: Indigeneity, Education and Society* 7, no. 1 (2018): 3.

9. Yazzie and Baldy, "Introduction," 2.

10. The players include Karolina Baran, Kathryn Yani, Stephanie Dodge, Nina Bakan, Laura Onderwater, and Natalia St. Lawrence.

11. Nick Dyer-Witheford and Greig de Peuter, *Games of Empire: Global Capitalism and Video Games* (Minneapolis: University of Minnesota Press, 2009), 36.

In this sense, Public Studio's practice approximates what the authors term "games of multitude" and "tactical play," which counteract prevailing systems of extractive capitalism and perform social critique.

12. The other poets are Adrienne Rich, Anne Sexton, Prageeta Sharma, and ineffable-hufflepuff.

13. In addition to female players, it would also be intriguing to invite forest ecologists to explore these games and examine what they reveal about their virtual silvicultures and the accuracy of their computer-generated representations of actual forest environments—although that is not to say that games should not be able to also portray fictional and imaginative habitats that make no claim upon ecomimesis, which is sometimes what games do best.

14. Anne Sexton, "Her Kind" (1960), in *The Complete Poems* (Boston: Houghton Mifflin, 1981).

15. For an overview of some of these green games, see Alenda Chang and John Parham, "Green Computer and Video Games: An Introduction," *Ecozon@: European Journal of Literature, Culture and Environment* 8, no. 2 (2017): 1–17. Chang and Parham state that their cause for hope in green games owes in part "to the medium's tendency to stress systems thinking, continuous feedback, and richly immersive experiences of diverse worlds, a fundamental similarity between games as informatics objects and ecology as a cybernetic science" (12).

16. Alenda Chang, "The Ecology of Games" (lecture, University of California, Santa Cruz, May 16, 2017, video recording), https://itunes.apple.com/us /itunes-u/2017-art-deans-lecture-series/id1234639108?mt=10; Alenda Chang, "Games as Environmental Texts," *Qui Parle* 19, no. 2 (spring/summer 2011): 57–84.

17. For a reading of media *as* and *about* nature, see Jussi Parikka, "Media Ecologies and Imaginary Media: Expansions, Contractions and Foldings," in *Medianatures: The Materiality of Information Technology and Electronic Waste*, ed. Jussi Parikka (London: Open Humanities Press, 2011), 34–50; and John Durham Peters, *The Marvelous Clouds: Toward a Philosophy of Elemental Media* (Chicago: University of Chicago Press, 2015).

18. In dislodging Pierce's classic semiotic taxonomy of icons (likeness between sign and reference) and indexes (existential connection between image and meaning) from the anthropocentric domain, Kohn argues that these are also signs nonhuman beings, or morphodynamic biota, use to signify the world and communicate between themselves, where life's reproduction depends on and is constituted by (nonhuman, nonlinguistic) representation. See Eduardo Kohn, *How Forests Think: Toward an Anthropology beyond the Human* (Berkeley: University of California Press, 2013); and Viveiros de Castro, *Cannibal Metaphysics*.

19. Eduardo Viveiros de Castro, "Exchanging Perspectives: The Transformation of Objects into Subjects in Amerindian Ontologies," *Common Knowledge* 10, no. 3 (2004): 467.

20. Aldo Leopold, *A Sand County Almanac: And Sketches Here and There* (Oxford: Oxford University Press, 1949), 139–40: "The cowman who cleans his range of wolves does not realize that he is taking over the wolf's job of trimming the herd to fit the change. He has not learned to think like a mountain. Hence we have dustbowls, and rivers washing the future into the sea."

21. See Corey Mead, *War Play: Video Games and the Future of Armed Conflict* (New York: Eamon Dolan / Houghton Mifflin Harcourt, 2013).

22. See Farocki's discussion of *Eye-Machine I–III* (2001–3), in which he addresses the concept of the "operational image": these images "do not portray a process but are themselves part of a process." Harun Farocki, "Eye / Machine III," artist's website, accessed December 17, 2019, http://www.harunfarocki.de /installations/2000s/2003/eye-machine-iii.html. See also Trevor Paglen, "Operational Images," *e-flux* 59 (November 2014), http://www.e-flux.com/journal /59/61130/operational-images/.

23. See Aubrey Anable, *Playing with Feelings: Video Games and Affect* (Minneapolis: University of Minnesota Press, 2018); and Jayne Gackenbach and Johnathan Bown, eds., *Boundaries of Self and Reality Online: Implications of Digitally Constructed Realities* (London: Academic Press, 2017).

24. See Henry Jenkins, "Game Design as Narrative Architecture," in *The Game Design Reader: A Rules of Play Anthology*, ed. Katie Salen and Eric Zimmerman (Cambridge, MA: MIT Press, 2006).

25. See Anita Sarkeesian's ongoing web series, *Tropes vs. Women in Video Games*, begun in 2011; and relatedly, Dustin Kidd and Amanda Turner, "The #GamerGate Files: Misogyny in the Media," in *Defining Identity and the Changing Scope of Culture in the Digital Age*, ed. Alison Novak and Imaani J. El-Burki (Hershey, PA: IGI Global, 2016); and Tracy Everbach and Jacqueline Ryan Vickery, eds., *Mediating Misogyny: Gender, Technology, and Harassment* (Chum, Switzerland: Palgrave Macmillan, 2018).

26. See Diana Beresford-Kroeger, *The Global Forest: Forty Ways Trees Can Save Us* (New York: Penguin, 2011), and in particular her chapter "Bioplan for Biodiversity," 48–51, which served as a guide for Public Studio.

27. *Symbiogenesis* is the term coined by biologist Lynn Margulis to define the relational ontology of cellular life, as referenced and developed by Donna Haraway in *When Species Meet* (Minneapolis: University of Minnesota Press, 2007), 15, and in *Staying with the Trouble: Making Kin in the Chthulucene* (Durham, NC: Duke University Press, 2016).

28. For more discussion of Earth law, or biocentric legality, and contemporary art, see my essay "Rights of Nature: The Art and Politics of Earth Jurisprudence," written for the exhibition *Rights of Nature: Art and Ecology in the Americas* (Nottingham Contemporary, January 24–March 15, 2015; curated by T. J. Demos and Alex Farquharson, with Irene Aristizábal) and published in 2015 on the website of Nottingham Contemporary,

http://nottinghamcontemporary.org. See also the 1974 classic text of Christopher Stone, asking "Should Trees Have Standing?" in courts of law, reprinted in *Should Trees Have Standing? 40 Years On*, ed. Anna Grear (Northampton, MA: Edward Elgar, 2012).

29. For further elaboration on rights of nature legality and global activism, see Cormac Cullinan, *Wild Law: A Manifesto for Earth Justice* (Claremont, CA: Green Books, 2002); David R. Boyd, *The Rights of Nature: A Legal Revolution That Could Save the World* (Toronto: ECW Press, 2017); and Maya K. van Rossum, *The Green Amendment: Securing Our Right to a Healthy Environment* (New York: Disruption Books, 2017). See also the websites for the Earth Law Library, http://www.gaiafoundation.org/earth-law-library; and the Indigenous Law Institute, http://ili.nativeweb.org/index.html.

30. Pablo Solón, "The Rights of Mother Nature," City University of New York, April 21, 2011, http://ashleydawson.info/2011/04/21/the-rights-of-mother-nature/.

31. In this regard, the video resembles recent green games such as Mountain, an innovative simulation video game developed by David O'Reilly in 2014, which pictures a mountain floating and slowly revolving in space. Over the course of the game that invites viewer identification with the nonhuman being—again following Aldo Leopold's eco-philosophy—the mountain is gradually hit by a range of everyday objects, shares thoughts through text communications, and after around fifty hours of running comes to an end by crashing into a passing star.

32. See Deborah Bird Rose, "Double Death," 2012, http://www.multispecies-salon.org/double-death/; and Deborah Bird Rose, "When All You Love Is Being Trashed," May 9, 2014, https://vimeo.com/97758080, accessed December 17, 2019.

33. Terri-Lynn Williams-Davidson, "Ts'uu K'waayga/Cedar Sister," in *Out of Concealment: Female Supernatural Beings of Haida Gwaii* (Vancouver: Heritage, 2017), 46–49. Many thanks to Williams-Davidson for bringing this catalog to my attention.

34. Haraway, *Staying with the Trouble*, 4–5.

CHAPTER FIVE: ANIMAL COSMOPOLITICS

1. For further description and documentation, see Gustafsson&Haapoja, *The Trial*, November 2014, http://www.gustafssonhaapoja.org/the-trial/.

2. Terike Haapoja, "A History of Othering," June 19, 2015, http://www.terikehaapoja.net/the-history-of-othering/. For a short video clip of the performance, see "Terike Haapoja&Laura Gustafsson—The Trial—Short Edit," December 16, 2014, https://vimeo.com/114677049.

3. See Aleksandra Jach, "History of Others: Interview with Laura Gustafsson and Terike Haapoja," *Anthropocene Index*, December 24, 2015,

http://theanthropoceneindex.com/article/32-History-of-Others.-Interview-with-Laura-Gustafsson-and-Terike-Haapoja.

4. Giorgio Agamben, *State of Exception*, trans. Kevin Attell (Chicago: University of Chicago Press, 2005); Haapoja, "A History of Othering."

5. Haapoja, "A History of Othering."

6. See Gustafsson&Haapoja, *The Trial*.

7. See Christopher D. Stone, "Should Trees Have Standing—Toward Legal Rights for Natural Objects," *Southern California Law Review* 45 (1972): 450–87; and the website of the Global Alliance for the Rights of Nature, therightsofnature.org/. The Stone precedent and the Nonhuman Rights Project are also referenced and discussed in Haapoja, "A History of Othering." Stone's concern was *Sierra Club v. Morton*, a lawsuit initiated by the environmentalist organization against Walt Disney Enterprises's ski resort development project in the Mineral King Valley, a wilderness area in the Sierra Nevada Mountains of California. The US Supreme Court rejected the case, claiming the Sierra Club had no property there, and thus no legal standing (the necessary basis upon which the case could proceed), although one dissenting judge, William O. Douglas, asked if the valley should not be able to assume personhood status and assert its rights, much like ships and corporations possess legal personhood: "So it should be as respects [to] valleys, alpine meadows, rivers, lakes, estuaries, beaches, ridges, groves of trees, swampland, or even air that feels the destructive pressures of modern technology and modern life." That opinion proved prescient, with contemporary legal activists attempting to establish the rights of nature as a valid basis of legal standing to this day.

8. Nonhuman Rights Project, "Client, Tommy (Chimpanzee): The NhRP's First Client," accessed December 17, 2019, https://www.nonhumanrights.org/client-tommy/. On May 8, 2018, a New York Court of Appeals denied the Nonhuman Rights Project's attempt to contest a lower court's ruling on the fate of chimpanzees Tommy and Kiko, with the court claiming that the case represents "a deep dilemma of ethics and policy that demands our attention. To treat a chimpanzee as if he or she had no right to liberty protected by *habeas corpus* is to regard the chimpanzee as entirely lacking independent worth, as a mere resource for human use, a thing the value of which consists exclusively in its usefulness to others. Instead, we should consider whether a chimpanzee is an individual with inherent value who has the right to be treated with respect'"—words that could have come right out of Haapoja and Gustafsson's *Trial*. Robby Berman, "Court Ruling Denies Appeal for Tommy and Kiko, but Not Their Rights," *Big Think*, May 9, 2018, https://bigthink.com/robby-berman/court-ruling-denies-appeal-for-tommy-and-kiko-but-not-their-rights.

9. David R. Boyd, *The Rights of Nature: A Legal Revolution That Could Save the World* (Toronto: ECW Press, 2017). For further links between rights of nature legality and artistic practice, see "Rights of Nature: The Art and Politics of

Earth Jurisprudence," my catalog essay for the exhibition *Rights of Nature: Art and Ecology in the Americas* (Nottingham Contemporary, January 24–March 15, 2015; curated by T. J. Demos and Alex Farquharson, with Irene Aristizábal), www.nottinghamcontemporary.org.

10. For the hour-long documentary excerpting moments from the hearings, see Compass, "Monsanto Hearings," accessed September 28, 2015, http://midwestcompass.org/monsanto-hearings. See also "COP21: Make It Work," May 2015, http://www.sciencespo.fr/public/en/content/cop21-make-it-work; and Bruno Latour, "From Realpolitik to Dingpolitik: Or, How to Make Things Public?," in *Making Things Public: Atmospheres of Democracy*, ed. Bruno Latour and Peter Weibel (Cambridge, MA: MIT Press, 2005). For an interview with Nabil Ahmed about the Inter-Pacific Ring Tribunal, see T. J. Demos, "West Papua Conflict: From Genocide to Ecocide: An Interview with Nabil Ahmed," Center for Creative Ecologies, March 2018, https://creativeecologies.ucsc.edu/west-papua-conflict-from-genocide-to-ecocide/.

11. For a historical and philosophical overview of Western human exceptionalism, see Gary Steiner, *Anthropocentrism and Its Discontents: The Moral Status of Animals in the History of Western Philosophy* (Pittsburgh: University of Pittsburgh Press, 2005).

12. For one useful articulation of cosmopolitics—the politics of building a common world—see Isabelle Stengers, "The Cosmopolitical Proposal," in Latour and Weibel, *Making Things Public*, 994–1003.

13. Terike Haapoja, opening speech for *The Party of Others*, 2011 (manuscript in author's possession). Thanks to Terike Haapoja for sharing her documents.

14. See Laura Gustafsson and Terike Haapoja, "Introduction: Museum of Nonhumanity Declares That Dehumanization Is History," in *Museum of Nonhumanity*, 2019 (manuscript in author's possession).

15. Félix Guattari, *The Three Ecologies* (1989), trans. Ian Pindar and Paul Sutton (London: Athlone Press, 2000); Félix Guattari, *Chaosmosis: An Ethico-Aesthetic Paradigm* (1992), trans. Paul Bains and Julian Pefanis (Bloomingdale: Indiana University Press, 1995).

16. I am thinking of work by such authors as Vine Deloria Jr. to Glen Sean Coulthard and Audra Simpson, from Angela Davis and Audre Lorde to Kimberlé Crenshaw and Keeanga-Yamahtta Taylor.

17. Rosi Braidotti, "Posthuman Critical Theory," in *Critical Posthumanism and Planetary Futures*, ed. D. Banerji and M. R. Paranjape (New Delhi: Springer India, 2016), 13, 22, citing Guattari's *The Three Ecologies*.

18. Kimberly TallBear, "Beyond the Life/Not Life Binary: A Feminist-Indigenous Reading of Cryopreservation, Interspecies Thinking and the New Materialisms," in *Cryopolitics: Frozen Life in a Melting World*, ed. Joanna Radin and Emma Kowal (Cambridge, MA: MIT Press, 2017); Zoe Todd, "An Indigenous Feminist's Take on the Ontological Turn: 'Ontology' Is Just Another Word

for Colonialism," *Urbane Adventurer: Amiskwacî* (blog), October 24, 2014, https://zoeandthecity.wordpress.com/2014/10/24/an-indigenous-feminists-take-on-the-ontological-turn-ontology-is-just-another-word-for-colonialism.

19. Donna Haraway, "Tentacular Thinking: Anthropocene, Capitalocene, Chthulucene," in *Staying with the Trouble: Making Kin in the Chthulucene* (Durham, NC: Duke University Press, 2016), 30.

20. See Genesis 1:26 (*The New Oxford Annotated Bible with the Apocrypha*, Oxford University Press, 1977): "Then God said, 'Let us make man in our image, after our likeness; and let them have dominion over the fish of the sea, and over the birds of the air, and over the cattle, and over all the earth, and over every creeping thing that creeps upon the earth.' "

21. For further discussion of extraction, see chapter 2. For overviews of extractive capital and slow environmental violence, see Macarena Gómez-Barris, *The Extractive Zone: Social Ecologies and Decolonial Perspectives* (Durham, NC: Duke University Press, 2017); Sandro Mezzadra and Brett Neilson, "On the Multiple Frontiers of Extraction: Excavating Contemporary Capitalism," *Cultural Studies* 31, nos. 2–3 (2017): 185–204; Andreas Malm, *Fossil Capital: The Rise of Steam Power and the Roots of Global Warming* (London: Verso, 2016); and Rob Nixon, *Slow Violence and the Environmentalism of the Poor* (Cambridge, MA: Harvard University Press, 2011).

22. Michel Serres, *The Natural Contract* (1990), trans. Elizabeth MacArthur and William Paulson (Ann Arbor: University of Michigan Press, 1995). The history of environmental thinking has also been importantly extended back to Marx, in John Bellamy Foster, *Marx's Ecology: Materialism and Nature* (New York: Monthly Review Press, 2000).

23. Anna Tsing, "Unruly Edges: Mushrooms as Companion Species," *Environmental Humanities* 1 (2012): 141; Haraway, *Staying with the Trouble*, 12. See also Anna Tsing, *The Mushroom at the End of the World: On the Possibility of Life in Capitalist Ruins* (Princeton, NJ: Princeton University Press, 2015).

24. Hugh Raffles, *Insectopedia* (New York: Pantheon, 2011); Thom van Dooren, *The Wake of Crows: Living and Dying in Shared Worlds* (New York: Columbia University Press, 2019); Jennifer Ackerman, *The Genius of Birds* (New York: Penguin, 2016). See also Eben Kirksey, Craig Schuetze, and Stefan Helmreich, "Introduction," in *The Multispecies Salon*, ed. Eben Kirksey (Durham, NC: Duke University Press, 2014), 1–24; and the Institute for Critical Animal Studies (http://www.criticalanimalstudies.org/).

25. Paulo Tavares, "In the Forest Ruins," *e-flux*, December 9, 2016, http://www.e-flux.com/architecture/superhumanity/68688/in-the-forest-ruins/; Eduardo Kohn, *How Forests Think: Toward an Anthropology beyond the Human* (Berkeley: University of California Press, 2013).

26. On animal nature-cultures, see "Breed," ed. Kristen Guest and Monica Mattfeld, special issue, *Humanimalia: A Journal of Human/Animal Interface Studies*

10, no. 1 (Fall 2018); and Brian Massumi, *What Animals Teach Us about Politics* (Durham, NC: Duke University Press, 2014). "Naturalcultural" is a term of Donna Haraway's, unhyphenated in order to grammatically signal the false binary that conventionally separates these unseparable contact zones of mutual origination and becoming. See Donna Haraway, *When Species Meet* (Minneapolis: University of Minnesota Press, 2007).

27. Anna Tsing, Heather Swanson, Elaine Gan, and Nils Bubandt, eds., *Arts of Living on a Damaged Planet* (Minneapolis: University of Minnesota Press, 2017), G12. See also Guattari's notion of "a new art of living" (*Chaosmosis*, 21).

28. Haapoja, "A History of Othering."

29. Giorgio Agamben, *The Open: Man and Animal*, trans. Kevin Attell (Stanford: Stanford University Press, 2004), 80.

30. Haapoja, "A History of Othering."

31. On the biopolitics of disability, see Jasbir Puar, *The Right to Maim: Debility, Capacity, Disability* (Durham, NC: Duke University Press, 2017).

32. Terike Haapoja, "The Party of Others: Platform," 2011 (manuscript in author's possession); Happoja, "The Party of Others: Opening Speech." Cf. the "undocumented political party" of refugee members of the Amsterdam-based We Are Here collective, as discussed in Jonas Staal, "Theater of the Stateless," *Propaganda Art in the 21st Century* (Cambridge, MA: MIT Press, 2019), 149–86.

33. Haapoja reports that she subsequently began to expand and develop *The Party of Others* in Guatemala and Mexico in 2014 but was only doing preliminary interviews and workshops. She explains that the Guatemala project was especially notable because most of the interviewees were Indigenous Mayans, which gave the project a whole different perspective, also making it less urgent, as these Indigenous folks, as with native traditions elsewhere, already share many of the project's assumptions of an expanded cosmology of personhood and rights beyond the human. Email to author, September 28, 2018.

34. Terike Haapoja, *The Party of Others*, 2011, accessed January 3, 2020, http://www.terikehaapoja.net/party-of-others/.

35. Haapoja, *The Party of Others*.

36. In the Finnish language, which lacks gendered pronouns, all things are referred to as "it"; consequently, Haapoja asked interviewees to refer to animals and natural entities as "they/them." Gustafsson&Haapoja are also currently experimenting with building an interspecies language school called Baaa-Bel, which would raise all sorts of questions about nonanthropocentric language and communication. Email to author, May 11, 2019.

37. Haapoja, *The Party of Others*. Cf. Stengers, "The Cosmopolitical Proposal," 1002: "As for the cosmopolitical perspective, its question is twofold. How to design the political scene in a way that actively protects it from the fiction that 'humans of good will will decide in the name of the general interest'? How to turn the virus or the river into a cause for thinking? But also how to

design it in such a way that collective thinking has to proceed 'in the presence of' those who would otherwise be likely to be disqualified as having idiotically nothing to propose, hindering the emergent 'common account'?"

38. Bruno Latour, *Politics of Nature: How to Bring the Sciences into Democracy*, trans. Catherine Porter (Cambridge, MA: Harvard University Press, 2004), 18. See also Latour and Weibel, *Making Things Public*.

39. Stefan Helmreich, *Alien Ocean: Anthropological Voyages in Microbial Seas* (Berkeley: University of California Press, 2009). The genealogy of the term *symbiopolitics* moves through "symbiogenesis," which biologist Lynn Margulis defined as the relational ontology of cellular life, and is discussed further in Haraway, *When Species Meet*, 15.

40. The classic text that challenges this regime of objectification is Peter Singer's *Animal Liberation: A New Ethics for Our Treatment of Animals* (New York: Random House, 1975). See also Martha Nussbaum and Cass Sunstein, *Animal Rights* (New York: Oxford University Press, 2004).

41. Haraway, *When Species Meet*, 18.

42. This restricted notion of intersectionality is productively challenged in Aph Ko and Syl Ko, *Aphro-ism: Essays on Pop Culture, Feminism, and Black Veganism from Two Sisters* (New York: Lantern Books, 2017); and Julia Feliz Brueck, ed., *Veganism in an Oppressive World: A Vegans of Color Community Project* (Lexington: Sanctuary, 2017).

43. See Agamben, *The Open*; and Eben Kirksey and Stefan Helmreich, "The Emergence of Multispecies Ethnography," *Cultural Anthropology* 25, no. 4 (2010): 545. For further discussion of recent artistic engagements of animal cultures, see Sven Lütticken, "Abstract Habitats: Installations of Coexistence and Co-evolution," *Grey Room* (Spring 2015): 102–27.

44. Haapoja, "A History of Othering."

45. Laura Gustafsson and Terike Haapoja, eds., *History According to Cattle* (Helsinki: Into Kustannus, 2015), 149.

46. Terike Haapoja and Laura Gustafsson, "A History According to Cattle," reprinted in *Art in the Anthropocene*, ed. Heather Davis and Etienne Turpin (London: Open Humanities Press, 2015), 297.

47. See Gustafsson and Haapoja, *History According to Cattle*, 42–43.

48. Scout Calvert, "Ready for the Robot: Bovines in the Integrated Circuit," *Humanimalia* 10, no. 1 (Fall 2018): 74–97.

49. Laura Gustafsson and Terike Haapoja, "Imagining Non-Human Realities," in *History According to Cattle*, 109.

50. I adapt the term *cosmological autism* from Kohn, *How Forests Think*. See also Gustafsson and Haapoja, *History According to Cattle*, 107. In "A History of Othering," Haapoja describes the Museum of the History of Cattle as "a holocaust museum of its own kind."

51. Gustafsson and Haapoja, "Imagining Non-Human Realities," 109.

52. Gustafsson and Haapoja, "Imagining Non-Human Realities," 109.

53. Gustafsson and Haapoja, "Imagining Non-Human Realities," 111.

54. On blackness and the (in)human, where representation is historically denied and contested, see Alexander G. Weheliye, *Habeas Viscus: Racializing Assemblages, Biopolitics, and Black Feminist Theories of the Human* (Durham, NC: Duke University Press, 2014).

55. Gayatri Chakravorty Spivak, "Can the Subaltern Speak?"; Kirksey and Helmreich, "The Emergence of Multispecies Ethnography," 555. For Arjun Appadurai, "anthropology survives by its claim to capture other places (and other voices) through its special brand of ventriloquism. It is this claim that needs constant examination." Arjun Appadurai, "Introduction: Place and Voice in Anthropological Theory," *Cultural Anthropology* 3, no. 1 (1988): 20.

56. Jacques Derrida, "And Say the Animal Responded?," in *Zoontologies: The Question of the Animal* (Minneapolis: University of Minnesota Press, 2003), 121–46.

57. See Barbara Smuts, "Embodied Communication in Nonhuman Animals," in *Human Development in the Twenty-First Century: Visionary Ideas from Systems Scientists*, ed. Alan Fogel, Barbara J. King, and Stuart G. Shanker (Cambridge: Cambridge University Press, 2007), cited in Haraway, *When Species Meet*, 26.

58. See Eric C. Brown, ed., *Insect Poetics* (Minneapolis: University of Minnesota Press, 2006); and Susan McHugh, *Animal Stories: Narrating across Species Lines* (Minneapolis: University of Minnesota Press, 2011).

59. Gregory Bateson, "Problems in Cetacean and Other Mammalian Communication," in *Steps to an Ecology of Mind* (New York: Ballantine Books, 1972), 369–83.

60. Massumi, *What Animals Teach Us about Politics*, 8.

61. Massumi, *What Animals Teach Us about Politics*, 2.

62. Massumi, *What Animals Teach Us about Politics*, 108n43.

63. Haapoja, "A History of Othering."

64. Massumi, *What Animals Teach Us about Politics*, 12.

CHAPTER SIX: TO SAVE A WORLD

1. John Asafu-Adjaye et al., "An Ecomodernist Manifesto," April 2015, 6, http://www.ecomodernism.org/s/An-Ecomodernist-Manifesto.pdf.

2. See Movement for Black Lives, "Platform," accessed January 3, 2020, https://policy.m4bl.org/platform/.

3. As I argued in T. J. Demos, *Against the Anthropocene: Visual Culture and Environment Today* (Berlin: Sternberg, 2017).

4. See Donna Haraway, *Staying with the Trouble: Making Kin in the Chthulucene* (Durham, NC: Duke University Press, 2016); Anna Tsing, Heather Swanson, Elaine Gan, and Nils Bubandt, eds., *Arts of Living on a Damaged Planet* (Minneapolis: University of Minnesota Press, 2017); and Jason Moore, *Capitalism in the Web of Life* (London: Verso, 2015).

5. The fairly generic and species-based terminology of the Anthropocene actually has a much longer genealogy, which I discuss in *Against the Anthropocene*.

6. Paul Crutzen and Eugene Stoermer, "The 'Anthropocene,'" *Global Change Newsletter* 41 (2000): 17–18.

7. Paul J. Crutzen, "Geology of Mankind," *Nature* 415, no. 23 (January 3, 2002): 23.

8. Paul Crutzen, "Albedo Enhancement by Stratospheric Sulfur Injections: A Contribution to Resolve a Policy Dilemma? An Editorial Essay," *Climatic Change* 77 (2006): 211–19. For Crutzen, the Cold War provided the opportunity to first research the atmosphere as theater of large-scale military intervention transformed by a hypothetical "nuclear winter," an experience that fed into his subsequent consideration of technology in the 1990s as a means of tackling climate change. See also Paul Crutzen and John W. Birks, "The Atmosphere after a Nuclear War: Twilight at Noon," in *Nuclear War: The Aftermath*, ed. Jeannie Peterson (New York: Pantheon Books, 1983), 114–25.

9. Simon Lewis and Mark Maslin, "Defining the Anthropocene," *Nature* 519, no. 7542 (March 12, 2015): 174–75; David Biello, "Mass Deaths in Americas Start New CO_2 Epoch," *Scientific American*, March 11, 2015; and Alexander Koch, Chris Brierley, Mark Maslin, and Simon Lewis, "European colonization of the Americas killed 10 percent of world population and caused global cooling," PRI, January 31, 2019, https://www.pri.org.

10. For additional historiographic discussion, see Karen Barad's recent speculative proposals for a defractive methodology unfolding from the insights in quantum field theory. According to her suggestion, highlighting time's in/determinacies, we might think 1945 *in and through* 1492, 1610, 1950, and 1962–66, and vice versa, where all prospective Anthropocene dates and resonant crisis points define a materially connected web of intra-active historical unfoldings and respective repositionings, a/causalities and in/consequences, that are significant but not totalizing. Karen Barad, "Troubling Time/s and Ecologies of Nothingness: Re-turning, Re-membering, and Facing the Incalculable," *New Formations* 92 (autumn 2017): 57.

11. For elaborations on the importance of dating the Anthropocene sensitive to colonial and racial history, see Heather Davis and Zoe Todd, "On the Importance of a Date, or Decolonizing the Anthropocene," ACME: *An International Journal for Critical Geographies* 16, no. 4 (2017): 761–80; and Kathryn Yusoff, "Golden Spikes and Dubious Origins," in *A Billion Black Anthropocenes or None* (Minneapolis: University of Minnesota Press, 2018), 23–64.

12. Asafu-Adjaye et al., "An Ecomodernist Manifesto," 6.

13. "Notes from the Editors," *Monthly Review* 66, no. 2 (June 1, 2014), https://monthlyreview.org/2014/06/01/mr-066-02-2014-06_0/. See also Colin McInnes, "Time to Embrace Geoengineering: Beyond Planetary Boundaries,"

The Breakthrough, June 27, 2013, http://thebreakthrough.org/programs/energy
-and-climate/time-to-embrace-geoengineering.

14. Michael Shellenberger and Ted Nordhaus, "The Death of Environmentalism: Global Warming Politics in a Post-Environmental World," 2004,
https://s3.us-east-2.amazonaws.com/uploads.thebreakthrough.org/legacy
/images/Death_of_Environmentalism.pdf. *Ecological modernization theory*, as
Richard York and Eugene Rosa explain, contends that "industrialization,
technological development, economic growth, and capitalism are not only
potentially compatible with ecological sustainability but also may be key drivers
of environmental reform." Richard York and Eugene A. Rosa, "Key Challenges
to Ecological Modernization Theory," *Organization and Environment* 16, no. 3 (September 2003): 274. The "politics of limits" refers to the Breakthrough Institute's
ultimate nemesis: Donella H. Meadows et al., *The Limits to Growth: A Report for the
Club of Rome's Project on the Predicament of Mankind* (London: Pan, 1974).

15. "Notes from the Editors," *Monthly Review*. For a thorough critique of the
manifesto and its pro-growth claims, see Jeremy Caradonna et al., "A Degrowth
Response to an Ecomodernist Manifesto," May 6, 2015, http://www.resilience
.org/stories/2015-05-06/a-degrowth-response-to-an-ecomodernist-manifesto.

16. Asafu-Adjaye et al., "An Ecomodernist Manifesto," 29.

17. On this debunking, see, for instance, David Harvey, *A Brief History of
Neoliberalism* (Oxford: Oxford University Press, 2005); and Naomi Klein, *This
Changes Everything: Capitalism vs. the Climate* (New York: Allen Lane, 2014).

18. Van Jones, "Vanity Fair: The Unbearable Whiteness of Green," *Huff-
post*, May 17, 2007, https://www.huffingtonpost.com/van-jones/vanity-fair-the
-unbearabl_b_48766.html.

19. For further criticism of the slippery discourse of sustainable development, see T. J. Demos, "The Art and Politics of Sustainability," in *Decolonizing
Nature: Contemporary Art and the Politics of Ecology* (Berlin: Sternberg, 2016), 31–62.

20. Christina Sharpe, *In the Wake: On Blackness and Being* (Durham, NC: Duke
University Press, 2016), 21. Meanwhile, there is hardly a mention of the terms
ecology, *climate*, or *atmosphere* in the recent 848-page catalog of Jafa's work, with
essays by Fred Moten, Tina M. Campt, Ernest Hardy, John Akomfrah, Hans
Ulrich Obrist, and Yana Peel, *Arthur Jafa: A Series of Utterly Improbable, Yet Extraordinary Renditions*, ed. Amira Gad and Joseph Constable (London: König and
Serpentine, 2018).

21. See Frieda Ekotto and Adeline Koh, eds., *Rethinking Third Cinema: The
Role of Anti-colonial Media and Aesthetics in Postmodernity* (Berlin: Lit, 2009); and
"The Militant Image: A Ciné-Geography," ed. Kodwo Eshun and Ros Gray,
special issue, *Third Text* 25, no. 1 (January 2011).

22. Alessandra Raengo, "Black Ontology and the Love of Blackness: Introduction," *Liquid Blackness* 3, no. 6 (December 2016), http://liquidblackness.com
/lb6-black-ontology-and-the-love-of-blackness/.

23. For discussion of the Black Anthropocene, where racialization is premised on exclusion as well as creative survival and critical resistance, and which stresses the formative influence of Octavia Butler's dystopian sci-fi and Earthseed series, see Stephanie LeMenager, "To Get Ready for Climate Change, Read Octavia Butler," *Electrastreet*, November 2017, https://electrastreet .net/2017/11/to-get-ready-for-climate-change-read-octavia-butler/; and Yusoff, *A Billion Black Anthropocenes or None*.

24. For further discussion of art and climate justice, see "Contemporary Art and the Politics of Ecology," ed. T. J. Demos, special issue, *Third Text* 120 (January 2013); Demos, *Decolonizing Nature*; and Yates McKee, "On Flooded Streets and Breathing-in-Common: Climate Justice, Black Lives Matter, and the Arts of Decolonization," in *Strike Art: Contemporary Art and the Post-Occupy Condition* (London: Verso, 2016), 181–236.

25. Robert D. Bullard and Beverly Wright, *Race, Place, and Environmental Justice after Hurricane Katrina: Struggles to Reclaim, Rebuild, and Revitalize New Orleans and the Gulf Coast* (Boulder, CO: Westview Press, 2009).

26. Neil Smith, "There Is No Such Thing as a Natural Disaster," *Understanding Katrina: Perspectives from the Social Sciences*, June 11, 2006, http:// understandingkatrina.ssrc.org/Smith/.

27. Stefano Harney and Fred Moten, "Michael Brown," *boundary 2* 42, no. 4 (November 2015): 82.

28. Robinson Meyer, "Donald Trump Is the First Demagogue of the Anthropocene," *The Atlantic*, October 19, 2016; Christopher Schaberg, "Trump in the Anthropocene," *Sierra*, February 1, 2017. According to Schaberg, "We have to acknowledge Trump as endemic to, and symptomatic of, the current state of our world. His bullying tweets and destructive executive orders; his prioritizing dirty fossil fuels over clean renewable energy; his 'us versus them' and 'America first' ethic all expose the very same pathologies that got us an 'Anthropocene' in the first place."

29. Rebecca Solnit, "Climate Change Is Violence," *Truthout*, February 5, 2015, http://truthout.org/articles/climate-change-is-violence.

30. Naomi Klein, "Why #BlackLivesMatter Should Transform the Climate Debate," *The Nation*, December 12, 2014.

31. See the larger discussion of this situation in the research project of Adrian Lahoud, "Climate Crimes," accessed January 3, 2020, https://www.vam .ac.uk/articles/project-focus-adrian-lahoud-climate-crimes.

32. Two recent contributions supporting movement in this direction are adrienne mare brown, *Emergent Strategy: Shaping Change, Changing Worlds* (Chico, CA: AK Press, 2017); and Shelley Streeby, *Imagining the Future of Climate Change: World-Making through Science Fiction and Activism* (Oakland: University of California Press, 2018).

33. See Environmental Protection Agency, "Environmental Justice Time-line," accessed January 3, 2020, https://www.epa.gov/environmentaljustice/environmental-justice-timeline; United Church of Christ's Commission for Racial Justice's landmark report, *Toxic Wastes and Race in the United States* (New York: Public Data Access, 1987), which revealed that "three out of every five Black and Hispanic Americans lived in communities with uncontrolled toxic waste sites" (xiv); and the important work of Robert D. Bullard, *Dumping in Dixie: Race, Class, and Environmental Quality* (Boulder, CO: Westview, 1990). More recently, see Lindsey Dillon and Julie Sze, "Police Power and Particulate Matters: Environmental Justice and the Spatialities of In/securities in U.S. Cities," *English Language Notes* (Fall/Winter 2016).

34. Jasbir Puar, "Hands Up, Don't Shoot!," in *The Right to Maim: Debility, Capacity, Disability* (Durham, NC: Duke University Press, 2017), xvii.

35. See Craig Owens, "The Allegorical Impulse: Toward a Theory of Post-modernism," in *Beyond Recognition* (Los Angeles: University of California Press, 1992), wherein allegory figures as "the epitome of counter-narrative, for it arrests narrative in place, substituting a principle of syntagmatic disjunction for one of diegetic combination. In this way allegory superinduces a vertical or paradigmatic reading of correspondences upon a horizontal or syntagmatic chain of events" (57).

36. Bruno Latour, "Love Your Monsters: Why We Must Care for Our Technologies as We Do Our Children," *Breakthrough* 2 (winter 2012), https://thebreakthrough.org/journal/issue-2/love-your-monsters.

37. Bruno Latour, *Facing Gaia: Eight Lectures on the New Climatic Regime*, trans. Catherine Porter (Medford, MA: Polity, 2017), 97.

38. Latour, "Love Your Monsters"; Klein, *This Changes Everything*, 279. That said, there are also progressive engineering models distinct from techno-fixes, including forest management practices, mangrove protection, and permaculture farming, all of which accelerate carbon sequestration through natural processes rather than fossil fuel–based machines, changing both the world and ourselves. See Troy Vettese, "To Freeze the Thames: Natural Geo-Engineering and Biodiversity," *New Left Review* 111 (May–June 2018).

39. For more critical overviews of geoengineering, see www.geoengineeringmonitor.org, a joint project of Biofuelwatch and ETC Group, with support from the Heinrich Böll Foundation; Linda Schneider, "Geo-engineering and Environmental Capitalism: Extractive Industries in the Era of Climate Change," *Science for the People*, Summer 2018, https://magazine.scienceforthepeople.org/geoengineering-environmental-capitalism/; and John Bellamy Foster, "Making War on the Planet: Geoengineering and Capitalism's Creative Destruction of the Earth," *Science for the People*, Summer 2018, https://magazine.scienceforthepeople.org/making-war-on-the-planet/. For

current proposals for developing a governance system based on functional, strategic, and normative demand rationales, see Sikina Jinnah, "Why Govern Climate Engineering? A Preliminary Framework for Demand-Based Governance," *International Studies Review* 20 (2018): 272–82. See also the overview of the dangers of the technology as explained in the document endorsed by more than one hundred civil society organizations, "Manifesto against Geoengineering," October 2018, http://www.geoengineeringmonitor.org/2018/10/hands-off-mother-earth-manifesto-against-geoengineering/.

40. See Kum-Kum Bhavnani, John Foran, Priya A. Kurian, and Debashish Munshi, eds., *Climate Futures: Re-Imagining Global Climate Justice* (London: Zed Books, 2019); and Dominic Roser and Christian Seidel, *Climate Justice: An Introduction* (New York: Routledge, 2016).

41. I discuss many of these formations further in the next chapter.

42. As sci-fi writer Kim Stanley Robinson puts it in a recent interview: "Justice is a climate-change technology of great power, so there is no need to set up false dichotomies as to which good cause we support. The good causes reinforce each other and we need them all at once. This is why capitalism has to give way to an ecologically based post-capitalism, which, in some features, will be aspects of socialism chosen democratically. We have to figure out a way to pay ourselves to do the work of survival." Javier Sethness, "Toward an Ecologically Based Post-Capitalism: Interview with Novelist Kim Stanley Robinson," *Truthout*, March 17, 2018, http://www.truthout.org/articles/toward-an-ecologically-based-post-capitalism-interview-with-novelist-kim-stanley-robinson.

43. Jedediah Purdy, *After Nature: A Politics for the Anthropocene* (Cambridge, MA: Harvard University Press, 2015): the risk of a "neoliberal Anthropocene" occurs when nature is consigned to "natural capital" via economic mechanisms, where techno-optimism forces our collective fate into the hands of markets and technology.

44. John Elkington, "Saving the Planet from Ecological Disaster Is a $12 Trillion Opportunity," *Harvard Business Review*, May 4, 2017.

45. Breakthrough Initiatives, accessed January 3, 2020, https://breakthroughinitiatives.org/.

46. See Rory Rowan, "Beyond Colonial Futurism: Portugal's Atlantic Spaceport and the Neoliberalization of Outer Space," April 18, 2018, http://www.e-flux.com/video/198108/e-flux-lectures-rory-rowan-beyond-colonial-futurism-portugal-s-atlantic-spaceport-and-the-neoliberalization-of-outer-space/. For one example, see https://www.planetaryresources.com, the website of Planetary Resources, founded in 2009, partnering with such corporations as Google, Bechtel, and Virgin Gallactic, and currently embarking on "the world's first commercial deep space exploration program."

47. A related point of comparison is Trevor Paglen's *Orbital Reflector* (2018), a satellite-experiment-as-artistic-gesture supported by the Nevada Museum

of Art, and launched into space via a SpaceX Falcon 9 rocket (belonging to the private Space Exploration Technologies Corporation owned by Musk). Once aloft, the kinetic sculpture was meant to inflate like a balloon, with reflective titanium dioxide powder coating its interior and making it visible from Earth. For a couple of months, it was to remain in low orbit, 350 miles from Earth, before disintegrating in the upper atmosphere without a trace. However, owing to the United States' record-long government shutdown, Paglen lost communication with *Orbital Reflector*, which ended up lost in space. Meant to initiate critical consideration of sky-bound technology going from satellites to space junk (which it inadvertently became), the project, in apparent complicity with SpaceX, also drew scrutiny away from justice-based politics and inequalities on the ground.

48. See Jackie Wang, *Carceral Capitalism* (Cambridge, MA: MIT Press, 2018); and Alleen Brown, Will Parrish, and Alice Speri, "Leaked Documents Reveal Counterterrorism Tactics Used at Standing Rock to 'Defeat Pipeline Insurgencies,'" *The Intercept*, May 17, 2017. Not only was a private counterinsurgency corporation, TigerSwan, employed against Standing Rock water protectors, but the FBI's terrorism taskforce investigated them as well.

49. See David Keith, *The Case for Geoengineering* (Cambridge, MA: MIT Press, 2013). Gates and Tar Sands tycoon Murray Edwards are among the key funders of Carbon Engineering. See the interactive geoengineering map designed by ETC Group and the Heinrich Böll Foundation that shows the global state of climate engineering research and experimentation, including nearly one thousand current projects: "Geoengineering Map," accessed January 3, 2020, https://map.geoengineeringmonitor.org/.

50. See Geoengineering Monitor and ETC Group, "Marine Cloud Brightening Project," accessed January 3, 2020, http://www.geoengineeringmonitor.org /wp-content/uploads/2018/04/geoeng_briefing-MCBP.pdf. Remarkably, none of these examples, which testify to the corporate domination of geoengineering research at present, is addressed in Holly Jean Buck's pro-tech apologia, *After Geoengineering* (London: Verso, 2019).

51. Achille Mbembe, *Critique of Black Reason*, trans. Laurent Dubois (Durham, NC: Duke University Press, 2017), 6.

52. Yuval Noah Harari, *Homo Deus: A Brief History of Tomorrow* (London: Harvill Secker, 2016). Bill Gates featured the book on his blog, in, "What if People Run Out of Things to Do?," May 22, 2017, https://www.gatesnotes.com/Books /Homo-Deus; and in Bill Gates, "What Are the Biggest Problems Facing Us in the 21st Century?," *New York Times*, September 4, 2018.

53. Joanna Zalinska, *The End of Man: A Feminist Counterapocalypse* (Minneapolis: University of Minnesota Press, 2018), 10.

54. Mark Lynas, *The God Species: Saving the Planet in the Age of Humans* (Washington, DC: National Geographic, 2011).

55. Harari, *Homo Deus.*

56. "Noam Chomsky on Midterms: Republican Party Is the 'Most Dangerous Organization in Human History,'" *Democracy Now!*, November 5, 2018, https://www.democracynow.org/2018/11/5/noam_chomsky_on_midterms _republican_party. At the same time, the US, along with the petrochemical industry, is a leading force in blocking any international regulation of climate engineering, which also works to legitimate further fossil fuel industry investment. See Jonathan Watts, "US and Saudi Arabia Blocking Regulation of Geoengineering, Sources Say," *The Guardian*, March 18, 2019.

57. Matthias Schrader, "Why Climate Change Skeptics Are Backing Geoengineering," *Wired*, March 28, 2018. "The future is bright for geoengineering," claimed Republican representative Randy Weber of Texas, chairman of the Energy Subcommittee of the House Committee on Science, Space and Technology and noted climate skeptic.

58. See Andy Parker, Joshua Horton, and David Keith, "Stopping Solar Geoengineering through Technical Means: A Preliminary Assessment of Counter-Geoengineering," *Earth's Future*, May 2018.

59. Arthur Jafa, with reference to Fred Moten, in conversation with Greg Tate, at the Hammer Museum, 2017: "Arthur Jafa & Greg Tate," July 5, 2017, https://www.youtube.com/watch?v=CAYSXam1vOA. See also Arthur Jafa, *My Black Death: On the Blackness of* BLACKNUSS (New York: Publication Studio, 2015).

60. Jafa in conversation with Tate, 2017.

61. Greg Tate, "The Changeling Mise-en-Scène—Arthur Jafa's Meta Love and the New Black Reportage," in *Love Is the Message, the Message Is Death* (New York: Gavin Brown's Enterprise, 2016), n.p.

62. "The Mundane Afrofuturist Manifesto," Artbound, November 18, 2015, https://www.kcet.org/shows/artbound/artbound-episode-the-mundane -afrofuturist-manifesto.

63. "The Mundane Afrofuturist Manifesto" was originally published by Rhizome in 2013. See Martine Syms, "The Mundane Afrofuturist Manifesto," December 17, 2013, http://rhizome.org/editorial/2013/dec/17/mundane -afrofuturist-manifesto/.

64. For further consideration of the emancipatory elements, chrono-politics, and sonic history of Afrofuturism, see Black Audio Film Collective's fictional documentary essay-film *The Last Angel of History* (1996); Kodwo Eshun, *More Brilliant Than the Sun: Adventures in Sonic Fiction* (London: Quartet Books, 1999); Kodwo Eshun, "Further Considerations on Afrofuturism," CR: *The New Centennial Review* 3, no. 2 (Summer 2003): 287–301; and "On Black Panther, Afrofuturism, and Astroblackness: A Conversation with Reynaldo Anderson," *Black Scholar*, March 13, 2018.

65. Martine Syms, "The Mundane Afrofuturist Manifesto." In this piece, Syms builds off the "Mundane Sci-Fi Manifesto" conceptualized by Geoff Ryman in 2007, although she notably injects social justice and progressive

political imperatives into her version. See "'Take the Third Star on the Left and on til Morning!' by Geoff Ryman," *Mundane-SF*, September 16, 2007, http://mundane-sf.blogspot.com/2007/09/take-third-star-on-left-and-on-til.html. See also Reynaldo Anderson and Charles E. Jones, eds., *Afrofuturism 2.0: The Rise of Astro-Blackness* (Lanham, MD: Lexington Books, 2015), x, which defines Afrofuturism 2.0 as "the early twenty-first century technogenesis of Black identity reflecting counter histories, hacking and or appropriating the influence of network software, database logic, cultural analytics, deep remixability, neurosciences, enhancement and augmentation, gender fluidity, posthuman possibility, the speculative sphere, with transdisciplinary applications and has grown into an important Diasporic techno-cultural 'Pan African' movement."

66. Aria Dean, "Notes on Blacceleration," *e-flux*, no. 87 (December 2017), http://www.e-flux.com/journal/87/169402/notes-on-blacceleration/; this article also develops accelerationist and Afrofuturist themes articulated in relation to sonic fiction in Eshun's *More Brilliant Than the Sun*.

67. Jafa discusses the notion of affective proximities, and his indebtedness to John Akomfrah for the idea, in his interview in Apsara Diquinzio, *Arthur Jafa: Matrix 272* (Berkeley: Berkeley Art Museum and Pacific Film Archive, 2018), n.p.

68. Nicholas Mirzoeff, "It's Not the Anthropocene, It's the White Supremacy Scene, or, the Geological Color Line," in *After Extinction*, ed. Richard Grusin (Minneapolis: University of Minnesota Press, 2018). On the current risks of "white environmentalism," see Danielle Purifoy, "On the Stubborn Whiteness of Environmentalism," *Inside Higher Education*, June 22, 2018, https://www.insidehighered.com/advice/2018/06/22/how-environmentalism-academe-today-excludes-people-color-opinion.

69. Mark Fisher, *Capitalist Realism: Is There No Alternative?* (London: Zero Books, 2009), 8.

70. As Kyle Powys Whyte observes, Native Americans—like other groups that have suffered slavery, dispossession, and genocide—"are already living in what our ancestors would have understood as dystopian or post-apocalyptic times." Kyle Powys Whyte, "White Allies, Let's Be Honest about Decolonization," *Yes Magazine*, April 3, 2018, https://www.yesmagazine.org/issues/decolonize/white-allies-lets-be-honest-about-decolonization-20180403. See the Mellon-funded Sawyer Seminar research project, titled "Beyond the End of the World," directed by the Center for Creative Ecologies, which is addressing this subject during the 2019–20 academic year. For more information, see the website of the Center for Creative Ecologies, http://creativeecologies.ucsc.edu/.

71. Keeanga-Yamahtta Taylor, *From #BlackLivesMatter to Black Liberation* (Chicago: Haymarket Books, 2016), 194. For further arguments for a new "insurgent universality" of political liberation expressed through solidarity beyond identity, see Asad Haider, *Mistaken Identity: Race and Class in the Age of Trump* (London: Verso, 2018).

72. "Robin D. G. Kelley & Fred Moten in Conversation," University of Toronto, April 3, 2017, https://www.youtube.com/watch?v=fP-2F9MXjRE. Moten also appears and speaks extensively in Jafa's 2012 video *Dreams Are Colder Than Death*. On the indivisibility of justice, see Angela Davis, *Freedom Is a Constant Struggle: Ferguson, Palestine and the Foundations of a Movement* (London: Haymarket Books, 2015).

CHAPTER SEVEN: THE GREAT TRANSITION

1. Among recent relevant analyses, see Achille Mbembe, "The Age of Humanism Is Ending," *Mail and Guardian*, December 22, 2016, http://mg.co.za/article /2016-12-22-00-the-age-of-humanism-is-ending; Alain Badiou, "Reflections on the Recent Election," November 15, 2016, http://www.versobooks.com/blogs /2940-alain-badiou-reflections-on-the-recent-election; "The Perfect Storm," ed. Sven Lütticken, Julieta Aranda, Brian Kuan Wood, Stephen Squibb, and Anton Vidokle, special issue, *e-flux*, no. 76 (October 2016), http://www.e-flux.com /journal/76/, on the question of contemporary fascism; and Jason Stanley, *How Fascism Works: The Politics of Us and Them* (New York: Random House, 2018).

2. Audra Simpson explained this perception in a lecture at the University of Minnesota on September 14, 2017.

3. Umair Irfan, "Report: We Have Just 12 Years to Limit Devastating Global Warming," *Vox*, October 8, 2018, https://www.vox.com/2018/10/8/17948832 /climate-change-global-warming-un-ipcc-report; Damian Carrington, "Humanity Has Wiped Out 60% of Animal Populations since 1970, Report Finds," *The Guardian*, October 31, 2018.

4. Amitav Ghosh, *The Great Derangement: Climate Change and the Unthinkable* (Chicago: University of Chicago Press, 2016).

5. For more on the California fires and visual culture, see T. J. Demos, "The Agency of Fire: Burning Aesthetics," *eflux* Journal #98 (February 2019), https:// www.e-flux.com.

6. Franco "Bifo" Berardi, *After the Future*, trans. Arianna Bove et al. (Oakland, CA: AK Press, 2011), 18–19.

7. Fredric Jameson, "The Cultural Logic of Late Capitalism," in *Postmodernism, or, The Cultural Logic of Late Capitalism* (Durham, NC: Duke University Press, 1992), 21; Mark Fisher, *Ghosts of My Life: Writings on Depression, Hauntology and Lost Futures* (London: Zero, 2014), 14.

8. BFAMFAPHD, "We Ask: What Is a Work of Art in the Age of $120,000 Art Degrees?," accessed January 4, 2020, http://carolinewoolard.com/system /bfamfaphd/.

9. MTL Collective, "From Institutional Critique to Institutional Liberation? A Decolonial Perspective on the Crises of Contemporary Art," *October* 165 (summer 2018): 194, citing Walter D. Mignolo, "Epistemic Disobedience, Independent Thought and De-Colonial Freedom," *Theory, Culture, and Society*

26, nos. 7–8 (2009): 1–23. On MTL's and Decolonize This Place's recent Whitney action, see Decolonize This Place, "After Kanders, Decolonization Is the Way Forward," *Hyperallergic*, July 30, 2019, https://hyperallergic.com; and T. J. Demos, "Climate Control: From Emergency to Emergence," *eflux Journal* #104 (November 2019), https://www.e-flux.com/journal/104/299286/climate-control-from-emergency-to-emergence/.

10. Damian Carrington, "'Brutal News': Global Carbon Emissions Jump to All-Time High in 2018," *The Guardian*, December 5, 2018.

11. Matthew Taylro, "Doctors Call for Nonviolent Direct Action over Climate Crisis," *The Guardian*, June 27, 2019.

12. Oliver Milman, "James Hansen, Father of Climate Change Awareness, Calls Paris Talks 'a Fraud,'" *The Guardian*, December 12, 2015; James Hansen, "The Peaceful Revolutionary Party," January 27, 2017, http://www.columbia.edu/~jeh1/mailings/2017/20170127_PeacefulParty.pdf.

13. For recent critical literature on the Green New Deal, see Sarah Lazare, "We Have to Make Sure the 'Green New Deal' Doesn't Become Green Capitalism: A Conversation with Kali Akuno of Cooperation Jackson," *In These Times*, December 12, 2018, http://inthesetimes.com/article/21632/green-new-deal-alexandria-ocasio-cortez-climate-cooperation-jackson-capital; DSA (Democratic Socialists of America) Ecosocialists, "An Ecosocialist Green New Deal: Guiding Principles," February 28, 2019, https://ecosocialists.dsausa.org/2019/02/28/gnd-principles/; and Indigenous Environmental Network, "Talking Points on the AOC-Markey Green New Deal," http://www.ienearth.org/talking-points-on-the-aoc-markey-green-new-deal-gnd-resolution/. Interestingly, Alexandria Ocasio-Cortez visited the Oceti Sakowin Camp in support of the #NoDAPL struggle before becoming a congresswoman, a visit that likely contributed to her motivation to support the Green New Deal.

14. For more on this long history and recent examples, see Andrew Boyd and Dave Oswald Mitchell, eds., *Beautiful Trouble: A Toolbox for Revolution* (New York: OR Books, 2012); and Catherine Flood and Gavin Grindon, eds., *Disobedient Objects* (London: V&A Publishing, 2014).

15. Elizabeth A. Povinelli, "What Do White People Want? Interest, Desire, and Affect in Late Liberalism," *e-flux conversations*, December 10, 2016, http://conversations.e-flux.com/t/elizabeth-a-povinelli-what-do-white-people-want-interest-desire-and-affect-in-late-liberalism/5845.

16. See Andrea Fraser, *2016: In Museums, Money, and Politics* (Cambridge, MA: MIT Press, 2018).

17. See, for instance, the recent issue of *Artforum* (May 2019) dedicated to art and activism. While it contains some discussion of collective activity, the issue—typical of conventional (market-friendly) institutional approaches—nonetheless largely privileges the artistic practice of exemplary individuals and their creative, original construction of mediagenic objects and performances.

In his short text "Art's Uprisings: Activism Now," editor David Velasco explains, "To be modern, art must follow a simple edict: Don't instrumentalize" (196). That modernist myth still largely informs Artforum's version of contemporary activist art.

18. See Andrea Fraser, "L'1% C'est Moi," Texte zur Kunst (August 2011); and Hito Steyerl, "Politics of Art: Contemporary Art and the Transition to Post-democracy," e-flux, no. 21 (December 2010). At the same time, I argue in earlier chapters of this book that artists might still do important work in conventional artistic spaces, redefining the perceptual and conceptual conditions of what environment and climate mean, and how life might be lived otherwise.

19. For Hegel, it was imperative to "exclude the beauty of Nature" from aesthetics, so as to realize self-conscious Spirit, where "artistic beauty starts higher than nature," and "everything spiritual is better than anything natural." See John Bellamy Foster and Paul Burkett, Marx and the Earth: An Anti-Critique (London: Haymarket Books, 2017), 51, citing Georg W. F. Hegel, Introductory Lectures on Aesthetics (1835) (New York: Penguin, 1993), 3–5, 11, 34. See also Andrew Biro, Critical Ecologies: The Frankfurt School and Contemporary Environmental Crises (Toronto: University of Toronto Press, 2011); Steven Vogel, Against Nature: The Concept of Nature in Critical Theory (Albany: SUNY Press, 1996); and Tim Benton, "Modernism and Nature," in Modernism: Designing a New World, ed. Christopher Wilk (London: Victoria and Albert Museum, 2006), 311–39.

20. Ghosh, The Great Derangement, 9.

21. In an earlier version of this chapter, I developed an analogy more specifically between nonfiction and documentary, while here I am stressing cultural activism as well. In some ways, all three share the same goal—to reflect on and intervene in the real—which precisely goes against modernism's aesthetics of abstraction and autonomy. It is this latter version of aesthetics that I see in terminal crisis today.

22. See Jason W. Moore, Anthropocene or Capitalocene? Nature, History, and the Crisis of Capitalism (Oakland, CA: PM Press, 2016); and T. J. Demos, Against the Anthropocene: Visual Culture and Environment Today (Berlin: Sternberg, 2017). For more discussion of the "neoliberal Anthropocene," as well as the dating and naming practices of geology, see chapter 6.

23. adrienne maree brown, Emergent Strategy: Shaping Change, Changing Worlds (Chico, CA: AK Press, 2017), 24; Shelley Streeby, Imagining the Future of Climate Change: World-Making through Science Fiction and Activism (Oakland: University of California Press, 2018).

24. Winona LaDuke, "The Dakota Access Pipeline: What Would Sitting Bull Do?," EcoWatch, August 30, 2016, http://www.ecowatch.com/dakota -access-pipeline-1991972867.html; Mario Blaser and Marisol de la Cadena, eds., A World of Many Worlds (Durham, NC: Duke University Press, 2018).

25. For an excellent overview, see Nick Estes, *Our History Is the Future: Standing Rock versus the Dakota Access Pipeline, and the Long Tradition of Indigenous Resistance* (London: Verso, 2019). He explains in a related interview: "[G]iven the opportunity to create a new world in that camp, centered on indigenous justice and treaty rights, society organized itself according to need and not to profit. And so, where there was, you know, the world of settlers, settler colonialism, that surrounded us, [and] there was the world of indigenous justice that existed for a brief moment in time. And in that world, instead of doing to settler society what they did to us—genociding, removing, excluding—there's a capaciousness to indigenous resistance movements that welcomes in non-indigenous peoples into our struggle, because that's our primary strength, is one of relationality, one of making kin, right?" "*Our History Is the Future*: Lakota Historian Nick Estes on Thanksgiving & Indigenous Resistance," *Democracy Now!*, November 28, 2019, https://www.democracynow.org.

26. See, for instance, Justseeds Artists' Cooperative's portfolio of graphics dedicated to Standing Rock and #NoDAPL, accessed January 4, 2020, https://justseeds.org/movement/standing-rock-no-dapl/.

27. Mary Louis Cappelli, "Standing with Standing Rock," *Social Text*; and Alexandra Deem, "Mediated Intersections of Environmental and Decolonial Politics in the No Dakota Access Pipeline Movement," *Theory, Culture & Society*, Vol. 36 (5) (2019), 113–131.

28. Wesley Clark said: "Many of us, me particularly, are from the units that have hurt you over the many years. We came. We fought you. We took your land. We signed treaties that we broke. We stole minerals from your sacred hills. We blasted the faces of our presidents onto your sacred mountain. Then we took still more land and then we took your children and . . . we tried to eliminate your language that God gave you, and the Creator gave you. We didn't respect you, we polluted your Earth, we've hurt you in so many ways but we've come to say that we are sorry. We are at your service and we beg for your forgiveness." "Veteran Wesley Clark Jr: Why I Knelt before Standing Rock Elders and Asked for Forgiveness," EcoWatch, December 22, 2016, https://www.ecowatch.com/veterans-standing-rock-elders-2160559817.html.

29. As discussed in Amber Hickey, "The Aesthetics of Decolonial Worlding" (PhD diss., UC Santa Cruz, 2018).

30. "Our History Is the Future: Lakota Historian Nick Estes on Indigenous Resistance to Climate Change," *Democracy Now!*.

31. Cited in Carolina A. Miranda, "The Artist Who Made Protesters' Mirrored Shields Says the 'Struggle Porn' Media Miss Point of Standing Rock," *Los Angeles Times*, Jan 12, 2017.

32. See the introduction to "Indigenous Peoples and the Politics of Water," ed. Melanie K. Yazzie and Cutcha Risling Baldy, special issue, *Decolonization: Indigeneity, Education and Society* 7, no. 1 (2018): 1–18.

33. Robin Wall Kimmerer and Kathleen Dean Moore, "The White Horse and the Humvees—Standing Rock Is Offering Us a Choice," *Nation of Change*, November 7, 2016, http://www.nationofchange.org/2016/11/07/white-horse-humvees-standing-rock-offering-us-choice/. For a wider background, see NYC Stands with Standing Rock Collective (Matt Chrisler, Jaskiran Dhillon, and Audra Simpson), "#Standing Rock Syllabus," 2016, https://nycstandswithstandingrock.wordpress.com/standingrocksyllabus/.

34. Standing Rock, in this regard, enacted the decolonization of water as water's privatization is continually threatened in the US. Not surprisingly, with Trump's recent declaration to approve further work on the pipeline, the movement has shifted to an international divestment campaign, to date removing more than $55 million from the leading financial institutions funding the DAPL construction (in fact, Seattle's Affordable Housing, Neighborhoods and Finance Committee just voted to divest $3 billion from Wells Fargo, one the project's leading financiers). Frances Madeson, "Defund DAPL Spreads across Indian Country as Tribes Divest," *Yes!* magazine, February 2, 2017, http://www.yesmagazine.org/people-power/defund-dapl-spreads-across-indian-country-as-tribes-divest-20170202.

35. Jaskiran Dhillon, "Introduction: Indigenous Resurgence, Decolonization, and Movements for Environmental Justice," *Environment and Society: Advances in Research* 9 (2018): 3. See also, in the same issue, Melanie Yazzi, "Decolonizing Development in Dené Bikeyah: Resource Extraction, Anti-capitalism, and Relational Futures," 25–39; and Paul Burnow, Samara Brock, and Michael R. Dove, "Unsettling the Land: Indigeneity, Ontology, and Hybridity in Settler Colonialism," 57–74.

36. Yazzi and Baldy, "Introduction," 2.

37. Kyle Whyte, "The Dakota Access Pipeline, Environmental Injustice, and U.S. Colonialism," *Red Ink: An International Journal of Indigenous Literature, Arts, and Humanities* (January/February 2017): 5. See also Nick Estes, "Fighting for Our Lives: #NoDAPL in Historical Context," *Red Nation*, September 18, 2016, https://therednation.org/2016/09/18/fighting-for-our-lives-nodapl-in-context/; and Nick Estes and Jaskiran Dhillon, eds., *Standing with Standing Rock: Voices from the #NoDAPL Movement* (Minneapolis: University of Minnesota Press, 2019).

38. As Estes observes, "Most [non-Indigenous] people think that decolonization would mean getting kicked off the land, or that Indigenous people would do to them what they did to Indigenous people in the past. It's a failure to imagine what a just future could look like. But it's also a failure to critically understand who owns the land in the United States and what the land is used for. Upward of 96 percent of agricultural lands are owned by white people, not Indigenous people. But these aren't just mom-and-pop farms out in rural South Dakota or Wyoming. These are large-scale industrial agricultural

operations with thousands and thousands of acres of land. Ted Turner, the media mogul, owns 200,000 acres of our treaty territory alone. He has the largest privately owned buffalo herd in the world. Worldwide, he owns 2 million acres of land. Why is it that a single white man can own that much land?" Nick Serpe, "Indigenous Resistance Is Post-Apocalyptic, with Nick Estes," *Dissent*, July 31, 2019, https://www.dissentmagazine.org.

39. Marisol de la Cadena, "Uncommoning Nature," *e-flux*, August 22, 2015, http://supercommunity.e-flux.com/authors/marisol-de-la-cadena/; and numerous calls for solidarity at: https://standwithstandingrock.net.

40. Estes, *Our History Is the Future*, 257. Needless to say, the social movements of decolonization and institutional liberation are of an entirely different paradigm than the "folk-politics" of immediacy, localism, and horizontalist direct democracy, as in Occupy, Spain's 15M, and Zapatismo, which are largely misunderstood and disparaged in Nick Srnicek and Alex Williams's *Inventing the Future: Postcapitalism and a World without Work* (London: Verso, 2015)—even while the latter does make valid points about the urgent need for the development of complex and global strategies to enable any transformative, counter-hegemonic politics today.

41. Mel Evans, *Artwash: Big Oil and the Arts* (Chicago: University of Chicago Press, 2015).

42. David Graeber, "The New Anarchists," *New Left Review* 13 (January–February 2002): 61–73. Graeber defines "creative direct action" as the "rejection of a politics which appeals to governments to modify their behaviour, in favour of physical intervention against state power in a form that itself prefigures an alternative" (62). See also David Graeber, *Direct Action: An Ethnography* (Chico, CA: AK Press, 2009).

43. Jodi Dean, "The Anamorphic Politics of Climate Change," *e-flux*, no. 69 (January 2016), http://www.e-flux.com/journal/69/60586/the-anamorphic -politics-of-climate-change/.

44. A recent selection of discussions of solidarity includes Corey Snelgrove, Rita Dhamoon, and Jeff Corntassel, "Unsettling Settler Colonialism: The Discourse and Politics of Settlers, and Solidarity with Indigenous Nations," *Decolonization: Indigeneity, Education and Society* 3, no. 2 (2014): 1–32; Black Lives Matter, "Black Lives Matter Stands in Solidarity with Water Protectors at Standing Rock," https://twitter.com/blklivesmatter/status/771876930870280193 ?lang=en; Clayton Thomas Muller, "The Rise of the Native Rights-Based Strategic Framework: Our Last Best Hope to Save our Water, Air, and Earth," in *The Winter We Danced: Voices from the Past, the Future, and the Idle No More Movement*, ed. Kino-nda-niimi Collective (Winnipeg: ARP Books, 2014), 365–78; Harsha Walia, "Decolonizing Together: Moving beyond a Politics of Solidarity Toward a Practice of Decolonization," in Kino-nda-niimi Collective, *The Winter We Danced*, 44–50; Matthew Wildcat, Mandee McDonald, Stephanie Irlbacher-Fox,

and Glen Coulthard, "Learning from the Land: Indigenous Land Based Pedagogy and Decolonization," in "Indigenous Land-Based Education," special issue, *Decolonization: Indigeneity, Education and Society* 3, no. 3 (2014): 1–25.

45. Eve Tuck and K. Wayne Yang, "Decolonization Is Not a Metaphor," *Decolonization: Indigeneity, Education and Society* 1, no. 1 (2012): 1–40.

46. Joe Curnow and Anjai Helferty, "Contradictions of Solidarity: Whiteness, Settler Coloniality, and the Mainstream Environmental Movement," *Environment and Society: Advances in Research* 9 (2018).

47. MTL Collective, "From Institutional Critique to Institutional Liberation?," 197. On the transnational alliance formations reaching across borders and engaging the politics of caste, class, gender, religion, environment, and indigeneity, from the local to the global, see Jai Sen, ed., *The Movement of Movements*, part 1, *What Makes Us Move?*, and part 2, *Rethinking Our Dance* (Oakland, CA: PM Press, 2017).

48. Angela Davis, *Freedom Is a Constant Struggle: Ferguson, Palestine, and the Foundations of a Movement* (Chicago: Haymarket Press, 2015).

49. Tony Bennett, *The Birth of the Museum: History, Theory, Politics* (New York: Routledge, 1995). For Bennett, the "exhibitionary complex," building off Michel Foucault's discussion of panopticism and its universal reign of visibility within unequal structures of power, forms part of the cultural infrastructure of the modern state, including institutions of behavior management, perceptual techniques, and disciplinary functions.

50. MTL Collective, "From Institutional Critique to Institutional Liberation?," 206.

51. Liberate Tate, "Confronting the Institution in Performance: Liberate Tate's Hidden Figures," *Performance Research* 20, no. 4 (2015): 83, citing Stefano Harney and Fred Moten, *The Undercommons: Fugitive Planning and Black Study* (Port Watson: Minor Compositions, 2013); and Michael Warner, *Publics and Counterpublics* (New York: Zone Books, 2002). See also the subsequent historical genealogy of institutional critique and a discussion of "instituent power" in MTL Collective, "From Institutional Critique to Institutional Liberation?"

52. See the continual coverage between December 2018 and May 2019, especially in *Hyperallergic*, beginning with Jasmine Weber, "Decolonize This Place Plans Action at the Whitney Opposing Tear Gas Manufacturer on Museum Board," *Hyperallergic*, December 7, 2018, https://hyperallergic.com/475016/decolonize-this-place-plans-action-at-the-whitney-opposing-tear-gas-manufacturer-on-museum-board/.

53. Not an Alternative, "Institutional Liberation," *e-flux*, no. 77 (November 2016), http://www.e-flux.com/journal/77/76215/institutional-liberation/.

54. Anonymous, "La ZAD: Another End of the World Is Possible: Learning from 50 Years of Struggle at Notre-Dame-des-Landes," April 9, 2018,

https://crimethinc.com/2018/04/09/la-zad-another-end-of-the-world-is
-possible-learning-from-50-years-of-struggle-at-notre-dame-des-landes.

55. Martin Legall, "The ZAD: An Autonomous Zone in the Heart of France," *Roar*, January 26, 2017, https://roarmag.org/essays/zad-autonomous-zone-france/.

56. Mauvaise Troupe Collective, *Defending the Zad* (Paris: Éditions de l'Éclat, 2015), 6.

57. John Jordan, "The Revenge against the Commons," April 24, 2018, https://zadforever.blog/2018/04/24/the-revenge-against-the-commons/.

58. Naomi Klein, *This Changes Everything: Capitalism vs. the Climate* (New York: Allen Lane, 2014), 294–95.

59. Mauvaise Troupe Collective, *Defending the Zad*, 20.

60. Anna Feigenbaum, Fabian Frenzel, and Patrick McCurdy, *Protest Camps* (London: Zed Books, 2013); Yates McKee, *Strike Art: Contemporary Art and the Post-Occupy Condition* (London: Verso, 2016); Flood and Grindon, *Disobedient Objects*.

61. Jordan, "The Revenge against the Commons." See also Anonymous, "La ZAD." For a history of communalism since the 1960s, see Iain Boal, Janferie Stone, Michael Watts, and Cal Winslow, eds., *West of Eden: Communes and Utopia in Northern California* (Oakland, CA: PM Press, 2012). For a study of recent European models, see "Journée de formation 'L'Art du Blocage'—Dimanche 30 octubre sur la zad," *Les Sentiers de l'Utopie: Le blog du livre-film d'Isabelle Fremeaux et John Jordan*, October 24, 2016, https://lessentiersdelutopie.wordpress.com/. I consider Jordan and Fremeaux's critical relation to past communal forms in T. J. Demos, "The Post-Natural Condition: Art after Nature?," in *Decolonizing Nature: Contemporary Art and the Politics of Ecology* (Berlin: Sternberg, 2017), 31–62.

62. Jordan, "The Revenge against the Commons."

63. See Jordan, "The Revenge against the Commons"; and the recent update, "Tank Goodness We Are Here," May 24, 2018, https://zadforever.blog /2018/05/24/tank-goodness-we-are-here/, which is signed by the residents of Moulin de Rohanne, the Rolandière, the 100 names, the Hulotte, Saint-Jean-du-Tertre, the FossesNoires, the Baraka and Nantes, jointly represented in the CMDO (Council for the Maintenance of Occupations), the latter a reference to the eponymous group in Paris in May 1968.

64. Dorian Batycka, "French Authorities Move to Evict Decade-Old Commune, Tearing Down Unique Structures," *Hyperallergic*, May 2, 2018, https://hyperallergic.com/440808/zone-a-defendre-eviction-france-commune -architecture/. It is also important to situate the discourse of the commons, which, if articulated in the Americas, would need to contend with decolonial politics, according to which the land is understood to have been stolen by settler colonialism, and where Indigenous positions would complicate if not reject activist calls to establish a commons. On this, see Tuck and Yang, "Decolonization Is Not a Metaphor."

65. Legall, "The ZAD"; Invisible Committee, *The Coming Insurrection* (Cambridge, MA: Semiotext(e), 2009).

66. Mauvaise Troupe Collective, *Defending the Zad*, 20.

67. Maxime Combes, "Yellow Vests: Macron's Fuel Tax Was No Solution to Climate Chaos," Global Justice Ecology Project, December 10, 2018, https:// globaljusticeecology.org/yellow-vests-macrons-fuel-tax-was-no-solution-to -climate-chaos/; Andreas Malm, "A Lesson in How Not to Mitigate Climate Change," December 7, 2018, https://www.versobooks.com/blogs?post_author =382718.

68. Thanks to the Otolith Group for the term *past potential futures*. For a discussion of the Commune's liberated politico-aesthetic practice, where a barricade could be an example of social justice art working toward a world of shared social wealth, see Kristin Ross, *Communal Luxury: The Political Imaginary of the Paris Commune* (London: Verso, 2015).

69. Anna Tsing, *The Mushroom at the End of the World: On the Possibility of Life in Capitalist Ruins* (Princeton, NJ: Princeton University Press, 2015).

70. Here I am building on the philosophical project of Jacques Rancière. See, for instance, Jacques Rancière, *The Politics of Aesthetics: The Distribution of the Sensible*, trans. Gabriel Rockhill (London: Continuum, 2004); Jacques Rancière, *Aisthesis: Scenes from the Aesthetic Regime of Art*, trans. Zakir Paul (London: Verso, 2011); and relatedly, Kathryn Yusoff, "Biopolitical Economies and the Political Aesthetics of Climate Change," *Theory, Culture and Society* 27, nos. 2–3 (May 2010): 73–99.

71. See Boyd and Mitchell, *Beautiful Trouble*, to which Jordan was a contributor; Mark Fisher, *Capitalist Realism: Is There No Alternative?* (Ropley, England: O Books, 2009); and Richard Smith, *Green Capitalism: The God That Failed* (London: College Publications, 2016).

72. The more recent work of Bifo recognizes this as well. See Franco "Bifo" Berardi, *Futurability: The Age of Impotence and the Horizon of Possibility* (London: Verso, 2017).

73. See the website of It Takes Roots, https://ittakesroots.org/; Stephen Spratt, Andrew Simms, Eva Neitzert, and Josh Ryan-Collins, *The Great Transition: A Tale of How It Turned Out Right* (London: New Economics Foundation, 2010); "The Leap Manifesto," issued by a broad coalition of Canadian authors, artists, national leaders, and activists in September 2015, https://leapmanifesto .org/en/the-leap-manifesto/; and the website of the ecosocialist coalition System Change Not Climate Change, http://systemchangenotclimatechange.org/.

74. Lazare, "We Have to Make Sure"; and Nick Estes, "A Red Deal," *Jacobin*, August 6, 2019, https://jacobinmag.com. For further discussion of how to radicalize the Green New Deal and keep it from the hands of green capital, see Thea Riofrancos, "Plan, Mood, Battlefield—Reflections on the Green New Deal," *Viewpoint*, May 16, 2019, https://www.viewpointmag.com.

INDEX

Page numbers followed by f indicate figures; those with a t indicate tables.

100; in Canada, 50, 53–58; in Greece, 44–46, 51–52; naturalization of, 109; socioenvironmental conditions of, 67; Trump's support of, 163–64

Exxon, 36, 54

Farage, Nigel, 77
Farocki, Harun, 107–9, 108, 224n22
fascism. See neofascism
Fisher, Mark, 165
Flanders, Elle, 3, 97–113
Flint, Michigan, 66
Forensic Architecture project, 76–77, 90–92, 220n47
Forensic Climatology, 56, 58
Forensic Oceanography, 3, 90–92, 91f
Forest Law (Biemann and Tavares), 54–55, 55f
Forman, Fonna, 3; Cross-Border Commons, 92–94, 93f
Foucault, Michel, 99–100, 126, 246n49
Fox, Josh, 178–79
fracking, 123–24, 178, 186
Franklin, Benjamin, 63–64
Fraser, Andrea, 171, 183
Friedrich, Caspar David, 30, 32
Friz, Anna, 98
Fund for Innovative Climate and Energy Research, 154
futurism, 2–3, 159–61; conflictual, 137–38; virtual, 42. See also Afrofuturism

gaming, 96–113; geontopolitics of, 97–107, 98f, 102f, 105f
Garza, Alicia, 13
Gates, Bill, 155–56; Carbon Engineering funding by, 237n49; Fund for Innovative Climate and Energy Research, 154; Hazari and, 15, 237n52
Gates, Henry Louis, Jr., 207n11
General Motors (GM), 11–12, 154
Geneva Conventions, 80

genocide, 119, 130; "climate," 148; of Indigenous peoples, 9–10, 141–42
geoengineering, 141–42, 147–52, 162, 237n49; criticism of, 2–3, 7, 156, 235n39; Latour on, 151; Republican Party support for, 238n56–57; techno-utopianism of, 137, 156–57. See also climate engineering
geontopolitics, 21, 48; of gaming, 97–107, 98f, 102f, 105f; Yazzie on, 101
geontopower, 16, 99–100
Ghosh, Amitav, 7–8, 59, 164, 172
Gilets Jaunes ("yellow vests") movement, 190
Gilroy, Paul, 33, 39
Glacier National Park (Montana), 59
Global Alliance for the Rights of Nature, 119
Global Witness (organization), 211n9
globalization, 5, 120; of "climate apartheid," 69; colonialism and, 9; of disaster capitalism, 8; of precarity, 3, 62
Goldin, Nan, 183
Gómez-Barris, Macarena, 46, 204n59
Gordon, Jessica, 174
Graeber, David, 180, 245n42
Grand Theft Auto (video game), 107
Greece, 3, 43–48; debt crisis in, 44, 52, 210n1; refugee crisis in, 50–52, 53f, 65, 82–84
green capitalism, 3, 11, 138, 170, 241n13; Anthropocene reasoning and, 8; white supremacy and, 13
Green New Deal, 170, 192, 241n13
greenhouse gases, 6, 12, 16; ocean acidity from, 36. See also climate change
Greenpeace, 12, 177
Griffith, D. W., 146–47
Gross, Lawrence, 9–10, 201n26
Guatemala, 92, 229n33
Guattari, Félix, 122–24, 205n65
Guevara, Paula Cabo, 44
Gustafsson, Laura, 3–4, 117, 125, 133

Gustafsson&Haapoja, 116–36; *Museum of Nonhumanity*, 122; *The Museum of the History of Cattle*, 122, 130–34, 131f, 132f; *The Party of Others*, 122, 125–29, 128f; *The Trial*, 116–21, 117f

Haacke, Hans, 183
Haapoja, Terike, 4, 117, 130; on artists' social role, 121–22, 133; on other-ing, 118, 125–27, 226n7. *See also* Gustafsson&Haapoja
Haida people, 115
Haiti, 62
Hall, Stuart, 28
Haner, Josh, 74, 75f, 84, 87
Hansen, James, 170
Harari, Yuval Noah, 15, 155–56, 237n52
Haraway, Donna, 5, 115, 210n33; on animal communicative capacities, 134; on generative sympoeisis, 122; on human exceptionalism, 123, 124; on "naturalcultural," 229n26; on Others, 129; on "symbiogenesis," 110, 224n27; on techno-organic hybrids, 132–33
Harman, Graham, 40
Harney, Stefano, 13–14, 148
Harper, Stephen, 58
Hartman, Saidiya, 202n29
Harvey, David, 46, 111
hauntologies, 39–42, 210n37
Hawking, Stephen, 153
Heartland Institute, 156
Hegel, Georg Wilhelm Friedrich, 165, 242n19
Heinrich Böll Foundation, 235n39, 237n49
Heise, Ursula, 208n19
Helferty, Anjai, 182
Heller, Charles, 90–91, 91f
Helmreich, Stefan, 129, 134
Hewlett Foundation, 154
Himalayan glaciers, 59
Hobbes, Thomas, 2

Holocene, 7, 9
homophobia, 12
Honduras, 47–48, 92
hooks, bell, 11, 210n32
Hoover Institution, 156
Hornborg, Alf, 15
Horne, Lena, 146
Houma Nation, 74
Houston, 62
Human Flow (Ai Weiwei), 82–87, 83f, 86f, 87f
Human Rights Watch, 84
"humanimalia," 124, 228n26
humanism, 122–23, 160; Chthulucene and, 5; environmental, 8, 15; neohumanism and, 11, 15, 140, 156–57. *See also* posthumanism
Hungary, 78
Hurricane Katrina, 81, 147, 220n38
hurricanes, 8, 74, 151

I Have Been Her Kind (video), 103
Idle No More movement, 174, 184
India, 92; Bangladeshi immigrants in, 58–59; rights of nature in, 120
Indigenous peoples, 106, 166, 222n7; cosmovisions of, 123, 229n33; genocide of, 9–10, 141–42; rights of, 173–79, 176f. *See also* Columbian exchange
Indonesia, 48, 120
"insect poetics," 134
Inter-Pacific Ring Tribunal, 120
Intergovernmental Panel on Climate Change (IPCC), 164
Internal Displacement Monitoring Centre, 79
International Convention for the Regulation of Whaling, 209n24
International Monetary Fund (IMF), 79, 120, 190
intersectionality, 4, 12, 129–30, 138; ecologies of, 11, 15, 19, 33–41, 52, 147; Guattari and, 122

www.ingramcontent.com/pod-product-compliance
Lightning Source LLC
Chambersburg PA
CBHW051211170526
45166CB00005B/1844